Project Management

Fifth Edition

ABSOLUTE
BEGINNER'S
GUIDE

Gregory M. Horine

que®

Project Management Absolute Beginner's Guide, Fifth Edition

ISBN-13: 978-0-13-764695-1

ISBN-10: 0-13-764695-X

Library of Congress Control Number: 2021950930

6 2024

Trademarks

Warning and Disclaimer

Special Sales

Editor-in-Chief
Mark Taub

Acquisitions Editor
Anshul Sharma

Development Editor
Patrice-Anne Rutledge

Managing Editor
Sandra Schroeder

Senior Project Editor
Tonya Simpson

Copy Editor
William McManus

Indexer
Erika Millen

Proofreader
Charlotte Kughen

Technical Editor
J. Boyd Nolan

Editorial Assistant
Cindy Teeters

Cover Designer
Chuti Prasertsith

Compositor
codeMantra

Pearson's Commitment to Diversity, Equity, and Inclusion

Pearson is dedicated to creating bias-free content that reflects the diversity of all learners. We embrace the many dimensions of diversity, including but not limited to race, ethnicity, gender, socioeconomic status, ability, age, sexual orientation, and religious or political beliefs.

Education is a powerful force for equity and change in our world. It has the potential to deliver opportunities that improve lives and enable economic mobility. As we work with authors to create content for every product and service, we acknowledge our responsibility to demonstrate inclusivity and incorporate diverse scholarship so that everyone can achieve their potential through learning. As the world's leading learning company, we have a duty to help drive change and live up to our purpose to help more people create a better life for themselves and to create a better world.

Our ambition is to purposefully contribute to a world where

- Everyone has an equitable and lifelong opportunity to succeed through learning

- Our educational products and services are inclusive and represent the rich diversity of learners

- Our educational content accurately reflects the histories and experiences of the learners we serve

- Our educational content prompts deeper discussions with learners and motivates them to expand their own learning (and worldview)

While we work hard to present unbiased content, we want to hear from you about any concerns or needs with this Pearson product so that we can investigate and address them.

Please contact us with concerns about any potential bias at https://www.pearson.com/report-bias.html.

Contents at a Glance

Table of Contents

About the Author

Gregory M. Horine is a certified (PMP, Certified Scrum Master, Six Sigma Green Belt) business technology and IT project management professional with a track record of successful results using servant leadership principles and a focused customer orientation. He has been consistently recognized for excellence in people management, leadership maturity, communication skills, problem-solving skills, and establishing long-term client relationships. Primary areas of expertise and strength include the following:

- Project management and leadership
- Complete project life-cycle experience across multiple industries
- Agile, waterfall, and hybrid application development
- Package implementation and integration
- Enterprise solution development
- Application release management
- Application development team management
- Project and portfolio management tools
- Data analysis and transformation
- Business process analysis and improvement
- Testing, quality, and risk management

In addition, Mr. Horine holds a master's degree in computer science from Ball State University and a bachelor's degree in both marketing and computer science from Anderson College (Anderson, Indiana).

Through his servant leadership approach, Mr. Horine has established a track record of empowering his teammates, improving project communications, overcoming technical and political obstacles, and successfully completing projects that meet the targeted objectives.

Mr. Horine is grateful for the guidance and the opportunities that he has received from many mentors throughout his career. Their patience and influence has helped form a rewarding career marked by continuous learning and improvement.

Dedication

This book is dedicated to the "students" that I constantly visualized in my mind as I developed this book—the bright and caring family that surrounds my life, including my wife, parents, siblings, in-laws, aunts, uncles, cousins, and grandparents.

This book is dedicated to my father, Nelson "Bud" Horine, who passed away in 2020. My "best man" who is, and will be, missed.

This book is also dedicated to the parents, families, practitioners, and researchers who are diligently fighting to rescue children from autism spectrum and bipolar disorders.

This book is dedicated to the brave individuals fighting for freedom and against the forces of censorship and tyranny.

This book is dedicated to my key inspirational sources: my incredible wife, Mayme (I still wake up every day with a smile in my heart knowing I am married to her), and my "fabulous five" children: Michael, Victoria, Alex, Luke, and Elayna (each one is a hero to me).

Acknowledgments

I am grateful for the patience, support, and teamwork demonstrated by the following individuals: my editor, Laura Norman; the Pearson Publishing team, my family; and my parents, Carla and Bud.

In addition, I want to acknowledge the talents and professionalism of Mr. Craig Thurmond for his graphical design contributions to this book.

We Want to Hear from You!

As the reader of this book, *you* are our most important critic and commentator. We value your opinion and want to know what we're doing right, what we could do better, what areas you'd like to see us publish in, and any other words of wisdom you're willing to pass our way.

We welcome your comments. You can email or write to let us know what you did or didn't like about this book—as well as what we can do to make our books better.

Please note that we cannot help you with technical problems related to the topic of this book.

When you write, please be sure to include this book's title and author as well as your name and email address. We will carefully review your comments and share them with the author and editors who worked on the book.

Email: community@informit.com

Reader Services

Register your copy of *Project Management Absolute Beginner's Guide* at quepublishing.com for convenient access to downloads, updates, and corrections as they become available. To start the registration process, go to quepublishing.com/register and log in or create an account.* Enter the product ISBN, 9780137646951, and click Submit. Once the process is complete, you will find any available bonus content under Registered Products.

*Be sure to check the box that you would like to hear from us in order to receive exclusive discounts on future editions of this product.

Figure Credits

Figure 8-1 © Microsoft Corporation

Figure 8-2 © Microsoft Corporation

Figure 12-1 © Microsoft Corporation

Figure 12-2 © Microsoft Corporation

Introduction

As organizations continue to move toward "project-based" management to get more done with fewer resources—and as the demand for effective project managers continues to grow—more and more individuals find themselves with the opportunity to manage projects for the first time.

In an ideal world, every new project manager candidate would complete certified project management training programs and serve as an apprentice before starting a first project manager opportunity, but...this is the real world. In many cases, a quicker, more accessible, and more economical alternative is needed to guide these candidates in managing projects successfully the first time.

Project Management Absolute Beginner's Guide, Fifth Edition, is intended to provide this alternative in a helpful, fun, and practical style.

About This Book

The objectives of this book include the following:

- To be a pragmatic guide that prepares a new project manager for the "real world."

- To be an easy-to-use tutorial and reference for any person managing a first project.

- To teach the key concepts and fundamentals behind project management techniques. When you understand these, you can apply them effectively independent of toolset, environment, or industry.

- To reduce the on-the-job learning curve by sharing the traits of successful projects and "lessons learned" from less-than-successful projects.

- To balance the breadth of topics covered with adequate depth in specific areas to best prepare a new project manager.

- To review the skills and qualities of effective project managers.

- To emphasize the importance of project "leadership" versus just project "management."

Consistent with the *Absolute Beginner's Guide* series, this book uses a teaching style to review the essential techniques and skills needed to successfully manage a project. By teaching style, I intend the following:

- Offers a mentoring, coaching style that is fun, easy to read, and practical.

- Assumes that the reader does not have previous hands-on experience with project management.

- Teaches the material as if an instructor were physically present.

- Presents the material in task-oriented, logically ordered, self-contained lessons (chapters) that can be read and comprehended in a short period of time (15 to 30 minutes).

- Emphasizes understanding the principle behind the technique or practice.

- Teaches the material independent of specific tools and methodologies.

- Teaches the material with the assumption that the reader does not have access to organizational templates or methodologies.

- Provides a summary map of the main ideas covered at the end of each chapter. Research has shown that this type of "mind-map" approach can drive better memory recollection when compared to traditional linear summary approaches.

OUT OF SCOPE

The scope of this book is clearly outlined in the table of contents, but as I cover later, it is always good to review what is out of scope to ensure understanding of the scope boundaries. Because the field of project management is extremely broad, and I needed to draw the line somewhere, this book focuses on the proper management of a single project. As a result, the following advanced project management subjects are not covered in this book:

- Program management

- Enterprise portfolio management

- Enterprise resource management

- Advanced project risk management

- Advanced project quality management

- Advanced project procurement management

- Advanced enterprise agile management

DISCLAIMER

Although there are definitely concepts, fundamentals, and techniques covered in this book that are of enormous assistance to anyone taking the PMP certification exam, this book is not intended to be an exam preparation guide.

The focus of this book is not on theory, academia, or the *PMBOK Guide* (PMI's *A Guide to the Project Management Body of Knowledge*). The focus is on getting the first-timer ready to manage a first project in the real-world environment.

Although the PMBOK is an admirable industry standard, it is updated every four years to better capture the evolving knowledge in the field and to improve the consistency and clarity of the standards. It is not intended to be a "how-to" guide for a first-time practitioner.

That being said, the latest PMBOK edition, Version 7, has undergone a significant shift toward principles and outcomes versus its historical focus on prescriptive processes, so it is more aligned with the spirit of this book now. In addition, there is a bonus chapter on PMP exam-preparation pointers in Chapter 26, "Powerful PMP Exam Tips," that was added in the Fourth Edition. This chapter is updated to account for the changes in PMBOK Version 7.

Who Should Read This Book?

Project Management Absolute Beginner's Guide, Fifth Edition, is recommended for any person who fits into one or more of the following categories:

- Individuals unsatisfied with other introductory project management books
- Individuals new to project management, such as
  - Technologists
  - Knowledge workers
  - Students
  - Functional managers
- Professionals taking a first project management assignment, such as
  - Team leaders
  - Project coordinators

- Project administrators

- Project support staff

- Experienced project managers needing a refresher course

- Experienced project managers with limited formal project management education

How This Book Is Organized

This book has been divided into five parts:

- Part I, "Project Management Jumpstart," sets up the general framework for our project management discussion and accelerates your project management learning curve, including an insightful review of successful projects and project managers.

- Part II, "Project Planning," reviews the processes that establish the foundation for your project.

- Part III, "Project Control," reviews the processes that enable you to effectively monitor, track, correct, and protect your project's performance.

- Part IV, "Project Execution," reviews the key leadership and people-focused skills that you need to have to meet today's business demands.

- Part V, "Accelerating the Learning Curve...Even More," provides experienced insights and tips to better handle real-life project situations that will further accelerate the knowledge base and skill level of the new project manager. Key topics include making better use of Microsoft Project, dealing with real-world situations, and other topics that a new project manager is likely to encounter in today's rapidly changing environment.

What's New in This Edition

While the key principles of project management, leading teams, and effective communication that this book has focused on since 2005 are timeless, this book has always been ahead of the curve in addressing leading-edge trends in projects and project management and in providing powerful tips to help reduce the learning curves for new project managers. Hot key trends in project management, such as agile approaches, leading virtual/remote teams, leading disparate teams, and cloud collaboration tools, have been included since the first edition.

However, it has been four years since the fourth edition, and adoption of many these leading-edge approaches and techniques have now become mainstream.

In this edition, existing sections have been enhanced with additional material on those trends mentioned before, especially agile approaches. We will explore the role of the Project Manager in the agile world, discuss the differences between a Scrum Master, a Product Owner, and a Project Manager, and talk about what to do if you are asked to serve as both the Project Manager and the Scrum Master. For those in the IT space, we will explore how the adoption of DevOps and DevSec-Ops impacts the project manager and the efforts they manage.

On top of that, all references to the PMBOK have been updated with the *PMBOK Guide – Seventh Edition* references (released in August 2021), and the chapter on PMP exam preparation (Chapter 26) has been updated accordingly.

Conventions Used in This Book

Throughout the book, I use the following conventions and special features:

- At the beginning of each chapter, you find a quick overview of the major topics that are expounded upon as you read through the material that follows.

- The end of each chapter provides a list of key points along with a visual summary map.

- You also find several special sidebars used throughout this book:

 NOTE   These highlight specific learning points or provide supporting information to the current topic.

 TIP   These highlight specific techniques or recommendations that could be helpful to most project managers.

 CAUTION   These highlight specific warnings that a project manager should be aware of.

IN THIS CHAPTER

- Clarify what project management is and "is not" (it's likely more than you think)
- Learn why projects are challenging to manage
- Understand why project management is the key to the future growth of any organization
- Learn why the future of project management is bright and why becoming a certified project manager might be a wise career move
- Review the latest trends in project management that might impact your first opportunity

1

PROJECT MANAGEMENT OVERVIEW

Because your perceptions surrounding project management will vary depending on work experiences, education, industry, and roles, it's important to establish some "common ground" before we venture down the road of learning what you must do to be successful in your first opportunity as a project manager.

This chapter provides the common ground by clarifying what constitutes project management and why project management is important to both your future and the future of your organization.

What Is Project Management...Exactly?

If you are like most people, you are "pretty sure" you know what projects are, and you "think" you know what project management is (and what a project manager does), but there's always a varying amount of uncertainty in those perceptions. So, let's start off by clarifying some key concepts.

Project management is simply the process of managing projects (and you thought this was going to be difficult). Although this definition is not particularly helpful, it does illustrate three key points:

- Project management is not "brain surgery." Yes, it covers a vast array of subjects, processes, skills, and tools, but the key fundamentals of project management are straightforward and are consistent across industries.

- To better understand project management, we need to understand what a project is. The nature of a project provides insights into the scope and challenges of project management.

- To better understand project management, we need to understand what is implied by the term *managing* and how this compares against traditional business management.

What Is a Project Exactly?

A *project* is the work performed by an organization one time to produce a unique outcome. By *one time*, we mean the work has a definite beginning and a definite end, and by *unique*, we mean the work result is different in one or more ways from anything the organization has produced before. Examples of projects include the following:

- Building a new house

- Developing a new software application

- Performing an assessment of current manufacturing processes

- Improving an organizational business process

- Writing a book

- Relocating a company's technology infrastructure to a new location or to a cloud platform

- Merging two organizations

- Developing a new medical device

This is in contrast to the operations of an organization. The operational work is the ongoing, repetitive set of activities that sustain the organization. Examples of ongoing operations include the following:

- Processing customer orders

- Performing accounts receivable and accounts payable activities

- Executing daily manufacturing orders

- Performing recommended equipment maintenance procedures

- Conducting customer account maintenance

To further explain the nature of projects (and project management) and how they compare to the ongoing operations of an organization, please review the summary in Table 1.1.

TABLE 1.1 Comparing Projects and Operations

Feature	Projects	Operations
Key Similarities	Planned, executed, and controlled	Planned, executed, and controlled
	Performed by people	Performed by people
	Resource constrained	Resource constrained
Purpose	Attain objectives and terminate	Sustain the organization
Time	Temporary	Ongoing
	Definite beginning and end points	
Outcome	Unique product, service, or result	Non-unique product, service, or result
People	Dynamic, temporary teams formed to meet project needs	Functional teams generally aligned with organizational structure
	Generally not aligned with organizational structure	
Authority of Manager	Varies by organizational structure	Generally formal, direct line authority
	Generally minimal, if any, direct line authority	

 NOTE The Project Management Institute (PMI) definition of *project* is a temporary endeavor to produce a unique product, service, or result. The temporary nature of projects indicates a beginning and an end to the project work or a phase of the project work. Projects can stand alone or be part of a program or portfolio.

To better clarify what projects are, let's take a look at how projects compare to products. With the increasing focus on product management and its adoption by organizations, there is often some confusion regarding how projects and products differ. We will touch on this distinction throughout the book, but to jump-start this understanding, please review the summary in Table 1.2.

TABLE 1.2 Comparing Projects and Products

Feature	Projects	Products
Relationship to Each Other	Create a product Update/improve a product	Result of a project
Purpose	Attain objectives and terminate	Generate revenue for organization and value to customers on ongoing basis
Focus	Execute the process to achieve objectives while managing constraints	Maximize value of the product
Time	Temporary Definite beginning and end points	Ongoing until product is retired
Key Similarities	Deliver value to customer Quality focus Resource and budget constraints	Deliver value to customer Quality focus Resource and budget constraints
Teams	Dynamic, temporary teams formed to meet project needs	Functional permanent team members Initial project team members may become part of permanent product team

Managing Projects

"Managing projects" means all of the following:

- Applying both the science and the art of planning, organizing, implementing, leading, and controlling the work of a project to meet the goals and objectives of the organization

- The process of defining a project, developing a plan, executing the plan, monitoring progress against the plan, overcoming obstacles, managing risks, and taking corrective actions

- The process of managing the competing demands and trade-offs between the desired results of the project (scope, performance, quality) and the natural constraints of the project (time and cost)

 NOTE The PMI definition of *project management* is the application of knowledge, skills, tools, and techniques to project activities to meet project requirements. Project management refers to guiding the project work to deliver the intended outcomes. Project teams can achieve the outcomes using a broad range of approaches (e.g., predictive, hybrid, and adaptive).

- The process of leading a team that has never worked together before to accomplish something that has never been done before in a given amount of time with a limited amount of money

Sounds like fun, doesn't it? I explain each of these key aspects of project management in subsequent chapters, and I discuss many of the specific tasks and responsibilities performed by the project manager in Chapter 2, "The Project Manager," but for now we just want to align our general understanding of project management.

An Academic Look

To further assist this alignment process, let's look at project management from a more academic level. PMI, the globally recognized standards organization for project management (www.pmi.org), had defined project management as a set of five process groups (see Table 1.3) and ten knowledge areas (see Table 1.4) in the first six editions of its standards. These references are taken from PMI's *A Guide to the Project Management Body of Knowledge*, Sixth Edition (*PMBOK Guide – Sixth Edition*).

However, with the latest edition, *A Guide to the Project Management Body of Knowledge*, Seventh Edition (*PMBOK Guide – Seventh Edition*), PMI made a significant update to respond to the changing landscape, to emphasize project value and outcomes, and to capture how successful practitioners were actually applying these processes and knowledge areas to deliver successful projects for their organizations. In addition, the new edition provides a foundation that is designed to be tailored to best meet the needs of the organization and individual project. With *PMBOK Guide – Seventh Edition*, PMI now defines project management as a set of twelve principles (see Table 1.5) and eight performance domains (see Table 1.6).

TABLE 1.3 Description of *PMBOK Guide* – Sixth Edition Project Management Process Groups

#	Process Group	Description	Common Terms
1	Initiating	Those processes performed to define a new project or a new phase of an existing project by obtaining authorization to start the project or phase.	"preliminary planning" "kicking off"
2	Planning	Those processes required to establish the scope of the project, refine the objectives, and define the course of action required to attain the objectives that the project was undertaken to achieve.	"defining" "developing the plan" "setting the stage"
3	Executing	Those processes required to coordinate the people and resources needed to implement the plan.	"making it happen" "getting it done" "coordinating"
4	Monitoring and Controlling	Those processes required to track, review, and regulate the progress and performance of the project; identify any areas in which changes to the plan are required; and initiate the corresponding changes.	"tracking progress" "keeping on course"
5	Closing	Those processes performed to formally complete or close the project, phase, or contract.	"client acceptance" "transition" "closeout" "close contract"

TABLE 1.4 Description of *PMBOK Guide* – Sixth Edition Knowledge Areas

#	Knowledge Area	Description	Common Deliverables
1	Project Integration Management	Processes and activities to identify, define, combine, unify, and coordinate the various processes and project management activities within the Project Management Process Groups.	Project Charter Project Plan Change Requests Work Results
2	Project Scope Management	Processes required to ensure that project includes all the work that is required and only the work that is required to complete the project successfully.	Scope Statement Work Breakdown Structure Formal Acceptance

#	Knowledge Area	Description	Common Deliverables
3	Project Schedule Management	Processes required to ensure timely completion of the project.	Network Diagram Task Estimates Project Schedule
4	Project Cost Management	Processes involved in planning, estimating, budgeting, financing, funding, managing, and controlling costs so the project can be completed within the approved budget.	Resource Requirements Cost Estimates Project Budget
5	Project Quality Management	Processes for incorporating the organization's quality policy regarding planning, managing, and controlling project and product quality requirements to meet stakeholders' expectations.	Quality Management Plan Checklists Quality Reviews
6	Project Resources Management	Processes required to make the most effective use of the people involved with the project.	Role and Responsibility Matrix Organization Chart Performance Evaluations
7	Project Communications Management	Processes required to ensure timely and appropriate planning, collection, creation, distribution, storage, retrieval, management, control, monitoring, and ultimate disposition of project information.	Communication Plan Status Reports Presentations Lessons Learned Knowledge Repositories
8	Project Risk Management	Processes of conducting risk management planning, identification, analysis, response planning, response implementation, and monitoring risk on a project.	Risk Management Plan Risk Response Plan Risk Log
9	Project Procurement Management	Processes necessary to purchase or acquire products, services, or results needed from outside the project team.	Procurement Plan Statement of Work Proposals Contracts
10	Project Stakeholder Management	Processes required to identify the people, groups, or organizations that could impact or be impacted by the project, to analyze stakeholder expectations and their impact on the project, and to develop appropriate management strategies for effectively engaging stakeholders in project decisions and execution.	Stakeholder Register Stakeholder Engagement Plan Project Schedule Issue Log Change Requests

Figure 1.1 summarizes the relationships among the project management process groups, based on *PMBOK Guide* – Sixth Edition.

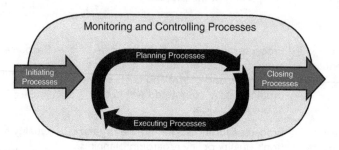

FIGURE 1.1

Project management process relationships.

 NOTE *PMBOK Guide* – Sixth Edition was released in 2017. *PMBOK Guide* – Seventh Edition was officially released in August 2021. PMI targets an update to the PMBOK every four years.

TABLE 1.5 Description of *PMBOK Guide* – Seventh Edition Twelve Principles of Project Management

#	Category	Principle Label	Principle Statement
1	Stewardship	Be a diligent, respectful, and caring steward	Stewards act responsibly to carry out activities with integrity, care, and trustworthiness while maintaining compliance with internal and external guidelines.
2	Team	Create a collaborative project team environment	Project teams that work collaboratively can accomplish a shared objective more effectively and efficiently than individuals working on their own.
3	Stakeholders	Effectively engage with stakeholders	Engage stakeholders proactively and to the degree needed to contribute to project success and customer satisfaction.
4	Value	Focus on value	Continually evaluate and adjust project alignment to business objectives and intended benefits and value.
5	Systems Thinking	Recognize, evaluate, and respond to system interactions	Recognize, evaluate, and respond to the dynamic circumstances within and surrounding the project in a holistic way to positively affect project performance.

#	Category	Principle Label	Principle Statement
6	Leadership	Demonstrate leadership behaviors	Demonstrate and adapt leadership behaviors to support individual and team needs and to promote project success.
7	Tailoring	Tailor based on context	Design the project approach based on the context, objectives, stakeholders, governance, and environment using "just enough" process to achieve the desired outcome while maximizing value, managing cost, and enhancing speed.
8	Quality	Build quality into processes and deliverables	Maintain a focus on quality that produces deliverables that meet project objectives and align to the needs, uses, and acceptance requirements set by relevant stakeholders.
9	Complexity	Navigate complexity	Continually evaluate and navigate project complexity so that approaches and plans enable the project teams to successfully navigate the project life cycle.
10	Risk	Optimize risk responses	Continually evaluate exposure to risk to maximize positive impacts and minimize negative impacts to the project and its outcomes.
11	Adaptability and Resiliency	Embrace adaptability and resiliency	Build adaptability and resiliency into the organization's and project team's approaches to help the project accommodate change, recover from setbacks, and advance the work of the project.
12	Change	Enable change to achieve the envisioned future state	Prepare those impacted for the adoption and sustainment of new and different behaviors and processes required for the transition from the current state to the intended future state created by the project outcomes.

 NOTE   The PMBOK Principles of Project Management reflect the influence of the values and principles captured in the Agile Manifesto.

TABLE 1.6   Description of *PMBOK Guide* – Seventh Edition Eight Performance Domains of Project Management

#	Performance Domain	Focus	Desired Outcomes
1	Stakeholders	Activities and functions associated with stakeholders	Productive working relationship with stakeholders

Stakeholder agreement with project objectives |

#	Performance Domain	Focus	Desired Outcomes
2	Team	Activities and functions associated with the people responsible for producing project deliverables	Shared ownership High performing team Applicable leadership and interpersonal skills demonstrated by all team members
3	Approach and Life Cycle	Activities and functions associated with the approach, cadence, and life cycle phases of the project	Approaches consistent with project deliverables Project life cycle that connects delivery of value from beginning to end of project Project life cycle that facilitates delivery cadence and approach required to produce the deliverables
4	Planning	Activities and functions associated with the initial, ongoing, and evolving organization and coordination necessary to deliver project deliverables and outcomes	Project progresses in an organized, coordinated, and deliberate manner A holistic approach to delivering project outcomes Evolving information is elaborated to produce the deliverables and outcomes Time spent planning is appropriate for situation Planning information is sufficient to manage expectations There is a process to adapt plans based on emerging and changing needs or conditions
5	Project Work	Activities and functions associated with the establishing project processes, managing physical resources, and fostering a learning environment	Efficient and effective project performance Processes are appropriate for the project and environment Appropriate communication with stakeholders Efficient management of physical resources Effective management of procurements Improved team capability due to continuous learning and process improvement

#	Performance Domain	Focus	Desired Outcomes
6	Delivery	Activities and functions associated with delivering targeted scope and quality	Project contributes to business objectives
			Project realizes intended outcomes
			Project benefits are realized in the time frame planned
			Project team has clear understanding of requirements
			Stakeholders satisfied with project deliverables
7	Measurement	Activities and functions associated with assessing project performance and taking appropriate actions to maintain acceptable performance	Reliable understanding of project status
			Actionable data to facilitate decision-making
			Timely and appropriate actions to keep project performance on track
			Achieving targets and business value by making informed and timely decisions based on reliable forecasts and evaluations
8	Uncertainty	Activities and functions associated with risk and uncertainty	Awareness of the holistic environment in which project occurs
			Proactively exploring and responding to uncertainty
			Awareness of the interdependence of all project variables
			Capacity to anticipate threats and opportunities and understand the consequences
			Project delivery with minimal impact from unforeseen events or conditions
			Opportunities are realized to improve project performance and outcomes
			Cost and schedule reserves are leveraged to maintain alignment with project objectives

 NOTE Project management is a broad field with great potential for specialized and in-depth study. There are entire books and training classes focused solely on advanced analysis of individual process groups, knowledge areas, principles, and performance domains.

Again, depending on your experiences, you might not have realized that project management consists of all the foregoing activities, and you might not actually perform all these activities as a project manager in your organization. However, it is important and helpful to understand how big your playing field is when learning something new. This book will not completely educate you on each of these process groups, knowledge areas, principles, or performance domains, but it will provide you with the knowledge, essential tools, and real-world insights to improve your effectiveness on your first project management assignment.

 TIP   We will review more of the changes in *PMBOK Guide – Seventh Edition*, in Chapter 26, "Powerful PMP Exam Tips."

What Is the Value of Project Management?

As the organizational operating environment continues to become more global, more competitive, and more demanding, organizations must adapt. They must become more efficient, more productive—they must do more with less. They must continually innovate. They must respond rapidly to a fast-changing environment. *How can they do this? How can they do this in a strategic manner? How can they do this and still have the proper management controls?* They can do this with effective project management. The strategic value points that effective project management can offer an organization include, but are not limited to, the following:

- Provide a controlled way to rapidly respond to changing market conditions and new strategic opportunities

- Maximize the innovative and creative capabilities of the organization by creating environments of focus and open communication

- Enable organizations to accomplish more with less cost

- Enable better leverage of both internal and external expertise

- Provide key information and visibility on project metrics to enable better decision-making management

- Increase the pace and level of stakeholder acceptance for any strategic change

- Reduce financial losses by "killing off" poor project investments early in their life cycles

NOTE *Stakeholder* is the term used to describe individuals and organizations who are actively involved in the project or whose interests might be impacted by the execution or completion of the project.

In addition to providing apparent value to any organization, project management also offers tremendous value to each of us as individuals. At a personal level, the value of effective project management

- Ensures that our work is put to the best use for the organization and is properly recognized

- Provides a career path that offers unique, challenging opportunities on each new project

- Provides a career path that requires all our abilities and knowledge, including our management, business, people, and technical skills

- Provides a career path that is high in demand and, generally, offers an increase in income

- Provides a career path that prepares you for organizational leadership positions

- Provides a career path that is recognized more each year as excellent preparation for CxO positions (as more CxO positions are filled by individuals with project management experience)

- Provides a career path that enables you to be on the front lines of strategic organizational initiatives and have major impact on the organization's future

Why Are Projects Challenging?

From what we've covered so far, from your own experiences, or from your reading of trade publications, you likely have some appreciation for the difficulty of completing a successful project. Although I address many common challenges in more detail throughout this book, let's review the key reasons why projects are challenging to manage:

- **Uncharted territory**—Each project is unique. The work to be done has likely never been done before by this group of people in this particular environment.

- **Multiple expectations**—Each project has multiple stakeholders that each have their own needs and expectations for the project.

- **Communication obstacles**—Due to natural organizational boundaries, communication channels, and team development stages, communication of project information must be proactively managed to ensure proper flow.

- **Balancing the competing demands**—Every project is defined to produce one or more deliverables (scope) within a defined time period (time), under an approved budget (cost) with a specified set of resources. In addition, the deliverables must achieve a certain performance level (quality) and meet the approval of the key stakeholders (expectations). Each of these factors can affect the others, as Figure 1.2 illustrates. For example, if additional functionality (scope, quality) is desired, the time and cost (resources needed) of the project will increase. This is a key focus of an effective project manager.

 NOTE The competing project demands are often referred to as the *triple constraint of project management*. Time and Cost (or Resources) are always two sides of the triangle. Depending on where you look, the third side is either Scope, Performance, or Quality. In either case, it's the "output" of the project. Additionally, many recent variations of this model have included the additional demand of Client Expectations.

FIGURE 1.2

Competing project demands (traditional model on left, modern model on right), summarizing the relationships between the natural competing demands of projects.

- **Cutting edge**—Often, projects have a strategic, innovative focus. As a result, they often deal with new, leading-edge technologies. In these cases, the project has more risks, more unknowns, and is much more difficult to estimate accurately.

- **Organizational impacts**—In addition to overcoming natural communication obstacles created by the project structure, the project manager must also manage overlaps in organizational approval and authority domains, contend with competing priorities for shared resources, deal with annual budget cycles that might not be aligned with the project's funding needs, and ensure that the project is aligned with the focus of the organization.

- **Collaboration**—Depending on the strategic level and scope of your project, your project team will consist of stakeholders across the organization from different functional areas that are likely not accustomed to working together. For project success, these different stakeholders must learn to work together and to understand the others' perspectives to make the best decisions for the project. Often, the project manager plays a key facilitating role in this collaboration process.

- **Estimating the work**—Estimating project work is difficult, yet the time and cost dimensions of the project are built on these work effort estimates. Given the facts that the work of the project is often unique (never been done before at all, never been done with these tools, and never been done by these people) and most organizations do not maintain accurate historical records on previous projects (that might have similar work components), it is difficult to accurately estimate the effort for individual work items, not to mention the entire project. This is especially difficult when the project entails the delivery of a solution when the full requirements are undetermined. This challenge in particular is why agile management has grown in popularity and use throughout many organizations.

Growing Demand for Effective Project Managers

With the value that project management offers any organization, it is easy to understand why more and more industries are adopting project management as the way to do business. As a result, if you check nearly any recent hiring survey or "hot" careers forecast, you will find project management near the top of this list.

With the business trends of global competition and increased worker productivity continuing for the foreseeable future, the demand for successful project managers will only increase. Even in industries and organizations that are experiencing staff reductions, the individuals who have the knowledge, the social intelligence, and the management competence to solve problems and get projects done are the individuals most valued and retained by the organization.

In addition, with the increased cybersecurity threats to organizational assets, the growing complexity of applications, the increasing adoption of project approaches requiring integration and teamwork of all organizational functions, and the ability to collect more and more data, the need for professionals who can understand these dynamics, clearly summarize and communicate to the organization, and still get things done successfully will just continue to rise for years to come.

Furthermore, many organizations have either compliance or competitive drivers requiring them to make process improvement. Common compliance drivers include new or updated process standards issued by a governing body applicable to the organization. Examples include acts of Congress (such as Health Insurance Portability and Accountability Act [HIPAA] compliance), government agencies (such as the Food and Drug Administration or Environmental Protection Agency), industry standards bodies (such as the International Organization for Standardization), and industry process models (such as Six Sigma Quality Model or the Capability Maturity Model Integration for software engineering or project management). Common competitive drivers include leveraging the latest best practices and methodologies applicable to the industry, market, and organization involved. Some examples include agile project management, product management, DevOps, and DevSecOps). In all these cases, effective project management is a requirement to ensure that these process improvements are made, sustained, and repeatable.

As the demand for effective project managers continues to grow and organizations continue to experience varying degrees of success with project management, more organizations are requiring their project managers to be certified. Specifically, they are requesting PMI's Project Management Professional (PMP) certification. Much like a master's of business administration (MBA) degree does not guarantee a person can run a profitable, growing business, the PMP certification does not guarantee a person can successfully manage a project. However, it does provide assurance that the individual has a baseline level of knowledge and experience, and it does indicate that the person takes her profession seriously.

Trends in Project Management

The pace of change in today's business and technology climate has never been greater. As a result, there are always new challenges facing today's project manager. Here are some other trends in business and project management that first-time project managers are likely to encounter (that they might not have just a decade or less ago):

- **Agile approaches**—Due to the pace of change, the need to adapt and generate products/systems quickly, and the difficulty in developing detailed work plans upfront, agile development methodologies are becoming the norm. And in most organizations, the transition to agile project approaches does not occur overnight. Thus, you are likely to encounter both growing pains and hybrid project approaches as an organization makes the transition. See Chapter 25, "The Fun Never Stops," for more information.

- **DevOps and DevSecOps**—Much like agile development, these IT methodologies require a culture shift in an organization and are focused on delivering value faster. These practices require integration and collaboration among traditionally disparate groups, process automation, and transparency to be successful.

- **Product management**—With the adoption of agile project management has come an organizational focus on product management. This focus can entail building teams and processes for the life of the product, not just the project; managing the entire life cycle of the product, not just the project; and aligning and leveraging organizational resources by product groups. In this environment, products are managed like long-running programs, and funding is typically done on an incremental basis.

- **Cybersecurity threats**—With the increased frequency, scale, and impact of cyber attacks, organizations are having to respond and update legacy systems quickly that were not designed with the necessary level of security in mind. In addition, any new system must be designed with these new requirements. See Chapter 25 for more information.

- **Mobile and Internet of Things (IoT) applications**—The growing use of mobile and wearable technologies, combined with the accelerating use of smart sensors in almost all devices, now enables organizations to offer services and collect both quality and quantity of data that seemed impossible just a few years ago. All of this has exponential impact on the variables that need to be tested.

- **Social media**—When used responsibly and with purpose both internal and external to the organization, social media is a powerful tool; however, if guidelines and security protocols are not established, it can be a problem.

- **Project management collaboration tools**—As the move to virtual teams was accelerated in response to the pandemic, the ability to set up and use a cloud-based collaboration work environment effectively is important. See Chapter 25 for more information.

- **Work management tools**—Many organizations are leveraging work management tools (such as Jira) to capture, manage, and monitor all work elements of a project and product (such as requirements, backlog, test defects, issues, risks, etc.).

- **HIPAA privacy compliance**—For many organizations and industries, HIPAA compliance is the first time they have had to set up procedures and systems to ensure specific data items are protected and not put at risk. This coincides with the general increased risk of all customer data being exposed due to cybersecurity threats. See Chapter 25 for more information.

- **Managing virtual, cross-functional, and multicultural teams**—With the continuous advancements in workgroup and communications tools, the increased integration of processes within an organization, and the continuous drive for increased organizational efficiencies, it is very likely that your project team will consist of members from different physical locations (virtual), different functional departments (cross-functional), or different cultures (multicultural, global). See Chapter 20, "Managing Differences," and Chapter 17, "Managing Project Communications," for more information.

- **Change agent**—Because most projects represent a change to business as usual, the project manager is expected to play a key role in leading the stakeholders through the change and acceptance process. See Chapter 16, "Leading a Project," and Chapter 18, "Managing Expectations," for more information.

- **Servant leadership**—Due to a lack of formal authority, the need to understand the requirements of all stakeholders, and the importance of facilitation, collaboration, and managing expectations, there is a growing awareness that a servant leadership style is paramount for effective project management. See Chapter 16 for more information.

- **Managing vendors**—With the increased outsourcing of non-core activities and the increased use of cloud services, more projects leverage one or more vendors (suppliers) to get work done. See Chapter 21, "Managing Vendors," for more information.

- **Working with PMOs and corporate governance processes**—If you are working in any type of corporate or multiple business unit environment, you most likely deal with a Project Management Office (PMO), a Product Line Management group, or other corporate governance processes. See Chapter 25 for more information.

Additional Resources

In addition to the PMBOK, PMI also provides specific standards documents or practice guides on the following:

- Program Management
- Portfolio Management
- Organizational Project Management Maturity Management (OPM3)
- Earned Value Management
- Project Risk Management
- Project Estimating
- Work Breakdown Structures
- Project Scheduling
- Project Configuration Management
- Project Management Competency
- Construction—Project Management
- Government—Project Management
- Requirements Management
- Business Analysis
- Change Management

In addition, I recommend the following online resources for insightful articles on project management:

- www.pmi.org
- www.projectmanagement.com
- www.mpug.com
- www.cio.com
- www.techrepublic.com/topic/project-management
- www.linkedin.com/learning

THE ABSOLUTE MINIMUM

At this point, you should have a high-level understanding of the following:

- The elements of project management
- What a project is and how it differs from operations and a product
- The common challenges of managing projects
- The value of effective project management to an organization
- The merits of project management as a career choice
- The latest business and project management trends that might impact your first opportunity

The map in Figure 1.3 summarizes the main points we reviewed in this chapter.

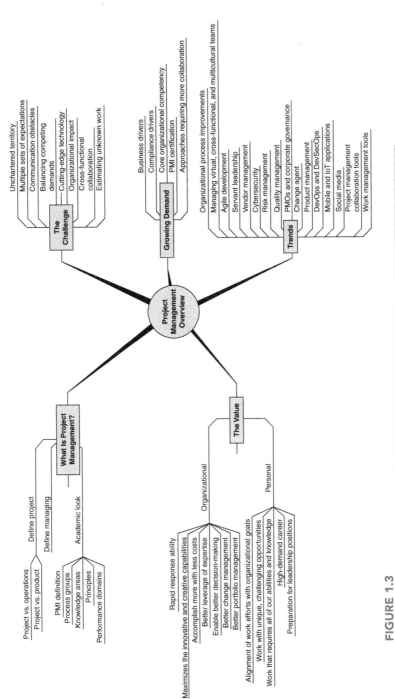

FIGURE 1.3

Project management overview.

2

THE PROJECT MANAGER

As we reviewed in Chapter 1, "Project Management Overview," the project manager has many activities to perform, challenges to overcome, and responsibilities to uphold over the life of a project. Depending on your individual experiences, your industry background, and the manner in which project management has been implemented, that review might have been quite enlightening to you.

To ensure that we have a common understanding of what a project manager does, in this chapter I review the different roles a project manager plays over the life of a project and discuss the prerequisite skills that you need to perform those roles. Most importantly, I accelerate your learning curve by sharing the characteristics of successful project managers and the common mistakes made by many others.

One Title, Many Roles

You've likely heard many of the analogies before to describe the role of project manager—the "captain" of the ship, the "conductor" of the orchestra, the "coach" of the team, the "catalyst" of the engine, and so on. There's truth and insight in each of the analogies, but each can be incomplete as well. To gain better understanding of what a project manager does, let's briefly discuss each of the key roles played by the project manager:

- **Planner**—Ensures that the project is defined properly and completely for success, all stakeholders are engaged, work effort approach is determined, required resources are available when needed, and processes are in place to properly execute and control the project.

- **Organizer**—Using work breakdown, estimating, and scheduling techniques, determines the complete work effort for the project, the proper sequence of the work activities, when the work will be accomplished, who will do the work, and how much the work will cost.

- **Point Person**—Serves as the central point of contact for all oral and written project communications.

- **Quartermaster**—Ensures the project has the resources, materials, and facilities it needs when it needs it.

- **Facilitator**—Ensures that stakeholders and team members who come from different perspectives understand each other and work together to accomplish the project goals.

- **Persuader**—Gains agreement from the stakeholders on project definition, success criteria, and approach; manages stakeholder expectations throughout the project while managing the competing demands of time, cost, and quality; and gains agreement on resource decisions and issue resolution action steps.

- **Problem Solver**—Utilizes root-cause analysis process experience, prior project experience, and technical knowledge to resolve unforeseen technical issues and take any necessary corrective actions.

- **Umbrella**—Works to shield the project team from the politics and "noise" surrounding the project, so they can stay focused and productive.

- **Coach**—Determines and communicates the role each team member plays and the importance of that role to the project's success, finds ways to motivate each team member, looks for ways to improve the skills of each team member, and provides constructive and timely feedback on individual performances.

- **Bulldog**—Performs the follow-up to ensure that commitments are maintained, issues are resolved, and action items are completed.

- **Librarian**—Manages all information, communications, and documentation involved in the project.

 NOTE   Although there is consensus that the disciplines and techniques used in project management can be applied in any industry, there is no consensus on whether individual project managers can be effective in a different industry.

There is no doubt that the more knowledge and experience that a project manager has in the subject matter area of the project, the more value they can offer. However, depending on the size of the initiative and the team composition, a project manager with different industry experience can bring tremendous value if that person is strong in the other four key skill categories discussed.

- **Insurance Agent**—Continuously works to identify risks and develop responses to those risk events in advance.

- **Police Officer**—Consistently measures progress against the plan, develops corrective actions, and reviews the quality of both project processes and project deliverables.

- **Salesperson**—An extension of the Persuader and Coach roles, focuses on "selling" the benefits of the project to the organization, serving as a "change agent," and inspiring team members to meet project goals and overcome project challenges.

Key Skills of Project Managers

Although a broad range of skills is needed to effectively manage the people, process, and technical aspects of any project, it becomes clear there is a set of key skills that each project manager should have. Although these skill categories are not necessarily exclusive of each other, let's group them into five categories to streamline our review and discussion:

1. **Project Management Fundamentals**—The "science" part of project management, covered in this book, including office productivity suite (such as Microsoft Office, email, and so on), project management software, project collaboration tool, and work management tool skills.

2. **Business Management Fundamentals**—Those skills that would be equally valuable to an operations or line-of-business manager, such as budgeting, finance, procurement, organizational dynamics, team development, performance management, coaching, and motivation.

   TIP Active listening is one of the secret weapons of effective project managers.

3. **Technical Knowledge**—The knowledge gained from experience and competence in the focal area of the project. With it, you greatly increase your effectiveness as a project manager. You have more credibility, and you can ask better questions, validate the estimates and detail plans of team members, help solve technical issues, develop better solutions, and serve more of a leadership role.

4. **Communication Skills**—Because communication is regarded as the most important project management skill by the Project Management Institute (PMI), I feel it is important to separate these out. Skills included in this category include all written communication skills (correspondence, emails, documents), oral communication skills, facilitation skills, presentation skills, and—the most valuable—active listening. *Active listening* can be defined as "really listening" and the ability to listen with focus, empathy, and the desire to connect with the speaker.

   NOTE The specific combination of skills required for a project manager to be successful on a given project varies depending on the size and nature of the project. For example, as a general rule, on larger projects, technical knowledge is less important than competence in the other skill categories.

5. **Leadership Skills**—This category overlaps with some of the others and focuses on the attitude and mindset required for project management. However, it also includes key skills such as interpersonal and general people relationship-building skills, adaptability, flexibility, people management, degree of customer orientation, analytical skills, problem-solving skills, and the ability to keep the big picture in mind.

   NOTE In *PMBOK Guide – Sixth Edition*, PMI combines these key skill sets into three groups in the PMI Talent Triangle (shown in Figure 1.2):

   Technical project management—The knowledge, skills, and behaviors related to specific domains of project, program, and portfolio management. The technical aspects of performing one's role.

Leadership—The knowledge, skills, and behaviors needed to guide, motivate, and direct a team, to help an organization achieve its business goals.

Strategic and business management—The knowledge of and expertise in the industry and organization that enhances performance and better delivers business outcomes.

I know, I know...after reading this, you are probably thinking either one or more of the following:

- "You must be kidding! I need to be good in all those areas to manage a project?"

- "Wait! I've been on projects before, and I've yet to see a project manager who could do all that."

- "Wait, you must be kidding! If anyone was excellent in all those areas, they'd be a CxO of our company."

To help address these thoughts, please understand two important observations:

1. Many projects are not successful.

2. You do not need to get an "A" in all these categories to be successful as a project manager.

The key is that the project manager has the right mix of skills to meet the needs of the given project. In addition, a self-assessment against these skill categories enables you to leverage your strengths, compensate for your deficiencies, and focus your self-improvement program.

Qualities of Successful Project Managers

Given the many roles played by a project manager, the broad range of skills needed, and the inherent challenges in successfully delivering a project, we need to find ways to accelerate the learning process. Two key ways to accelerate our learning are understanding the qualities of successful project managers and understanding the common mistakes made by project managers.

Successful project managers do not share personality types, appearances, or sizes, but they do share three important features:

- They excel in at least two of the five key skill categories (Project Management Fundamentals, Business Management Skills, Technical Knowledge, Communication Skills, Leadership Skills) and are either good enough in the other categories or staff their teams to compensate for their deficiencies.

- They avoid the common mistakes described in the next section.
- They bring a mindset and approach to project management that is best characterized by one or more of the following qualities:
  - **Takes ownership**—Takes responsibility and accountability for the project, leads by example, and brings energy and drive to the project; without this attitude, all the skills and techniques in the world will only get you so far.
  - **Savvy**—Understands people and the dynamics of the organization; navigates tricky politics; has the ability to quickly read and diffuse emotionally charged situations; thinks fast on their feet; builds relationships; leverages personal power for benefit of the project.
  - **Intensity with a smile**—Balances an assertive, resilient, tenacious, results-oriented focus with a style that makes people want to help; consistently follows up on everything and their resolutions without annoying everyone.
  - **Eye of the storm**—Demonstrates ability to be the calm eye of the project hurricane; high tolerance for ambiguity; takes the heat from key stakeholders (CxOs, business managers, and project team); exhibits a calm, confident aura when others are showing signs of issue or project stress.
  - **Strong customer-service orientation**—Demonstrates ability to see each stakeholder's perspective; able to provide voice of all key stakeholders (especially the sponsor) to the project team; has strong facilitation and collaboration skills; has excellent active listening skills.
  - **People-focused**—Takes a team-oriented approach; understands that methodology, process, and tools are important, but without quality people it's very difficult to complete a project successfully.
  - **Always keeps "eye on the ball"**—Stays focused on the project goals and objectives. There are many ways to accomplish a given objective, which is especially important to remember when things don't go as planned.
  - **Controlled passion**—Balances passion for completing the project objectives with a healthy detached perspective, which enables them to make better decisions, to continue to see all points of view, to better anticipate risks, and to better respond to project issues.
  - **Healthy paranoia**—Balances a confident, positive outlook with a realism that assumes nothing, constantly questions, and verifies everything.
  - **Context understanding**—Understands the context of the project—the priority that their project has among the organization's portfolio of projects and how it aligns with the overall goals of the organization.

- **Looking for trouble**—Constantly looking and listening for potential risks, issues, or obstacles; confronts doubt head-on; deals with disgruntled users right away; understands that most of these situations are opportunities and can be resolved upfront before they become full-scale crisis points.

15 Common Mistakes of Project Managers

Although we review many of the common errors made in each of the fundamental areas of project management throughout this book (so you can avoid them), understanding the most common project management mistakes helps focus our efforts and helps us to avoid the same mistakes on our projects. The following are some of the most common mistakes made by project managers:

1. Not clearly understanding how or ensuring that the project is aligned with organizational objectives.

2. Not properly managing stakeholder expectations throughout the project.

3. Not gaining agreement and buy-in on project goals and success criteria from key stakeholders.

4. Not developing a realistic schedule that includes all work efforts, task dependencies, bottom-up estimates, and assigned leveled resources.

5. Not getting buy-in and acceptance on the project schedule.

6. Not clearly deciding and communicating who is responsible for what.

7. Not utilizing change control procedures to manage the scope of the project.

8. Not communicating consistently and effectively with all key stakeholders.

9. Not executing the project plan.

10. Not tackling key risks early in the project.

11. Not proactively identifying risks and developing contingency plans (responses) for those risks.

12. Not obtaining the right resources with the right skills at the right time.

13. Not aggressively pursuing issue resolution.

14. Inadequately defining and managing requirements.

15. Insufficiently managing and leading the project team.

Project Manager Versus Scrum Master Versus Product Owner

With the increasing adoption of agile project approaches, and the Scrum agile methodology in particular, there is often some initial confusion about how a Project Manager fits in this environment, since the Scrum methodology does not define a Project Manager role. And frankly, many organizations struggle to figure out how to leverage their existing project managers as they transition to agile and Scrum project approaches. Often, it is this struggle that leads to the confusion and the uncertainty surrounding the Project Manager role.

In summary, once you understand the role of the Scrum Master, the Product Owner, and the Project Manager, it's much easier to see the importance of each role and why they are all needed for a successful agile Scrum project.

 NOTE   The Scrum Guide is the official process and terminology document published by Scrum.org. The co-creator of the Scrum agile process, Ken Schwaber, founded Scrum.org as a mission-based organization to help people and teams solve complex problems by applying Scrum through training courses, certifications, and ongoing learning, all based on a common competency model.

Let's briefly discuss each role to jump-start this understanding:

- **Scrum Master**—A defined Scrum Guide role that is focused on the core team and guiding them through the Scrum process. The Scrum Master is both a coach and a facilitator for the development team, the Product Owner, and often the organization. This role is focused on the work process, alleviating bottlenecks and continuously striving for process improvement.

- **Product Owner**—A defined Scrum Guide role that is focused on maximizing the value of the product being delivered. The Product Owner is responsible for defining the backlog items (for example, requirements and features), setting priorities, and providing feedback to the core development team after each sprint (work increment).

- **Project Manager**—Serves as overall leader and manager of the project itself. This role works with the Scrum Master and Product Owner to ensure that the needs of the organization and business are being met. The Project Manager is responsible for delivering the project on time, within budget, and within the agreed-upon scope. In addition, the Project Manager handles building the team, securing the budget, development and maintenance of project schedules, delivering project communications, managing project issues and risks, and coordinating release deployments.

Seems fairly straightforward, right? So where does the confusion come into play? In my experience, the confusion stems from one, if not all, of these factors:

- Some of the traditional Project Manager functions are shared by the Scrum Master and the Product Owner.

- The Scrum Master and/or Product Owner roles have not been properly staffed and/or individuals lack the requisite Scrum training.

- A single individual is serving a combination of these roles.

Is it possible for a single person to serve a combination of these roles? Sure, but it does run the risk of highly compromising the Scrum process. The most common scenario that can be successful is one in which the Project Manager also serves as the Scrum Master, but this does assume the Project Manager has the appropriate skills, training, and time to serve both roles properly. In general, the more aligned the organization is with the Scrum agile roles, and the more mature an organization becomes with successfully leveraging the Scrum approach, the clearer the differences and the importance of each of these roles become.

THE ABSOLUTE MINIMUM

At this point, you should have a high-level understanding of the following:

- The different roles played by the project manager
- The five key skill areas every project manager should master
- The common qualities of successful project managers
- The common mistakes made by project managers
- The difference between a Project Manager, Scrum Master, and Product Owner on an agile project
- The Scrum guide is available from Scrum.org at this url: https://www.scrum.org/resources/scrum-guide

The map in Figure 2.1 summarizes the main points we reviewed in this chapter.

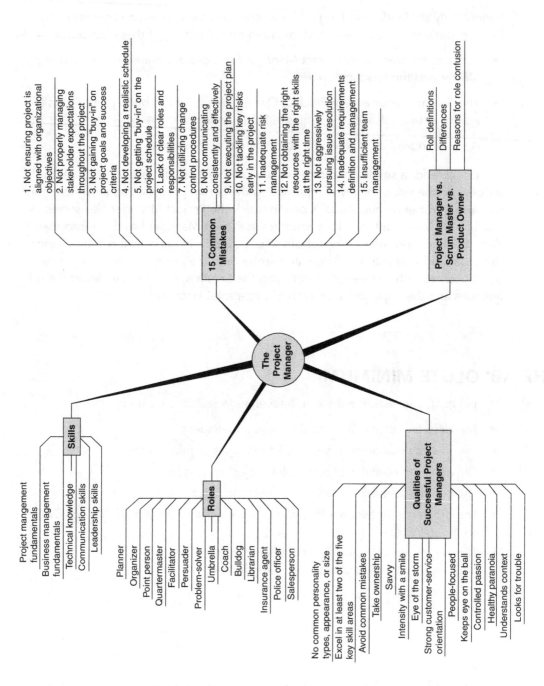

FIGURE 2.1

IN THIS CHAPTER

- Learn what comprises a successful project
- Understand the common characteristics of troubled projects
- Review the common characteristics of successful projects
- Find out which tools are indispensable to most project managers

ESSENTIAL ELEMENTS FOR ANY SUCCESSFUL PROJECT

In this chapter, we continue the accelerated learning approach started in the previous chapter. Anytime you are learning a new skill set, especially one that is as broad as project management, one of the most effective ways to reduce your learning curve and focus your mental energies is to understand what successful people do in the field and, equally important, understand what not to do.

With this philosophy in mind, we take a step up in this chapter and look at projects as a whole and not just the project manager position. We review the leading causes of troubled projects and discuss the common principles, techniques, and tools underlying most successful projects. With this foundation in place, you will better understand the purpose and the value of the fundamentals covered in the rest of this book and, as a result, be much better positioned for success on your project management assignments.

What Exactly Is a Successful Project?

You would think it would be relatively straightforward to describe the attributes of a successful project. Well, let's just say this endeavor has kept more than a few spin doctors, politicians, and history revisionists employed throughout organizations across our great land. Why is this the case? There are several reasons for this:

- There is a lack of universal harmony of what comprises project success metrics. It seems that every project management educational source and organizational process maturity standard has a slightly different definition of project success.

- For many projects, the acceptance and success criteria are never established or agreed to by all key stakeholders.

- In many cases, an organization might define a project as successful even when some of the textbook criteria for project success (such as schedule, cost, and client expectations) are not completely met. This is often the case if the project achieved strategic business or organizational objectives.

- In other cases, a cancelled project might be a successful project if there was a plan for one or more go/no-go decision points.

From a utopian, academic standpoint, the ultimate successful project would be defined as a project that

- **Delivers as promised**—The project produces all the stated deliverables.

- **Completes on time**—The project completes within the approved schedule.

- **Completes within budget**—The project completes under the approved budget.

- **Delivers quality**—The project deliverables meet all functional, performance, and quality specifications.

- **Achieves original purpose**—The project achieves its original goals, objectives, and purpose.

- **Meets all stakeholder expectations**—The complete expectations of each key stakeholder are met, including all client acceptance criteria, and each key stakeholder accepts the project results without reservation.

- **Maintains "win-win" relationships**—The needs of the project are met with a "people focus" and do not require sacrificing the needs of individual team members or vendors. Participants on successful projects should be enthusiastic when the project is complete and eager to repeat a similar experience.

TIP An excellent technique is to identify, document, review, and approve any criteria that will be used to measure the success of the project during the project definition and planning processes.

Learning from Troubled Projects

Before we review the common traits of many successful projects, you can learn a lot from less-than-successful projects. From my experience, the reasons for project troubles can be generally classified into two groups: project-level issues and organizational-level issues.

One of the key differences in the two groups is the level of control that the project manager has over these factors. For project-level issues, the project manager has tremendous influence on these matters. In most cases, the project manager can either avoid the issue or take action to resolve it if it does occur. For issues at the organizational level, the project manager cannot generally fix the problems, but the project manager can certainly have influence on them by asking the right questions, anticipating the associated risks and issues, focusing extra efforts to compensate for the issues, and developing contingency plans to minimize the impact on the project.

Also, please note that these issues are not exclusive. In most cases, there is overlap, and if you have one of these factors present in a project, you will generally have others. Table 3.1 summarizes these issues, gives specific examples of each, and notes what type of issue it is (organizational, project, or both).

TABLE 3.1 Common Reasons for Troubled Projects

Reason	Example(s)	Type	Key Learning Point
Project not aligned	Project not aligned with business unit or organizational goals; project not aligned with other projects	Org.	Verify alignment before project kicks off
Lack of management support	Insufficient funding; insufficient resources; issues not resolved; senior management performance criteria not aligned with project success criteria	Org.	Understand project impact of organizational structure; ensure proper senior management involvement in project organization; advocate PMO and steering committee structures

Reason	Example(s)	Type	Key Learning Point
Lack of stakeholder buy-in	Purpose and goals not clear; "trust" relationship not established; inadequate communications; mismatched expectations; all stakeholders not involved	Both	Gain acceptance of project purpose, goals, and success upfront; ensure all stakeholders are identified and consulted; constantly communicate and validate understanding
Inadequate project sponsor	Inactive, unengaged sponsor; lack of leadership; ethical issues; not handling organizational issues; not supportive of project management process	Org.	Educate sponsors on their roles and responsibilities; gain formal authorization of project and the project management position; understand sponsors' motives and incentives
Too many project sponsors	Conflicting project goals; lack of ownership; political battles	Org.	Relates to the need for proper project alignment and clear roles and responsibilities
Lack of clarity on roles and responsibilities	Inefficient work efforts; missed deadlines; lower team morale; delayed issue resolution	Both	Use *Responsibility Matrix* to clarify all roles and responsibilities; review roles and responsibilities with each individual; validate expectations in advance
Poor communication	Inconsistent, incomplete, or nonexistent status information on key project metrics; inadequate tracking and monitoring of project progress; not listening to stakeholder concerns or feedback; not using proper mediums for certain project communications; messages are not clear or occur too frequently	Project	Develop a project communications plan that is acceptable to all stakeholders; establish tracking and monitoring mechanisms during planning; constantly seek questions and feedback; understand each stakeholder's perspective; clearly set context of each message
Price wars	Due to budget reduction measures or market pressures, management agrees to perform project at or below estimated costs	Org.	Develop complete, detailed project budgets; communicate associated risks; improve negotiating skills
Resource conflicts	Lack of dedicated team members; key resources not available when scheduled	Org.	Develop project resource plan; gain commitments from resource managers; encourage centralized organizational structure for resource planning/deployment

Reason	Example(s)	Type	Key Learning Point
Inadequate project manager	Lack of leadership; inexperienced or untrained project manager; ineffective project manager	Both	Organizational commitment to PM education; use of PM mentorship programs
Underestimate change impact	Not understanding the complete effects on both existing processes and people that the change introduced by the project will have; not properly preparing or planning for the change	Org.	Use project sponsor and business process owners to champion the new process; involve additional stakeholders to understand their needs and solicit their support; plan for the necessary communications and training (change management plan); plan for the disruptive deployment period; utilize pilot approaches to minimize impact
Inadequate planning	Management does not require or allow time for proper planning; incomplete scope or deliverables list; incomplete work identification; lack of detailed schedule; inadequate risk identification; assumptions not documented; lack of schedule and budget contingency	Both	Educate senior management on the value of proper planning; use standard methodology for project planning; gain formal acceptance of project plan before proceeding; develop realistic project schedule and budget, as well as tools and processes to keep updated; identify and document project risks and mitigation strategies
Lack of change control management	Scope of work increases without proper schedule, budget, or resource adjustments; changes occur to deliverables, schedule, or budget without proper notification and approval	Project	Utilize formal change control procedures to properly assess and communicate any change to the scope, schedule, budget, and targeted project deliverable
Lack of completion criteria	Missed stakeholder expectations; increased costs or missed deadlines due to rework; lack of smooth transition from one phase to another	Both	Ensure success criteria are established during planning phase; define user acceptance criteria for project deliverables; define exit criteria for project phases

Reason	Example(s)	Type	Key Learning Point
Inadequate progress tracking	Inability to measure project status and probability for success; inability to review project at key points to make go/no-go decisions	Both	Establish and execute periodic status meetings and reporting (weekly in most cases); review project at scheduled intervals against established criteria to determine whether project should progress into next phase
Unforeseen technical difficulties	Effort spent resolving technical issues drives missed schedules and increased costs; unproven technology does not meet user expectations	Project	Structure project to deal with high-risk technical challenges early in the project; prove the technology before making additional investment; leverage technical expertise to support team capabilities
Poor requirements definition and/or management	Documented requirements not aligned with actual objective, workflow, or process; updated/changed requirements not implemented; delivered product is not adequate; stakeholders not satisfied	Both	Utilize requirements gathering techniques that elicit engaged participation and make it easier for stakeholders to visualize final deliverable; evaluate how requirements are reviewed and approved; establish a process to manage and communicate updates to requirements

CAUTION   A good project manager can still end up managing a troubled project. Sometimes, your best project management work might be in minimizing the damage from a troubled project.

Learning from Successful Projects

After reviewing what makes a project successful and the common ills that befall many troubled projects, you likely have a good sense of the qualities and traits shared by most successful projects. Although no two projects are ever the same, and every project has its own unique set of challenges, there is a common core of principles that successful projects share. By understanding these, new project managers can better prioritize and better focus their project management efforts. These qualities are generally true about successful projects:

- The project is aligned with organizational goals.

- The project has effective management support.

- The project has effective leadership.
- All key stakeholders are in agreement on the purpose, goals, and objectives of the project.
- All key stakeholders share a common vision of the project results.
- All key stakeholders share realistic expectations for the project results.
- The project results meet the expectations of the key stakeholders.
- Stakeholder expectations are constantly managed and validated throughout the project.
- An investment is made in proper planning.
- The project scope, approach, and deliverables are clearly defined and agreed upon during planning.
- Each stakeholder and team member's role(s) and responsibilities are clearly communicated and understood.
- A high priority is placed on accurate and complete work effort estimates.
- A realistic schedule is developed and agreed upon.
- The project team is results-focused and customer-oriented.
- Requirements are effectively defined and properly managed.
- Project communications are consistent, effective, and focused on understanding.
- Project progress is measured consistently from the current baseline.
- Project issues and subsequent action items are aggressively pursued.
- There is a strong sense of collaboration and teamwork.
- Expectations and changes surrounding scope, quality, schedule, and cost are closely managed.
- Project resources are skilled and available when needed.
- The project team proactively identifies risk and determines mitigation strategies to reduce project exposure.
- The project team anticipates and overcomes obstacles to ensure the project meets objectives.

Essential Project Manager Toolkit

Although there are many facets of project management and many lessons to be learned from both troubled projects and successful projects, there is an essential set of tangible tools that any project manager needs to have to best manage any project. Table 3.2 lists these essential tools and why they are important.

The important principles to remember regarding project management tools are as follows:

- Any planning document needs to be reviewed and agreed to by appropriate project stakeholders and team members.

- Separate documents are not always needed. Smaller projects might combine relevant information (especially "plan" documents) into a single "grouped" document.

- The essential tools represent the key information and thought processes that are needed to effectively manage the project.

TABLE 3.2 Essential Project Manager Tools

Tool	Description	Value	Notes
Project Charter	Authorizes project and the project manager	Provides official notice to the organization	Might not always be a formal document; at a minimum, get an email notification
Project Definition Document	Defines project purpose, objectives, success criteria, and scope	Key for managing expectations, controlling scope, and completing other planning efforts	Core tool
Requirements	Defines the specifications for product/output of the project	Key for managing expectations and controlling scope	Core tool; document or database
Project Schedule	Shows all work efforts, properly estimated, with logical dependencies, assigned to responsible resources scheduled against a calendar	Key for directing all project team work efforts; key for managing expectations; allows for impact and what-if simulations when things change	Core tool

Tool	Description	Value	Notes
Status Reports	Periodic reviews of actual performance versus expected performance	Provides essential information to stakeholders; allows for timely identification of performance variances	See Chapter 10, "Controlling a Project," and Chapter 17, "Managing Project Communications," for more details
Milestone Chart	A summary of the detailed project schedule showing progress against key milestones	Allows stakeholders to see high-level project progress on one page	Detailed schedule roll-ups can be difficult to read and interpret; incorporate into status report
Project Organization Chart	Shows all project stakeholders and the working relationships among them	Allows team members to get a better understanding of the project roles and organizational dynamics	On smaller projects, might be combined with project plan or project definition document
Responsibility Matrix	Defines all project roles and indicates what responsibilities each role has	Key for managing expectations; establishes accountability	On smaller projects, might be combined with project plan or project definition document
Communication Plan	Defines the how, what, when, and who regarding the flow of project information to stakeholders	Key for managing expectations; establishes buy-in	On smaller projects, might be combined with project plan or project definition document
Quality Management Plan	Defines the approaches and methods that will be utilized to manage the quality levels of project processes and results	Key for managing expectations regarding quality, performance, and regulatory compliance matters; impacts work efforts and project schedule; establishes accountability	On smaller projects, might be combined with project plan or project definition document
Staffing Management Plan	Lists how project resources will be acquired, when they are needed, how much they are needed, and how long they will be needed	Key for building schedule; key for properly managing resources	Might also include role profiles, rates, training needs; on smaller projects, might be combined with project plan or project schedule
Risk Response Plan	Lists each identified risk and the planned response strategy for each	Communicates potential issues in advance; proactive measures help reduce impact to project	On smaller projects, might be combined with project plan or project definition document

Tool	Description	Value	Notes
Project Plan	Formal, approved document that is used to manage project execution	Includes all other supplemental planning documents; key output of project planning	On smaller projects, might be combined with project definition document
Deliverable Summary	Defines and lists all deliverables to be produced by the project	Key to managing expectations; ensures proper visibility, tracking, and reporting of targeted deliverables	Might be combined with status reports; might be part of project definition document
Project Log	Captures essential information for each project risk, issue, action item, and change request	Ensures proper visibility, tracking, and reporting of items impacting the project	Core tool
Change Request Form	Captures essential information for any requested change that impacts scope, schedule, or budget	Allows change item to be properly assessed and communicated before action is taken	Core tool
Project Repository	The location where all pertinent project information is stored	Key part of managing project information; project team knows where to find current project documents	Identified in project plan and/or configuration management plan; most are digital but might have physical location, too
Project Notebook	Used by project manager to maintain official record of important project documents and deliverables	Part of managing project information	Electronic and/or hardcopy versions; frequently incorporated into project repository

THE ABSOLUTE MINIMUM

At this point, you should have a solid understanding of the following:

- What defines a successful project and why it is not always easy to measure
- The common reasons why projects get into trouble and what you can do to avoid them
- The key principles that serve as the foundation for most successful projects
- The essential project management tools and why they are important

The map in Figure 3.1 summarizes the main points reviewed in this chapter.

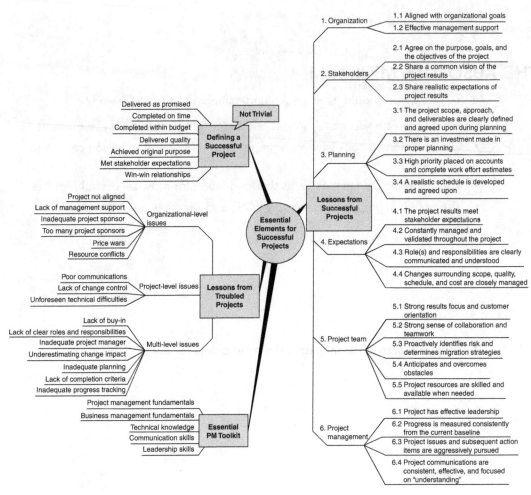

FIGURE 3.1

Essential elements for any successful project overview.

IN THIS CHAPTER

- Understand the importance of defining a project correctly

- Learn what questions must be answered to properly define a project

- Understand how defining a project relates to planning a project

- Review the essential elements for a Project Definition document

- Learn how to determine whether a project has been properly defined

4

DEFINING A PROJECT

The journey begins...

The first stop on our journey down Project Management Boulevard is also the most important because it builds the foundation for all other project management activities and sets the stage for our eventual project success (or failure).

The irony of this is that, depending on your organization and industry, you (the project manager) might be the primary agent in getting this done, or you might not be involved at all until after project definition is complete.

In either case, you need to know how to properly define a project and how to evaluate whether a project definition performed by others is complete before starting any detailed project planning efforts.

With all this in mind, we will review the critical importance this step plays, the key questions that must be answered and agreed upon, the "must-have" elements of your Project Definition document, and the success criteria for the project definition process.

Setting the Stage for Success

Pick your cliché of choice here: "getting everyone on the same page," "singing from the same songbook," "dancing to the same beat," "pointed in the same direction," or "painting the picture." They all apply, and they all communicate the importance of getting the key project participants to agree on the answers to these seven basic project definition questions:

1. Why are we doing this? (Purpose)

2. What organizational-level goal(s) does this project support? (Goals and Objectives)

3. How does this project fit with the other projects that are going on? (Scope, Project Context, Project Dependencies)

4. What is the expected benefit from this project? (Expected Benefits, Business Case, Value, Success Criteria)

5. What are we going to do? (Scope)

6. Who is affected by this and who must be involved? (Stakeholders)

7. How will we know when we are done and whether the project was successful? (Success Criteria)

Gaining consensus on these questions is paramount to managing the organizational-level factors that get projects in trouble (such as alignment with organization and management support) and to controlling key project-level factors that impact project success: stakeholder expectations and scope management.

 NOTE   As with all project management processes, the time and rigor invested should be consistent with the size and risk level of the project.

As a general guideline, 20% of the total project duration should be invested in definition and planning activities.

How Does Defining a Project Relate to Project Planning?

Many people think of "defining a project" as part of the project planning process, and they are correct. It is the first step. However, it is important to make the distinction for several reasons:

- Logistically, before you develop a detailed and complete project plan, you need to know the parameters and boundaries for the project.

- Politically, you need to know the key stakeholders are in agreement with the project mission (project purpose, goals, objectives, and success criteria) before proceeding.

- Practically, the work to properly define a project is often not trivial. In fact, many process-focused and disciplined organizations handle "project definitions" as separate projects. Common examples include business case development, cost-benefit analysis, selection, proof-of-concept models, and assessment projects.

- Historically, people have learned that detailed project planning and general project management are inefficient, and difficult at best, if project definition is not performed.

- Financially, effective execution of the project definition process enables the organization to leverage portfolio project management processes. This enables the organization to better invest its limited resources in initiatives that offer the greatest return.

PORTFOLIO PROJECT MANAGEMENT

Portfolio project management is a management practice that brings rigor and diligence to the project definition process. It is a management practice that enables executives to make better decisions regarding which projects to fund, gives them visibility to all targeted enterprise projects throughout the project life cycle, and applies a consistent set of performance metrics and criteria to better compare project performance. It is a management practice that attempts to bring an end to projects that are not organizationally aligned, not prioritized, not resourced properly, and not monitored closely. Some of the key benefits of this approach to an organization include the following:

- Requires each potential project to be fully defined upfront.

- Engages the executives in the project selection and prioritization process, using a consistent, objective approach.

- Ensures that individual work efforts are prioritized and focused on the most important projects.

- Maintains executive visibility on targeted projects. This helps maintain organizational alignment.

- Enables executives to identify troubled projects earlier. This provides them more options, and it enables them to reallocate valuable resources much quicker.

Project Definition Document

We've referred to "gaining consensus" and "getting agreement" as the answers to the important project-defining questions several times. How do you do this? You write them down and get everyone to formally sign off on this document. We will refer to this document as the Project Definition document. This section reviews both the must-have elements and good-to-have elements of the Project Definition document.

CAUTION   There are many different names for the Project Definition document. Some of the most common alternative names are Project Brief, Project Charter, Project Initiation, Scope Statement, and Statement of Work.

I use Project Definition because this term best describes the purpose of the document.

TIP   Whenever you define what is in scope, it's a good idea to note what related work is out of scope. This helps clarify understanding and expectations regarding project scope.

As a rule, any work item related to your defined scope that someone could assume is included, but is not, should be listed as out of scope.

Required Elements

First, let's review the must-have informational elements that should be included in your Project Definition document:

- **Purpose**—This section should answer the "Why?" question and clearly communicate the expected business value. It should reference the organizational objective being supported, the business problem being solved, and its relative priority level.

- **Goals and Objectives**—This section is derived from the Purpose and communicates the targeted outcomes for the project. It should answer the "What are you going to accomplish?" question.

- **Success Criteria**—Closely related to Goals and Objectives, this section should list the measurable, verifiable results that determine the success level of this project. This section is often referred to as Critical Success Factors.

- **Project Context**—This section documents how this project relates to other projects within the product program and within the organization as a whole. This section should also describe how the project fits within the organization and business process flow.

- **Project Dependencies**—Closely related to Project Context, this section clearly documents any dependencies that could affect the results or success factors of this project.

- **Scope Specifications**—This section clearly designates the organizational, process, systems, and functional specification boundaries for the project. This section should be a high-level breakdown of the Goals and Objectives.

- **Out-of-Scope Specifications**—This section clearly indicates the high-level work items that are related to (or associated with) this initiative but that are not part of this project, to better communicate what is considered to be in scope.

 NOTE To expedite the process of getting agreement on the Project Definition document, walk through an initial draft that you develop with the stakeholder group rather than starting with a blank slate.

The process of project definition and project planning is a process of iterative refinement (or what PMI refers to as *progressive elaboration*), so your draft helps facilitate the discussions, negotiations, and modifications that need to occur among the stakeholders.

- **Assumptions**—This section clearly communicates the underlying basis or things to be considered true in regard to any other aspect of this document. In most cases, the Scope, Out-of-Scope, Assumptions, and Constraints sections combine to clearly define what work will be performed by this project.

- **Constraints**—This section lists any business event, schedule, budgetary, resource, or technical factor that will limit the options available to the project.

- **Risks**—This section lists any uncertain event or condition (risk) that, if it occurs, could have a negative effect on one or more project success criteria (schedule, budget, quality, and so on). For each risk, it is good to list the related causes, the perceived negative effects, the likelihood it will occur, and the planned response strategy and action items. See Chapter 14, "Managing Project Risks," for more details.

- **Stakeholders**—Lists all the individuals, business units, and organizations involved in the project, the role(s) each is expected to play, and an indication of how they relate to one another. Including a project organization chart and a stakeholder-role description table is highly recommended here.

- **Recommended Project Approach**—Highlights the recommended approach to getting the work of the project done and why it is selected over any other options as a way to better describe the intent of the initiative. This section should note any key strategies, methodologies, and technologies to be used.

TIP An agile project approach should be considered when the requirement details are not well understood, when there is a lack of consensus on the product vision, or when there is high risk involved.

Additional Elements to Consider

These are informational elements that might not always apply but, if appropriate, are recommended additions to the Project Definition document.

CAUTION The Project Definition document is a living document and should be updated to reflect the evolving circumstances, issues, and needs surrounding the project.

Changes are okay. The changes just need to be announced, reviewed, and approved by the relevant stakeholders.

- **Alternative Project Approaches**—This section lists the approach details for any alternatives that were considered.

- **Organizational Change Issues**—Because most projects result in a change to the status quo, and the most common oversight in projects is not adequately realizing, planning, and preparing for the change impact to current customers, business processes, and personnel, it is highly recommended that this area be a focus from the start of the project.

- **Policies and Standards**—Given the priority that standardization, compliance, process improvement, security, and quality have in most organizations, it is highly recommended that any policy, regulation, or standard that will be applied to the project or the results of the project be identified from the start of the project.

- **Preliminary Cost, Schedule, and Resource Estimates**—Generally, there is some preliminary "ballpark" expectation for the cost, timing, and resource needs of this project. In many cases, these will be noted as either project objectives or project constraints. The most valuable information here is not necessarily the date or the dollar amount, but an explanation for what is driving the figures presented.

 TIP Use a visual project scope summary to gain a clearer picture of project purpose, context, goals, and change impact among key stakeholders.

- **References to Supporting Documents**—For any situation, where the results of a preliminary or related project served to define the need or details for this project, always include a reference to those supporting documents. Common examples would be a Business Case, Cost-Benefit Analysis, Assessment Results, Requirements Document, and Business Process Engineering Studies.

- **Visual Scope Summary**—For most projects, a visual summary of the project scope can be an invaluable tool for communicating the objectives, boundaries, and change elements of the project. It can help validate the definition of the project, identify potential risks, and greatly improve the common understanding of the project stakeholders. Especially for any project that is introducing significant change, the effort to create this visual summary is one of the best investments you'll make. The creation of a visual scope summary definitely falls into the "art" part of project management—there is not a single way to do this. The specific tool or medium used can vary depending on skill set and tools available. The specific approach depends on the nature of the project. For product and construction projects, a prototype or visual drawing of the target can be used. For projects impacting business processes, a variant of a flow diagram (process, data, system) showing current state and proposed future state can be very effective. There is no right answer—you just need to be effective.

 TIP For anyone who has not attended a Goal Setting 101 course, let's do a quick review of SMART goals.

Actually, I've seen three different definitions of SMART goals, and they all apply. In each, the first two parts and the last part are consistent   -

Definition #1—SMART goals are **S**pecific, **M**easurable, **A**chievable, **R**ewarding, and **T**ime-based.

Definition #2—SMART goals are **S**pecific, **M**easurable, **A**ttainable, **R**elevant, and **T**ime-based.

Definition #3—SMART goals are **S**pecific, **M**easurable, **A**greed-To, **R**ealistic, and **T**ime-based.

Perhaps the acronym should be SMAAARRRT. For projects, the third definition is more important due to the "Agreed-To" element.

Project Definition Checklist

A project definition checklist can help you determine whether your project is defined properly and whether you are ready to proceed to the next iteration of detailed planning. If you find that your project is not properly defined, the following options are available:

- Resolve any gaps with appropriate stakeholders before moving on to the next phase.

- If the project has already been defined, work to resolve these gaps during the detail planning phase.

- If gaps cannot be resolved, then handle as project risks or issues (whichever is appropriate for the specific gap).

General

- Is it clear why this project is being undertaken?

- Is there a clear picture of the desired results of this project?

- Is there a clear picture of how this project fits within the organizational landscape?

- Is there a gap between available and needed funds?

- Have the success factors been identified? Are they complete? Are they SMART?

- Have any future-state performance targets been defined as success factors? Are they SMART?

- Is the gap between the current state and the desired future state clearly documented and understood?

- Has the expected change impact on existing business processes, customers, systems, and staff been clearly documented?

- Do you understand who is funding the project initiative?

> **TIP** Use a Project Organization Chart to effectively summarize the project team members and the key stakeholders (see Chapter 5, "Planning a Project").

Scope

- Does project scope indicate boundaries among impacted processes, systems, and organizations?

- Is project scope defined clearly enough to show when scope creep is occurring?

- Have any external process or system interfaces that will be impacted by this project been identified?

- Has the process workflow between business units or business functions been properly considered?

- Have the organizational and geographic boundaries been clearly defined?

- Does project scope include related items that are out of scope?

- Does project scope include any other organizational or technology-based initiative that is needed to fully support the project objective?

- If project scope includes any requirements, have the requirements been properly validated?

- Have any and all project constraints been identified?

- Have any and all project assumptions been identified?

- Are there any known policies, regulations, or standards that apply to this project (such as procurement, quality, security, regulatory compliance, and so on)?

> **CAUTION** As with all project documents, make sure you have a way to control changes to the Project Definition document and that you have proper backups of it.
>
> Your Configuration Management Plan (discussed in Chapter 12, "Managing Project Deliverables") documents this.

Stakeholders

- Has the project sponsor been identified and engaged?
- Is each affected business unit and business process step represented on the project team?
- Is each customer group represented on the project team?
- Are all stakeholders identified in a project organization chart?
- Are the reporting relationships indicated in the project organization chart?
- Are project roles described and assigned to each stakeholder?
- Have you identified which stakeholders form the core management steering committee?
- Have you identified which stakeholders need to review and approve any requested changes to the project definition?

Project Approach

- Does the recommended approach explain why it is selected over the alternatives?
- Are the proposed technologies, strategies, and methodologies documented?

Other

- Are the project definition elements documented?
- Is the Project Definition document under configuration management (version control)?
- Have high-level risks and planned responses been identified?
- Have the preliminary timeline and budget been stated? Are the supporting reasons and assumptions documented?

Acceptance

- Have all stakeholders reviewed, agreed upon, and approved the Project Definition document?
- Have the project and the project manager been officially authorized?

THE ABSOLUTE MINIMUM

At this point, you should have a solid understanding of the following:

- A properly defined project greatly increases the odds for project success.
- The project and the project manager position should be officially announced and formally authorized to proceed.
- The primary project management tool for defining a project is the Project Definition document.
- The key skills used by the project manager when defining a project are facilitation, interviewing, negotiation, and general interpersonal skills.
- The Project Definition document should clearly communicate why the project is being undertaken, how it fits within the organization, what it will accomplish, the boundaries for the project work, who will be involved, and how project success will be measured.
- Two effective visual tools for communicating the definition of a project are the Project Overview Map and the Project Organization Chart.
- The Project Definition document is a living document throughout the project. However, any changes to the document must be approved by the same set of original stakeholders.
- All stakeholders in the project must be identified.
- All major stakeholders must approve the Project Definition document.

The map in Figure 4.1 summarizes the main points reviewed in this chapter.

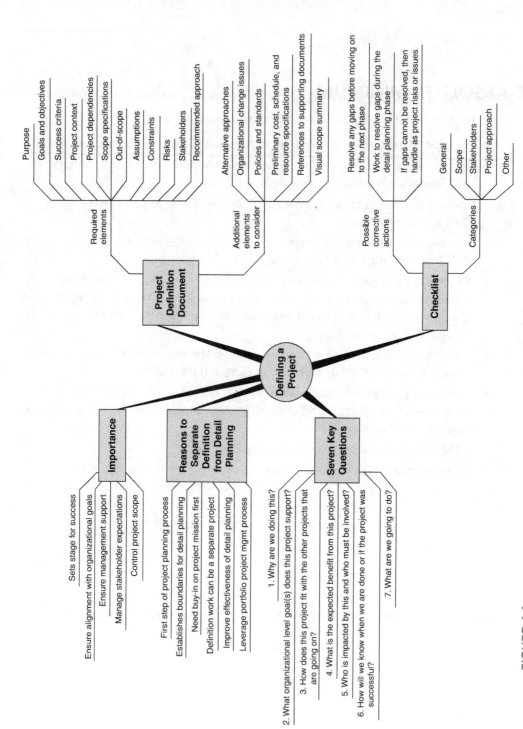

FIGURE 4.1

Defining a project overview.

IN THIS CHAPTER

- Understand the key principles of effective project planning
- Learn the important questions that project planning should answer
- Understand that a project plan is not a Microsoft Project file
- Review the essential elements for a project plan
- Find out how to develop a project plan
- Discover how to avoid the common project planning mistakes

5

PLANNING A PROJECT

The journey continues . . .

As is true with defining a project, project planning is essential for project success. In defining a project, we come to an agreement on what we will do and who will be involved. In planning a project, we focus on how the work will be done. This involves both how the deliverables will be developed and how the project will be managed. Thus, project planning involves the traditional areas of work tasks, resources, schedule, and costs, and it also sets the stage for managing project changes, project communications, project quality, project risks, project procurement activities, and the project team. Each of these factors directly impacts stakeholder expectations and our ability to successfully control and execute the project.

Unfortunately, there are many misconceptions about project planning, and often it is performed incompletely or incorrectly.

With this in mind, we review the key principles of project planning, how to properly plan a project, the key planning questions that must be answered and agreed upon, the must-have elements of your project plan document, and the success criteria for the project planning process.

It is also worth noting that even if you find yourself managing an agile project, these principles still apply. The agile process anticipates change and expects the project team to refine the work plan based on the outcomes of each iteration.

 NOTE A planning technique that is often used to deal with the realities of planning project work is called *rolling wave planning*, which plans work *details only* for the *next* project phase. The planning for the subsequent phases is kept at a high level. As part of the closing process and review of the current phase, the work details for the next phase are then planned out.

In fact, this concept is inherent in the agile project management approach, where planning is ongoing throughout the project and focuses on performing detail planning for each timebox (iteration, sprint).

Key Project Planning Principles

Although most reasonable people will at least acknowledge there is value to planning at a logical level, many of those same people are less than emotionally committed to the practice. Why is this? Generally, it is because the project planning they have witnessed has violated one or more of the following key project planning principles:

- **Purpose**—The purpose of project planning is to develop a plan that enables the project to be executed and controlled, as shown in Figure 5.1.

- **Multiple passes required**—Project planning is not a one-time activity performed at the beginning of a project. For starters, it generally takes several iterations to get to a comprehensive plan given the multitude of inputs that must be integrated and the number of stakeholders that need to agree on the plan. In addition, as things happen and we learn more, plans will need to be adjusted and details ironed out as the project moves along.

- **A project plan *is NOT a Microsoft Project file***—Before we go any further, let's make sure we are clear on a few key terms. A project plan is not a project schedule or a work breakdown structure (WBS).

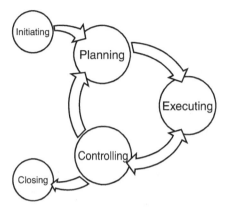

FIGURE 5.1

Highlights the interactions between the planning, executing, and controlling project management processes.

 NOTE A project plan is an all-encompassing document that is used as the basis for controlling and executing a project.

- **Give me one of them**—The planning exercise and the planning team must have control over one of the traditional project success factors (scope, time, cost, or performance). Senior management can set all but one of these factors, but at least one must be left to the project.

 CAUTION A Microsoft Project file (or anything else resembling a project schedule, timeline, or WBS) is not a project plan.

A project plan generally references other documents and supplemental plans, including a WBS and project schedule.

- **Proactive project management**—Effective planning enables a proactive project management approach. Before the execution of the project gets underway, we ask the questions and determine the approaches we will take to manage the project and stakeholder expectations regarding project communications, stakeholder responsibilities, quality management, risks, responses to specific performance variances, procurement management, and project team management.

TIP   Change control, communications, risk, and quality project management are excellent examples of proactive project management.

The team approach to project planning greatly increases its acceptance and commitment level to the project plan.

- **Stay down from the mountain**—Project planning is not the time for the top-down, Mount Olympus approach to management. Project planning is the time for questions, facilitation, interaction, and feedback.

    Specifically, you need to conduct a stakeholder analysis on all your management and customer stakeholders to validate the project definition elements, understand their expectations and communication needs, and review procedures for dealing with critical issues, risks, change requests, and performance variances.

    In addition, the team members who will be *doing* the work should be heavily involved in *defining* and *estimating* the details of the work to be performed. (We address this further in Chapter 6, "Developing the Work Breakdown Structure," and Chapter 7, "Estimating the Work.") This approach leads to a better definition of the work required and a higher commitment level toward scheduled work assignments.

Important Questions Project Planning Should Answer

Think of project planning as a process of asking questions and working with your team to get the answers. While the process of defining a project answers some key fundamental questions to get us started, such as the following, it does not answer all of them:

- Why are we doing this project?

- What is the project supposed to accomplish?

- Who are the key stakeholders? The sponsor? The customers?

It is the process of "detail planning" a project that allows us to answer the questions we need to address to implement and manage the project. These important questions focus on both the work to produce the targeted deliverables and the work to manage the project. Some of these key questions include the following:

TIP   Always get sign-off from appropriate stakeholders to confirm agreement and understanding.

- How exactly will the deliverables be produced?

- What processes or approaches will work best to get us the results we need?

- What work tasks must be performed to produce the deliverables?

- Who will do the work?

- What other resources (facilities, tools) will the team need to do the work?

- Where will the work occur?

- How long will it take to do the work?

- When will the work be done?

- How much will this project cost?

- What skills, skill levels, and experience are needed for each role? When do we need them?

- When do we need each resource? How do we get resources?

- Who is responsible and accountable for what?

- How will changes be controlled?

- How do we ensure acceptable quality in deliverables and in the process?

- How will we keep stakeholders informed and get their feedback, and what mediums are best?

- How will we track issues? How will critical issues be escalated?

- How do we handle variances? What is the threshold for senior management? What communication needs to occur?

- What risks exist? What are our response strategies?

- How will version control be conducted?

- How will project information be maintained and secured?

- How will we manage the project team? What training needs exist? How will their performance be evaluated? How will we orient any new team member?

 TIP   As you visit with stakeholders during detail planning, make sure to validate their project definition understanding and expectation.

Reconfirm that the business case for the project is still valid after the detailed project planning exercise is complete.

- If we are leveraging external resources (vendors, suppliers), how do we manage their performance?

- How will project performance be measured and reported?

- And ultimately, do I have a plan that will enable me to execute and control this project?

As we determine these answers, we capture them in the project plan. We can then review the project plan with our key stakeholders to ensure we have agreement and understanding. Next, let's step through a typical project plan, review what each section is for, and determine how we go about getting this information.

Building a Project Plan

The first step in building a project plan is to validate the elements of the Project Definition document. Depending on the length of time between acceptance of the project definition and the start of detail planning, you might need to confirm that there have been no changes in the purpose, objectives, success criteria, and scope of the project with your key stakeholders.

 TIP To simplify the review process and minimize future document modifications, capture any information that is shared, needs to be reviewed separately, or is likely to be updated frequently in its own document.

Common examples are assumptions, WBS, communications plan, project schedule, requirements, project organization chart, and responsibility matrix.

- **Validate project definition**—This section should reference the Project Definition document and includes all required elements of a Project Definition document. The key task here is to revalidate the business case for the project. This is especially important if there has been a time lag between project definition and detail project planning, or if the planning exercise results in time and cost estimates significantly greater than originally estimated during project definition.

- **Determine what needs to be done**—This section should provide any additional details regarding the project approach (how this will be done), the targeted deliverables that will be produced, and all the work that is required to complete the project. This process is explained in greater detail in Chapter 6.

This section normally refers to a list of deliverables and to the WBS.

- **Determine acceptance criteria**—This information can be part of other components, such as the deliverables list, WBS, project approach, or quality management plan, and might not be its own section. However, to validate that all required work has been identified and to improve the quality of work estimates, it is best to clearly document (somewhere in the project plan) what the acceptance criteria are for each deliverable and for each project phase.

- **Determine resource needs**—Based on the tasks and activities that need to be performed, determine the type and quantity of resources needed. Resources include people (roles), facilities, and tools. These resource needs should be determined when developing the WBS with the team members who will be doing the work.

  To assist the acquisition and management of these resources, all resource needs should be documented (resource management plan). For people resources, document the role description and the prerequisite skills, skill levels, and experiences.

  As part of the scheduling process, the timing of resource needs should be noted and finalized in the resource management plan. A sample resource management plan is illustrated in Figure 5.2.

Role	Team Member	Training Needs	Projected Start Date	Projected Roll-off Date	Percent Allocation
Technical Leader	B Gates	• Advanced Enterprise Web Development	6/1/2021	10/30/2021	80%
Business Process Leader	S Jones	• Process Modeling • Power PowerPoint User	6/1/2021	10/30/2021	100%
Lead Developer	L Gregory	• Advanced Enterprise Web Development	6/15/2021	10/30/2021	100%
Lead Analyst	E Michael	• Rational Test Studio	6/1/2021	10/30/2021	100%
Test Manager	Q Victoria	• Advanced Load Testing	6/15/2021	10/30/2021	100%
Developer	R Alexander	• Accelerated OO Development	7/15/2021	9/30/2021	100%

FIGURE 5.2

Basic example of a resource management plan.

- **Acquire resources**—After the resource needs are documented, we can now begin the process of acquiring those resources. The key questions to be answered here are

  - Will I be able to get the quality of resource requested?

     NOTE The responsibility matrix is often referred to as a RACI ("Ray-Cee") matrix or RASIC ("Ray-Sick") matrix. The acronyms represent each level of potential responsibility.

    R—Responsible

    A—Accountable

    C—Consulted

    I—Informed

    R—Responsible

    A—Approve

    S—Support

    I—Informed

    C—Consulted

  - Will I be able to get this resource in-house, or will I need to obtain it from an external supplier/vendor?

  - Will the resource be available when needed?

  - How will this impact my cost estimates and budget?

- **Estimate the work**—After we know what all the work activities are, and we know what level of resource will be doing the work, we can now estimate the effort and duration for each activity. Due to the critical importance and difficulty of this step, we review this in greater detail in Chapter 7.

- **Develop the schedule**—Now that we understand the required resources and estimated effort for each work task, we are in position to identify the relationships between these tasks and build a schedule to complete the work. Due to the critical importance and common errors in this step, we review this in greater detail in Chapter 8, "Developing the Project Schedule."

At a minimum, schedule information should be available in at least one summary form (such as a milestone summary, an example of which is depicted in Figure 5.3) and always available in complete detail.

TIP To help identify relevant stakeholders, make sure to understand the complete business workflow process(es) and how each person involved is impacted by your project objectives.

Project Milestone	Original Est. Completion Date	Revised Est. Completion Date 06/15/07	Variance
Plan Phase Toll-Gate	Apr 30, 2021	-	-
Design Phase Toll-Gate	Jun 15, 2021	Jun 22, 2021	1 week
Iteration 1 Development Complete	July 15, 2021	July 22, 2021	1 week
Iteration 2 Development Complete	Aug 15, 2021	Aug 29, 2021	2 weeks
Iteration 3 Development Complete	Sep 15, 2021	Sep 30, 2021	2 weeks
Stress Testing Complete	Sep 30, 2021	Oct 15, 2021	2 weeks
User Acceptance Testing Complete	Oct 30, 2021	Nov 15, 2021	2 weeks
Deploy Phase Toll-Gate	Nov 7, 2021	Nov 22, 2021	2 weeks
Pilot Site Implementation	Nov 17, 2021	Nov 29, 2021	2 weeks
Pilot Implementation Review	Dec 15, 2021	Jan 15, 2022	4 weeks
Close Phase Toll-Gate	Dec 22, 2021	Jan 22, 2022	4 weeks

FIGURE 5.3

Example of a milestone schedule summary that tracks any approved schedule variances.

- **Update roles and responsibilities**—This step has two parts:

  First, if any new role has been identified, then update the stakeholder-role description table (first mentioned in the Project Definition document) with the name of the required role and the specific responsibilities that role has. After specific individuals are assigned to roles, the project role responsibility chart can be updated to reflect role assignments. An example of a partial project role responsibility chart is presented in Figure 5.4.

  Second, for each significant work package listed in the WBS, map the responsibility level that each role has regarding that item. This mapping is routinely captured in a responsibility assignment matrix. An example of a partial project responsibility assignment matrix is presented in Figure 5.5.

  This summary map is a powerful tool to help stakeholders clearly understand their roles and what is expected of them.

Project Role	Project Responsibilities	Assigned Team Member
Project Sponsor	* Responsible for championing the project and communicating all aspects of the project to other senior management stakeholders * Has ultimate authority over and is responsible for the project and/or the program * Approve changes to the scope and provide the applicable funds for those changes	T. Terrific
Project Manager	* Provide direction and oversight to the initiative * Work with stakeholders to ensure that expectations are met * Develop and manage project plan * Design and execution of a project communications plan * Measure, evaluate, and report progress against the project plan * Provide project status reports * Coordinate and manage activities of project personnel * Resolve project issues * Conduct scheduled project status meetings * Establish documentation and procedural standards for the project * Perform quality review of deliverable documents * Maintain project communication with the Client Project Manager * Review and administer Project Change Control Procedures	M. Yost
Technical Leader	* Provide technical leadership on the design of application architecture * Lead resolution of any application development issues * Facilitate technical design sessions * Provide quality assurance to technical deliverables	B. Gates
Quality Assurance Manager	* Provide quality assurance to the overall project processes, procedures, and deliverables * Work with Project Leadership to ensure project expectations are met	N. Reed
Business Process Leaders	* Provide business competence to the project team * Participate in information gathering sessions * Provide pertinent strategic business documentation and information * Assist in the identification of business critical processes * Validate viability of recommendations * Serve as primary user acceptance testers	S. Jones G. Griffey

FIGURE 5.4

A partial role responsibility chart for a software development project.

Role	Team Member	Approved Budget	Current State Process Flow	Requirements Document	Change Impact Analysis	Configuration Mgmt Plan	Disaster Recovery Strategy	Deployment Plan	Project Plan	QA Plan	Risk Response Plan	Future State Process Flow	Test Cases	Test Plan	Training Plan	System Design Document
Project Sponsor	T Terrific	A	I			A			A	A	A	A	A	I	I	A
Project Manager	M Yost	R	C		R	R		S	R	A	R	C	C	A	C	A
Technical Leader	B Gates	S	C	A	C	I	R	S	A	A	A	C	C	C	C	A
Business Process Leader	S Jones	C	A		A	C		A	A	A	A	A	A	A	R	A
Lead Developer	L Gregory		C	C			S		C	C	C	I	C		I	R
Lead Analyst	E Michael		R	R	C	I		R	A	C	C	R	S	S	S	S
QA Manager	N Reed	I		I	I	C	I		C	A	R	C	I	A	A	A
Test Manager	Q Victoria		I		I			I	R	A	C	C	R	R	R	C
Developer	R Alexander		I	I			S		I	C	I	C	I	C		C

Legend: R=Responsible; A=Approve; S=Support; C=Consulted; I=Informed

FIGURE 5.5

A partial RASIC responsibility matrix.

- **Update project organization**—Also previously mentioned in the Project Definition document, this section lists all the individuals, business units, and organizations involved in the project, the role(s) each is expected to play, and an indication of how they relate to one another. A project organization chart as shown in Figure 5.6 is highly recommended here.

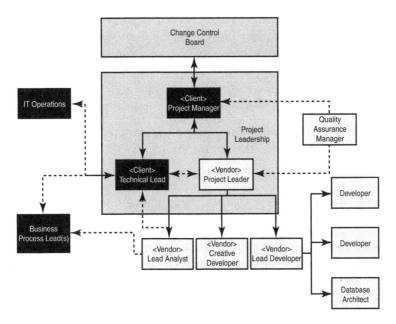

FIGURE 5.6

A project organization chart for an outsourced software development initiative.

NOTE The risk management process can impact the project plan throughout the project because it is a continuous, proactive project management activity.

- **Determine project costs and budget**—Now that we have our resource needs and a preliminary schedule, we can tabulate estimated project costs and a phased project budget. We discuss this in greater detail in Chapter 9, "Determining the Project Budget."

- **Determine project control system**—Specifically, we need to get agreement on how the performance of the project will be measured, how often, and how it will be reported. In addition, we need to determine how performance variances should be managed. Frequently, this information is documented in either the project plan itself, the project communications plan, or the quality management plan. We discuss this in greater detail in Chapter 10, "Controlling a Project."

- **Plan for change**—All plans are subject to change. The difference with successful projects is that they anticipate the changes and establish procedures in advance to review, assess, and manage any request or any factor that affects the key performance factors (scope, quality, time, and cost). These procedures help to ensure that the right people are involved in the process and that the right people are informed of any change decision. We discuss this in greater detail in Chapter 11, "Managing Project Changes."

 CAUTION The project plan document and its components are living documents and can be updated to reflect the evolving circumstances, issues, and needs surrounding the project.

Changes are okay. The changes just need to be announced, reviewed, and approved by the relevant stakeholders.

- **Plan for project information**—There are two primary objectives of this step, which are to determine the following:

  - Where will the project repository be located? Who can access it? Who controls it?

  - How will changes to project deliverables be managed and controlled?

  This information is frequently maintained in a configuration management plan. We discuss this in greater detail in Chapter 12, "Managing Project Deliverables."

 NOTE The formality and detail of each Project Plan section or supplemental plan varies depending on project need, project size, industry, and organizational culture.

- **Plan for issues**—All projects have issues and actions that must be taken to resolve them. The difference with successful projects is that they establish a process in advance to closely track these issues and establish a procedure in advance to escalate any critical issue to the appropriate management stakeholders. We discuss this in greater detail in Chapter 13, "Managing Project Issues."

- **Plan for quality**—Another proactive management approach is to determine the quality standards and policies that project deliverables and processes must meet. For planning, the significance is that additional roles, work activities, and costs will likely affect the project schedule and the project budget. We discuss this in greater detail in Chapter 15, "Managing Project Quality."

- **Plan for communications**—Another aspect of proactive management is to determine the information and communication needs of each project stakeholder. These needs should be determined as part of the stakeholder analysis. The work efforts associated with delivering project communications should be accounted for in both the WBS and the project schedule. We discuss this in greater detail in Chapter 17, "Managing Project Communications," and in Chapter 18, "Managing Expectations."

- **Plan for team management**—Although we have already taken key steps to lay the groundwork for an effective project team by involving them in the planning process, establishing clear role descriptions, and scheduling clear assignments, there are additional steps to consider, including training needs and performance evaluation. We discuss this topic in greater detail in Chapter 19, "Keys to Better Project Team Performance."

- **Plan for procurements**—This step is closely linked to resource planning. If resources need to be obtained externally, then the work to manage the procurement process must be planned and added to the WBS, project schedule, and project budget. We discuss this in greater detail in Chapter 21, "Managing Vendors."

Summary of Supplemental Project Plan Components

The previous section introduced several new planning components, in addition to the core work plan, budget, and control elements you can expect, and referenced the impact that several of them have on the overall project planning effort. To help summarize and organize this information, see Table 5.1.

TABLE 5.1   Summary of Supplemental Project Plan Components

Project Plan Component	Purpose	Key Elements/Notes	Impact on Project Planning
Change Control Plan	Describes how the project success factors (scope, cost, schedule, quality) will be managed and how changes will be integrated.	Can include assessment of expected stability of project scope.	Proactive approach; manages expectations.
Communications Plan	Describes how the information and communication needs of project stakeholders will be met.	Often documented and presented in tabular form.	Communications management plan details must be added to WBS and project schedule.
Configuration Management Plan	Describes how changes to project deliverables and work products will be controlled and managed.	Should include both technical work products and project documentation.	Proactive approach; manages expectations.
Procurement Management Plan	Describes how the procurement process will be managed.	Contract types; roles of project team and procurement department.	Remaining procurement management tasks must be added to project schedule. Constraints of scheduling procurement activities with third-party vendors might impact the project schedule.
Quality Management Plan	Describes the project quality system.	Should address both project work products and the project processes.	Cost and schedule adjustments might be needed to meet quality standards. Quality assurance and quality control activities must be staffed and added to the project schedule.
Responsibility Matrix	Lists the project roles and responsibilities. Cross-references roles with assigned resources.	RACI matrix.	Ensures all required resources are accounted for.

Project Plan Component	Purpose	Key Elements/Notes	Impact on Project Planning
Resource Management Plan	Indicates when project resources are needed on the project (start and end dates).	Impact if resource cannot meet all skill requirements. Impact if resource must be acquired at rates higher than estimated.	Cost baseline, work estimates, and project schedule are in flux until the final resources are acquired.
Risk Management Plan	Describes how the risk management process will be structured and performed.	Describes the process to be used.	Ensures risk management tasks are added to WBS and project schedule.
Risk Response Plan	Describes the response strategies for identified risks.	Risk Log. Details action steps to be taken if risk event occurs.	Risk response strategies might entail the allocation of additional resources, tasks, time, and costs. Budget reserves, contingency plans.
Variance Management	Describes how performance (cost, schedule) variances will be managed.	Documents planned responses to different variance levels.	Proactive approach; manages expectations.

 NOTE To assist with the review and acceptance process of the project plan, consider the following:

1. Distribute the project plan and components to reviewers in advance of the official review meeting.

2. Prepare a summary presentation of the project plan.

3. Encourage open, honest feedback.

4. Seek understanding and buy-in first; then and only then, ask for the acceptance sign-off.

Project Plan Checklist

Here's a quick checklist that can help you to determine whether your project is planned properly and whether you are ready to proceed to execute your project:

- Have you answered all the questions in the section, "Important Questions Project Planning Should Answer"?

- Have you reviewed your WBS, work effort estimates, project schedule, and project budget against their respective checklists?

- Has the project plan been reviewed and approved?
- Was the project plan signed off in a review meeting? In person?

THE ABSOLUTE MINIMUM

At this point, you should have a solid understanding of the following:

- Project definition is focused on what the project will do. Project planning is focused on how the project will get it done.
- A project plan is an all-encompassing document that provides the basis for project execution and control, and it is not a Microsoft Project file.
- The project plan document should clearly communicate what work will be performed, who will do it, when they will do it, who is responsible for what, and how the project will be managed, monitored, and controlled.
- The project plan document and its components are living documents throughout the project. However, any change to the document must be approved by the same set of original stakeholders.
- The key skills used by the project manager when planning a project are facilitation, analytical, organizational, negotiation, and general interpersonal and leadership skills.
- All major stakeholders must approve the project plan document, preferably in person.
- A sign-off does not have to be a physical document signature. It can also be an email or a verbal acceptance (if it is documented in meeting minutes). However, the risk of misunderstandings is usually increased.

The map in Figure 5.7 summarizes the main points reviewed in this chapter.

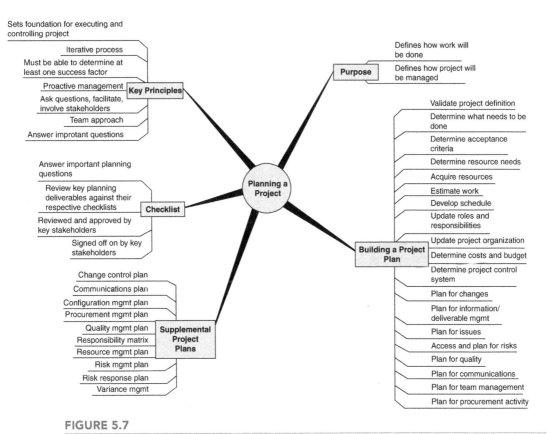

FIGURE 5.7

Planning a project overview.

DEVELOPING THE WORK BREAKDOWN STRUCTURE

If you were to ask anyone off the street what they think of when they hear "project management," you are likely to hear "planning." And if you further ask them what they mean by "planning," you are likely to hear "schedule" or "work plan." Yes, even to the uninitiated, people know that project managers plan and develop work schedules, if they do nothing else.

Yet, the process of understanding all the work that needs to be done and building a realistic project schedule continues to be the Achilles' heel of project management.

In this chapter, we begin our close review of the schedule development process by exploring the power and the purpose of the work breakdown structure (WBS). By performing this step correctly, we will do a much better job at the other detail project planning activities, such as identifying resources, identifying risks, getting better estimates, building a realistic schedule, and developing an accurate project budget. In addition, a solid WBS enables us to better manage stakeholder expectations and the critical success factors throughout the project life cycle.

As part of this review, we clarify exactly what a WBS is (and is not); we examine why the WBS is crucial to our other project management activities; we identify how to develop an effective WBS and how to avoid the common miscues in this arena; and we discuss why these WBS development principles are still applicable for an agile project.

What Exactly Is a WBS?

As I mentioned in Chapter 1, "Project Management Overview," project management is not brain surgery and does not require advanced logic and reasoning skills to achieve winning results (I'm a great example of this). In most cases, the disciplines and terms used in project management are very common sense and obvious in nature. A WBS is a classic case. As the terms defining the acronym indicate, a WBS is a logical breakdown (decomposition) and representation (hierarchical structure) of the work required by the project.

A WBS can take one of two forms: graphical or outline. See Figures 6.1 and 6.2 for examples of each.

Both types have their place in your toolbox. The graphical form is best for communicating the top three to five levels of work activity to senior management or customer stakeholders. The outline form is best for capturing the details needed for cost and schedule development.

 NOTE   A WBS is a logical, hierarchical, and organized task list developed with the team.

A WBS shows the work and any interim deliverables that are required to produce the major project deliverables identified in the project definition process. In most cases, the WBS reflects the components that make up the final deliverables and the approach (methodology) used to develop, integrate, and validate them. In short, the WBS is an organized task list.

By simply doing this, we create an organized picture that allows us to see—and more importantly, allows our stakeholders to see—all the work required to accomplish the project objectives. You can begin to see the power of the WBS in managing expectations.

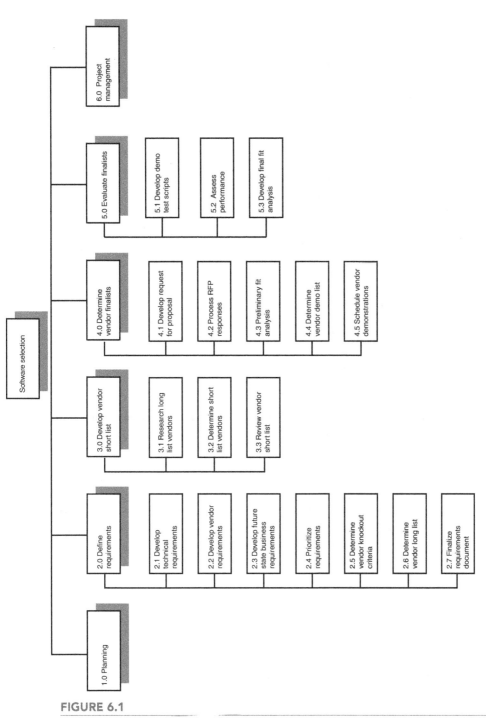

FIGURE 6.1

Partial graphical WBS for a software selection project.

```
□ Software Selection Project
    □ 1 Planning
        1.1 Determine selection strategies
        1.2 Determine final schedule
    □ 2 Define Requirements
        2.1 Develop Technical Requirements
        2.2 Develop Vendor Requirements
        2.3 Develop Future State Business Requirements
        2.4 Prioritize Requirements
        2.5 Identify Vendor Knockout Criteria
        2.6 Determine Vendor Long List
        2.7 Finalize Requirements Document
    □ 3 Develop Vendor Short List
        3.1 Research Vendors on Long List
        3.2 Determine Vendor Short List
        3.3 Review Vendor Short List
    □ 4 Develop Vendor Finalist List
        ⊞ 4.1 Develop Request for Proposal (RFP)
        ⊞ 4.2 Process RFP Responses
        4.3 Develop Preliminary Fit Analysis
        4.4 Determine Vendor Demonstration List
        4.5 Schedule Demonstrations
    □ 5 Evaluate Finalists
        5.1 Develop Demo Test Scripts
        □ 5.2 Assess Performance
            ⊞ 5.2.1 Assess Package Performance
            ⊞ 5.2.2 Assess Vendor Performance
        ⊞ 5.3 Develop Final Fit Analysis
        5.4 Review Final Fit Analysis
        5.5 Make Final Recommendation
    ⊞ 6 Project Management
```

FIGURE 6.2
_____

Partial outline WBS for a software selection project.

Also, by doing this, we employ the primary secret weapon of managing large, complex projects, which is "You don't!" You break the work into chunks and manage many smaller components.

I'm not going to spend a great deal of time on explaining how to create a WBS and how to break down the higher-level work of a project because I think most analytical people do this naturally, and the details of the work decomposition depend on the specifics associated with your organization and industry. In fact, many organizations leverage standard WBS templates to ensure any new project includes the recommended work items.

 TIP   Always clarify terms with your project team and project stakeholders in any communication.

For an official repository of project terms, the use of a project glossary document can be helpful.

However, what I will spend time on is making sure you are clear on terminology, making sure you understand how this step fits into the overall schedule development process, and reviewing the best practices of WBS development.

Isn't WBS Just Another Name for the Project Schedule?

Many industries and organizations routinely use the following terms in an interchangeable fashion: WBS, project plan, project schedule, and work plan. As you know by now, these terms do represent different project management elements and should not be used interchangeably. However, as with all less-than-ideal practices, there are reasons they develop. Understanding the reasons is always helpful and, in this case, can provide additional insights as to why projects can get into a troubled state.

When you think about the process for developing a schedule (see Figure 6.3), determining the work (detail tasks) that is required is the first step.

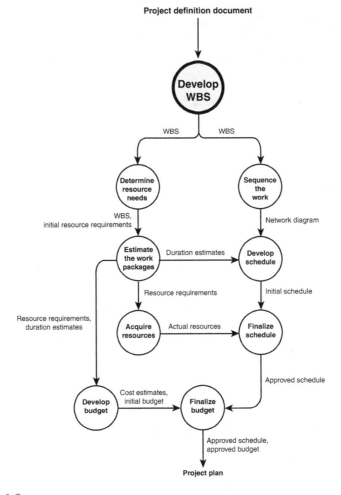

FIGURE 6.3

The role of the WBS in the development of the project schedule.

After you have identified the work tasks, you can determine what resources are required for each task, how much effort each task will take (process details discussed in Chapter 7, "Estimating the Work"), and what logical dependencies exist between the tasks (details covered in Chapter 8, "Developing the Project Schedule"). At this point, you can begin to construct the first of several iterations of a project schedule.

Sounds logical enough—so, where's the problem?

In general, the problems lie with the use and application of project scheduling software such as Microsoft (MS) Project. Here's a common scenario:

- Joe Manager is told to build a work plan for the project.

- Joe goes to his desk and opens up MS Project and starts entering and organizing the tasks that need to be performed.

- Joe enters estimated durations and start and end dates for some of the key or most visible tasks.

- Joe presents results to his supervisor for review.

 NOTE   Avoid judging a current work practice or process or the people involved before you understand why it is done this way or how it evolved to the current point.

This approach keeps you results-focused, improves your ability to develop solution alternatives, increases your effectiveness in leading change, and enhances your relationships with all stakeholders.

So, what did Joe present to his boss? A WBS? It does have work tasks listed. A project schedule? It was created in MS Project. A work plan? That's what his boss asked for. Well, what you probably have here is a high-level WBS and an initial milestone schedule summary, at best. This example illustrates how an inadequate project planning and schedule development process combined with inadequate training on the project scheduling software can lead to terminology confusion. Table 6.1 summarizes these terms and the factors that lead to their interchangeable use.

TABLE 6.1   Terms Used for Planning Project Work

Term	Description	Key Factors	Notes
Project Plan	All-encompassing planning document used as basis for execution and control.	Often incorrectly used to describe project schedule or work plan.	Common tendency to think of project "scheduling" software as project "management" software.

Term	Description	Key Factors	Notes
Project Schedule	Shows when the work will be done and by whom. Drives project execution.	Many "schedules" are more like task lists (WBS) because the task dependencies and resource assignments are not properly captured.	Inadequate training on project scheduling software; inadequate schedule development and review process.
Work Plan	A generic term used to refer to either of the other three.	Usually refers to project schedule.	Need to clarify terms upfront.
WBS	WBS hierarchical representation of work to be performed.	WBS often created with project scheduling software (MS Project); WBS templates often created and saved with project scheduling software (MS Project). For agile projects, WBS can be captured as the Product Roadmap with breakdown of epics, stories, enablers, and tasks.	Use of project scheduling software is acceptable as long as the proper process is followed.For agile, a product management tool can be used (e.g., Jira).

Key Differences Between the WBS and the Project Schedule

The key differences between the WBS and the project schedule include the following:

- **Task dependencies**—WBS does not show them; a project schedule does.
- **Scheduled tasks**—WBS does not show when tasks occur; a project schedule shows start and end dates for each task.
- **Task assignments**—WBS does not show who is assigned to an individual task; a project schedule does.

Different Types of Breakdown Structures

Another factor that can impact understanding of the WBS term and concept is that many industries utilize other breakdown structures and related acronyms that can confuse this subject. Therefore, to better understand what is meant by a WBS, you should be familiar with these other types of breakdown structures, as listed in Table 6.2, and how they are different from a WBS.

CAUTION Any work not defined in the WBS is considered to be outside the project scope.

TABLE 6.2 Different Types of Breakdown Structures

Acronym	Description	Notes
CWBS	Contractual WBS	Defines the level of reporting between the seller and buyer. The CWBS is not as detailed as the WBS used to manage the actual work.
OBS	Organizational Breakdown Structure	Maps work components to organizational units.
RBS	Resource Breakdown Structure	Maps work components to individuals.
BOM	Bill of Materials	Describes the physical components needed for the project.
PBS	Project Breakdown Structure	The PBS is actually the same as the WBS. This term is only used in areas where the term WBS is incorrectly used to refer to a BOM.

Why Is the WBS Important?

The Project Management Institute (PMI) considers the WBS the most important tool of the project manager. Why?

More than any other project management tool, the WBS provides the foundation for defining and organizing the work needed to fulfill the project objectives. Through the WBS, the work to produce the targeted deliverables is structured, assigned, scheduled, tracked, and reported. Through the WBS, the work of the project is effectively represented and communicated to all stakeholders. A well-done WBS accomplishes the following objectives for the project manager:

TIP A well-done WBS can become a template for similar, future projects.

- **Manage the pieces**—It provides a mechanism to manage any project size or complexity. Through decomposition, you can manage the pieces (work packages) rather than the whole project.

- **Better work definition, fewer changes**—It enables identification of all necessary work for the project and only the necessary work. It also reduces the number of items that slip through the cracks as well as the "Oh, I didn't think of that!" moments.

- **Better estimates, better planning**—It improves the accuracy of cost, duration, and resource estimates.

- **Better control**—It defines a baseline for performance measurement and control.

- **Clear responsibilities**—It facilitates clear responsibility assignments at both an individual and an organizational level.

 NOTE Major deliverables should come from the project definition document and are likely second-level WBS elements.

There is no one way to organize a WBS. It should be organized in a manner that emphasizes the most important aspects and that best communicates the entire scope of the project to your stakeholders.

- **Stakeholder buy-in on scope work effort**—It facilitates understanding and buy-in of the project scope, the project approach, the work effort involved, and alignment between scope and work from each stakeholder.

- **Tighter management integration**—It provides a mechanism to relate the work directly to schedule, budget, and resource allocation plans.

- **Better team performance**—It enables team members to easily understand how their work fits into the overall project, how it affects the work of other team members, and to stay focused on deliverables.

- **Risk factors identified early**—Through decomposition of the work, a more complete and effective risk analysis can be performed during project planning.

- **Confidence increases**—When people see that the work of the project is structured, definable, and doable, their confidence level in the project increases.

The Process of Building a WBS

Now that you understand what a WBS is and the importance it plays in your project, let's review the key techniques, guidelines, and principles in building an effective WBS.

In general, the process of breaking down work is something we do frequently and is a straightforward logical endeavor. However, there are frequently two common challenges in the WBS development process:

- Where do I start?

- Where do I stop?

Getting Started

To start the work decomposition process, think about the following:

- Does a template WBS exist as part of your methodology or from a past project that you can use?
- What are the major deliverables?
- What is the project approach? The project life cycle? The major project phases?
- Think through the entire project. What does the end look like?

To continue the work decomposition process, think about these questions:

- Can you break down this WBS element (deliverable) into subcomponents?
- How exactly will the deliverables be produced? What processes and methods will be used?
- How do you ensure acceptable quality in deliverables and in the process?
- Can you make adequate costs and duration estimates from this level of detail?

Guidelines for Effective WBS

Here are a few guidelines regarding the development of the project WBS that you want to keep in mind:

 NOTE The WBS should always be defined at least one level lower than what is required for management reporting purposes. This enables you to better identify the source of any issues or variances.

In general, the more detail in the WBS, the more accurate the work estimates and the better level of control. However, there is a balance. Too much detail and you will incur excessive costs performing data collection, tracking, and reporting. Too little detail and you incur higher risks and are unable to effectively manage.

- *All* the work of the project is included in the WBS.
- The WBS should be deliverable focused.
- All deliverables are explicit in the WBS.
- The WBS should be developed with the team.

- The WBS is refined as the project progresses.

- The WBS is a top-down decomposition and is logical—the summary tasks go with lower-level tasks.

- The WBS should be organized in a manner that emphasizes the most important aspects of the project and that best communicates the entire scope of the project to your stakeholders.

- The lowest level of the WBS is the work package or activity level and is used for schedule and cost development. This is the level where effort and cost can be reliably estimated.

 CAUTION   Most troubled projects have WBS elements that are too large. If each lower-level element should be completed within the standard reporting period (every week or every two weeks), it is much easier to track actual progress and to take any corrective actions.

- Unique identifiers are assigned to each item in the WBS to allow for better management reporting of costs and resources.

- WBS elements should be consistent with organizational and accounting structures.

- The coding scheme should clearly represent a hierarchical structure.

- Review and refine the WBS until all key project stakeholders are satisfied.

- Each WBS element represents a single deliverable and should be an aggregation of lower-level WBS elements.

- Each WBS element has only one parent.

- Upper levels of the WBS represent major deliverables or project phases.

- The WBS should include project management tasks and activities.

- The WBS should include and isolate any work needed to integrate components and deliverables.

- The WBS should account for any subcontracted or externally committed deliverable.

- The WBS should represent all work needed to ensure completeness, correctness, and acceptance of deliverables.

- The depth of WBS depends on three key factors:
  - Amount of project risk
  - Reporting requirements
  - Balance of control versus costs

 NOTE These are solid guidelines—not rules. The most important thing to remember is to size the work package to the level you need for effective management and control. Again, setting the maximum size to correspond to your reporting period is an excellent idea.

The level of depth (granularity) for the work package level in a WBS (lowest levels) will vary. It depends on what level of detail the project manager needs for effective management and control of the project.

In a program, or on large projects, the work package level might represent efforts in the hundreds of hours. In these cases, it is expected that the teams assigned to these work packages (or subprojects) will define the detail activities and tasks needed to complete the work package. From a practical standpoint, these teams should develop their own WBS that can then be rolled up into the master WBS.

Knowing When to Stop

The other aspect of WBS development that creates frequent uncertainty is knowing when to stop. To determine whether you have enough detail in your WBS, review these questions for each lower-level item:

- Can each lower-level item be estimated, scheduled, budgeted, and assigned to a responsible party?

- Do you need more detail to make it easier to estimate effort, assign work, track costs, or measure progress?

- You will read about common rules of thumb for the proper size of work packages. The most common rules are 8/80 and 4/40, which means no task should be less than 8 hours or more than 80 hours, or in the case of 4/40, it would be less than 4 hours or more than 40 hours.

- In addition, consider further decomposition of the lower-level item, if any of the following are true:

  - The work cannot be completed within the standard reporting period for the project.

  - There are specific risks associated with a smaller portion of the work element.

  - More than one individual or group is responsible.

  - More than one deliverable is included.

  - More than one work process is included.

  - There is a time gap involved.

  - The resource requirements for the work element are not consistent.

The importance of the WBS cannot be overemphasized. Because the correctness and completeness of the WBS has a direct impact on how well we determine our resource needs, estimate the work efforts, and properly sequence the work, it is the foundation that drives our schedule and most of our planning efforts.

Do I Need a WBS for an Agile Project?

You might be wondering if this WBS development process applies to you if your organization is using agile project management. Let me assure you...it does. The main difference is when this work breakdown occurs. For an agile project, the targeted work items are prioritized and details refined on an iterative basis rather than attempting to do it all upfront. In addition, the tool that manages the Product Backlog (the work items yet to be completed) would capture all of the WBS work packages. But in the end, the quality of your schedule and your ability to manage expectations are dependent on the degree that all of the work required was accounted for in the plan. Missing work items are a common reason why all the planned work for an agile iteration or sprint was not completed within the designated time box. Of course, this is one of the advantages of the agile development approach. The inherent feedback loops and iterative planning processes for each work iteration help identify these gaps sooner and allow you to adjust plans accordingly.

THE ABSOLUTE MINIMUM

At this point, you should have a solid understanding of the following:

- A WBS is a logical breakdown of all the work to be performed by the project.
- A WBS is neither the project schedule nor the project plan.
- The WBS should be developed with the project team.
- The WBS is a vital tool to the project manager.
- Avoid judging a current work process or the people involved before you understand *why* it is done this way or *how* it evolved to the current point.
- You learned how to evaluate a WBS.
- You learned how to avoid the common challenges and issues with WBS development.
- The WBS is the foundation for developing a realistic schedule, determining project resource needs, and figuring an accurate project budget.
- The work packages included in the WBS should be detailed enough to support effective management and control.
- The maximum size of a WBS work package should correspond to the standard reporting period for the project.
- For an agile project, the WBS is essential, corresponds to the Product Backlog, and is continuously refined.

The map in Figure 6.4 summarizes the main points reviewed in this chapter.

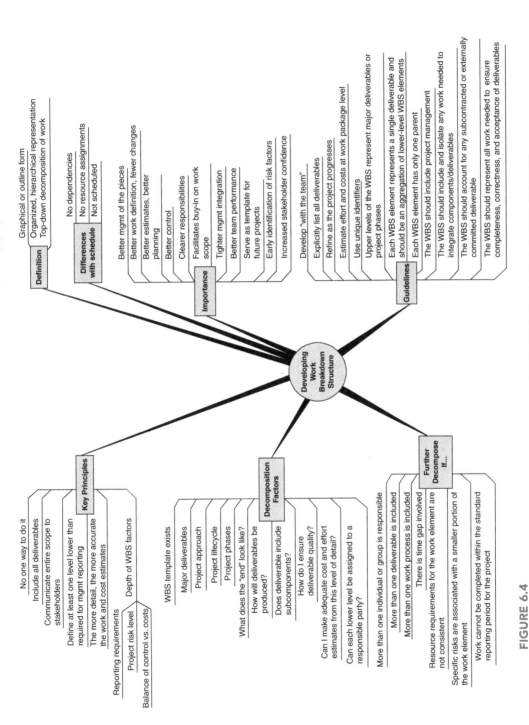

FIGURE 6.4

Developing a work breakdown structure overview.

7

ESTIMATING THE WORK

Estimating. Nothing else symbolizes the challenges of project management better. Negotiate with senior management and customers to prevent "ball park" estimates from becoming your targets; team with subject matter experts (SMEs) and knowledge workers to develop accurate estimates for work that has never been done in these conditions, with these tools, by these people; assess your risks; educate stakeholders on the estimating process; and continuously manage the time-cost-quality equilibrium. Plus, you likely must do all of this in an organization that has not made the investment to improve estimating accuracy. Is it any wonder we love this job? For most people and most organizations, you would need a moving truck to carry all the baggage that comes along for the ride when estimating is discussed.

The baggage accumulates from political battles, misunderstandings, a sense of no control, and past troubled projects. As a result, there are complete educational courses and books in the marketplace that cover nothing but estimating—not to mention the many reputable therapists that can improve your emotional and spiritual well-being (just kidding; it's not *that* bad).

This chapter shows you how to leave that moving truck behind and take control of the estimating process. It can be done. First, we review how estimating the work fits in with the overall schedule development process and how it is an integral part of how we manage risk on the project. Then, we examine the key estimating techniques and methods and how to use them. And finally, we discuss the common reasons for poor estimates and review the golden guidelines of estimating. This will enable you to improve your estimating accuracy and get it right the first time.

 NOTE Accurate estimates build the foundation for a realistic schedule and an accurate project budget.

Next Step in the Schedule Development Process

Before we get into the details of estimating, let's make sure we are clear on where estimating falls in the schedule development and planning process. If someone stopped you on the street and asked you for an estimate, what is the minimum information that you would need? You would need to know what the estimate is for—what work is to be done. And you would need to know who is going to do it—what type of resources will be involved in performing the work. This flow is shown in Figure 7.1. Estimating the work should occur after you have identified the work and after you have thought about what resources are needed for the project.

It sounds so simple, doesn't it? Then why is this so tough? Well, we cover this in more detail later in this chapter, but these two basic prerequisites are where most estimating woes originate. There is often not a clear or complete understanding of the work to be performed by the person doing the estimate, and the relationship between the work estimate and the resource doing the work is not defined or communicated. In addition, there is the challenge of estimating work that has not been done before in exactly these conditions.

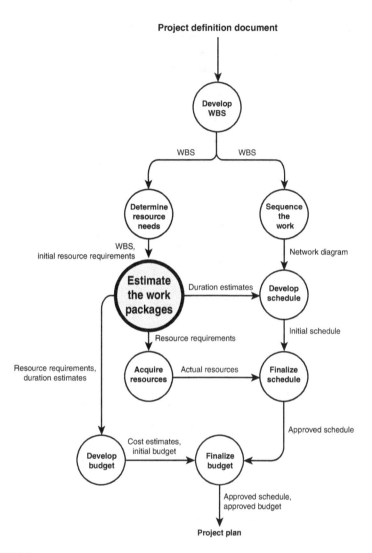

FIGURE 7.1

The step of estimating the work in the development of the project schedule.

Yet, estimating the work effort is a cornerstone activity for planning the project. From these work estimates, we determine the project costs (see Chapter 9,
"Determining the Project Budget"), develop the project schedule (Chapter 8,
"Developing the Project Schedule"), and identify key project risks. This relationship is illustrated in Figure 7.2.

FIGURE 7.2

The foundational role that the WBS and the work estimates play in the overall planning process.

Managing the Risk, Managing the Estimates

There lies the key challenge. How do you manage the uncertainty that is naturally involved with the estimating process? Because these estimates form the foundation for the project schedule and the project budget, you must implement techniques and approaches that enable you to properly manage this risk and the expectations of your stakeholders.

Although this subject of estimating and risk could easily slip into a review of statistics, probability, standard deviations, skewed distributions, and Monte Carlo analysis, we will not go there. In many real-world environments, these advanced concepts and techniques are not utilized to estimate work and to manage the associated risk, and these topics would be outside the scope of this book. Our focus is understanding the impact that estimating work has on our overall risk management approach and what we can do to minimize those risks.

Estimating the work is a fundamental risk analysis step. Not only do you estimate work efforts, but you also identify the assumptions that support the estimate and the key risk factors that might affect the accuracy of those estimates. These key outputs are depicted in Figure 7.3.

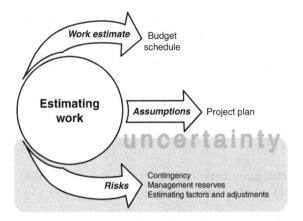

FIGURE 7.3

Estimates are key inputs for scheduling, budgeting, and risk management.

Reasons for Estimating Woes

Before we review the key estimating techniques and methods that we need to know to best plan our projects and manage our risk, let's first take a deeper look at the common reasons for estimating woes on many troubled projects:

- **Improper work definition**—The number one reason for inaccurate work estimates is inadequate definition of the work to be performed. This includes the following:

  - Estimates based on high-level or incomplete requirements.

  - Estimates based on incomplete work—work elements (packages) not accounted for in the WBS.

  - Estimates based on lack of detailed work breakdown.

  - Estimates made without understanding the standards, quality levels, and completion criteria for the work package.

- **Wrong people estimating**—Another key reason for inaccurate work estimates is that the wrong people make the estimates. Although it might be appropriate for management to make ballpark estimates during the early defining and planning stages, when firm commitments must be made, it is best to have the people who have experience doing the work make the estimates (or at least review and approve any proposed estimate made by someone else).

- **Poor communications**—This reason hits on the process of facilitating estimate development. This category includes events such as

  - Not sharing all necessary information with the estimator.

  - Not verifying with the estimator what resource assumptions and other factors the estimates are based on.

  - Not capturing and communicating the estimate assumptions to all stakeholders.

- **Wrong technique used**—We cover this in greater detail in the next section, but this category includes events such as

  - Making firm budget commitments based on top-down or ballpark estimates rather than bottom-up estimates.

  - Not asking for an estimate range or multiple estimates.

  - Not leveraging the project team.

  - Not basing estimates on similar experiences.

- **Resource issues**—This is a specific case where it's not really an estimate issue but an issue with the assumptions supporting the estimate. This is when the person assigned to do the work is not producing at the targeted level or when there are performance quality issues with any of the materials, facilities, or tools. Without documented assumptions, these issues can appear as inaccurate estimates to stakeholders.

- **Lack of contingency**—In many cases, especially on projects involving new technologies and new processes, the identified risk factors are not properly accounted for in the work estimates. The uncertainty level in specific work estimates needs to be identified and carried forward into the project schedule and budget as part of the contingency buffer or management reserve.

- **Management decisions**—In many situations, senior management influence and decisions impact the estimating accuracy level. This category includes events such as

  - Senior management making firm budget commitments based on initial, high-level estimates and not accounting for accuracy ranges.

  - Senior management not willing to invest time or resources to get detailed, bottom-up estimates.

  - Estimators factoring their estimates for senior management expectations rather than the actual work effort.

- Management requesting that estimates be reduced to make the work meet the budget or schedule goals.

- Management decisions to bid or accept work for less than estimated cost.

- No use of management reserve to account for risk or uncertainty.

Powerful Estimating Techniques and Methods

There are several key estimating techniques you should know about. Table 7.1 lists these techniques and summarizes the key characteristics of each.

TABLE 7.1   Estimating Techniques

Estimating Technique	Key Characteristics	Notes
Analogous (top-down) estimating	Used in early planning phases and project selection. Utilizes historical information (actual duration periods from previous projects) to form estimates.	Reliable if WBS from previous projects mirror the WBS needed for this project.
Bottom-up estimating	Used to develop detailed estimates. Provides estimate for lowest level of the WBS (work package). Provides the most accuracy.	Best technique for identifying risk factors. Takes most time and money to develop.
Effort distribution estimating	Uses project phase percentages to estimate. Example would be Initiation Phase—10% Plan Phase—10% Elaboration Phase—20% Construction Phase—40% Deploy Phase—20%	Used in organizations that use common methodology and/or that do similar projects. Can be used if enough information is known for one of the major project phases.
Heuristic estimating	Based on experiences. "Rule-of-thumb" estimating. Frequently used when no historical records are available.	Also known as Delphi technique and expert judgment.

Estimating Technique	Key Characteristics	Notes
Parametric estimating	Uses historical data and statistical relationships. Developed by identifying the number of work units and the duration/effort per work unit. Examples include the following: Lines of code for software development. Square footage for construction. Number of sites for network migration.	Also known as quantitative-based estimating. Can be used with other techniques and methods.
Phased estimating	Estimates the project phase by phase. Provides for a detailed, bottom-up estimate for the next phase and a higher level, top-down estimate for the other phases. Best technique to use on high-risk and agile projects.	Incorporates "re-estimating" as part of the management approach. Best use of estimating resources. Excellent risk management tool.

For each estimating technique (approach), there are one or more methods that can be leveraged. Table 7.2 lists these methods and summarizes the key characteristics of each.

TABLE 7.2   Estimating Methods

Estimating Method	Key Characteristics	Notes
Expert judgment	Relies on SME in targeted work area.	Used most effectively with bottom-up estimating.
Historical information	Relies on actual durations from past projects. The three types are project files, commercial databases, and project team members.	Many organizations do not accurately capture this information. Recollection of project team members is the least reliable source. Critical to improving estimate accuracy in an organization.

Estimating Method	Key Characteristics	Notes
Weighted average (PERT)	Uses three estimates for each activity (weighted average): optimistic, most likely, pessimistic $E = (O + 4M + P) / 6$ Each estimate is captured for each activity.	Used mainly on large-scale or high-risk projects. Excellent risk management technique. This technique is time consuming. PERT = Program Evaluation and Review Technique.
Risk factors	Adjusting an original estimate based on one or more risk factors. Used in conjunction with other methods.	Common risk factors affecting effort estimates include complexity (technical, process), organizational change impact, requirements (volatility, quality), and resources (skills, costs, and so on).
Team (consensus) estimating	Uses multiple SMEs to develop independent estimates. Facilitation meeting used to reconcile differences and develop consensus estimates.	Best for identifying assumptions and other risk factors. Avoids one person being accountable for estimate. Allows for multiple historical perspectives to be taken into account. Allows SMEs from different backgrounds to complement one another.

 TIP   There are two primary reasons estimating should be performed (or approved) by the person doing the work: more accurate estimates and higher commitment levels to the project.

As with all other planning activities, work estimates are refined and improved as more is learned about the project. At a minimum, each project (or project phase) should be estimated three times. Each estimate provides a greater degree of accuracy. To better understand this concept and to better educate others in your organization, see the three levels of estimate accuracy recognized by PMI in Table 7.3.

TABLE 7.3   Estimate Accuracy Levels

Level	Accuracy Range	Generally Used During
Order of magnitude	–25% to +75%	Initiating (defining) phase
Budget	–10% to +25%	Planning phase
Definitive	–5% to +10%	Planning phase

NOTE I have no doubt that the use of buffers and historical information when developing work effort estimates is a common, everyday practice in your real-world experience…or maybe not.

They represent a clear example of why leadership, negotiation, and communication skills are so important for project managers.

Best Practices

Now that we have an overview of the estimating techniques and methods that are available to us, and we have a feel for the estimating mistakes that are commonly made, let's review the estimating best practices of successful organizations and projects:

- Should be based on the work breakdown detailed in the WBS.

- Estimating should be performed (or approved) by the person doing the work.

- The work estimates for lower-level WBS items should be less than the standard reporting period for the project (typically one or two weeks).

- As discussed in Chapter 6, "Developing the Work Breakdown Structure," if the work estimate is not less than this, it is a good sign the task needs further decomposition.

- Estimating should be based on historical information and expert judgment.

- Estimates are influenced by the capabilities of the resources (human and materials) allocated to the activity.

- Estimates are influenced by the known project risks and should be adjusted accordingly to account for those risks.

- When estimating effort for something unprecedented or high risk, where the confidence level in any estimate is low, leverage timeboxing and proof-of-concept models to improve knowledge quickly, so you can derive better estimates. This approach is a key aspect of agile projects.

NOTE Critical chain management (scheduling) is an increasingly popular technique of estimating and scheduling work. We take a closer look at this approach in Chapter 25, "The Fun Never Stops."

- All bases and assumptions used in estimating should be documented in the project plan.

- When asking an SME for an activity estimate, make sure to provide the following whenever possible:
  - Project definition document (context, approach, assumptions, and constraints)
  - WBS
  - Applicable standards, quality levels, and completion criteria for the work package
- When asking an SME for an activity estimate, make sure to ask for the following at a minimum:
  - An estimate range (not just a single value)
  - Factors driving that range
  - Assumed resource level, skills, and productivity
  - Assumed quality level and acceptable completion criteria
- Estimates should be given in specific time ranges.
- To manage high-risk projects, the following estimating techniques are recommended:
  - Use of phased and bottom-up estimating techniques
  - Use of the average weight and team consensus estimating methods
- For high-risk projects where the organization lacks significant previous experience or process knowledge, consider outsourcing the planning phase to an outside firm as an assessment engagement.
- A project's time and cost estimates should be based on project needs and not dictated by senior management. The project manager should work with senior management to reconcile any differences.
- Reserve time (contingency and buffer) should be added to either the project schedule or to individual activity duration estimates to account for the level of risk and any uncertainty that exists.
- Historical information is vital to improving estimates. If you don't measure actual performance, you will not have the feedback to improve estimating accuracy.

 NOTE Many of these estimating best practices are part of the agile project management approach. In particular, the ones that focus on estimating work packages defined in the WBS (epics, stories, enablers, and tasks, in the agile vernacular), the team doing the work provides the estimates, relying on historical performance of the team, accounting for risk in the estimates as part of the planning process, and using timeboxes and proof-of-concept models on high risk items. We take a closer look at this approach in Chapter 25.

 NOTE For agile projects, there are techniques for estimating work items for iteration (or sprint) planning. We take a closer look at these techniques in Chapter 25.

THE ABSOLUTE MINIMUM

At this point, you should have a solid understanding of the following:

- It takes time and money to develop accurate estimates.
- Any estimating technique improves results if it is used consistently by leveraging lessons from the past.
- To get science in the process, estimates must be compared to actual performance.
- Multiple estimating techniques can be used together. The art is knowing when to use which technique and knowing how much accuracy is required for the business decision at hand.
- Many variables beyond the control of the project team, such as changing specs, team turnover, and failed technology, can invalidate original estimates.
- Project managers should never work independently when making estimates.
- Organizations must make a conscious effort to establish rigor and procedures to estimating to improve accuracy over time.
- All stakeholders are responsible for estimates.

The map in Figure 7.4 summarizes the main points reviewed in this chapter.

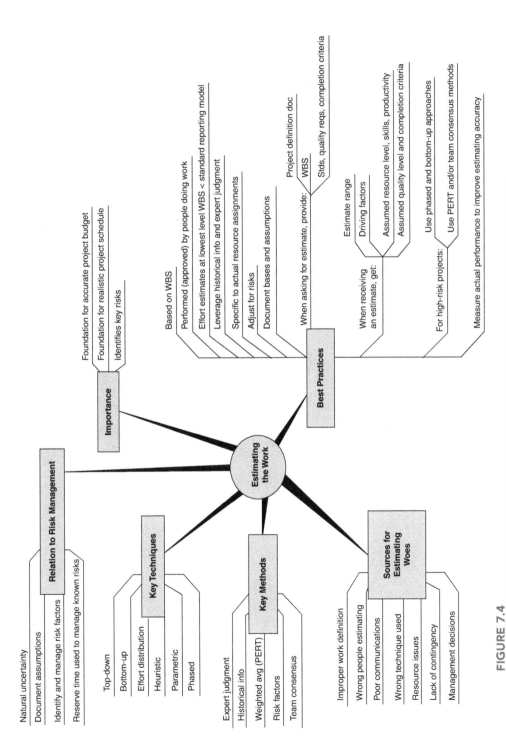

FIGURE 7.4

Estimating the work overview.

IN THIS CHAPTER

- Understand why the project schedule is vital to a successful project
- Review the process for creating a realistic schedule
- Learn the characteristics of a good schedule
- Learn how to avoid the common mistakes that even experienced project managers can make when building a schedule
- Review the options for effectively presenting your schedule to others

DEVELOPING THE PROJECT SCHEDULE

It's funny, really. The one activity that the common person associates with project management is planning, and the main output from this planning effort is a schedule. Yet, it is a challenge to find a project manager who can develop one accurately. Although scheduling is one of the two primary technical aspects of project management, it is a common technical weakness of many project managers.

Why is this? Well, from my own experience, I can state at least four reasons: lack of time for proper planning, lack of education on the schedule development process, lack of training with the scheduling software, and a belief that a detailed schedule is not necessary. I believe this issue is one of the fundamental reasons why many organizations started project management offices (PMOs)—internal support and governance organizations to improve project performance. Unrealistic project schedules have an adverse impact on resource management and project investment decisions.

Of course, as a reader of this book, you will know the proper process for developing a schedule, you will understand the necessity of a detailed schedule, and you will have plenty of ammunition to use when negotiating for project planning time. Combined with proper knowledge of the scheduling software you are using, you will possess a key strength for successful project managers and be a key asset to your stakeholders. Given that, let's continue our review of the overall schedule development process.

In this chapter, we emphasize the vital importance of the project schedule, step through the process for developing a realistic schedule, and highlight the areas where people often go astray. This will lead to a schedule that your stakeholders will believe and accept, and it will provide you with the foundation to properly execute and monitor the project.

And yes, this process and these principles still apply for an agile project or hybrid agile project. While the approach for performing the work is iterative and detail planning for each iteration is an ongoing process, there is generally still a need for an integrated master schedule that accounts for all aspects of the project and maps the elements of the product roadmap to planned releases and iterations (sprints). We will review a few more specifics in Chapter 25, "The Fun Never Stops".

The Impact of the Project Schedule

The project schedule is the tool that merges all the work tasks to be performed, their relationships, their estimated durations, and their assigned resources to a calendar. Examples of partial schedules are illustrated in Figures 8.1 and 8.2. For most, specialized scheduling software (such as Microsoft [MS] Project) is used to produce a project schedule. For those managers who use Microsoft Project, I discuss how to make better use of this tool in Chapter 23, "Making Better Use of Microsoft Project."

As mentioned earlier in the book, the project schedule is often referred to as the "project plan" in error. Although not technically correct, it is easy to understand why this term is often used. The project schedule serves as the chief integration point for most, if not all, of your project planning efforts. The project schedule reflects (or should reflect, when the schedule development process is complete) all the following:

- Work breakdown structure (WBS)

- Resource plan

- Work estimates

- Key milestones

- Responsibility assignments (RASIC)

- Quality management plan

- Risk management plan

- Communications management plan

- Procurement management plan

- Staff management (training) plan

Software Selection Project Schedule

ID	O	Task Name	Work	Duration	Start	Finish	Predecessors	Resource Names
0		Software Selection Project	1,112 hrs	46.5 days	Mon 1/12/04	Tue 3/16/04		
1		1 Planning	32 hrs	2 days	Mon 1/12/04	Tue 1/13/04		
2		1.1 Determine selection strategies	24 hrs	8 hrs	Mon 1/12/04	Mon 1/12/04		Technology Advisor,Business Analyst,Project Leader
3		1.2 Determine final schedule	8 hrs	8 hrs	Tue 1/13/04	Tue 1/13/04	2	Project Leader
4		2 Define Requirements	144 hrs	11 days	Wed 1/14/04	Wed 1/28/04	1	
5		2.1 Develop Technical Requirements	24 hrs	24 hrs	Wed 1/14/04	Fri 1/16/04		Technology Advisor
6		2.2 Develop Vendor Requirements	16 hrs	8 hrs	Mon 1/19/04	Mon 1/19/04	5	Technology Advisor,Business Analyst
7		2.3 Develop Future State Business Requirements	16 hrs	16 hrs	Tue 1/20/04	Wed 1/21/04	6	Business Analyst
8		2.4 Prioritize Requirements	48 hrs	16 hrs	Thu 1/22/04	Fri 1/23/04	5,6,7	Technology Advisor,Business Analyst,Project Leader
9		2.5 Identify Vendor Knockout Criteria	12 hrs	4 hrs	Mon 1/26/04	Mon 1/26/04	8	Technology Advisor,Business Analyst,Project Leader
10		2.6 Determine Vendor Long List	12 hrs	4 hrs	Mon 1/26/04	Mon 1/26/04	9	Technology Advisor,Business Analyst,Project Leader
11		2.7 Finalize Requirements Document	16 hrs	16 hrs	Tue 1/27/04	Wed 1/28/04	10	Business Analyst
12		3 Develop Vendor Short List	56 hrs	7 days	Tue 1/27/04	Wed 2/4/04		
13		3.1 Research Vendors on Long List	40 hrs	5 days	Tue 1/27/04	Mon 2/2/04	10	Technology Advisor
14		3.2 Determine Vendor Short List	8 hrs	1 day	Tue 2/3/04	Tue 2/3/04	13	Technology Advisor
15		3.3 Review Vendor Short List	8 hrs	1 day	Wed 2/4/04	Wed 2/4/04	14	Technology Advisor
16		4 Develop Vendor Finalist List	120 hrs	18.5 days	Thu 1/29/04	Tue 2/24/04		
17		4.1 Develop Request for Proposal (RFP)	64 hrs	8 days	Thu 1/29/04	Mon 2/9/04	4	
18		4.1.1 Create Request for Proposal	32 hrs	32 hrs	Thu 1/29/04	Tue 2/3/04		Business Analyst
19		4.1.2 Approve Request for Proposal	24 hrs	24 hrs	Wed 2/4/04	Fri 2/6/04	18	Business Analyst
20		4.1.3 Distribute Request for Proposal	8 hrs	8 hrs	Mon 2/9/04	Mon 2/9/04	19	Business Analyst
21		4.2 Process RFP Responses	24 hrs	1.5 days	Mon 2/16/04	Wed 2/18/04	17FS+5 days	
22		4.2.1 Vendor RFP Responses Due	0 hrs	0 days	Mon 2/16/04	Mon 2/16/04		
23		4.2.2 Review and Summarize Vendor Responses	16 hrs	8 hrs	Tue 2/17/04	Tue 2/17/04	22	Technology Advisor,Business Analyst
24		4.2.3 Research Vendor References	8 hrs	4 hrs	Wed 2/18/04	Wed 2/18/04	23	Technology Advisor,Business Analyst
25		4.3 Develop Preliminary Fit Analysis	16 hrs	16 hrs	Wed 2/18/04	Fri 2/20/04	21	Technology Advisor
26		4.4 Determine Vendor Demonstration List	8 hrs	8 hrs	Fri 2/20/04	Mon 2/23/04	25	Technology Advisor
27		4.5 Schedule Demonstrations	8 hrs	8 hrs	Mon 2/23/04	Tue 2/24/04	26	Project Leader
28		5 Evaluate Finalists	400 hrs	25.5 days	Tue 2/10/04	Tue 3/16/04		
29		5.1 Develop Demo Test Scripts	48 hrs	24 hrs	Tue 2/10/04	Thu 2/12/04	17	Technology Advisor,Business Analyst
30		5.2 Assess Performance	224 hrs	8 days	Tue 2/24/04	Fri 3/5/04	16	
31		5.2.1 Assess Package Performance	128 hrs	6 days	Tue 2/24/04	Wed 3/3/04		
32		5.2.1.1 Working Session - Vendor A	12 hrs	4 hrs	Tue 2/24/04	Tue 2/24/04	16	Technology Advisor,Business Analyst,Project Leader
33		5.2.1.2 Working Session - Vendor B	12 hrs	4 hrs	Wed 2/25/04	Wed 2/25/04	32	Technology Advisor,Business Analyst,Project Leader
34		5.2.1.3 Vendor "A" Demonstration	48 hrs	16 hrs	Wed 2/25/04	Fri 2/27/04	32,29,27,33	Technology Advisor,Business Analyst,Project Leader
35		5.2.1.4 Vendor "B" Demonstration	48 hrs	16 hrs	Fri 2/27/04	Tue 3/2/04	34	Technology Advisor,Business Analyst,Project Leader
36		5.2.1.5 Record Demo Scores	8 hrs	8 hrs	Tue 3/2/04	Wed 3/3/04	35	Business Analyst
37		5.2.2 Assess Vendor Performance	96 hrs	8 days	Tue 2/24/04	Fri 3/5/04		
38		5.2.2.1 Research vendor references	48 hrs	16 hrs	Tue 2/24/04	Thu 2/26/04	16	Technology Advisor,Business Analyst,Project Leader
39		5.2.2.2 Possible Site visits	48 hrs	16 hrs	Wed 3/3/04	Fri 3/5/04	31	Technology Advisor,Business Analyst,Project Leader
40		5.3 Develop Final Fit Analysis	80 hrs	5 days	Fri 3/5/04	Fri 3/12/04	30	
41		5.3.1 Perform Fit-Gap analysis for each option	16 hrs	8 hrs	Fri 3/5/04	Mon 3/8/04		Technology Advisor,Business Analyst
42		5.3.2 Assess risk for each option	16 hrs	8 hrs	Mon 3/8/04	Tue 3/9/04	41	Technology Advisor,Business Analyst
43		5.3.3 Develop high-level schedule and budget forecast	16 hrs	8 hrs	Tue 3/9/04	Wed 3/10/04	42	Technology Advisor,Business Analyst

FIGURE 8.1

An example of a partial schedule displayed in table form.

FIGURE 8.2

An example of a partial schedule displayed in Gantt chart form.

In addition to providing this vital integration role, the project schedule is important to the project manager for these reasons as well:

- **Drives project budget**—Because most of your project costs are a factor of time (we cover this in more detail in Chapter 9, "Determining the Project Budget"), the project schedule is a main driver for your project budget. If the schedule is inaccurate, your budget is likely incorrect, too.

- **Drives resource schedule**—Your schedule drives the timing of your resource needs. Especially in organizations where resources are shared across projects or centrally managed, the accuracy of the schedule is key to efficient resource management.

- **Essential for managing expectations**—With a well-developed schedule, you have the best tool for managing stakeholder expectations regarding the schedule-cost-quality equilibrium. A well-developed schedule illustrates the earliest date a project can be completed given the project's current requirements and constraints. This is an invaluable tool when negotiating the final schedule with senior management or customers and when assessing the impact of any change to any equilibrium factor during the execution of the project.

- **Allows project performance to be measured**—With a well-developed and approved project schedule, you have the capability to establish a baseline for how the project is actually performing. We discuss this in more detail in Chapter 10, "Controlling a Project."

- **Provides for "what-if" analysis capabilities**—Another important ability that a well-developed schedule provides is the ability to perform what-if analysis during the execution of the project. Over the course of a project, things happen that can negatively affect project performance. At these times, you need to know what corrective actions can be taken to possibly get the project back on schedule. Without a well-developed schedule, you cannot quickly determine the effect of implementing a given schedule compression technique, such as fast-tracking, crashing, or limited overtime.

 NOTE Although any scheduling software can assist in what-if analysis, Microsoft introduced this capability in the Microsoft Project Professional tool starting with the 2010 version by allowing the user to inactivate tasks in the primary schedule file. See Chapter 23 for more information on this.

The Goal of the Schedule Development Process

I've used terms such as "realistic" and "well-developed" to describe the type of project schedule we want to develop. Before we continue, let's clarify what the goal of the schedule development process should be. The schedule development process should generate a project schedule that meets the following criteria:

- **Complete**—The schedule must represent all the work to be done. This is why the quality and completeness of the WBS is so important.

- **Realistic**—The schedule must be realistic with regard to time expectations.

- **Accepted**—The schedule must have buy-in from team members and stakeholders.

- **Formal**—The schedule must be documented and formalized.

After reviewing this list, you probably see why so many projects are troubled from the start. Although there are many factors that can adversely affect project performance and cause us to replan, reschedule, or take corrective actions, an improper schedule should not be one of them. Of course, by understanding the lessons discussed in this chapter and in this book, you will be well on your way to developing solid project schedules every time.

Key Inputs for Building a Schedule

The first step in building a schedule is to review the key inputs. Let's make sure we are clear on these and where we are in the overall schedule development and planning process. To build a project schedule, you need five key inputs:

- **WBS**—List of organized tasks, the work to be done (covered in Chapter 6, "Developing the Work Breakdown Structure").

- **Effort estimates**—Amount of effort and time each task will take (covered in Chapter 7, "Estimating the Work").

- **Task relationships**—The logical dependencies that exist between work tasks. I review this step in this chapter.

- **Resources**—The actual personnel and equipment needed to perform the work between work tasks (referenced throughout Part II, "Project Planning," and covered in more detail in this chapter).

- **Risk responses**—Measures taken to deal with the uncertainty surrounding effort and resource estimates; usually in the form of additional time (contingency buffer) added to the schedule.

Due to the amount of important information and the critical nature of two of these inputs (developing the WBS and estimating the work packages), we reviewed them in their own chapters. In this chapter, we take these two key inputs together with the other three (sequence the work, develop schedule, and finalize schedule) to develop a realistic schedule, as depicted in Figure 8.3.

 NOTE Due to the number of inputs, trade-offs, and feedback points, the schedule development process is a natural, iterative process.

Expect to continuously loop through this process and refine your inputs until a final, approved schedule is achieved.

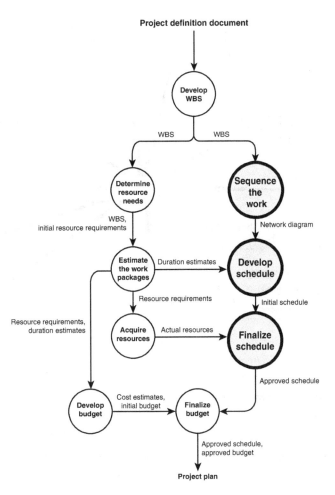

FIGURE 8.3

The schedule development points to be reviewed in this chapter.

Creating a Schedule

Because we are on this wavelength, let's go ahead and review the key steps involved in building a project schedule. The steps are also summarized in Figure 8.4. We will follow up this section with a more in-depth look at a few of these:

1. **Identify the work tasks (WBS)**—Identify the work tasks that need to be performed (reviewed in Chapter 6, but might need to be revisited as you iterate through the process).

FIGURE 8.4

The ten steps involved in creating a schedule.

2. **Estimate the effort for each work task**—Based on specific resource types, estimate the amount of effort each task will require (covered in Chapter 7, but might need to be revisited until resource assignments are finalized).

3. **Determine task relationships (network diagram)**—Identify which tasks have to be done before others can begin and which tasks can be done at the same time (in parallel).

4. **Assign resources**—Assign the roles, personnel, and equipment that will perform each task.

5. **Develop preliminary schedule**—If you have not already, capture all these inputs using your preferred scheduling software.

6. **Perform "reality" check**—This is a key, often overlooked, step in the process to make your schedule realistic. This step includes a review of resource allocation and calendar setup.

7. **Shorten the schedule**—In this step, you determine the critical path and look for ways to reduce the time required to complete the critical path tasks.

8. **Account for risk responses**—If any of the risk responses includes adding a contingency buffer to any specific task or to the entire schedule, make sure to include this in the schedule, too.

9. **Walk through the schedule**—In this important step, the proposed schedule is presented for review and feedback. At a minimum, the schedule should be closely reviewed first by the core project team and then by the key stakeholders (management, customers).

 CAUTION   A common reason for unrealistic schedules is that the schedule does not account for all the logical dependencies that exist. The schedule generally reflects an earlier completion date than what is actually possible.

10. **Finalize schedule**—Incorporate feedback from stakeholders; make any adjustments for actual resource assignments, final risk responses, and success factor trade-offs; get formal acceptance of schedule.

Let's take a closer look at a few of the key steps.

 TIP   Become knowledgeable and proficient at the scheduling software you use. Many unrealistic schedules originate with a project manager who does not understand how to best use the tool. For those who use Microsoft Project, make sure to check out Chapter 23.

Determining Task Relationships (Sequencing the Work)

In this step, we think about what needs to be done first and what can be done at the same time. We want to capture the logical relationships that exist between the tasks in our WBS. The traditional technique used to capture these relationships is the network diagram. An example of a network diagram is pictured in Figure 8.5.

FIGURE 8.5

Example of a partial network diagram showing logical sequence of tasks.

Unlike most introductory project management books, I'm not going to spend five to ten pages (or more) on traditional network diagram topics such as types of network diagrams (Activity-on-Node, Activity-on-Arrow, GERT), dependency types (Finish-to-Start, Start-to-Finish, Start-to-Start, Finish-to-Finish), or mathematical analysis scheduling techniques (Critical Path Method, PERT, and Monte Carlo simulation). Why? Because unless you are in a specialized industry, these techniques are not used very often, and most project scheduling software will take care of this for you (if you know how to use it). Of course, if you plan to take the PMP, you will need to hone your knowledge of these concepts.

The whole idea here is to look at your work visually and think about in what order (sequence) the work needs to occur. This is an exercise in logic. In many cases, this step is an excellent team activity. At this time, you don't want to concern yourself with resource constraints: just focus on logical sequence of the work. When you complete this task, you want to be clear on three things:

CAUTION Avoid entering start and end dates for tasks. These dates establish constraints in the scheduling software and can give you unexpected results.

If you have a hard, fixed milestone date that must be honored, then leverage a separate milestone task or, if you're using Microsoft Project, the "deadline" task attribute.

- For each task, what other tasks must be completed first?

- For the project, what tasks could be done at the same time (concurrently, in parallel)?

- For the project, where are your external dependencies? What tasks can't start until an external event or task has completed?

TIP A team-based schedule development approach should be pursued whenever possible for two primary reasons: higher quality schedule and team ownership of the schedule.

Team collaboration tools like Mindjet's MindManager can be very effective for these activities.

Building the Preliminary Schedule

Now that we have our key inputs (WBS, task relationships, effort estimates, and resource assignments), we are ready to build our initial schedule. There are a few keys to remember here:

- Use scheduling software and be properly trained in how to use it.

 NOTE A schedule is considered "preliminary" until resource assignments are confirmed.

VALUE OF SCHEDULING SOFTWARE

If you are not an advocate of scheduling software, or you need to help convince someone else in your organization, please note the following benefits provided by scheduling software:

- Critical path analysis
- Project and resource calendars
- Schedule calculation
- Resource leveling
- Facilitate what-if analysis
- Provide for top-down planning
- Baseline management

- If you've completed the other steps well up to this point, this step is much easier. For each task you want to schedule, you need to enter the following information:

  - Task name

  - Estimated effort

  - Predecessor task

  - Assigned resource

- Understand the relationship between work, duration, resources, and productivity.

 CAUTION Overallocated resources and misaligned schedule calendars are two of the most common causes of unrealistic project schedules.

The duration of a task is dependent upon the number of resources (and their productivity rate) that are assigned to the total work effort.

- Using the scheduling software, locate the critical path. Often, the software differentiates the tasks that comprise the critical path in some way, such as showing these tasks in red font.

The critical path is the longest path through your network and represents the minimum amount of time it will take to complete the project.

- Although the overall schedule development process should be a team-based activity, a single person generally performs the construction of the actual schedule, due to the nature of the software.

 NOTE Frequently, in the real world, project managers need to schedule to hard milestone dates or need to develop a schedule with less-than-complete work details. See Chapter 24, "When Reality Happens," for helpful recommendations.

Perform Reality Check

In this step, we need to make sure the schedule is reasonable and is aligned with the organizational culture. The primary checkpoints are to check for proper allocation of resources and check for proper use of calendars.

When checking for proper allocation resources, you want to do two things: remove unrealistic work allocations and optimize the use of your resources.

This activity is commonly referred to as *resource leveling*. Most scheduling software systems provide a function to do this for you, but proceed with caution—the software does not always get this right. As a result, you can have a less-than-optimal schedule.

I recommend, especially if you are just beginning, that you manually level the allocation of your resources. As a result, you will learn more about your scheduling software and become more intimate with your schedule.

 NOTE The only way to shorten a schedule is to compress the critical path time.

Review the resource schedule and look for any allocation that is more than the maximum hours per day or per week. In other words, if Joe Analyst is allocated for 16 hours on Monday, you have an unrealistic expectation. An adjustment needs to be made. The three common responses to resource overallocation situations are the following:

- Utilize other resources. Assign one or more of the affected tasks to an available resource.

- Establish a predecessor relationship. If Joe is the one who must perform each task, make the start of one task dependent on the finish of the other(s).

- Modify the priority level of one or more of the tasks and let the software perform its resource leveling function.

To check for proper use of calendars, verify the following:

- Are nonworking days accounted for (holidays or weekends)?

- Are the number of work hours per day consistent with the organization's expectation? Are eight hours of productivity per day assumed or something different?

- For part-time resources or resources with special work schedules, are individual calendars assigned to them that reflect this reality?

Shorten the Schedule

On most projects, your preliminary schedule will not be the schedule presented to the stakeholders for approval. Due to either stakeholder expectations or an external deadline that must be met, an effort must be made to compress or shorten the schedule without reducing the scope of the project. The key to this effort is the critical path.

TIP You can also deploy techniques to shorten the project schedule during project execution as a corrective action to a schedule variance.

Clearly document and communicate all assumptions used in building the schedule.

The critical path determines the earliest (the soonest) your project can be completed given the current task relationships and estimated durations. As a project manager, you want to be very clear about which tasks comprise the critical path for two reasons:

- If you can reduce this critical path (or change it), you might be able to complete the project sooner.

- Any slippage in the completion of a critical path task pushes out the completion date for the entire project.

The common techniques to consider are detailed in Table 8.1.

TABLE 8.1 Techniques for Compressing the Project Schedule

Technique	Definition	Key Issue(s)
Crashing	Adding resources to critical path activities only.	Certain activities cannot be completed faster by adding resources. Additional resources often add overhead that can negate any time savings. Crashing can increase project costs.
Fast tracking	Performing critical path activities in parallel.	Fast tracking is a high-risk technique that increases the probability of rework.
Process improvements	Gaining productivity increases based on different work processes, technologies, or machinery.	New approaches can increase project risks. Process improvements are not always available.
Limited overtime	Increasing the number of hours per day or week available to work on project tasks.	Overtime is most effective when used for limited periods of time. Overuse can lead to issues with team morale and quality of work.

Walk Through the Schedule

In our pursuit of both a more realistic schedule and a schedule that our stakeholders feel ownership for, you need to walk through the schedule with at least two groups—and if at all possible get a third quality-based review.

- **Review with project team**—First, present the proposed schedule to your project team. Seek their feedback on all aspects: complete task listing, correct resource assignments, logical task sequence, reality factors, and so on. Make any necessary adjustments.

- **Quality review**—This review is not always possible, but whenever possible, have an experienced and knowledgeable project scheduler review your proposed schedule before you submit it to your stakeholders. Especially if you are just gaining experience at this, this input and training can be invaluable.

- **Review with project stakeholders**—Present the proposed schedule to key stakeholders. Seek feedback and questions on all aspects: verify resource assignments, risk responses, key milestones, and so forth. There are two keys to this step: one, the form and manner in which the schedule information is presented (making it as reviewer-friendly as possible), and two, investing the time to have a real-time, interactive review session.

Presenting the Schedule

One element of project planning and project management that is often overlooked is effectively communicating the project schedule to the various project stakeholders. Although presenting a detailed, tabular view of the schedule to the core team is acceptable, the use of visual summary representations of the schedule is highly recommended when presenting the schedule to other stakeholders. The common methods of presenting a project schedule summary are detailed in Table 8.2.

TABLE 8.2 Methods for Presenting a Project Schedule Summary

Method	Key Attributes	Benefits	Notes
Milestone chart	This is a bar chart that shows start and end dates, major deliverables, and key external dependencies.	Highlights key decision and completion points as well as any external dependencies.	Milestone tables are also used (same information, no bar chart).
Gantt chart	This is a bar chart that shows the various levels of the WBS.	Easy to read, incorporates the WBS, and can easily show actual progress against estimates.	Usually does not show interdependencies.
Timeline summary	Combines aspects of a milestone chart and a Gantt chart.	Summarizes critical path, key milestones, and relative duration of key activities. Excellent for executive presentations.	Microsoft Project (starting with 2010) offers a feature called Timeline View that makes this method much easier to generate.

Method	Key Attributes	Benefits	Notes
Network diagram	A network diagram uses nodes and arrows. Date information is added to each activity node.	Highlights the critical path and shows project logic (flow).	For presentations, the summary task level of the WBS is generally used; otherwise, a network diagram is best suited for wall display.
Modified WBS	Uses the project WBS organization with status information added to each node.	Shows progress against original work breakdown organization. Easy to read.	Similar to network diagram type representations.

THE ABSOLUTE MINIMUM

At this point, you should have a solid understanding of the following:

- Schedule development is an iterative, team-based activity.
- The project schedule is a critical component of the project plan and integrates all the key planning activities.
- The project schedule drives the project budget and the resource schedule.
- The project schedule is the project manager's most effective tool in managing expectations regarding the key success factors (time, cost, and quality).
- The five key inputs for the schedule are the WBS, effort estimates, task relationships, assigned resources, and planned risk responses.
- Many reasons for an unrealistic schedule originate with an inadequate schedule development process and inadequate training with the scheduling software.
- Document and clearly communicate all scheduling assumptions.

The map in Figure 8.6 summarizes the main points reviewed in this chapter.

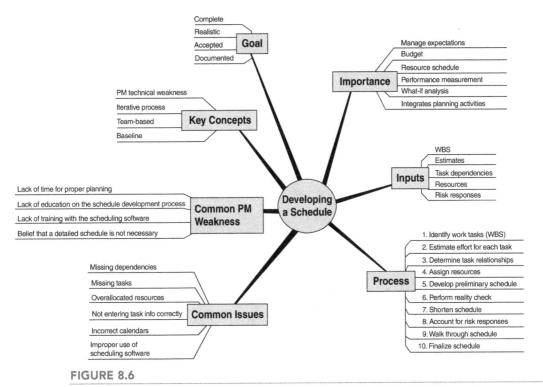

FIGURE 8.6

Overview of developing a schedule.

IN THIS CHAPTER

- Understand why the project budget is important to project success
- Review the process for figuring a realistic budget
- Learn the key project budgeting principles
- Understand the common mistakes people make when building a project budget

DETERMINING THE PROJECT BUDGET

It's one of the key success factors for projects—completing the project within budget. Yet, for many project managers, especially those managing internal projects, it's the success factor they have the least awareness about. There are several reasons why this occurs, and it does vary by industry, but most of the reasons have to do with organizational management structures and organizational budgeting and cost-controlling policies.

For our purposes, in this age of increased accountability of project investment decisions, we will assume you need to establish a project budget and need to track costs against it as the project is executed.

Because this is an introductory project management book, we avoid any discussion of advanced financial topics and instead put our focus on the "need-to-know" fundamentals for figuring your project budget. In this chapter, we emphasize the importance of the project budget, review the process and key principles for developing a realistic budget, and highlight the areas where people often go astray. This leads to a budget that has credibility with your stakeholders and provides you with the foundation to effectively track project costs and manage project execution.

The Impact of the Project Budget

Even if you find yourself in an environment where it is not expected that you develop a project budget (instead you are asked to primarily manage schedule and scope), I strongly encourage you to do two things:

- **Do it anyway**—Develop a project budget anyway. This exercise builds your project management skills, enables you to recognize project performance issues sooner, and better prepares you for senior management discussions about your project.

- **Follow the money**—You should have determined this as part of project definition, but just in case you haven't, make sure you are totally clear on who is financially sponsoring the project and who controls any finance-based decisions to be made about your project. This awareness is key in your efforts to manage expectations and to understand the political aspects of your project.

The project budget estimates all the costs the project will incur, and when they will be incurred. It is a key component of the overall project plan. The project budget is important for the following reasons:

- **Planning validator**—Because the project schedule is a main driver for the project budget, the budget can serve as an excellent cross-reference for the validity of the schedule and vice versa. By looking at the schedule from a cost perspective, you might see resource or budget issues that were not obvious before. Inversely, the schedule input is key for validating the project budget because the budget needs to account for all the time a resource is required on the project.

- **Performance measurement**—By measuring project progress against a cost baseline, you can better measure the true performance of your project along the way, and in most cases, identify issues and risks much sooner. This is the basis for an advanced project controlling technique called earned value management, which we discuss in Chapter 10, "Controlling a Project."

- **Managing expectations**—The budget impacts stakeholder expectations in several ways. The initial budget sets the expectation of what the total project costs should be. If the budget is not developed properly, then you are bound to have an expectation issue. If the project budget is predefined and serves as a cost ceiling for the project, then it helps you to set stakeholder expectations regarding project schedule and project scope.

- **Cash flow management tool**—Your schedule drives the timing of your resource needs. Especially in organizations where resources are shared across projects or centrally managed, the accuracy of the schedule is key to efficient resource management.

- **Justifying project investment**—With more projects accountable to a project selection process and to financial return on investment expectations, it is increasingly important to establish the cost baseline for the project and monitor closely.

 CAUTION Make sure your project budget accounts for all cost factors and for the entire life cycle of the effort.

Principles of an Effective Budget

Before we get into the details of building a project budget, let's review the fundamental principles that guide this process:

- **Iterative process**—Budget development is an iterative process, just like all project planning. The various facets of project planning interrelate and have natural feedback loops. With the project budget, there are strong dependencies on organizational policies and on the schedule development process. As a result, it usually takes several cycles to fully develop the budget and come to an agreement.

- **Total life cycle**—The budget should address the total project life cycle. This is a common oversight, especially for the operational phases of the project.

- **Time-phased**—Not only do we need to budget cost totals, but we need to know when these costs will be incurred for both cash flow management and project control reasons. The goal of the project budgeting process is to establish a cost baseline.

- **Comprehensive**—The budget should account for all project costs. There is a tendency to only account for obvious resources needed for the project (labor or new equipment). As part of our focus on making the budget (like the schedule) complete and realistic, we cover all the costs that need to be considered later in this chapter.

- **Include a buffer**—A buffer, normally referred to as management reserve, should be allocated to the project budget. The management reserve is primarily there to deal with known risks (a risk response), the estimating uncertainty factor, and the overall planning uncertainty factor (hidden work, rework, hidden costs, and change requests). In addition, if you have a long-term project or an international project, you might need a buffer for monetary factors such as inflation and exchange rates. Of course, these should be noted as risks in these situations.

- **Document assumptions**—Budget assumptions are documented like all other project assumptions. Any assumption made as part of the budgeting process should be documented and clearly communicated. As with all assumptions, you can document them within the targeted deliverable (in this case the budget document spreadsheet), or add them to the designated repository for project assumptions (commonly either a separate assumptions document, the project definition document, or project plan).

Creating a Project Budget

The actual process of developing a project budget is straightforward. The general challenges lie more with omissions and the foundation on which the budget is based. In this section, we review the details of the development budget and finalize the budget steps depicted in the general project planning process flow in Figure 9.1.

Sources of Project Costs

The first step in building a project budget is to identify your costs. This sounds easy enough, right? Let's review the cost sources that you need to consider. These cost sources are summarized in Figure 9.2.

- **Labor costs**—One of the key budget cost items. Budget should reflect a line item for each person or role—whichever makes the most sense for your project. Costs are based on resource rates and estimated work durations. When dealing with external labor, these costs are a key component of the business relationship and normally easy to obtain. However, it can be difficult getting rates for internal resources. In most organizations, either the human resources or finance department should have standard labor rates for internal resources based on role.

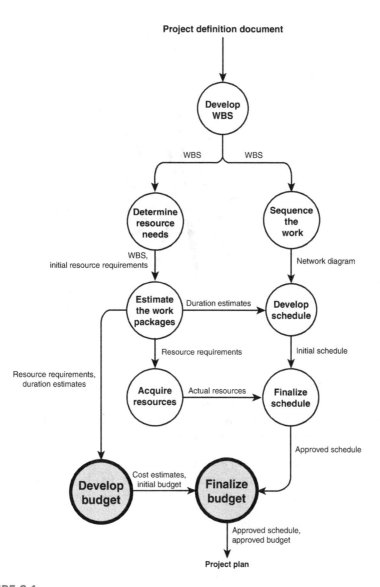

FIGURE 9.1

The budget-focused planning steps.

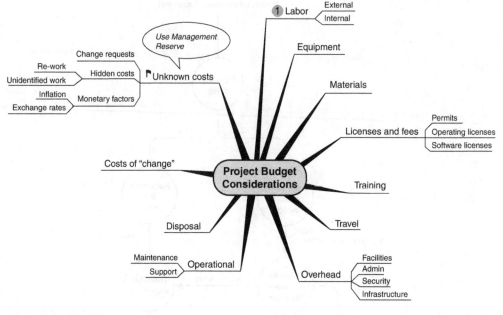

FIGURE 9.2

The budget costs to consider.

- **Equipment**—This category generally includes the tools that the project team requires to complete the work of the project. For budget purposes, the keys with the equipment category are twofold:

  - **Completeness**—Using a bottom-up estimating approach should identify all equipment needs from a task perspective. For knowledge-based projects, you need to account for software-based tools, too.

  - **Expense versus capital**—You should work with accounting to determine whether your equipment costs need to be expensed at full cost against your project or whether your project just needs to reflect depreciation cost. Different factors can influence this decision, but the most common one is whether the equipment will be used by more than one project.

- **Materials**—This category includes those items that are needed to build the product. The information is generally found in the product specifications document. In dealing with vendor relationships, you either acquire or confirm material costs by reviewing vendor responses to the formal procurement documents.

- **Licenses and fees**—This category includes costs such as software licenses, cloud-based software expenses or Software as a Service (SaaS) fees, building permits, and so on.

- **Training**—This category includes the cost of any training your project team needs to do their work and any training your users need to use the final product.

- **Travel**—This category includes the travel and lodging costs to be charged to the project that will be incurred by any project team member while doing the work of the project.

- **Operational costs**—This category includes the costs associated with the maintenance and support of the final product.

- **Disposal costs**—This category includes the costs associated with the disposal or removal of whatever the project is replacing.

- **Overhead costs**—This category includes the common overhead costs incurred by any project. Items typically included are facilities, administrative assistance, security, and technology infrastructure. Depending on the organization, these costs might not be allocated to individual projects or there might be a predetermined percentage or amount that is used by all projects.

- **Costs of "change"**—A focal point of project planning is to consider the change impact that the project will have. This category includes any costs (change management programs or initial productivity loss) that can directly attribute to the change factor. These costs should have been considered during the project selection phase as part of a cost-benefit analysis or return-on-investment analysis. In addition, these costs might be accounted for in the other budget categories. The important thing here is to think about these costs upfront during planning.

- **Unknown costs**—This category is often covered by the management reserve and addresses common cost items like change requests, re-work, and unidentified work. If your project deals with different currencies, it can also cover inflation factors and exchange rate fluctuations.

 NOTE Most project scheduling software programs offer a resource schedule that shows the total hours (and total costs) that each resource incurs over the desired time period. This feature can be very helpful to your budgeting process.

Developing an Initial Budget

After you have your resource requirements and work duration estimates, you can start to develop the budget. Like the estimates for work, it is best to estimate your costs at the work-package level. By taking a bottom-up approach, you are in the best position to identify all your resource needs and develop a more realistic budget. In addition, many industries and organizations have cost estimate models that can be leveraged, too. These models are best used during initial planning activities and as a cross-reference and validation tool for your detailed planning efforts.

Unless your organization has invested in an enterprise project management application with an emphasis on project costing or you have advanced skills in project scheduling software, I recommend the use of spreadsheet software (such as Microsoft Excel) for your project budget. I favor the spreadsheet approach for three principal reasons:

- **Capture all costs**—The spreadsheet approach enables you to easily capture all your project costs (and not just labor costs, which is the primary cost element captured by your schedule).

- **Flexible**—The spreadsheet approach offers flexible options in how you set up and organize your budget. It can also be used to track your project costs during project execution.

- **Easy analysis**—The spreadsheet approach comes with built-in analysis and reporting capabilities that can be easily leveraged.

The two keys for setting up your project budget are to set a line item for each cost source and to use columns for each time phase (period) that will be tracked.

Finalizing a Budget

As the schedule nears completion and the actual resources have been identified, you can finalize the project budget. Besides firming up rates on resources and estimates on other cost factors, there are several objectives to accomplish in this step:

- **Validate procurement tasks scheduled**—Make sure that all the tasks dealing with procuring resources (labor, equipment, and materials) are accounted for in the project schedule (and WBS). Common tasks include ordering, delivery, setup, and payment.

- **Reconcile task costs versus resource costs**—In most cases, there will be gaps between resource assignments on the schedule, or resources will not always be scheduled at maximum capacity. Much of this depends on how efficiently resources are leveled. Nevertheless, if your resource costs are based solely on assigned tasks, your budget might not reflect the actual resource costs you will incur. For example, Joe Analyst might have only 26 estimated work hours assigned one week but is fully booked at 40 hours the following week. You can't afford to release Joe for the small gap that exists, so the project is generally accountable for all his time both weeks. This situation also depends on the level of responsibility the project has for maximizing resource usage, the level of resource planning done in the organization, and how time is reported.

A good rule of thumb is to calculate personnel costs by taking their rates multiplied by a given calendar time period. For example, if I know Joe Analyst is on my project for 12 weeks, and I know he is generally a full-time resource, I calculate a resource cost for Joe by taking Joe's hourly rate × 40 hours × 12 weeks. This is likely to give me a truer cost estimate—at least a more conservative one.

- **Finalize management reserve**—Based on all known risk factors, finalize the buffer amount to be added to the project budget. The specific amount varies depending on risk level, industry practices, and management philosophy.

Common Budget Challenges

Let's take a quick review of the common challenges that a project manager faces when figuring a project budget. By increasing awareness of these factors, you can work proactively to avoid them in your own situation.

- **Based on weak foundation**—The budget is built on the planning foundation created by the WBS, resource estimates, effort estimates, and the project schedule. An inadequacy in any of these elements is directly reflected in the budget.

- **Missing cost categories**—The budget must reflect all the costs that will be incurred or at least all the costs that the project is accountable for by the sponsoring organization. See the "Sources of Project Costs" section for the list of cost sources that should be considered.

- **No profit margin**—For projects that are sold to clients, do not forget to include the profit margin in your project budget and in your pricing decisions.

- **Budget is preallocated**—In many organizations, due to the nature of their budgeting cycles and level of project management maturity, the budgets for projects are established (from high-level estimates) before the complete work of the project is defined. In these cases, the budget is often the dominant constraint on the project; as a result, it limits the amount of work that can be completed and the resourcing options available.

- **Labor costs not tracked**—This is mostly an issue for internal projects because in many organizations it can be difficult for the project manager to define and track labor costs, especially for internal staff. The most common reasons for this include the following:

  - Organizational policy that project managers do not track internal labor costs.

  - Organizational policy to treat internal labor as "sunk costs."

  - A mismatch between time reporting system and procedures and the needs of the project.

    This last reason is important to understand and might limit your cost-tracking options, or at least the level of detail information you can obtain.

THE ABSOLUTE MINIMUM

At this point, you should have a solid understanding of the following:

- If the other planning activities have been done well, establishing a project budget is a very straightforward process.
- The project budget is vital for managing expectations, accurately measuring project performance, and managing cash flow.
- An effective project budget is time-phased, addresses the complete project life cycle, and accounts for all project costs.
- The project budget is a critical component of the project plan and integrates the project schedule, resource plan, procurement plan, and risk response plan.
- The WBS, work estimates, and project schedule provide the foundation for a solid project budget.
- Spreadsheet software is usually the best tool to use for project budgeting.

The map in Figure 9.3 summarizes the main points reviewed in this chapter.

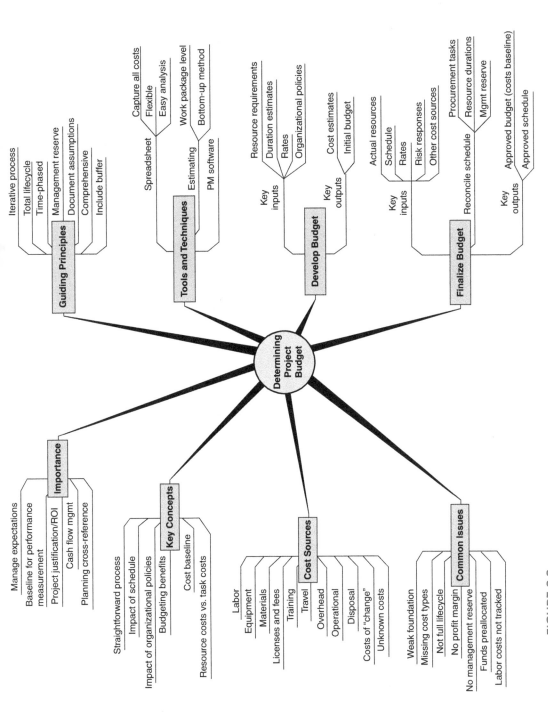

FIGURE 9.3

Overview of figuring a budget.

IN THIS CHAPTER

- Clarify what we mean by "controlling" a project
- Understand why project planning is so important to controlling a project
- Learn the principles of an effective project control system
- Learn powerful techniques that simplify project control
- Understand why earned value management is the best technique for measuring project performance, yet the least used
- Review the essential principles of project status reporting

CONTROLLING A PROJECT

Now that we have our project plan, we are ready to implement it. From a project management perspective, implementing a project plan involves two general categories of activities: project execution and project control. These activities are performed in parallel to complete the work of the project, report project progress, and keep the project on track. For the purposes of this book, we will address the process-focused activities in Part III of the book, "Project Control," and the people-focused aspects in Part IV, "Project Execution."

Although there are entire books and courses that address just single aspects of project control and project execution, we focus on the "need-to-know" fundamentals that will greatly reduce your learning curve and accelerate your effectiveness as a project manager.

This chapter serves as an excellent bridge between the "Project Planning" part we just completed and the "Project Control" part we are just beginning. In this chapter, we clarify what "controlling a project" really means, emphasize the key principles of a project control system, highlight the impact that project planning has on this effort, review powerful techniques that should always be considered, and discuss how to avoid the common challenges faced by most project managers. Finally, to summarize the key fundamentals of controlling a project, we study the lessons that can be learned from project recovery missions. This will lead to an understanding that will enable you to develop an appropriate project control system that best meets the needs of your next project.

What Is Project Control?

What do you think of when you hear "project control"? Micromanager? Confrontation? Inflexible? Military-style leadership? Theory X management? Fortunately, none of these terms accurately describe project control. Project control consists of the information systems and the management procedures that enable you to answer questions such as

- Are we on track?
- Are we on budget?
- Are we on schedule?
- Are we delivering what we said we would?
- Are we meeting quality and performance standards?
- Are we meeting stakeholder expectations?
- What have we accomplished?
- Will the project objectives be met?
- What deviations/variances exist?
- What corrective actions are we taking?
- What caused these variances?
- What risks are we monitoring?
- What issues do we need to resolve?
- What lessons have we learned?

Officially, the Project Management Institute (PMI) defines the Monitoring and Controlling Process Group as those processes required to track, review, and regulate the progress and performance of the project; identify any areas in which changes to the plan are required; and initiate the corresponding changes.

Although accurate, this definition does not clearly communicate all the aspects of project control that we need to understand, and it does not emphasize the most important aspect—prevention.

PDA: The Principles of Project Control

An easy way to remember what project control is all about is to think *PDA*. PDA stands for Prevention, Detection, and Action. Let's take a closer look at these fundamental principles of project control:

- **Prevention**—As with your own health, the secret to wellness is strengthening your immune system and minimizing contact with harmful agents. In other words, don't get sick in the first place. The same principle applies to effective project control. The best way to keep your project on track is to prevent (or at least minimize) variances from occurring. How do you do this? This takes your entire array of project management skills, but a few key activities include investing in planning, communicating effectively, monitoring risk factors continuously, resolving issues aggressively, and delegating work clearly.

TIP Controlling project performance is all about PDA—Prevention, Detection, and Action.

TIP "Lessons learned" are important resources for improving performance on the current project and on future projects.

- **Detection**—For this aspect of project control, think radar system or early warning system. Project control should provide early detection of variances. The sooner we can act on a variance, the more likely we are to get the success factor back on track. The key for early detection is to have the tracking systems and work processes in place that allow for the timely measurement of project results. Common examples of detection methods are performance reporting, review meetings, and development methodologies that emphasize early and frequent product generation. Two important concepts to note here are that to have a variance, you must be comparing actual results to a baseline of some type, and a variance can apply to any of the critical success factors, including stakeholder expectations and quality, not just schedule, cost, and scope.

- **Action**—Although the prevention aspect has a strong action orientation too, this principle goes hand-in-hand with early detection. For project control to be effective, the detection of a variance must be able to trigger an appropriate and timely response. The three most common action types are corrective actions, change control procedures, and lessons learned. Often, as part of the planning for project control, specific variance thresholds are established that dictate what variances and corrective actions can be managed by the project team and what things need the immediate attention of senior-level management.

Components of Project Control

To better clarify what is involved with project control, let's review some of the key project management processes that are involved. To reiterate, project control involves more than just these processes. Your leadership, communication, interpersonal, analytical, and team management skills are equally, if not more, important to this endeavor. However, without these fundamental management processes in place, as depicted in Figure 10.1, you will have a much more challenging time.

- **Performance reporting**—The process for measuring and communicating project status to the targeted stakeholders. Information generally is focused on the performance of critical success factors against baseline targets, key issues, corrective actions, and forecasted metrics.

FIGURE 10.1

The project management processes involved with project control.

- **Change control management**—The process for reviewing, approving, and coordinating any request to alter the project scope, schedule, or budget. We address this in greater detail in Chapter 11, "Managing Project Changes."

- **Configuration management**—The process for controlling changes, updates, and versions of project deliverables. We discuss this in greater detail in Chapter 11 and in Chapter 12, "Managing Project Deliverables."

- **Issue management**—The process for identifying, tracking, and resolving issues that could affect the project's critical success factors. We address this in greater detail in Chapter 13, "Managing Project Issues."

- **Risk management**—The process for identifying, monitoring, and responding to project risks. We address this in greater detail in Chapter 14, "Managing Project Risks."

 CAUTION It is important to know that a project is the most at risk, and most likely to change, at the beginning of the project.

- **Quality management**—The process for ensuring that work processes and project deliverables meet quality expectations. We address this in greater detail in Chapter 15, "Managing Project Quality."

- **Procurement management**—The controlling processes specifically used to manage any suppliers and vendors involved in the project.

- **Requirements management**—The process to ensure all requirements are identified correctly, documented, and tracked throughout the project. This is an excellent scope and change control technique that is mentioned again later in this chapter.

Management Fundamentals for Project Control

As a project manager, there are a few management fundamentals to consider when establishing your project control system:

- **Focus on priorities**—Understand what is important to the project and to the organization. Understand that whatever receives your focus will become important. Make sure there is alignment between the two.

- **Scale to project**—The level of rigor and detail in your project control system should be consistent with the level of risk in the project. It should also be consistent with the project budget. In other words, projects with either low risk or small budgets should not be burdened with a project control system that is designed for larger, mission-critical projects.

- **Think "process"**—You do not want to spend all your time and energy putting out fires, trying to get basic status information, and feeling like you are not in control of your project. You want to establish a natural system of control for the project; you want to plan it in advance. This applies to the project as a whole and to each individual team member's contribution.

- **Expect changes**—Project control does not mean prevent changes at all costs. Conversely, project changes should be expected, planned, and well-managed.

- **Invest in thorough planning**—The more energy spent in planning, the easier it is to control a project. If the project is defined properly, work is planned from the bottom up, risks have been identified, stakeholders are in agreement on project objectives, and the project control system has been accounted for, then keeping the project on track should take much less effort.

 CAUTION 15% Completion Rule—No project recovers from a variance at the 15% completion point. If you underestimated the near term, you are generally off on the long term, too.

- **Consider organizational culture**—Depending on the level of project management maturity in your organization, you might need to consider a gradual implementation of project controlling procedures to achieve greater acceptance and effectiveness. Again, just make sure you focus on top priorities.

- **Set expectations**—Remember to think "project control" in your project communications. Ensure that each team member understands what is expected from the project and from their individual role. In addition, make sure that the project team sees the discipline and priority that you place on all project control procedures.

- **Be consistent**—An important element to both effective project control and effective project communications is consistency. Project performance needs to be measured and reported on a consistent, regular basis. This approach is key for both early detection of variances and for establishing a culture of accountability to project assignments.

- **Pay attention early**—Just to follow up on the last point: make sure to pay close attention to your project early on. According to a study of more than 800 projects for the Department of Defense since 1977, the outcome of a project was no better than its performance taken at the 15% completion point. Thus, if a project was behind schedule and/or over budget at the 15% completion point, it did not recover from this variance. The general consensus is that this happens for two key reasons: lax project controls in the early stages and poor estimating. If the estimates were off for the immediate work efforts, they are unlikely to be more accurate further down the timeline. We discuss how to handle a variance in the "Variance Responses" section later in this chapter.

- **Track assumptions and constraints**—Often, the key assumptions and constraints for a project are identified during project planning then subsequently forgotten: "out of sight, out of mind." Also, many projects do not have a system in place to capture new or changing assumptions and constraints as the project moves forward. One suggestion is to track these alongside issues, risks, and key action items.

 NOTE The nature of agile project management approaches entails many of these project controlling fundamentals, especially the focus on priorities, expecting changes, setting expectations, being consistent, establishing a natural control process, scaling to match the needs of the project, and factoring the organizational culture.

Powerful Techniques for Project Control

So far, we have covered the value and importance of planning your control system. In this section, we'll take a look at some powerful project control techniques that you'll want to consider during your planning efforts and then implement during the execution of your project.

 CAUTION Make sure your status meetings are scheduled and conducted in a purposeful, value-added manner. Be cognizant of the cost involved in pulling the targeted resources together. Focus on improving team synergy, project communications, managing expectations, and accountability to the team.

- **Small work packages**—This was a point of emphasis during our discussion on building a work breakdown structure (WBS). Recall that there are two primary reasons for advocating small work packages: more accurate estimates and better control. From a control perspective, if your work packages are scheduled to complete within one (or at the most, two) reporting period, it is much easier to detect a delayed or troubled task. With earlier notice, you are more likely to resolve the variance and protect the project's critical success factors.

- **Early and frequent work packages**—In addition to small work packages, which help identify progress variances early, you should look for opportunities and approaches that emphasize prototyping (at a minimum) or early and frequent generation of the actual product result that is reviewed with the key stakeholders. This is the key aspect of agile-type methodologies. This helps identify any variances with requirements and stakeholder expectations as early as possible. And with earlier notice, you are more likely to resolve the variance and protect the project's critical success factors.

- **Baselines**—A fundamental control principle is to manage to baselines. First, establish a baseline. This is generally applied to the critical success factors of schedule and budget, but you can apply it equally as well to product-oriented aspects of the project, especially requirements. Second, measure and report performance against the baseline. Third, maintain the baseline unless there is a formal agreement to reset the baseline. We discuss this in greater detail in Chapter 11.

- **Status meetings**—The simplest, and most widely known, technique is the status meeting. Consistent and regular status meetings help to keep everyone honest, accountable, and on their toes—especially if work assignments are small and have clear completion criteria. In addition, status meetings are powerful tools for improving project communications and managing expectations.

- **Completion criteria**—This starts during project definition with defining the acceptance criteria for the project, and it continues for each deliverable and work assignment. Answer this question in advance for each deliverable and work assignment: "How will we know when it is done?" Understanding the completion criteria upfront increases productivity and avoids many of the issues associated with status reporting on work tasks, especially the infamous "I'm 90% done" syndrome.

 NOTE The "90% done" phenomenon refers to the phenomenon where task progress is reported as on schedule up to the 90% completion point. Then, the last 10% ends up taking most of the total task time to complete.

This can occur on projects when task status is reported subjectively by the resource assigned to the task and when there is no clear completion criteria for the task.

- **Reviews**—Reviews are a key technique for ensuring quality and managing expectations on project deliverables, and they can take many forms. The principle here is to plan for the review-feedback-correction cycle on most, if not all, of your key deliverables. Common examples of reviews are process reviews, design reviews, audits, walkthroughs, and testing. In addition, reviews can be combined with predefined milestones and checkpoints.

NOTE Agile projects leverage many of these project controlling techniques, especially the focus on small work packages, early and frequent work packages, frequent milestones and reviews, closely tracking requirements, completion criteria for all work items, and daily status/checkpoint meetings.

- **Milestones and checkpoints**—A key feature of most proven project methodologies is the use of predefined milestones and checkpoints. These markers are important points to stop, report progress, review key issues, confirm that everyone is still on board, and verify that the project should proceed with its mission. Besides being a powerful expectations management tool, these predefined points allow project sponsors and senior management to evaluate their project investments along the way and, if warranted, redirect valuable resources from a troubled project to more promising pursuits.

- **Track requirements**—A simple, yet often neglected, technique to help control both scope and expectations is the use of a *requirements traceability matrix*. The traceability matrix provides a documented link between the original set of approved requirements, any interim deliverable, and the final work product. This technique helps maintain the visibility of each original requirement and provides a natural barrier for introducing any "new" feature along the way (or at least provides a natural trigger to your change control system). In addition, the traceability matrix can link the specific test scenarios that are needed to verify that each requirement is met.

 NOTE If requirements and test cases are captured in a database or work management system, the traceability can be easily achieved with the proper data relationships.

- **Formal sign-offs**—Formal sign-offs are a key aspect of change control management, especially for projects that are client-vendor oriented. The formal record of review and acceptance of a given deliverable helps to keep expectations aligned and minimize potential disputes. Most importantly, the use of a formal sign-off acts as an extra incentive to make sure the appropriate stakeholders are actively engaged in the work of the project.

 TIP Focus your project performance reports on answering the big three questions:

- Where do we stand (with regard to the critical success factors)?
- What variances exist, what caused them, and what are we doing about them?
- Has the forecast changed?

- **Independent QA auditor**—The use of an independent quality assurance auditor is another specific example of the "review" technique mentioned earlier, and it's often a component of project QA plans. In addition, the quality audit can be focused on product deliverables, work processes, or project management activities. The power of this technique is in establishing the quality criteria in advance and in making the project accountable to an outside entity.

- **V method**—The *V method* is a term used for a common validation and verification approach that ensures that there is a validation and verification step for every deliverable and interim deliverable created. The left side of the V notes each targeted deliverable, and the right side of the V lists the verification method to be used for each deliverable directly across. The diagram in Figure 10.2 helps illustrate this method.

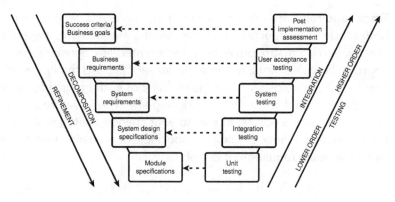

FIGURE 10.2

V method approach for a software development project.

- **Escalation thresholds**—Escalation thresholds sound much more ominous than they actually are. The purpose of escalation thresholds is to determine in advance what issues and variances the project team can handle and what issues or variances demand attention by senior management. Often, these thresholds are defined as percent variances around the critical success factors. For example, if the cost variance is greater than 10% or schedule variance is greater than 15%, engage senior management immediately for corrective action steps. The key value of this technique is that it helps to define tolerance levels, set expectations, and clarify when senior management should get involved in corrective action procedures.

NOTE Performance reporting requirements should be captured as part of the project communications plan.

Performance Reporting

As we have touched on several times already, another key aspect of project control is measuring and reporting project performance. We could easily spend an entire chapter (or two) reviewing the various options, factors, and challenges involved with this process. However, if you keep the following principles in mind, you can adapt your performance reporting process to best meet the needs of your project environment:

- **Answer the big three questions**—As a rule, key stakeholders want to know the answers to the following three questions when reviewing project performance:

  1. Where do we stand (with regard to the critical success factors)?

  2. What variances exist, what caused them, and what are we doing about them?

  3. Has the forecast changed?

- **Measure from current baseline**—If you are going to report project performance with a variance focus, you must establish and maintain your performance baselines. Any change to the performance baselines is controlled via your change control procedures.

- **Think "visual"**—Another key concept in reporting is to think visually. Most people are visual and spatial learners and will grasp the important project performance metrics more quickly if they are presented in a visual format. The use of bar charts, graphical schedule summaries, and stoplight indicators (red, yellow, and green) for key metrics are good examples of this technique.

- **Think "summary page"**—Along this same theme, you generally want to provide your key status information in no more than one to two pages. If it is appropriate to have details that will take more than one or two pages, it is recommended that you provide a one-page summary upfront.

- **Highlight accomplishments**—A part of the status report's function is to serve as a public relations tool for the project, so make sure key accomplishments are highlighted prominently.

- **Show forecasts**—In addition to reporting how the project has performed to date, remember to show the forecasted schedule and cost metrics. Often, this information is shown as Estimate At Completion (EAC) and Estimate To Complete (ETC) figures. Specifically, highlight any changes to these figures from the last reporting period.

NOTE   If the variance is due to estimating errors or estimating assumptions that have not held up, you should update your estimates and assumptions based on your actual experiences, and use this new information as the basis for the revised baseline.

- **Highlight key issues, risks, and change requests**—This is a natural category when assessing project performance. Make sure any key issues, risks, and change requests are included on status reports. I discuss these in greater detail in subsequent chapters.

- **Avoid surprises**—An important point about consistent, performance-based status reporting is that stakeholders are aware of and knowledgeable about overall project status and are not caught off guard with project developments. To this extent, depending on the audience for any status report, you might want to communicate with specific stakeholders in advance of any official report distribution. Always remember that you should not surprise anyone— especially your sponsors and accountable senior management stakeholders.

- **Adapt to meet stakeholder needs**—This is an example of the customer service orientation and servant leadership qualities of effective project managers. Be prepared to offer examples of performance reports that have worked well for you in the past, but most importantly, go into any project looking to understand the information needs for this given environment. Show enthusiasm and willingness to adapt to the customer's standards or to develop custom formats to best meet the stakeholders' needs.

- **Deliver with appropriate frequency**—Consistent with a management fundamental mentioned earlier, the frequency of performance reporting must be appropriate for the project. The process of gathering information and reporting performance needs to be quick enough and occur often enough to be useful and relevant.

CAUTION   Approved change requests would cause a baseline revision, too.

Variance Responses

As previously mentioned, the first goal of our project control system is to prevent any variance. However, we also realize variances and changes will occur—this is the nature of the project beast. Thus, the remaining goals of project control are centered on early detection and appropriate response. Let's review the general response options that are available to us as project managers when a variance occurs:

- **Take corrective actions**—The preferred option, whenever possible, is to understand the root cause of the variance and then implement action steps to correct the variance. When performance measurement is frequent, it is more likely that action can be taken that will make a difference. Examples of corrective actions include adding resources, changing the process, coaching individual performance, compressing the schedule (fast-tracking or crashing), or reducing scope (this would be documented as a change request, too).

- **Ignore it**—In cases where the variance is small (and falls within an acceptable threshold range), you might choose to take no action to resolve the deviation. Even in these cases, it would be advisable to log the variance as a risk factor.

- **Cancel the project**—There might be times when the appropriate response is to cancel the project altogether. This response is more likely on projects where one or more key assumptions have not held or when one or more of the critical success factors has a very low tolerance for any deviations.

- **Reset baselines**—While taking corrective action is the preferred option for performance variances, there are times when the variance cannot be eliminated. This is common on knowledge-based projects and common on projects where the estimating assumptions have not held. In these cases, a decision to reset the performance baselines is made and approved. From that point on, performance is measured from this revised baseline. This is part of the change control procedures we discuss more in Chapter 11.

 CAUTION   Earned Value Management (EVM) is the best project control technique for early detection of project performance variances.

Leveraging Earned Value Management Concepts

Earned Value Management (EVM) (otherwise known as variance analysis) is the best project control technique for early detection of performance variances. The technique was developed nearly 40 years ago for the United States government to better manage contract payments to vendors. Ever since, EVM has grown in popularity and acceptance across many industries and now is regarded as the preferred project control technique by PMI. However, it has not been accepted as standard practice in all industries, and it is usually a technique found in organizations or industries that are relatively mature in their management processes. Thus, we could spend an entire chapter on a technique that might not be part of your organizational culture yet. In addition, if you work in one of these process-mature environments, you are less likely to be reading this book, and you will likely have many additional resources to address the details of earned value.

Still, there is tremendous value in a quick review of EVM. An awareness of the fundamental concepts will help you in your project controlling and performance reporting endeavors.

- **Assess cost performance and schedule performance together**—The main value of EVM is that it enables you to measure and track both schedule and cost performance. Evaluating project performance on just one of these indicators does not always give you the true picture and does not allow you to detect variances as early.

- **Each work package has a planned value**—The planned value of any work package is the budgeted cost of the work scheduled to complete the work package. The important point here: Estimate the cost of each work package in your schedule. Also, this means that the project as a whole has a baseline schedule and budget.

- **At any point, the project has an "earned" value**—The earned value of a project is the budgeted cost of the work actually completed. In other words, how many work packages (or partial work packages) have been completed at this time? The value is expressed in budgeted cost terms, not actual costs. This enables you to perform cost analysis by comparing budgeted versus actual costs for the work completed. The important point to consider: Be aware of the costs you expected to incur for the work that has been completed.

Before we introduce an example EVM graph, let's review the other key terms and concepts that comprise EVM. Table 10.1 summarizes these key elements.

 CAUTION A negative performance index value is not favorable. It means that you're behind schedule or over budget.

TABLE 10.1 Earned Value Management Elements

Element	Definition	Notes
Planned Value (PV)	Budgeted cost of work scheduled.	Performance baseline.
Earned Value (EV)	Budgeted cost of work performed.	For the work performed, what was the budgeted cost?
Actual Costs (AC)	Actual costs of work performed.	For the work performed, what were the actual costs?

Element	Definition	Notes
Cost Variance (CV)	Earned Value – Actual Costs CV = EV – AC	A negative number means you are over budget.
Schedule Variance (SV)	Earned Value – Planned Value SV = EV – PV	A negative number means you are behind schedule.
Cost Performance Index (CPI)	Earned Value / Actual Costs CPI = EV / AC Numerical representation of project cost performance.	CPI < 1 means your project is costing you more than you planned. CPI > 1 means you are taking less money to do the project.
Schedule Performance Index (SPI)	Earned Value / Planned Value SPI = EV / PV Numerical representation of project schedule performance.	SPI < 1 means your project is behind schedule. SPI > 1 means you are ahead of schedule.
Budget at Completion (BAC)	Total baseline project.	The original project budget.
Estimate at Completion (EAC)	Budget at Completion / Cost Performance Index EAC = BAC / CPI	Based on current cost performance, what will be your total cost?
Estimate to Complete (ETC)	Estimate at Completion – Actual Costs ETC = EAC – AC	Subtract AC from EAC to get estimated remaining costs.

EVM takes the planned value (PV), or what you planned to do at an estimated cost, and compares it against the estimated cost of the work performed (EV) and against the actual cost of work performed (AC), or what actually got done. These metrics provide a wealth of information about whether the project tasks are taking longer than they should (schedule variance, or SV), or whether they are actually requiring more work effort to complete (cost variance, or CV). In addition, the estimate-at-completion metric (EAC) helps you forecast final project performance and determine whether any corrective action needs to take place.

To illustrate how EVM could be used for performance reporting, see Figure 10.3.

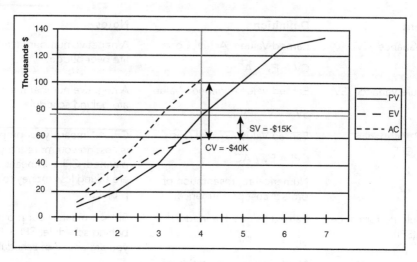

FIGURE 10.3

Depicts EVM metrics for the fourth time period on a sample project.

In this example, the report provides EVM data for the fourth reporting period. At this time, the Planned Value = $75K, the Actual Costs = $100K, and the Earned Value = $60K. On this project, we can tell the following by analyzing this report:

- There has been a cost variance from the start. It could be the actual resource costs have been higher.

- Also, for the first three weeks, the project was ahead of schedule. More work was completed than planned. This was a likely factor for the actual costs being higher too.

- During the past reporting period, something has occurred that delayed progress. The project is now behind schedule (and the cost variance has increased significantly).

Many of the project management software tools, such as Microsoft Project, include these EVM calculations. To be useful, the schedule must include all assigned resources, individual resource costs, and current progress measurements.

Common Project Control Challenges

Although we've touched on several challenges facing project managers when attempting to control their projects, let's run down the top reasons for difficulty in the project control arena:

- **Time and cost accounting logistics**—The logistical and organizational culture issues relating to time reporting and project costs tracking can prove detrimental to timely and accurate performance reporting. During planning, you want to understand and clarify how project time and cost information is reported and how quickly you can get this data. You might need to establish project-specific time reporting or approval procedures to ensure the integrity of your control system.

- **Project manager reluctance, multitasked**—The project manager might be reluctant to request WBS-level time reporting by project team members, especially if this is not part of the organizational culture. In addition, the project manager might be overallocated and might not be able to invest enough time to performing the project controlling duties. This is most common when the project manager has assigned other project roles to themself or when the project manager is assigned to multiple projects.

- **No change control**—The most common reason for project control difficulty is the lack of change control procedures. This is most problematic when the project scope has increased without the proper reconciliation with the project schedule and budget.

- **No completion criteria**—When clear completion criteria for work assignments are not established, you are more likely to have rework cycles, more difficulty in accurately reporting progress or status, and more likely to experience the 90% done phenomenon.

- **No baselines**—This should be obvious by now, but if a schedule and budget baseline are not established and controlled, then you will not be able to accurately measure for performance variances. Without this ability, you are less likely to detect problems early—when they are small and more manageable.

- **No requirements traceability**—This is definitely an issue for controlling scope and stakeholder expectations. The lack of a formal tracking procedure between original requirements and final products increases the odds of missed work and scope creep.

- **Not consistent**—When control procedures are not consistently implemented, it is difficult to detect performance variances early, and it is more difficult to get project team members to follow the defined control procedures.

- **Measuring progress accurately**—Accurately measuring progress is a natural challenge on work assignments with intangible final products, especially on any project where status is estimated. However, this challenge is further complicated when work definition is vague, completion criteria are not established, or work efforts are not reported on a daily basis.

- **Impact of hidden work**—This hits at the heart of work definition and change control. Any effort spent on unidentified work, unplanned rework cycles, or out-of-scope work adversely affects the accuracy and effectiveness of project control procedures.

- **Virtual/distributed teams**—When project team members are not physically located together, it can be more difficult to get information, detect potential issues, measure work progress, and ensure understanding of work expectations. We talk more about this in Chapter 20, "Managing Differences."

Lessons from Project Recoveries

To really understand what is important for controlling a project, let's review what occurs during a typical project recovery. For clarification, a project recovery is an attempt to turn around a troubled project. If there is ever a case where project control is absolutely critical, it is when you are trying to heal a sick project.

The first thing that senior management will do to recover a project is to make sure there is an effective project manager in charge. This might mean anything from validating the current project manager, bringing in someone new, pulling someone up from the project team, or providing a mentor to the current project leadership. After the project leadership is solidified, most recovery missions involve the following activities:

- **Review planning principles**—The planning principles are revisited. A focus is placed on establishing priorities and objectives, clarifying acceptance criteria, gaining consensus, and reviewing roles and responsibilities.

- **Reset baseline**—As a final step in the replanning step, key milestones are set and new baselines are set for cost and schedule performance.

- **Frequent status checks**—To facilitate better communications, prevent additional obstacles, reinforce the visibility of the recovery mission, and emphasize individual accountability, team status meetings are conducted daily. In some situations, these checkpoints are even more frequent. It depends on the nature of the project.

- **Aggressive issue resolution**—One purpose of the frequent status checks is to gain visibility of any new or potential issue. The resolution of any new issue is aggressively pursued. These become top priorities for project leadership.

- **Ensure clarity**—Another technique normally employed in successful project recoveries is an extra effort to ensure clear understanding of all communications, expectations, and work assignments. When focus and efficiency are of paramount importance, the criticality of clear communications and mutual understanding is obvious.

- **Increase visibility and accountability**—This has been referenced indirectly already, but it is worth emphasizing again. A major reason that project recoveries often work is because people know they are more accountable for their efforts due to the increased visibility with senior management. For both the individual and the organization, the recovery mission helps to prioritize efforts and align resource allocations.

THE ABSOLUTE MINIMUM

At this point, you should have a solid understanding of the following:

- The principles of project control are prevention, detection, and action.

- Project control consists of the information systems and the management procedures that enable us to answer the key questions regarding project performance.

- Key components of project control include performance reporting, change control management, configuration management, issue management, risk management, quality management, procurement management, and requirements management.

- The key management fundamentals of project control include focus on priorities, scale to project needs and organizational culture, set up natural control processes, expect project changes, be consistent, and pay particular attention to early project performance.

- Powerful project control techniques include using small work packages, managing to project baselines, conducting regular and effective status meetings, establishing clear completion criteria for each deliverable (and the project), conducting proper reviews, tracking requirements, and getting formal sign-offs.

- Performance reporting should communicate status with regard to critical success factors, any variances, and any changes to the performance forecast.

- The possible responses to an identified variance include taking corrective action, accepting it, resetting the performance baselines, and canceling the project.

- EVM is the best project control technique for early detection of project performance variances.

The map in Figure 10.4 summarizes the main points reviewed in this chapter.

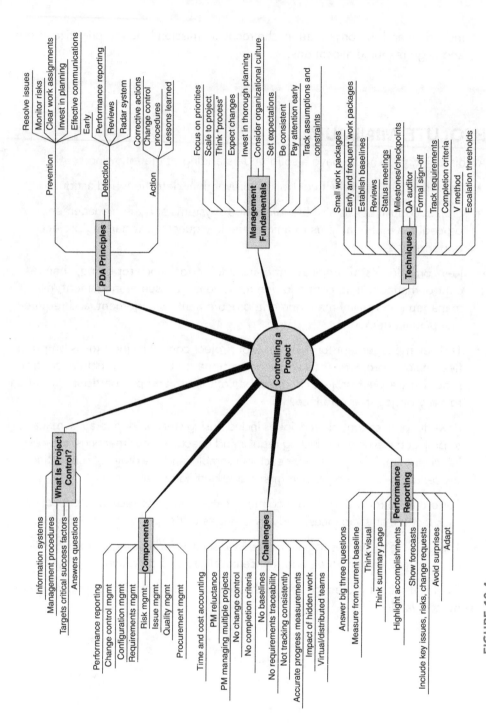

FIGURE 10.4

Overview of controlling a project.

IN THIS CHAPTER

- Understand what is meant by a project change and project change control

- Understand why scope changes occur

- Understand why good project managers take project change control seriously

- Learn the key management fundamentals for successfully handling project changes

- Understand why project change control is needed for agile projects too

- Review the essential components of an effective project change control system

- Find out how to reduce project changes

- Understand the common mistakes with managing project changes and how to avoid them

MANAGING PROJECT CHANGES

For many people, project control equals "managing project changes," and managing project changes equals preventing "scope creep." Although this belief is not completely accurate, the perception cannot be ignored. The ability to manage and control the change elements on a project, particularly the project scope, is a key to project success and a key performance indicator for a project manager. To manage project changes effectively, a project manager must utilize all of their skills and demonstrate project leadership. In addition to being an insightful measure of individual project management maturity, it is not uncommon for organizations that are in the early stages of adopting project management business approaches to look at how well project changes are being managed to determine whether project management is making a difference.

TIP The ability to effectively manage and control project changes is a trademark of a mature project manager.

Although it sounds like there is a lot riding on this ability to manage project changes (and there is), the process is not difficult if you follow the key success principles and understand how to avoid the common errors.

In this chapter, we continue our review of project control by taking a focused look at managing project changes. We clarify what we mean by "managing project changes," understand what drives most project scope changes, review the success principles of managing project changes, emphasize the essential elements of a project change control system, review powerful techniques that should help reduce the number of changes we need to manage, and make sure we are aware of the common challenges faced by many project managers in this arena in the past.

NOTE *Scope creep* is a common term used to describe uncontrolled expansion of project scope. Scope creep is legendary for causing project delays and cost overruns.

What Exactly Is a Project Change and What's the Big Deal, Anyway?

A *project change* is a change in any of the critical success factors (scope, schedule, costs, quality, and project acceptance criteria). The big deal is not that there is a change. In fact, for many projects, changes—especially scope expansions—are expected and encouraged. The big deal is uncontrolled change. Why? Because a change in any of the critical success factors affects the other factors, which then impacts project performance and the project's ability to achieve the success criteria, which then impacts stakeholder perceptions and satisfaction levels. For example, an expansion in project scope increases the work of the project. At a minimum, the increased work affects project schedule and project costs. In many cases, the increased work also impacts resource plans and adds new risks. On projects with contractual arrangements, the increased scope will likely have contract implications and needs to be formally managed to protect all parties involved.

Thus, any time a change occurs, the project needs a way to recognize the change, evaluate the impact of the change, communicate the change, and make planning adjustments if the change is accepted. This mechanism is commonly referred to as a *project change control system*. We review the key elements of this system later in this chapter.

 NOTE   A project change is a change in any of the critical success factors (scope, schedule, costs, quality, and project acceptance criteria).

Now, if you find yourself managing an agile project, you might be tempted to think "I don't need to worry about this change stuff, since change is encouraged and part of the innate process." Not so fast, my friend. We will talk more about this in Chapter 25, but while agile approaches do have built-in processes to identify, prioritize, and manage scope changes, that does not mean the changes won't impact the budget, alter the schedule, or require additional resources. All of this requires proper management. And this is especially true for contractual projects.

 TIP   Agile projects still need proper change control management.

Project Change Types—More Than Scope

As mentioned earlier, a project change is a change to any of the critical success factors and not just scope. Although scope changes are generally responsible for 80% or more of the project changes, and we discuss these in greater detail in the next section, it is important to recognize that any of the following would also constitute a project change (and should be controlled using the project change control system):

- An expansion or reduction of project scope

- An expansion or reduction of product features

- An expansion or reduction in performance requirements

 CAUTION   For agile projects, the frequency of scope-related change requests is reduced, since the project definition and/or contract does not normally contain scope/product details and is focused on the critical success factors and business value objectives. However, if there are requests identified that will impact the baseline schedule or budget, a change request should be leveraged.

- An expansion or reduction in quality requirements

- A significant change in the target milestone dates

- A shift in the implementation or deployment strategy

- An increase in resource costs

- An expansion or reduction in the project budget

- A change in any of the project objectives

- A change in any of the final acceptance criteria, including return on investment forecasts

- A change in any of the project assumptions, constraints, or dependencies, especially regarding resources and work effort estimates

- A shift in project roles or responsibilities, especially on projects with contractual arrangements

- A decision to reset the performance baselines due to an unrecoverable performance variance

Relation to Configuration Management and Organizational Change Management

To further clarify what is meant by a project change, let's review two other change-related components of project management: configuration management and organizational change. This is a common area of confusion because change control management, configuration management, and organizational change management are somewhat interrelated, they all deal with change, and they all are a part of project management. As illustrated in Figure 11.1, we are focused on change control management in this chapter. Table 11.1 summarizes the key differences between the three.

FIGURE 11.1

Change control management.

TABLE 11.1 Comparison of Change-Related Components of Project Management

	Change Control Management	Configuration Management	Organizational Change Management
Target	Project critical success factors	Project deliverables and product	Organizational impact of the project results
Primary Concern	Project performance; stakeholder expectations	Integrity of project deliverables; tracking changes in project deliverables	Preparing individuals, organizational units, and customers for the changes
Related Terms	Change control; scope management	Document management, versions, and builds	Change management
Discussed In	This chapter	Chapter 12	Chapters 18 and 20
Notes	Focus on scope can overlap with configuration management	Can be part of project's overall Change Control Plan	Not regarded as a project control activity

Fundamentals for Managing Project Change

There are seven key management principles for effective project change control:

- **Plan for changes**—Change control does not mean preventing changes at all costs. Conversely, project changes should be expected, planned, and well managed. The two keys here are selecting the proper project approach (methodology) and setting up a project change control system (to be discussed next). For projects with an innovation focus or a volatile set of requirements, an iterative or agile development-type approach that expects deliberate scope expansion or scope clarification should be utilized.

- **Set up a change control system**—If your organization does not already have a defined procedure for project change control, then you need to set up a change control system for your project. We discuss the details later in this chapter. The key benefits for establishing a formal change control system include the following:

  - Helps protect the integrity of the project performance baselines

  - Ensures that the right people are involved in the decision-making process

  - Helps manage stakeholder expectations

  - Enhances the credibility and professionalism of the project manager

  - Prevents issues and confrontations when changes do occur

- **Educate stakeholders**—Whether you adopt an existing change control system or develop your own, you need to step through the change control process with your stakeholders. Do not assume that because the procedure is documented that individuals understand it or their roles and responsibilities within it.

- **Use the system**—This might seem obvious, but it is a common pitfall. Make sure to utilize the change control system that you have defined. If the project manager does not consistently follow the process, no one else will either.

- **Minimize scope changes**—This is the great balance of managing project changes. On the one hand, you plan for changes and set up a system to manage those changes when they do occur; on the other hand, you work diligently on influencing those factors that are responsible for project changes, especially scope changes, to minimize their occurrence. The keys here include the following:

  - Keep the team focused on the project objectives, the big picture.

  - Listen carefully. You must understand immediately when a critical gap is identified.

  - Limit, if not totally avoid, any unnecessary changes by either the customer or the team.

  - Educate stakeholders on the impact of their change request.

  - Encourage any scope change request that is not an absolute, must-have feature to be scheduled for a follow-up project (cycle, iteration, or phase).

     NOTE While it might seem contradictory, the fundamental principle of "minimizing scope changes" as described here actually aligns with the agile approach. In the agile approach, the focus is always on delivering the most value with the least product (minimum viable product). The agile planning process keeps the team focused on "high value" work items, identifies/communicates the cost of any new work item to the customer, and encourages "lesser priority" work items to remain in the product backlog for a future iteration.

- **Overcommunicate**—For effective stakeholder management, make sure that all project changes are clearly communicated and understood by all key project stakeholders.

- **Be a watchdog**—As a project manager, you must be continuously alert and mindful about anything that could impact your critical success factors. In particular, you need to understand what can cause unplanned scope changes to occur—and then work to prevent their occurrence.

What Causes Unplanned Scope Changes?

To better manage project changes and project risks, and to minimize the number of scope changes, it is important to understand the leading causes for unplanned scope changes on a project.

- **Shift in business drivers**—Due to the dynamic nature of the business world today, things can change quickly. These business changes can have an immediate impact on existing projects. Examples of business drivers that can alter a project's scope include

  - Available budget/funding for the project

  - New government regulations

  - Changing target market for the product

  - Time-to-market pressures

  - New business opportunities

  - Changing customer priorities

  - Unexpected market or world events

- **Shift in project acceptance criteria**—This one addresses changes in any one of the following: the targeted completion date, financial return on investments, client satisfaction ratings, quality levels, other expected benefits, or the stakeholders who need to approve.

- **Shift in technology**—With the move to shorter-duration and phased projects, this is not as much of an issue as it has been in the past. However, there are still times when new technology becomes available during a project that will significantly meet the needs of the customer much better than what is currently planned.

- **Poor scope statement**—If the scope statement is incomplete, ambiguous, inconsistent with project assumptions, or does not address the complete business workflow process, you are much more likely to have project scope changes. Of course, this would happen only on projects that you inherited and would never happen on projects that you helped define. Right?

- **Poor requirements definition**—There are entire training courses on requirements definition and requirements management due to the importance they play in project success. Suffice to say, the more gaps that you have in your requirements, the more scope changes you are likely to have. For your awareness, here is a list of the leading reasons for poorly defined requirements:

- Ineffective or wrong techniques used to gather requirements

- Communication breakdowns between analysts and stakeholders

- Requirements not aligned with project scope

- Requirements not addressing complete process workflow

- Documented requirements not meaningful to targeted audience

- Requirements not reviewed for inconsistencies

- Requirements not verified for correctness and completeness

- Missing stakeholders

- User sign-off without a real understanding of what the documented requirements mean

Essential Elements of a Project Change Control System

At the heart of managing project changes well is a project change control system. The specifics of project change control systems can vary depending on industry, organization, and project importance, but every change control system should possess certain essential principles, guidelines, and components.

Principles

Effective project change control systems follow these key principles:

- Any proposed scope change is documented, evaluated, and approved before it is implemented.

- The appropriate stakeholders are involved in the evaluation and approval process.

- Any change request is thoroughly assessed for impact to other project critical success factors, especially project schedule and budget.

- The appropriate management level approves any change request before it is implemented.

- All project changes are documented and communicated to all stakeholders.

- Any stakeholder is permitted to submit a project change request.

- The rules are firm, the roles and responsibilities are clearly defined, and the workflow process meets the needs of all stakeholders.

 TIP Capture completion criteria for any scope-related change request.

Guidelines

In addition to the principles we reviewed, these guidelines should be considered for an effective project change control system:

- **Re-baseline**—The project plan should be updated to reflect the acceptance of any change to the critical success factors. A new performance baseline should be established.

- **Multiple paths**—The change control system should consider multiple process paths based on estimated impact of the change request and the thresholds negotiated with senior management. This allows the appropriate stakeholders and management levels to be involved when needed and at the right time.

- **Focus on buy-in**—Especially on proposed scope changes, make sure the right stakeholders are involved, understand the need and impact of the proposed change, and agree to the action plans before proceeding.

- **Aligned with contract**—If your project involves contractual arrangements, make sure the project's change control process is aligned with the change control process used to manage the contract with the vendor(s).

Components

There are no requirements from a technology perspective when it comes to project change control systems. They can leverage manual processes or utilize enterprise software packages. The key is that the following components be present, understood, and utilized:

- **Change request form**—This form is used to capture the pertinent details of the proposed change and the key information resulting from the impact assessment. Table 11.2 lists recommended form sections and corresponding data fields.

TABLE 11.2 Recommended Change Request Form Sections and Fields

Section	Data Fields
Identification	Change Request Number (ID)
	Date Received
	Date Revised
	Project Number (ID)
	Project Name
	Organization/Client Reference
Requester Information	Requester Name
	Organization/Department
	Contact Info (Email, Phone, and so on)
Change Information	Description of Change Request
	Reason for Change (Issue, Benefits, and so on)
	Priority
Impact Assessment	Stakeholders Impacted
	Deliverables Impacted
	Required Work Tasks
	Estimated Effort Impact (Hours)
	Estimated Cost Impact
	Estimated Schedule Impact
	Expected Benefits
	Completion Criteria
Status Information	Status (Submitted, Assigned, Evaluated, Pending Decision, Closed)
	Assigned To
	Assigned Date
	Decision (Approved, Deferred, Rejected)
	Decision Date
	Target Implementation Date/Milestone
Approvals	Approval Signatures

NOTE Ultimately, the determination of any change request is a consensus-based, cost-benefit decision made by the stakeholders accountable for the project.

- **Unique identification number**—When a change request is submitted for evaluation, a unique identification number should be assigned to facilitate better communications and tracking.

- **Change request tracking log**—The tracking log communicates summary information on all project change requests. Minimal information includes identification, impact summary, and current status. Spreadsheets and databases are common tools for tracking logs.

- **Change control board (CCB)**—The minimum set of project stakeholders who need to review and approve any change request impacting the project's critical success factors.

TIP Make sure your CCB is comprised of stakeholders who can represent each business process or functional group affected by your project. This organization helps provide a holistic, objective evaluation of each change request, and it helps prevent the addition of changes with marginal business value.

Powerful Techniques for Minimizing Project Changes

Although we want to be prepared for project changes when they occur, we want to spend most of our energy preventing the need for changes in the first place. The following techniques are powerful change prevention actions we can take:

- **Clear project definition**—The more effort spent upfront to get agreement on clear project objectives and success criteria from the appropriate stakeholders, the less likely we are to get change requests during the project.

- **Solid requirements definition**—As mentioned before, the more complete requirements are defined and understood, the likelihood of scope changes are reduced.

- **Trace requirements**—There is nothing like linking any work specification to its original source to control project scope. By tracing and showing the relationship from the original business objectives down to the detail design specification, you can identify (and possibly eliminate) any scope expansion when it is first proposed. If the proposed feature does not link directly to a higher-level specification, it is a potential scope change.

- **Formal acceptance sign-offs**—Formal sign-offs are a key aspect of change control management, especially for projects that are client-vendor oriented. The formal record of review and acceptance of a given deliverable helps to keep expectations aligned and minimize potential disputes.

- **Engaged stakeholders**—Although formal sign-offs do act as strong "stick" incentives to get stakeholders involved, there is nothing like having professional, knowledgeable, and engaged stakeholders who are committed to doing their best as the best weapon against unplanned scope expansion. A team of people who want to work together and get the job done can accomplish the work at hand with a less formal level of project management.

 TIP Rather than capturing assumptions and constraints in various project documents, capture them together in a single document. This makes it easier to communicate, update, and track throughout the project.

- **Use the right project approach**—This technique is more about risk management, but change control and risk management are very intertwined. As mentioned before, if you know there is likely to be a high degree of change, structure your project in a manner that allows for deliberate, planned scope expansion (prototyping, iterations, cycles, early and frequent product reviews, and so on). For all projects, the following approaches help reduce the number of project changes:

  - Emphasis on project definition and planning

  - Shorter timeframes (1 year or less is preferred)

  - Pilot tests

  - Phased implementations

  - Go/no-go decisions at phase ends

- **Use WBS to illustrate impact**—This technique might not prevent change requests from being submitted, but it can help you classify something as a change (and not part of the intended scope), and it can help you communicate the effect of the proposed change. By reviewing your detailed WBS, you can show that the work for the proposed feature was never accounted for, and you can show what other work items will be affected by adding the proposed change.

- **Defer to post-implementation**—This is another technique that will not prevent change requests, and that might not be applicable to all project situations; however, if it does work, it can reduce impact on the project success factors. If the change request is legitimate but is not absolutely critical to the initial release (there is not a workaround, it does not adversely affect the customer experience), you can guide the CCB to defer the request to a future project or a post-implementation phase.

- **Track assumptions and constraints**—This definitely is part of your risk response plan, too, but part of your watchdog mindset is to keep a close eye on the project assumptions and constraints. If these change, your project will definitely be impacted.

Common Project Change Control Challenges

Before we end this chapter on managing project changes, let's look at the challenges faced by many project managers. Here's a list of things to either avoid or be on the lookout for:

- **The obvious**—Be sure to set up a change control system as part of your approved project plan—and then use it.

- **Can't say "no"**—Use your change control system and don't automatically agree to accept a scope change request without running it through the process. This is a common issue with project managers who have a fear of confrontation. Use your system as an objective third party to minimize direct confrontations.

- **Can't say "yes"**—Some project managers take the other extreme. They are so paranoid about scope creep that they do not listen to consider legitimate scope changes, often overlooking changes that are needed to meet the project objective. Again, keep the focus on the big picture (the project objectives) and exercise your change control system.

- **Overreliance on formal sign-offs**—Formal sign-offs are important and valuable; however, they should represent genuine agreement and understanding. Verify that you have real understanding and buy-in before proceeding.

- **Not the "gold" you want**—Be on the lookout for *gold-plating*, the term given to extras or features added to the work product by the project team but not requested by the customer. This is a common reason why schedule delays occur and why unnecessary risks occur on projects. Also, the same issue can manifest itself in a work process. A technician might want their work to be perfect rather than just meet the specifications for the project. This is another reason why a team approach to estimating and planning can be so valuable.

- **Is it really a change?**—Not that this ever happens, but sometimes stakeholders do not agree on what really is an official change. I know—it's hard to believe. Especially in contractual arrangements, the issue isn't always "Is it a change?" but rather "Do I have to pay for it?"—a slightly different matter. There are no silver bullets here. Most of the disagreements occur because of ambiguity or inconsistencies in the specifications. Just do the other things previously mentioned, and you should have a solid foundation to deal with this, if it ever happens.

- **The impact of the change**—In most cases, the individuals who need to assess the impact of a proposed change, especially scope changes, are members of the existing project team—who have current work assignments. Be aware of the impact that this unplanned effort could have on the project, and guide the CCB accordingly.

- **Inadequate impact analysis**—You are exercising your change control system. The change request is being assessed. You are in good shape—right? Probably. Just make sure the analysis performed on the impact is complete. At the minimum, verify the following on any change request assessment:

  - Has the total work effort been accounted for? All supporting processes? All impacted deliverables?

  - Have the implications of the request been completely considered?

  - Have all impacted stakeholders been considered?

- **Beware of the little guys**—On most projects, there will always be one or more of those small, minor scope changes. Sometimes they are clear changes; other times, they fall into a gray area. In an effort to build relationships and please the customer, many project managers do not document these if they feel the change requires minimal effort to implement. Be very careful here. Before you know it, you can easily have a series of these little changes that, when added up, can affect your project. In addition, you must manage the expectations you are setting if you overuse this technique. As a rule, I would encourage you to at least document every change—no matter how small. For small ones, you might choose to group them into a single change request.

THE ABSOLUTE MINIMUM

At this point, you should have a solid understanding of the following:

- The ability to manage and control the change elements on a project, particularly the project scope, is a key to project success and a key performance indicator for a project manager.
- A project change is a change in any of the critical success factors (scope, schedule, costs, quality, and project acceptance criteria).
- The seven key management principles for effective project change control are the following:

  1. Expect and plan for changes.

  2. Set up a change control system.

  3. Educate stakeholders on process.

  4. Use the system.

  5. Work to minimize scope changes.

  6. Ensure that all changes are communicated and understood.

  7. Be alert to anything that could impact the critical success factors.

- The chief causes of unplanned scope changes include shifts in business drivers, project acceptance criteria, and technology, and inadequate scope statements and requirements definition.
- Completion criteria should be captured for any scope-related change request.
- Agile projects still need proper change control, especially for any requested changes that impact the baseline budget and/or schedule.
- Powerful techniques for minimizing project changes include a clear project definition, a solid requirements definition, effective traceability of requirements, getting formal acceptance sign-offs, implementing the right project approach, and assembling a team of engaged stakeholders.

The map in Figure 11.2 summarizes the main points reviewed in this chapter.

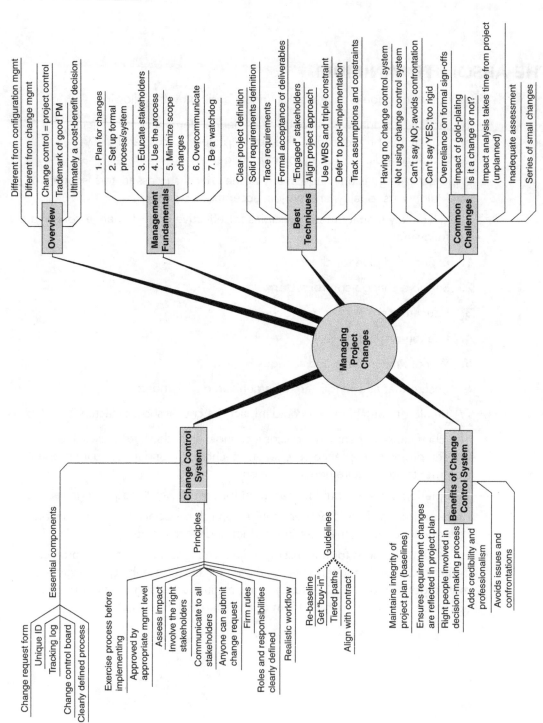

Overview
- Different from configuration mgmt
- Different from change mgmt
- Change control = project control
- Trademark of good PM
- Ultimately a cost-benefit decision

Management Fundamentals
1. Plan for changes
2. Set up formal process/system
3. Educate stakeholders
4. Use the process
5. Minimize scope changes
6. Overcommunicate
7. Be a watchdog

Best Techniques
- Clear project definition
- Solid requirements definition
- Trace requirements
- Formal acceptance of deliverables
- "Engaged" stakeholders
- Align project approach
- Use WBS and triple constraint
- Defer to post-implementation
- Track assumptions and constraints

Common Challenges
- Having no change control system
- Not using change control system
- Can't say NO; avoids confrontation
- Can't say YES; too rigid
- Overreliance on formal sign-offs
- Impact of gold-plating
- Is it a change or not?
- Impact analysis takes time from project (unplanned)
- Inadequate assessment
- Series of small changes

Managing Project Changes

Change Control System

Essential components
- Change request form
- Unique ID
- Tracking log
- Change control board
- Clearly defined process

Principles
- Exercise process before implementing
- Approved by appropriate mgmt level
- Assess impact
- Involve the right stakeholders
- Communicate to all stakeholders
- Anyone can submit change request
- Firm rules
- Roles and responsibilities clearly defined
- Realistic workflow

Guidelines
- Re-baseline
- Get "buy-in"
- Tiered paths
- Align with contract

Benefits of Change Control System
- Maintains integrity of project plan (baselines)
- Ensures requirement changes are reflected in project plan
- Right people involved in decision-making process
- Adds credibility and professionalism
- Avoids issues and confrontations

FIGURE 11.2

MANAGING PROJECT DELIVERABLES

An excellent indicator of the experience level, professionalism, and overall project management maturity of an individual is how much effort and thought this person gives to the management of the actual project work products (deliverables).

Why do I say this? This area of project management is one of the most neglected, yet it is a foundational element of managing risk, quality, and stakeholder expectations on any project. Without it, you will inevitably incur additional work efforts, lower quality, and more costs—which generally leads to missed project objectives and disappointed stakeholders.

In this chapter, we clarify what we mean by "managing project deliverables," emphasize the key principles of a project deliverable management system, review the best tips and techniques for keeping your deliverables under control, and discuss how to avoid the common challenges faced by most project managers in this area.

 TIP   Other terms related to configuration management include document management, software configuration management, and content management, to name a few.

"Managing Project Deliverables" Means What, Exactly?

By *managing project deliverables*, we mean the process by which the project work products are controlled. The work products can include anything resulting from project activities, including any deliverable, document, or project management item. And by *control*, we mean managing the changes to the actual work products themselves. The most common term for this process is *configuration management*. As discussed in Chapter 10, "Controlling a Project," this process is related to the project change control system, yet it is different. The change control system manages changes to a critical success factor (time, cost, scope, and quality) for the project.

The exact nature and details of this process will vary by project and the types of deliverables involved. The project planning document that defines this process is generally called the *configuration management plan*.

Configuration management is often neglected because it is an unglamorous, mundane aspect of project management that requires a certain discipline to carry out. In addition, this area of project management tends to fall victim to many ill-advised assumptions and the notion that this is just common sense and will just happen automatically. Real-world experience would say otherwise. Especially in the digital age, if you do not think about where your project files will be stored, who has access to them, how they will be protected, how changes will be made, and how changes will be tracked, your project is carrying a significant risk—and in most cases, an unidentified risk.

In many organizations today, enterprise configuration management tools are being implemented to better protect and control all digital assets of the organization, especially documents. However, this movement is not universal across all industries or organizations yet, so you may likely still need to develop your own project-specific procedures to address the needs of your project.

"Why Do This? It's Too Much Work!"

You might work in an environment where configuration management is an integral part of the project management approach, so this is not even an issue for you. For others, it is often tempting, as previously mentioned, to not give this area proper attention. So let's answer the question, "Why should we do this?" Why should we plan out the details for how specific work products are going to be managed? From the collective experience of project managers across the land (not that any of these have happened to me or anything), here are a few reasons why:

- **Where is that file?**—The ability to quickly locate project information for a key stakeholder or to help resolve an important issue.

- **Lost productivity**—Avoid instances of lost productivity when the work of one team member is overwritten by another team member, or when the product configuration you are testing does not have the latest versions of all components—thus making the test run invalid.

- **Baseline? What baseline?**—Avoid instances where you cannot go back to or restore previous versions of work products.

- **Who made that change?**—Avoid instances where you cannot clearly tell (or explain) when changes were made and who made them.

 TIP   If you are not using digital signatures or email confirmations for work product acceptance, be sure to scan the signed acceptance forms and store them in the project repository.

- **Who approved that change?**—Avoid instances where changes are made to work products that are not properly reviewed and approved. To say the least, this can lead to quality and customer satisfaction issues.

- **That will never happen to us**—A major or minor disaster occurs that wipes out one or more work products. Where is your backup copy? Can you recover?

- **We said we would do what?**—On projects with numerous deliverables and work products, it is easy to lose sight of the minor or auxiliary work items. A basic deliverable tracking mechanism can go a long way in preventing this from occurring.

- **I've got your official sign-off right here…now where did that go?**—Assuming you have official client acceptance of your key deliverables, make sure you have a way to protect this evidence going forward.

NOTE The entire concept of document management started with the legal industry.

- **You have no choice**—In many environments, there are legal, regulatory, or process compliance requirements that must be met. In each of these cases, having control over work product changes is an absolute must. Most of this activity is focused on protecting the integrity of the work product and providing associated audit trials (evidence).

- **The ultimate reason: negotiating power**—There is tremendous political power in having tight control over project work products. If targeted work products are officially approved, you have a clear audit trail on any changes to those work products, and those official sign-offs are protected, you are well positioned to deal with any scope or requirements dispute. In addition, a historical record of all project management work products, such as project schedules, issue logs, status reports, and meeting minutes, can be very valuable in negotiating new issues.

TIP The three fundamental principles of managing project work products are identify, protect, and track. Managing project deliverables can also be summarized by another important principle: CYA—Cover Your Assets. Assume you will have to legally prove your project's case in court someday.

Identify, Protect, and Track: The Principles of Managing Work Products

Managing project work products is a strong example of the preventative aspects of project control. If you have a solid process in place, and you are using it, everything rolls along as expected. It's only when you have a gap in this area that it attracts attention from stakeholders—generally unwanted attention. The principles of managing project work products are simple and can be boiled down to three management fundamentals:

- **Identify**—Define all the work products that need to be managed. Make sure all the work products are identified, not just the major ones and not just the product deliverables. For each deliverable type, you might need a different configuration management process. This is often true when dealing with both digital and tangible deliverables and when dealing with documents and software components. This can also be true when there are limitations with the configuration management tools that are available.

NOTE Depending on the type of work products you have, and the type of configuration management tools that you are utilizing, you might have more than one project repository, such as one for all digital documents and another for software modules.

- **Protect**—Protect the integrity of the work product. This means that you need to be able to control who has access to the work product, control what changes can be made by each person, and recover the work product in the event of an unexpected accident or disaster. The access control can have several layers, but the most common aspects are facilities access, network access, and a separation of duties between development and operational roles. In addition, this means protecting any contractually significant approvals or sign-offs.

- **Track**—Be able to trace your steps and track the changes that are made to a work product. Common terms associated with this principle are "version control" and "revision history." The other important aspect of this principle is the ability to provide status on the current state of all managed work products.

Best Practices

Whether you utilize manual or automated processes, here is a list of techniques that you should consider for your configuration management process:

- **Establish central repository**—First and foremost, define a central repository for the project where all project work documents will be stored. Make sure access to the repository can be controlled and that the appropriate stakeholders have access to it.

- **Define review/revision/approval process**—Define which work products need to be reviewed and approved when any change is made, who can make those changes, who needs to approve those changes, and the associated workflow that needs to be followed.

- **Define a "gatekeeper"**—Experience has shown tremendous value in establishing someone as the official librarian for the project repository. This person is responsible for controlling access to the repository, updating the repository, and ensuring that the configuration management procedures are being followed.

- **Implement access controls**—Ensure that the project repository is only accessible to authorized stakeholders and the granted access level is aligned with their role on the project. This becomes more important every day as the need to protect digital assets increases.

- **Establish a common directory structure**—To better organize work products and to make it easier to find them when you need them, it is recommended to define a directory structure that is aligned with the project phases and workflow process.

- **Establish file-naming conventions**—Also in the spirit of better organization of work products, it is recommended to define a common convention for naming project work products. The conventions provide consistency and help improve project communications and stakeholder expectations as well.

- **Establish search keyword conventions**—Given the growing popularity and use of Internet search engines, people are more accustomed to searching for what they need by the use of keywords. This can be especially helpful if the project repository directory structure is large or has multiple layers, and search capability can be a tremendous timesaver if it is less than obvious where a given work product can be found.

 NOTE Some configuration management tools and project collaboration tools automatically index all contents (think Google). In this case, the need for predefining keywords is greatly reduced, if not eliminated.

- **Establish version numbering scheme**—If these guidelines do not exist for your organization already, determine the rules that will govern the versioning scheme for each category of work product. Common elements to consider include version number format, differences between major and minor versions, and conventions to be followed.

- **Establish baselines**—This is a key best practice, especially before any milestone-type event on the project, such as phase end, tollgate, start of a testing phase, or releasing work product to a client. To effectively deal with any quality issues and client expectations, you must be able to clearly define (and maintain) the configuration of a work product at a given point in time.

- **Use standard document sections**—To help encourage effective configuration management practices, it is recommended to develop work product templates that contain standard document sections. Recommended document sections include the following:

  - Title page

  - Revision history page

  - Approval page

  - Standard header and footer formats/data

- **Use a deliverable tracker**—This is a powerful technique that can be utilized regardless of the sophistication of your process. Develop a mechanism to identify and track the status of your project work products. For lack of a better term, I will call this your deliverable tracker. This can be done with a simple spreadsheet program. Table 12.1 summarizes the key recommendations for your deliverable tracker.

 TIP   Execute a test of your backup recovery procedures to verify they are working correctly—before you actually need them.

TABLE 12.1   Deliverable Tracker Recommendations

Element	Definition	Notes
Work Product Name Project Phase	Targeted work product. Name of the project phase.	Can be a column/field, or you can use separate tab/sheet for each project phase.
Modification Type	Normally, values here are either Created or Updated.	Value may be created in one phase and updated in one or more later phases.
Work Product File Name	Actual file name of the work product.	Tip: Hyperlink to its repository location.
Version	Current version number of work product.	
Status	Current status of the work product in this project phase.	In-process, completed, approved. Tip: Use color to visually represent the work product status.
CM Indicator	Flag indicating whether this work product is under Configuration Management control.	Most will be YES.
Owner	Person responsible for the change.	
Target Completion Date	Scheduled completion date.	
Completion Date	Actual completion date.	
Approver	Person/group who must approve the change.	
Target Approval Date	Scheduled approval date.	
Date Approved	Actual approval date.	

- **Back it up**—Make sure that your project repositories have proper backup procedures in place and that they are actually working. You will be glad you did.

- **Address needs of different work product types**—A single configuration management process might not be adequate for your project. You should develop specific configuration management procedures for each type of work product you are managing.

 NOTE Configuration management tools include document management tools, software configuration management tools, enterprise project management tools, enterprise (and web) content management tools, records management tools, and workflow/collaboration tools.

- **Leverage configuration management tools**—Although effective configuration management procedures can be executed using clearly defined manual procedures—and a fair amount of discipline and a central control point—the process is much easier with configuration management tools. The tools enable you to control access to the repository, control the revision process (only one person can check out the work product for edit at a time), and provide an automatic audit trail.

 TIP Ensure appropriate team members are properly educated and trained on the configuration management tools and procedures.

Use archive folders to maintain access to previous versions and improve organization.

- **Define product configuration build/release process**—On any project that deals with a product that is composed of multiple components, a process is needed that properly integrates the components into a final product. This is especially true for any product that represents a system. This process enables you to establish a baseline configuration.

- **Define product/system release deployment process**—Similar to the previous best practice, but this is focused on moving (promoting) project work product through the development life-cycle process. Specifically, this practice occurs when deploying a new work product into a test environment and the production environment. For many digital work products/systems, there are setup aspects that need to be manually configured and/or environment preparation tasks that must be performed by authorized system administrators. It is imperative that all these tasks and dependencies be clearly understood and communicated.

- **Separation of duties between development and operations**—Closely related to the previous best practice, this one is focused on the actual team members involved in the deployment process. Whenever possible, it is best to have a different set of people responsible for the deployment, setup, and management of IT services/resources into a production environment versus the development and testing of those services/resources. This separation forces all needed steps and changes to support the release deployment to be documented and communicated; it keeps the responsibility for management of the production environment with a team that is independent of the development groups; and it improves the integrity and security controls of the production environment.

 NOTE To be compliant with most digital system security standards, this separation of duties is now a requirement.

- **Develop configuration management plan**—This is where you document all of the configuration management best practices you are going to utilize for your project. The configuration management plan enables you to communicate the procedures and rules that the project will follow and to gain agreement on the plan. We discuss some recommended sections for the configuration management plan in the next section.

- **Leverage archive folders**—A simple but powerful technique to help you manage (and not lose) project information is to always create an archive folder within a specific project directory to hold any previous versions, as illustrated in Figures 12.1 and 12.2. This is especially useful for digital work items that are not managed by a configuration management tool. This practice also has the added benefits of better organization and better visibility of the most current work items.

FIGURE 12.1

Sample use of archive subfolder.

FIGURE 12.2

Sample contents of archive subfolder showing previous versions.

Configuration Management Plan

The Configuration Management Plan (CM Plan) is first defined during the project planning process and is part of the overall project plan. Like all planning documents, the level of detail included in the CM Plan should be consistent with the risk levels, compliance requirements, and composition of the project team. As a guide, Table 12.2 lists the minimum topics that should be covered in a CM Plan.

TABLE 12.2   Recommended Sections for Configuration Management Plan

Element	Definition	Notes
Targets	The project work products to be managed.	Usually all project work products.
Repository	The location and definition of the central project repository.	Depending on work product types, there might be more than one. There should be only one document repository.
Directory Structure	Defines the organization of the project repository.	Usually organized by project phases and work product type.

Element	Definition	Notes
File Naming Conventions	Defines the conventions to be used for naming project files.	Should include project name and work product name at a minimum.
Keyword Conventions	Defines the list of keywords that can be associated with the work product.	Essential if team/organization/tool wants to leverage search capabilities to find/locate items and not manage overhead of directory structures and file-naming conventions, and the tool does not automatically index all contents.
Tools	Lists the configuration management tools to be utilized on the project.	
Process and Procedures	Defines how work products are introduced into the repository and how revisions are made to them. Defines the review and approval process for any work product requiring authorization before a change can be official.	Might reference subconfiguration management plans if multiple tools are used or needed.
Roles and Responsibilities	Defines the key roles in the configuration management process and what each project team member can do.	The key role is the librarian.
Reporting	Defines how configuration management status will be reported and what metrics are needed for this project.	Deliverable tracker.
Audits	Defines how the configuration management process will be audited for compliance and when those audits will occur.	Often a part of the QA review process.
Relation to other CM Plans	Indicates whether other configuration management plans are involved and how they integrate with the overall project plan.	Supplier CM Plans. Specific work product–type CM Plans.

CAUTION A common planning oversight is not factoring the CM activities into the task assignments or not allocating specific CM roles. As a result, the individuals assigned to CM activities are often overallocated. Thus, when time is tight, the CM activities are the first to go.

TIP For whatever CM tools you leverage, make sure there is a CM tool expert either on your team or available to the core project team.

Common Challenges and Pitfalls

We've addressed the challenges you will have on your project if you do not have a CM Plan, but even with a CM Plan, there are still some remaining pitfalls that you need to be on the lookout for:

- **Not following the plan**—One of the first things to go when the realities of the project hit is execution of the CM Plan. There are two things you can do to help make sure the CM Plan is executed:

    - Use an independent auditor (such as a QA Lead) and include the CM activities as part of the quality review process.

    - Make sure to include the CM activities in the WBS and project schedule.

- **Tool difficulties**—As stated before, configuration management tools should be leveraged whenever possible, and in some cases, they are absolutely mandatory. That being said, the proper use of these tools is not automatic. If you are going to use a tool, you need to make sure the right team members are trained on how to properly use the tool, and you need to verify that the tool works correctly.

THE ABSOLUTE MINIMUM

At this point, you should have a solid understanding of the following:

- The benefits of properly managing project work products include increased productivity (by avoiding lost work), enhanced professional credibility, audit-proofing your project, and increased customer satisfaction.

- The principles of managing project work products are identification, protection, and tracking...and, of course, CYA.

- The CM Plan documents the processes and procedures that will be utilized to ensure that project work products are protected and changes are controlled.

- Like other elements of the project, make sure stakeholders understand the value of the CM Plan and are properly trained on how to use the process.

- Make sure your backup recovery procedures work correctly before you actually need them.

- Consider web-enabled configuration management tools for virtual project team environments.

- For other helpful information on IT configuration management, check out CMCrossroads at www.cmcrossroads.com, or search for "IT service management" or "ITIL."

The map in Figure 12.3 summarizes the main points reviewed in this chapter.

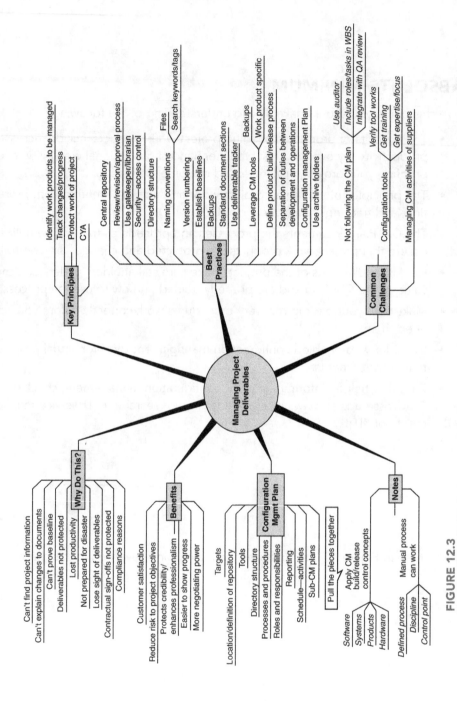

FIGURE 12.3

Overview of managing project deliverables.

13

MANAGING PROJECT ISSUES

Projects are dynamic; projects often deal with the new and the leading edge; and projects involve people. As a result, circumstances change, misunderstandings occur, assumptions don't hold, political agendas collide, problems arise, and risk events happen. These situations are categorized as *project issues*, and they all have the potential to adversely affect the project's capability to accomplish its objectives.

To minimize the potential effect of these obstacles on our project objectives, we need to have a proactive plan for effectively managing project issues. In this chapter, we focus on the key elements of that plan. We review the principles, best practices, and project manager skills that are essential to effectively managing project issues. In addition, we touch on the important elements of your issue management system and make sure you are aware of the common challenges faced by project managers in this arena.

 NOTE　A common source of confusion in the project management arena is the terminology used for project issues. For our purposes, I am differentiating between issues, risks, and defects.

Issues are events that have occurred or situations that exist which will adversely affect the project outcome if not resolved.

Risks are potential issues (more on these in Chapter 14, "Managing Project Risks").

Defects are issues that result from the project's quality management procedures (testing, reviews, and so on).

The workflow processes for each are slightly different.

The Goals, Objectives, and Principles of Project Issue Management

Managing project issues is an example of proactive project management. Through solid planning, effective stakeholder management, and insightful risk management, you can reduce the number of issues your project will encounter, but you cannot eliminate them. The goal of project issue management is to detect issues as early as possible. The earlier an issue is identified, the greater the chance of resolving the issue before it can affect any of the project's critical success factors.

The objective of project issue management is to identify, record, track, resolve, and communicate all issues that might adversely impact the project. Translated: write them down (so you don't lose sight of them) and take care of them (get on it). To accomplish this objective, we need to review the associated principles. The principles of issue management fall into two main categories: an administrative process and a project manager mindset.

- **Administrative process principles**—To properly manage project issues, there are a few administrative fundamentals to adhere to:

  - **Document the issues**—You need somewhere to log the issues as they are identified. We discuss the log details later in this chapter.

  - **Track until closure**—Use the log to make sure issues remain visible until they are resolved.

  - **Align with project needs**—Ensure the overall process matches the communication and workflow needs of the project.

- **Cost-effective approach**—Keep things in perspective. Don't buy a BMW when a Chevrolet is all you need.

- **Project manager mindset principles**—More than anything, effective issue management is an attitude and an approach. The following terms describe the mindset principles that a project manager needs to have in this arena:

  - **Ringmaster**—As the project manager, you operate as the focal point for tackling project issues. You are the gatekeeper. You are the one who must get the right people involved at the right time to make sure issues are resolved. In addition, some issues require the input of several different parties to resolve. You need to facilitate this process.

  - **Smiling bulldog**—Your goal is to resolve issues as quickly as possible and to stay with them until they are resolved. Be persistent. This is the "bulldog" mentality. However, you need to do this with a smile. Leverage your interpersonal strengths to do this, while still building relationships.

  - **Swivel-head**—Just as with risks, you need to constantly be looking for trouble—that is, trouble for your project. Sometimes issues come disguised as questions or nonverbal communications. When in doubt, ask questions and verify. The effect of most issues can be mitigated if they are detected early and resolved quickly with the right buy-in.

  - **Goaltender**—Just as good goaltenders do not let anything get by them, good project managers let no issue go unnoticed or unresolved. In addition, the subtle intensity displayed by the project manager here helps to set expectations with the project team and signals to all stakeholders that they will be held accountable for getting issues resolved.

  - **Disciplined**—To be effective, you need a fair amount of discipline. You need the discipline to log the issues and follow the process. In the whirlwind of most project environments, it is easy to let these slip.

Key Features of Issue Management Systems

The actual details of the issue management system are not complicated, and in most situations they share many similarities with your change control system and risk tracking system. Although issue management systems vary in complexity and sophistication depending on your organization and the needs of your project, all issue management systems should possess the following key features:

- **Clear process**—Clearly define and communicate how issues are submitted, how they will be resolved, how and when outstanding issues will be reviewed, and what is needed to officially close an issue. This is not complicated; generally, it's very commonsense stuff here.

- **Escalation procedures**—This is part of the overall issue resolution process, but not always thought about in advance. Define the types of issue that warrant escalation to higher levels of management. Generally, there is a single escalation process for a project, which is leveraged for anything affecting the critical success factors (issues, changes, or risks).

- **Issue log**—This is the mechanism used to document and track project issues. The most common mechanism is a spreadsheet, but there are limitations to this method. Other options include database systems and collaboration tools. There are pros and cons to each choice. The important thing is to use a tool that matches the needs of your project.

 NOTE Although the spreadsheet approach to an issue log has limitations, just the fact that you are documenting issues and actively managing them will put you light years ahead of many project environments.

- **Issue log administrator**—Someone needs to serve as the central control point for the issue log. Usually, this will be you, the project manager.

- **Issue data points**—Although the specific mechanism used for the issue log and the exact information needs vary across projects, there is a core set of data points that should be considered for any issue logged. The recommended data points are listed in Table 13.1.

TABLE 13.1 Recommended Issue Log Data Points

Element	Definition	Notes
Issue ID	Unique ID that can be used to clearly track this issue.	Best practice.
Issue Type	Category of issue—domain values will vary depending on project.	Example set—Technical, People, Business, Supplier.
Issue Name	The short name for the issue.	Generally fewer than 40 characters.
Issue Status	The current state of the issue. This should be aligned with the process workflow established for issue resolution.	Example set—Open, Assigned, Resolved, Closed. In some settings, Open and Closed values might be sufficient.
Issue Priority	Summarizes the importance and severity of the issue.	Typical domain—Critical, High, Medium, Low.
Issue Details	The full details of the issue.	

Element	Definition	Notes
Potential Impact	Lists the potential impact to the project critical success factors if issue is not resolved.	
Date Submitted	Date issue is identified and accepted.	
Submitted By	Person who originated the issue.	
Date Assigned	Date issue assigned to someone for follow-up.	
Assigned To	Person assigned to take action on the issue.	
Target Due Date	Target date for issue resolution.	
Date Updated	Date that issue log entry was last updated.	
Date Resolved	Date that issue is resolved.	This field might not be needed in many cases. Date Closed might suffice.
Date Closed	Date the issue is closed.	
Progress Notes	Contains updates and information regarding action items, findings, and steps to resolution.	
Related Items	In many cases, one issue is associated with other issues or spawns other issues/action items. It is good to track this association.	Might also be used to link to supporting documents.

 NOTE   The details of the issue log depend on the intended audience and general communication needs of the project.

Options for an Issue Log

Let's take a look at the available tool options for your issue log. The most popular options are word processor, spreadsheet, database, and collaboration/workflow tools. There are advantages to each, and each can be appropriate in the right scenario. Table 13.2 provides a comparison summary for your issue log options.

 CAUTION   Complex issues tend to linger and can come back to bite you. Take charge of these right away.

TABLE 13.2   Comparison of Issue Log Options

Options	Pros	Cons	Best Scenario
Word Processor	Low cost. Simple. Portable. "Quick and dirty."	Limited filtering. Limited access, visibility. Cumbersome as log grows. Manual processes needed.	Cost is key factor. Team is co-located. Only one person needs to update log. Collaboration needs are minimal. Low complexity level in issues tracked.
Spreadsheet	Low cost. Simple. Leverage sorting, filtering, and reporting capabilities of spreadsheet program. Portable.	Limited access, visibility. Cumbersome as log grows. Manual processes needed.	Cost is key factor. Team is co-located. Only one person needs to update log. Collaboration needs are minimal. Some need for sorting and filtering of data.
Database	Allows for multiuser updates. Better data relationships. Better reporting. Enforces process and business rules.	Increased setup and admin time. Increased costs. Not as portable. Training might be needed.	Many team members need to have access and update capabilities.
Collaboration/ Workflow Tools	Web-enabled. All advantages of database tool. Maps process flow. Automatic notifications.	Increased setup and admin time. Increased costs. Training might be needed.	Workflow process is more involved. Team is distributed, virtual. Communication needs are nontrivial.

TIP   As with all aspects of project management, always be looking for ways to improve your processes to better fit the needs of your current project and future projects.

Due to strong relationships and natural links between project issues, action items, risks, defects, and change requests, some organizations use a common log for all of them. Just add a data point called Item Type.

This approach can make logging and tracking simpler, especially if one person is responsible for maintaining the log in each of these areas. However, you must know how to properly use your tool to best report information from this central log.

Best Practices

The work of project issue management is straightforward. However, several techniques are proven to be effective and help you avoid the common mistakes in this aspect of project control.

- **Assign unique ID**—Make sure to assign a unique number to each logged issue. This simplifies the ongoing communication and tracking process.

- **Assign one person responsible**—As with other work tasks, assign a specific person responsible for any follow-up action items and for complete resolution to the issue.

- **Facilitate resolution to complex issues**—There are times when issues do not have a clear owner or need the collaboration of several parties to resolve. As the project manager, you must either assign someone to facilitate this process or take ownership of the facilitation process yourself.

- **Resolve issues at the lowest level**—Always attempt to deal with problems at their lowest level. You can resolve issues faster and at less cost. More importantly, you will earn the confidence of upper management by protecting their time and only engaging them when it is warranted. Again, make sure to establish the escalation triggers with your senior management stakeholders during planning, so you are clear about their expectations.

- **Go after root cause**—A common error in dealing with issues is not to deal with the actual source of the problem (root cause). Sometimes, political reasons might hamper your efforts to deal with the root cause, but whenever possible, do the proper analysis to get to the real problem and address it. If you do not, the issue will likely return for another visit.

- **Get buy-in on due date and ownership**—Apply the same approach to assigning issues as you do (or should) with assigning scheduled work tasks. For better issue management, make sure to spend the time with the person designated to take action on the issue and get agreement on when the action can be completed and that this is the right person to do it.

- **Adapt process and data points**—Even if your organization has a standard approach or methodology for issue management, don't be afraid to adapt the workflow process or the tracked data points to better fit the needs of the project.

- **Review issues frequently**—At a minimum, review any outstanding issues during each status review meeting. (This should be included in your communications plan.) As a good practice, follow up on outstanding issues every day and make sure the necessary steps and actions are occurring to get to a resolution.

- **Train project team on process and tools**—This is not as important for projects where the issue log is mostly a management tool just for the project manager (you). However, in any situation where collaboration tools are being utilized or multiple people are involved in the process, make sure the project team is properly prepared to leverage the system.

Some Special Situations

On this subject of managing project issues, a couple of special situations often come up. Let's discuss them briefly.

- **Visibility of issue log**—Usually on projects where there are multiple organizations (especially vendors and suppliers), you will want to manage multiple issue logs (same for risk logs, too). Why? Quite simply, there are things you are concerned about that might affect your project that you need to bring to the attention of your organization's management but that you are not ready to share with all project stakeholders. This is simply a matter of expectations management and not sharing your dirty laundry prematurely. A common example is with resource productivity on a fixed price engagement—a definite issue for your organization but not a real concern of the customer.

- **Logging issues that cycle in less than a reporting period**—Depending on how often the issue log is updated, there are often cases where an issue is identified, evaluated, and resolved before it can actually be logged. Of course, on many projects, this is a standard operating procedure. However, it is often difficult to exercise the discipline to log these issues after the fact. It is strongly recommended that you find the willpower (or assign someone) to get this accomplished. From a lessons learned and audit perspective, you will be glad you did. Plus, it boosts the "What did we accomplish?" section of your status report.

THE ABSOLUTE MINIMUM

At this point, you should have a solid understanding of the following:

- Managing project issues has two key components—an administrative process and a project management mindset. The mindset is far more important.
- The terms that best describe the desired project manager mindset are ringmaster, smiling bulldog, swivel-head, goaltender, and disciplined.
- The difference between project issues, risks, and defects:

    - Issues are events that have occurred or situations that exist that will adversely impact the project outcome if not resolved.

    - Risks are potential issues.

    - Defects are issues resulting from the project's quality management procedures (testing, reviews, and so on).

- Project issues must be identified, recorded, tracked, resolved, and communicated.
- Key issue management best practices include resolving issues at the lowest possible level, going after the root cause of any issue, assigning a specific person responsible for each issue, getting buy-in on ownership and due date from the person assigned the issue, and frequently reviewing the issue log with the project team.
- Whenever an issue needs the input of more than one person to resolve, the project manager should facilitate the resolution process.
- The issue management system needs to match the specific communication and workflow needs of the project team and the project stakeholders.

The map in Figure 13.1 summarizes the main points we reviewed in this chapter.

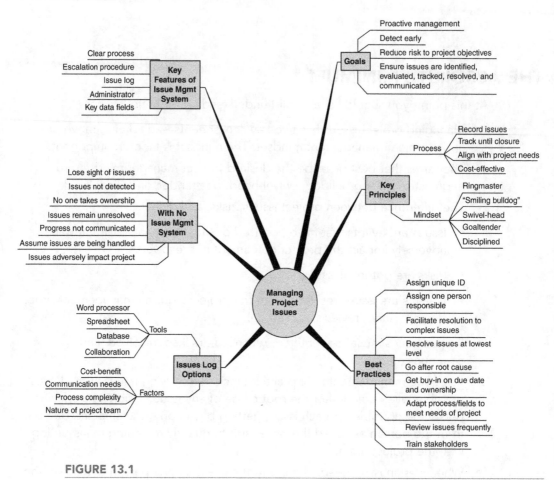

FIGURE 13.1

Overview of managing project issues.

IN THIS CHAPTER

- Understand why managing risks is what project management is all about
- Learn the key principles of controlling project risks
- Discover the value of managing project risks in a systematic manner
- Find out the essential steps and tools for effective risk management
- Realize that there is a common set of project characteristics that are responsible for most project risks
- Understand why many project risks are actually self-inflicted during the project planning process

14

MANAGING PROJECT RISKS

Managing project risks is the ultimate in proactive project management. It is the project manager's radar system. The goal of project management is to achieve the project's critical success factors, including meeting the targeted business objectives and client expectations. The goal of managing project risks is to identify and prepare for any potential threat to the project's critical success factors before it actually occurs. As a result, risk management is the essence of managing projects. Nothing impacts the decisions we make regarding general project approach, level of planning rigor, staffing, project control procedures, and overall contingencies more than the risks facing the project. Yet, there might be no aspect of project management that has a wider array of real-world implementations.

As a result, there is often a sense of confusion and uncertainty regarding the proper project risk management approach to take. In this chapter, we clarify all of this. We review the core principles, key process steps, and best practices that are essential to managing project risks. We share insights on how to identify common project risks, review the proven strategies that work best in controlling project risks, and highlight the typical risk management problems, so you can avoid them.

 TIP The essence of project management is risk management.

Key Risk Management Principles

A proactive management philosophy underlies the key principles of project risk management. By effectively managing project risks using these principles, a project manager remains in control of the project at all times, enables better project decisions, and provides the project the best opportunity for success.

The key principles to managing project risks include the following:

- **It's all risk management**—All project management is risk management. The current approaches and rules of modern project management—especially those surrounding portfolio management, project definition, and project planning—are all risk management focused. From past experiences, we now know how to structure a project for total success and how to greatly increase the likelihood the project will achieve its objectives.

 NOTE The primary reason for the increasing use of agile project approaches is for managing risk. With an agile approach, an organization manages the risks related to undefined customer requirements, building the wrong product, not prioritizing the high-value features, and/or delivering a viable product to market too late.

- **"Healthy paranoia"**—It's all attitude, even if it is a little psycho. Effective project managers take responsibility for managing risks on their project—believe me, no one else wants the job. As a result, you must strike the balance between having a paranoid outlook about your project (constantly thinking about what could go wrong) and doing everything you can to make sure the project is executed as planned.

- **Appropriate**—The level, type, and visibility of risk management should be consistent with the level of risk and the importance the project has to the organization. The cost of the risk response should not be greater than the impact loss the risk event might cause.

- **Systematic**—Any factor or risk that could impact the project should be identified, quantified, and assessed for possible effects to the project. This includes all people, process, technology, organizational, and environmental influences.

- **Continuous**—The identification of risks is an iterative process. Risk identification is repeatedly performed throughout the project, not just at the beginning.

- **Relentless**—The project manager and the organization must be committed to risk management for the entire project life cycle.

- **Focused**—Focus on the risks that you can control—starting with the high-priority risks.

 NOTE Per PMI, project risks can be reduced up to 90% if they are properly managed.

 NOTE The best risk profiles are ones that are specific to your industry, organization, and project type.

The Essential Process for Managing Project Risks

To be consistent with our principles, we need a systematic approach that enables us to focus time and resources on the highest priority risk elements. The power in the process is not in its complexity—it's relatively simple and straightforward—the power is in the management approach it inspires.

Let's review the essential steps for managing project risks:

- **Identify**—This is the critical step of identifying the risks to the project. The best way to start this process is also the best way to leverage the lessons from the past—use a *risk profile*. A risk profile, also referred to as a risk checklist or risk assessment form, lists the common sources of project risk that you need to consider. Although most risk profiles help you evaluate the majority of risk factors that are common to all projects, including the listing later in this chapter, the best risk profiles are ones that are specific to your industry, organization, and project type. In addition, the less experience that you have in project management or in the project domain, the more you should facilitate this process with the key stakeholders and subject matter experts on your project team.

- **Determine probability**—For each risk factor that has been identified, determine the likelihood that the risk event will occur. The goal is to quantify the uncertainty as much as possible, although in reality, this is still a judgment call. Common methods include numeric scales (1–5, 1–10) and subjective scales (High, Medium, Low).

- **Assess impact**—For each risk factor, determine the potential impact the risk event would have on the project critical success factors if it occurred. Like the probability element, the goal is to quantify the potential impact as much as possible. Generally, the same type of scale is used here, too. It is a good idea to document the specific impact (which critical success factor) and the magnitude of the impact.

- **Prioritize**—Now that we have a probability and an impact level, we tabulate a final ranking for each risk factor by combining the two values. If you have used numeric scales, this is straightforward; just multiply the two values together to get a final score. If you have used qualitative scales (L, M, H), you should be able to easily translate these to numeric values (1, 2, 3) to figure your final score. This step shows you the highest priority, most important risks, and the ones where you need to focus your initial efforts.

CAUTION   These steps focus on qualitative analysis and are more than sufficient for most projects, especially if a team approach is taken for this process. However, if you are in a situation or industry that requires more precise risk analysis, you will need to leverage a second phase of analysis called numerical (or quantitative) analysis. Techniques such as decision tree analysis and Monte Carlo simulations are frequently used here. Please consult an advanced project risk management course or text for instruction in this area.

- **Develop responses**—Document a response plan for each risk using one of the five risk response options detailed later in this chapter. Planning efforts are iterative in nature because risk response strategies might entail the allocation of additional resources, tasks, time, and costs to the project plan.

- **Get buy-in**—Review the risk response strategies with the key stakeholders to increase their awareness, get their feedback (if you have not already), and get their acceptance of the planned approaches.

- **Monitor**—Don't stop. Nothing stays the same. Continue to keep your eye on the risk factors—watch for triggers to activate other planned responses, be mindful of the appearance of new risk factors, and don't totally forget about the low-level risks. Either via circumstances changing or initial miscalculations, you might find some of these have a higher probability of occurring (or higher impact) than originally perceived.

Risk Response Options

 CAUTION For those planning on taking the PMP exam, note that risk management planning and risk response planning are two distinct activities.

Most people tend to think "mitigation" when they think of risk management. However, there are actually five risk response options. Table 14.1 reviews each response strategy and provides examples of each.

TABLE 14.1 Summary of Risk Response Options

Risk Response	Description	Examples/Notes
Avoidance	Avoiding the risk.	Reducing the scope to remove high-risk tasks.
	Changing the project plan to eliminate the risk.	Adding resources or time.
	Changing the project plan to protect a project objective from the impact.	Adopting a proven approach rather than a new one.
		Removing a "problem" resource.
Acceptance	Accepting the consequences of the risk.	Active acceptance.
		Passive acceptance.
	The project plan is not changed to deal with the risk.	No action.
	A better response strategy cannot be identified.	Contingency allowance (reserves).
		Notifying management that there could be a major cost increase if this risk occurs.
Monitor and prepare	Accepting the risk for now.	Contingency plan.
	Closely monitor the risk and proactively develop alternative action plans if the event occurs.	Fallback plan.
		Establish criteria that will trigger the implementation of the response plans.
Mitigation	Taking action to reduce the likelihood the risk will occur.	Adopting less-complex approaches.
		Planning on more testing.
	Taking action to reduce the impact of the risk.	Adding resources or time to the schedule.
	Reducing the probability is always more effective than minimizing the consequences.	Assigning a team member to visit the seller's facilities frequently to learn about potential delivery problems as early as possible.

Risk Response	Description	Examples/Notes
		Providing a less-experienced team member with additional training.
		Deciding to prototype a high-risk solution element.
Transference	Transferring ownership of the risk factor.	Outsourcing difficult work to a more-experienced company.
	Shifting the consequence of a risk and the ownership of the response to a third party.	Fixed price contract.
		Contracts, insurance, warranties, guarantees, and so on.
		Used most often for financial risk exposure.
		Does not eliminate the risk.

Key Risk Management Tools

One aspect of the risk management process described in the *PMBOK Guide* that many people find difficult to grasp is the reference to *unfamiliar tools and techniques*. Table 14.2 summarizes many of these tools and techniques to assist your learning and review process.

The risk assessment questionnaire contains questions that pertain to project size, structure, and technology. The risk assessment questionnaire is broken down by risk categories, subcategories, and criteria that rate risk level according to Low, Medium, or High.

 CAUTION As the project size and complexity increases (see size and complexity factors in Table 14.3), the level of risk can increase exponentially.

TABLE 14.2 Summary of Risk Management Tools

Risk Tool	Description	Notes/Examples
Risk profile	A questionnaire or checklist to guide the identification of project risk factors.	Should be specific to industry, organization, and project type.
Risk assessment	Generally synonymous with risk profile. Frequently will contain criteria to establish Low, Medium, and High risk levels.	Often used interchangeably for risk profile or risk checklist.
Risk register (log)	Used to document the identified risks, probability score, impact score, priority, and planned response strategies.	May be combined with other project logs.

Risk Tool	Description	Notes/Examples
Risk management plan	Describes how the risk management process will be structured and performed.	Describes the process to be used.
Risk response plan	Describes the response strategies for identified risks.	Risk log. Details action steps to be taken if risk event occurs.
Probability/impact matrix	Used to establish general High, Medium, and Low classifications for a risk factor. Cross-references the probability score with the impact score.	Generally developed at the organizational level to improve the consistency of risk rankings.

The Common Sources of Project Risk

The first key to managing risk on your project is to know where to look for it. The good news is that 80% or more of all risks originate from the same sources on every project. After you know the project characteristics that contribute to higher risk levels and the common sources of most project risks, you can quickly and effectively identify risk factors for any project. These factors should be first evaluated during project definition and are the main reason why several iterations of planning are often necessary. In Table 14.3, most of the key project risk factors are listed to better guide your risk identification activities. Note that many of these are emphasis points for project definition and detail project planning.

TABLE 14.3 Common Sources of Risk

Risk Source Category	Examples/Factors
Project size and complexity	Effort hours
	Calendar time
	Estimated budget
	Team size (number of resources)
	Number of sites
	Number of business units
	Number of system interfaces
	Number of dependencies on other projects
	Number of dependencies on other systems
	Degree of business change

Risk Source Category	Examples/Factors
Requirements	Volatile requirements
	Unrealistic or aggressive performance standards
	Complex requirements
Change impact	Replacement or new system
	Impact on business policies
	Impact on business processes
	Impact on organizational structure
	Impact on system operations
Organization	Changes to project objective
	Lack of priorities
	Lack of project management buy-in and support
	Inadequate project funding
	Misallocation and mismanagement of resources
Sponsorship	Lack of strong executive commitment
	Lack of clear ownership
	Loss of political support
Stakeholder involvement	All key stakeholders not identified
	Missing buy-in from a key stakeholder
	Stakeholder needs not completely identified
	Key stakeholders not fully engaged
Schedule	Estimate assumptions not holding true
	Schedule contingency not adequate
Funding	Reduction in available capital
	Cash flow issues
	Inflation or exchange rate factors
Facilities	Adequate for team productivity requirements
	Adequate for project security requirements

Risk Source Category	Examples/Factors
Team	Full-time or part-time roles
	Location of team members
	Can't find desired resources
	Lack of experience
	Lack of business knowledge
	Lack of skills
	Lack of commitment
	Personal issues
	Lack of prior experience working together
Technology	Missing technical data
	Use of unproven technology
	Use of nonstandard technology
	Development approach
	Level of complexity
Vendors and suppliers	Contract types
	Risk-reward elements
	Procurement process
	Experience with vendor/supplier
External factors	Changing weather conditions
	Changes in legal and regulatory environment
	Approvals from governmental agencies
	Political changes
Business factors	Time-to-market
	Mergers and acquisitions
	Economic events
	Market conditions
Assumptions and constraints	Might create schedule, cost, resource, or quality risks

Risk Source Category	Examples/Factors
Project management	Lack of experience
	Poor leadership
	Poor communications
	Lack of contingency plans
	Inadequate risk management

Although most sources of risk are inherent attributes of project initiatives or are outside the project manager's control (as the preceding table summarized), there is another common source of project risks that is generally self-inflicted. These are the project risks we create by not performing adequate project definition or detail project planning.

 NOTE Unidentified or unacknowledged project planning defects are the most common source of unknown risks.

 NOTE Technically, these factors are actually planning defects. They become project risks only if they are not corrected before planning is complete.

For a complete listing and explanation of those factors, you can review Part II, "Project Planning." For a quick review, Table 14.4 lists many of the key factors. Please note that some risk source categories are listed again in this table. This is intentional. In some areas, there are universal, inherent factors that contribute to project risk, and there are other risk factors that are introduced due to inadequate project planning. One example is the project schedule. Estimate assumptions not holding true and inadequate contingency buffer are inherent risks on any project. However, a poorly developed schedule is self-inflicted and a result of project planning deficiencies. Yet, it can be as devastating to your project critical success factors as anything.

TABLE 14.4 Common Project Planning Sources of Risk

Risk Source Category	Examples/Factors
Project management	Improperly defined project deliverables
	Incomplete planning
	Improper procedures
	Not defining clear roles and responsibilities
	Lack of contingency plans
	Inadequate risk management
	Inadequate attention to the right details
	Inadequate resource staffing
Project definition	Unrealistic objectives
	Inconsistent objectives
	Incomplete scope definition
	Inconsistent scope definition
	Improperly defined project deliverables
WBS (and project schedule)	Not reviewed and approved by stakeholders
	Missing tasks
	Lack of team understanding
	Missing project management activities
	External dependencies not identified and understood
Project schedule	Missing task dependencies
	Tasks not clearly assigned
	Resources overallocated
	Calendar realities not factored
	Inadequate contingency or reserve
Project budget	Poorly developed cost estimates
	Missing cost sources
	Inadequate contingency or reserve
Requirements	Incomplete or poorly defined requirements
Assumptions and constraints	Not completely defined

Typical Problems

As with any project management process, there are always challenges and things for which you should be on the lookout. Let's first review the four general problems that are typical with managing project risk:

- **Undetected risks**—These are the risks that will get you because you didn't even see them coming. The most common reasons for this are project managers not having the proper risk management mindset, project team members not raising awareness of specific risk factors, and planning defects that are not detected.

- **Unacknowledged risks**—These occur in dysfunctional organizations or in immature project management organizations. For whatever reason, often political in nature, an obvious risk factor is not formally acknowledged and, as a result, not properly managed. This is the proverbial "elephant in the room." A common example of this is an impossible schedule deadline.

 CAUTION In some cases, organizations knowingly accept the risk of abbreviating the project definition and planning steps to meet other objectives.

- **Not enough process**—It is not uncommon to see this area of project management totally ignored, at least from a systematic standpoint.

- **Too much process**—On the other end of the spectrum, I have often seen gung-ho, analytical project managers overdo the risk management process. They can spend so much time on risk management that planning is never completed, or they get so focused on risks that they become overly cautious and won't take any chances. Remember: project risk management is not about avoiding all risks.

In addition to the major problems typically found, a number of other smaller issues are common to the risk management process we discussed earlier. Table 14.5 summarizes those common gaps.

TABLE 14.5 Summary of Common Risk Management Gaps

Risk Management Process	Common Gaps
Risk management planning	No risk management plan.
	Risk management plan equals risk response plan.
Risk identification	Performed only once and not proactively managed.
	Process is incomplete.
	Missing entire types/categories of risk.
	Confusing issues with risks.
Risk qualitative analysis	The organization has not established standard practices/tools.
	The probability of occurrence is not calculated for each risk.
	The impact of each risk is not determined.
	Risks are not prioritized.
	Risk quantitative analysis is not limited to high-priority risks.
Risk response planning	Response strategies are not documented.
	No risk response plan is in place.
	Response strategies are not appropriate for risk severity.
	The project plan is not updated to implement and monitor responses.
Risk monitoring and control	The risk response plan is not maintained.
	Risk identification is not continued.
	The project plan is not updated to implement and monitor responses.
	Responses are not reevaluated.
	Progress is not tracked, or task owners are not held accountable.

Powerful Risk Control Strategies

This section breaks out of the strict risk management process and considers some powerful strategies you should consider to either deal with the high-priority risks you now have or reduce the number of new risks from occurring as your project goes forward.

- **Tackle high risks first**—Develop a work plan that attacks your high-risk factors right out of the gate Why? If you are going to have a problem, it is best to know sooner than later. If something is not feasible or acceptable, determine

this as soon as possible, so senior management can decide whether the
project is worthy of organizational investment and resources.

- **Use iterative, phased approaches**—By breaking the work of the project into
multiple iterations and phases, you provide a systematic method of providing tangible output to the stakeholders sooner and more often. The multiple
points of review and feedback with the stakeholders enable you to better control your greatest risk—stakeholder expectations and satisfaction.

- **Test it like you mean it**—This strategy overlaps with quality management but
is worth emphasizing here too. There's no better way to avoid and reduce
risks with a new work product than to use effective, prioritized testing. An
effective test plan will identify defects before the final project work item is
deployed to production or made available to the customer audience.

 NOTE   Agile approaches emphasize these first three risk
control strategies: tackle high risks first, use iterative, phased
approaches, and use prioritized testing.

- **Verify deployments**—And for those in the IT software world, this strategy is
focused on verifying the deployment of the project work product into a new
environment. Often, this is referred to as a "smoke test" and is commonly
used with IT services and resources. The project work item might have met
all requirements, but if it is not deployed and set up correctly in the target
environment, the customer will not be able to tell the difference.

 NOTE   For those in the IT space, DevOps (or DevSecOps)
approaches emphasize these last two risk control strategies:
prioritized/continuous testing and verifying deployments through
continuous build, integration, and deployment processes.

- **QA the planning process**—This strategy has been mentioned before but
is worth mentioning again: Be sure to do a quality review on the planning
process. This step helps identify planning defects that, if undetected, will
become unknown risks with a high-impact potential.

- **Leverage independent QA audits**—Leveraging an independent, experienced, and objective viewpoint can be a powerful way to identify risk factors
and determine the best response strategies. This can be especially useful in
project situations where the key stakeholders are inexperienced, the climate is
very political, or multiple vendors are involved.

Are You Sure It's a Risk?

Before we end our review of managing project risks, it is worth mentioning that one common problem associated with project risk management is terminology and the proper labeling of risks. This is more of an academic issue, and generally, the subtle differences are not key factors on projects. To make sure you avoid problems here, Table 14.6 quickly reviews the definition of terms closely related to project risk and clarifies those distinctions.

TABLE 14.6 Summary of Risk-Related Terms

Term	Definition	Notes
Risk	An uncertain event that could negatively impact the project critical success factors, if it occurs.	A threat. Probability of occurrence must be between 0% and 100%.
Issue	An active problem that could impact the project critical success factors.	A risk event that has actually occurred.
Constraint	A limit that must be planned around.	Factual. Constraints can introduce other risks.
Assumption	Factor considered to be true, real, or certain.	Assumptions can include accepted risks. Assumptions can introduce other risks.
Dependency	An external event that must occur for the project to accomplish its objectives.	Identified during planning along with risks, constraints, and assumptions.
Defect	A discrepancy between what is (actual) and what should be (expected). Mentioned here because planning and overall project management defects can become project risks if not identified and corrected.	Detailed planning efforts are important here. The key source for many unknown risks.

THE ABSOLUTE MINIMUM

At this point, you should have a solid understanding of the following:

- The essence of project management is risk management.
- The level of risk management should be consistent with the size, importance, and risk level of the project.
- Managing risks is an integral part of project planning.
- Risk management is a continuous, iterative process throughout the project life cycle.
- Project risks need to be identified, recorded, tracked, resolved, and communicated.
- Risk events that actually occur become project issues.
- The five risk response strategies include acceptance, avoidance, mitigation, transfer, and monitor.
- The best risk profiles are ones that are specific to your industry, organization, and project type.
- Unidentified or unacknowledged project planning defects are the most common source of unknown risks.
- The best ways to control risk are through solid project management, effective project planning, and a relentless desire to protect the project.

Figure 14.1 summarizes the main points reviewed in this chapter.

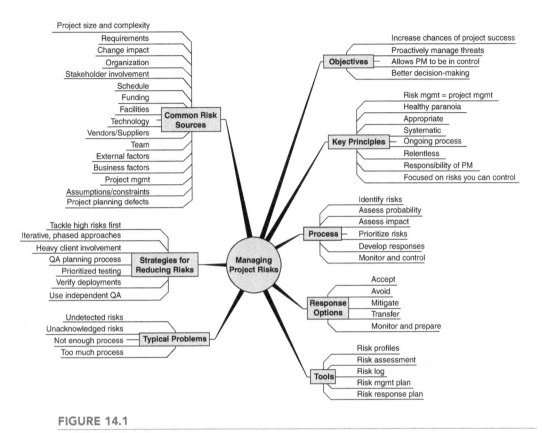

FIGURE 14.1

Overview of managing project risks.

MANAGING PROJECT QUALITY

Quality is one of the critical success factors for any project and one of the key tenets of modern project management. Yet, project quality is often misunderstood and poorly managed. Why is this?

Suppose a project delivers a technically sound, zero-defect product, but the project is over budget and the customer is not satisfied. Do you have project quality in this case or not?

Your organization may already need to comply with an industry quality standard (ISO 900x/1000x, ISO/TS 16949, IATF 16949, GxP, CMMi [Capability Maturity Model Integration]) or already employ one of the popular quality methodologies (Total Quality Management, Six Sigma, Continuous Improvement). Do you need to worry about project quality or not?

In this chapter, we explore these questions and address many more fundamental project quality topics. We clarify what project quality means and how it relates to managing project risks, project requirements, and client expectations. We review the core principles, key tools, and best practices of project quality management, including the critical quality techniques that are often overlooked by many project management texts. In addition, we share insights into the typical challenges surrounding managing project quality, so you can avoid them on your first (or next) project.

NOTE As mentioned in the book's introduction, this chapter does not address advanced quality management concepts that are more the domain of operational quality management programs. The review of quality control tools such as Pareto analysis, statistical sampling, control charts, fishbone diagrams, or trend analysis, and the review of quality management pioneers (such as Dr. W. Edwards Deming, Dr. Joseph Duran, and Philip Crosby) is left to other textbooks and courses that have a primary quality management focus.

What Is "Project Quality"?

What do you think of when you hear the word "quality"? Testing? Zero defects? Audits? Overhead? If you answered yes to any of these, you might be surprised to know how PMI defines quality. To PMI, *quality* equals "conformance to requirements and fitness of use." Well, of course it does. Simply translated, this means that the project produces what it said it would and that what it produces satisfies real customer needs. In other words, did the project deliver on the targeted requirements and were the requirements on target? Did your understanding of client needs translate into client satisfaction?

You might be thinking, "Greg, isn't this what a project is supposed to do?" or "You know, Greg, this sounds an awful lot like managing requirements." Exactly. Although there are aspects of managing quality that are unique, mainly verifying that the work is complete and correct, most elements of managing project quality are fused tightly with other aspects of project management, especially requirements (scope) management, expectations management, risk management, team management, and procurement management.

In the same way that we said project management is risk management in the previous chapter, we could also say project management is quality management, too. After all, most of the best practices now recommended for project management (and discussed in this book) have quality concerns as their foundation. From clearly defining the project, to the approach we take to accomplishing the work, to the project team we assemble, to the focus on customer buy-in, it's all there to give the project the best opportunity to deliver the solution requirements and meet the expectations of the client—in other words, to deliver project quality.

Unique Aspects of Managing Project Quality

Although project quality management is tightly integrated with all aspects of managing a project, there are a few aspects that are unique to this endeavor (after all, there must be some reason we have a separate chapter on it). The unique elements of managing project quality include the following:

- **Focus on quality-based requirements**—Ensure that all the quality, compliance, and security standards that the project is accountable for are identified, both from the customer and other governing stakeholders.

- **Focus on value-added requirements**—Work to understand the requirements, often unspoken if not probed, that go beyond the base functional requirements and will have the greatest impact on the customer satisfaction level of the final solution.

- **Focus on product and process**—Quality management addresses both *product* (goods and services) quality and *process* quality, especially the *project management* process.

- **Focus on verification**—Determine the game plan for ensuring that all the requirements will be met to the satisfaction of the relevant stakeholders. How will you validate whether the work of the project is on target? How will you prove the work is complete and correct?

Principles of Managing Project Quality

The seven key principles of project quality management originate from a proactive, customer-focused management philosophy and are consistent with other project management practices we have reviewed. By utilizing these principles, a project manager keeps the quality requirements aligned with both the project and the key stakeholders and gives the project the best opportunity to deliver on the quality success factor.

The seven key principles to managing project quality include the following:

- **Identify targets**—This is the critical first step in the process. Make sure you identify both the customer's quality expectations as part of the requirements gathering process and the quality/compliance/security expectations demanded from other key stakeholders, whether these are internal quality departments or external compliance agencies. This is the most common reason for not meeting quality expectations—they are never completely identified.

 TIP Quality is planned in, not inspected in. Effective project management is quality-focused.

- **Plan it**—Quality is planned in, not inspected in. After you determine the quality level requirements, you must then decide how to meet these requirements. With the quality level targets clearly identified, you can structure the overall approach of the project, allocate resources, and assign necessary tasks to give yourself the best opportunity to meet the quality expectations. In some form or another, you should document and communicate your plan for quality management on the project. Often, this is accomplished using a Quality Management Plan document, which is part of your overall project plan.

- **Right-size it**—Like other project management processes, use the appropriate level of rigor and formality to meet the needs of the project. In other words, match the investment in quality procedures with the risk level and other critical success factors. For example, does the project need to produce a zero-defect product that must pass FDA validation audits, or is the project more exploratory in nature—a "quick-and-dirty" initiative?

- **Set expectations**—This principle focuses on two key aspects. One, make sure the customer's quality expectations are aligned with the project's needs and the quality management approach to be taken. And two, if the effort (time, costs) to satisfy all quality requirements conflicts with either the schedule or budget constraints on the project, then you must facilitate a compromise via risk analysis and planning scenarios that results in a prioritization of quality management efforts or an adjustment in critical success factor balance.

- **Stay customer-focused**—Underlying the entire project quality management philosophy is a focus on the customer experience. This means doing things such as defining requirements from the customer's perspective, asking the right questions to uncover the other requirements that will affect the customer's perception of the final solution, validating from the customer's perspective, and clearly communicating (and getting buy-in) on why other quality requirements must be satisfied, too.

- **Trust, but verify**—This is a tangible example of an overall project management principle: assume nothing. Whether it is work assigned to a project team member, a supplier, or some other external party, always perform some level of verification to ensure the resulting work package meets the targeted completion criteria.

- **It's up to you!**—The project manager has ultimate responsibility for the project quality. Although many aspects of quality management are organizational in nature, and you need the support of senior management to make it stick, you are still responsible for the quality success criteria, as you are for the entire project. To this extent, this is why this chapter is focused on elements the project manager can control or influence.

Powerful Tools and Techniques for Project Quality

We emphasized the value and importance of planning your quality management system. In this section, we highlight ten of the most powerful quality-focused tools and techniques that you want to consider during your planning efforts, document in your Quality Management Plan, and then implement during the execution of your project.

- **Requirements traceability matrix**—A simple, yet often neglected technique to help control scope, expectations, and quality is the use of a requirements traceability matrix. The traceability matrix provides a documented link between the original set of approved requirements, any interim deliverable, all testing (verification) methods employed, and the final work product. This technique helps to ensure that the final work product(s) satisfy the targeted requirements and that all those requirements were properly validated.

- **Checklists**—Checklists are simple, yet powerful. They clearly capture and communicate the quality standards that the targeted work package must meet, and they improve project team productivity. They are flexible—separate checklists can be developed for each work product or project management process. They provide a mechanism to capture the lessons learned from past projects. They provide a mechanism to document the verification performed on the work package.

- **Templates**—The development and use of templates provides a way to both communicate and control the use of certain standards and to help standardize the resulting work packages and procedures across projects. In addition, templates can capture lessons-learned information (mostly updates and improvements based on prior experiences), provide guidance, and greatly improve the productivity level of a project team.

- **Reviews**—Reviews are a key technique for ensuring quality and managing expectations, and they can take many forms. The principle here is to plan for the review-feedback-correction cycle on most, if not all, of your key deliverables. Common examples of reviews are peer reviews, inspections, client walkthroughs, audits, testing cycles, sprint/iteration reviews, and milestone reviews.

- **Completion criteria**—This starts during project definition with defining the acceptance criteria for the project, and it continues for each deliverable and work assignment. Answer this question in advance for each deliverable and work assignment: "How will we know when it is done?" Understanding the completion criteria upfront increases productivity and avoids much of the rework that can occur when quality requirements are not understood upfront.

- **Small work packages**—You've seen this one before, too. In addition to reasons previously mentioned—more accurate estimates and better control—small work packages provide a finer level of quality control, too. By establishing completeness and correctness completion criteria for each work package and verifying each work package along the way, we provide many more opportunities to detect quality discrepancies as early in the project as possible. By doing this, we can take corrective actions when the costs are lower and time is still available.

- **Independent audits**—The use of an independent auditor is another specific example of the review technique mentioned earlier. The power of this technique is in establishing the quality criteria in advance and making the project accountable to an outside entity.

 NOTE Make sure the work and responsibilities associated with the project quality system are reflected in the WBS and project schedule.

- **Standards**—In many situations, specific quality standards either do not exist or have not been formally developed. In these cases, it is my recommendation that you establish project standards upfront that will be captured in both work assignments and quality checklists. And if at all possible, facilitate this standards development with the project team—you'll be glad you did.

- **V method**—The *V method* is a term used for a common validation and verification approach that ensures that there is a validation and verification step for every deliverable and interim deliverable created. While this method is traditionally associated with waterfall project approaches, the principles do apply and are used in agile approaches too. An overview of this method is illustrated in Figure 15.1. The left side of the "V" notes each targeted deliverable and the right side of the "V" lists the verification method used for each deliverable directly across. This method enables us to check quality along the way rather than waiting to the end to discover there are quality defects.

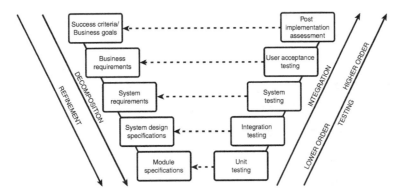

FIGURE 15.1

Illustration of V-method approach for software development project.

- **Quality Management Plan**—This is the document that describes and communicates the project's quality management system to the project stakeholders. Specifically, the Quality Management Plan should address most of these questions:
  - What is the scope of the quality management system?
  - How will either internal or external quality-based groups be involved?
  - What quality standards must be met?
  - What approaches, tools, and techniques will be employed?
  - How will the standards be enforced?
  - How will quality defects or discrepancies be tracked and reported?
  - How will each deliverable be validated?
  - What are the expected costs?

Powerful Quality Strategies

In addition to the powerful quality tools and techniques we reviewed earlier, there are five other key strategies related to managing project quality that we need to discuss:

- **Use customer-focused project approaches**—This might be self-evident by now, but utilize project approaches that accomplish the following:
  - Fully engage the customer throughout the project life cycle.
  - Partner the project team with the targeted customers.

- Enable the customer to provide feedback on "solution-like" deliverables as soon as possible.

- Emphasize prevention and early detection of quality defects.

- Popular, modern-day project approaches and techniques that fall into this category include the following:

  - Iterative development

  - Quality function deployment (QFD)

  - Prototyping

  - Computer simulation

  - Agile development

  - Scenario and use case development

  - Storyboarding

- **Take customer's perspective**—From the development of requirements to the testing approach, make sure to take the customer's perspective. In particular, the testing environment needs to simulate the real-world customer environment to the greatest extent possible. Without this approach, your verification procedures are incomplete at best and misleading at their worst.

- **Pre-verify deliverables**—To better manage client expectations, including confidence in the project team, make sure to conduct an internal quality check on any deliverable that will be reviewed by the client. Make sure to schedule these internal verification steps, too.

- **Focus on the people**—There is no better quality management technique than to have people who are good at what they do, who take pride in their work, and who are focused on the customer experience. The project management processes of staffing, managing, and leading a team are key project quality factors.

- **Leverage expertise**—A great way to deal with unanticipated project quality issues is to structure the team with one or more mentors (or coaches). Because many organizations do not have an effective way to formally pass along the lessons from the past, this strategy is an effective way to leverage the wisdom that lies within the social fabric of the organization. The two positions that are most needed are a mentor for the project manager and a technical mentor for the technical aspects of the project. In many cases, the technical mentor might actually provide the QA function for the technical deliverables.

- **Prioritize testing**—This is part of taking the customer perspective approach, and it also incorporates the importance of understanding where your key risks lie with the targeted work product. In situations where testing resources or schedules are limited, it is imperative to verify the high-risk areas first.

Typical Quality-Related Challenges

To both relate some additional experiences that you have endured or observed and reemphasize some of the key points covered so far, let's take a quick look at some common project quality-related challenges:

- **Forgot to pop the question**—This problem can be found on projects that are guilty of not having an organized quality approach and on projects with formal methodology coming out their ears. Always ask clients what "quality" means to them. Again, do not assume anything, especially here.

- **"Good intentions, but..."**—Many projects start off great. The Quality Management Plan is fully developed and approved, but then...nothing. Stuff happens and the quality management procedures are never carried out.

- **"We can't afford it"**—There is a common misconception in many organizations that quality-focused efforts are overhead and cost too much. This perception originates from two main sources. One, projects in these organizations are likely managed very informally, so to add quality management seems like a major investment. Two, the quality standards don't seem to add value. In some cases, this might be true. In either case, better understanding, communication, and salesmanship are needed. The real question to be asked is, "Can you afford not to focus on quality?" Historical data shows that in most cases, the cost of poor quality (nonconformance) is much greater than the cost of prevention.

- **Not factored in the schedule**—Especially on projects where the quality procedures are an afterthought, the actual quality tasks (reviews, audits, and so on) are never factored into the project schedule.

- **Quality resources overallocated**—In many project situations, the individuals who are designated for quality assurance roles are also fulfilling other roles. If the quality assurance role was not properly allocated and assigned to project tasks, you might have an overallocated resource. In this case, or when other pressure events occur, the quality assurance hat is often the first to go for these multirole team members.

- **Testing takes more than one cycle?**—An age-old dilemma on projects that require one or more testing phases on the targeted product is how much time to allocate for each phase. The common mistake is to officially schedule a testing phase as if it will be completed in the initial test cycle. I have yet to see this happen.

- **Avoid gold-plating**—Traditionally, *gold-plating* is a term associated with project scope management, and it refers to the practice of doing more (adding additional features) than what the requirements (specifications) call for without undergoing proper change control procedures. This is also an issue for project quality management for two reasons. One, the gold-plated features might introduce new quality risks into the equation. And two, the gold-plated features might do nothing to improve the actual deliverable quality, yet they can require additional time and costs.

- **No risk analysis**—On the one hand, many project managers are guilty of not identifying or being aware of the quality standards they are accountable for. On the other, there are project managers who blindly accept all the quality standards without properly assessing the impact to the project objectives and other critical success factors. Always assess the impact of meeting each quality standard, especially the schedule and cost impact. Decisions on priorities and risk response strategies may be needed to deal with the impact.

- **Forgot to smoke test**—For any work product that must be deployed or set up in a new environment, ensure that the actual deployment was correct before turning it over to the final customer. This is common for IT services, products, and resources, and this checkpoint is commonly referred to as a *smoke test*.

In summary, most aspects of managing project quality are interwoven into the fabric of solid project management practices. If you manage with a focus on key criteria, your projects will be well positioned to meet their quality objectives. These criteria include the following:

- The customer

- Requirements/scope

- Clear communication

- Clear completion/acceptance criteria

- Small work packages

- Prevention

- Verification

- Skilled resources and high-performing teams

 NOTE Agile project approaches incorporate many of the quality principles, strategies, and techniques reviewed in this chapter.

THE ABSOLUTE MINIMUM

At this point, you should have a solid understanding of the following:

- The level of quality management should be consistent with client expectations, project needs, and project risk level.

- Managing project quality is tightly connected with managing requirements, project scope, project risks, suppliers, and client expectations.

- The process of managing project quality enables you to go from identifying customer needs to achieving customer satisfaction.

- Specifically, project quality procedures answer the question: How do I verify that the work is complete and correct?

- Quality is doing what you said you would do.

- Quality management addresses both *product* (goods and services) quality and project management quality.

- The project manager has ultimate responsibility for the project quality.

- Effective quality management is consistent with effective project management.

- Two key aspects of project quality that are often overlooked are managing the project team and managing requirements.

- Historically, the costs of prevention are significantly less than the costs of quality defects.

- Essential tools for project quality management are the Quality Management Plan, checklists, reviews, requirements traceability matrix, audits, verification procedures, and clear completion criteria.

- Checklists and templates allow quality expectations to be clearly communicated and enforced. They also provide a way to pass along lessons learned from past projects.

- To ensure overall project quality, ensure each deliverable along the way meets quality expectations.

- For additional information on quality function deployment, visit the Quality Function Deployment Institute at www.qfdi.org.

The map in Figure 15.2 summarizes the main points reviewed in this chapter.

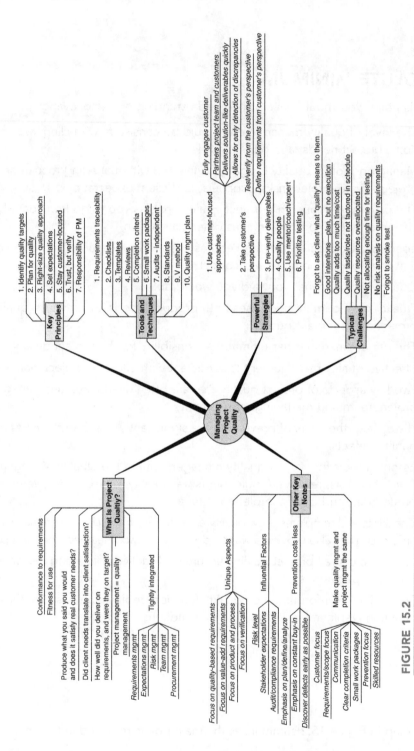

FIGURE 15.2

Overview of managing project quality.

IN THIS CHAPTER

- Understand why project leadership is important
- Understand the difference between managing and leading a project
- Understand why "old-school" management approaches don't usually work on projects
- Review the common behaviors of effective project leaders
- Understand where leadership is needed on a project
- Discover the 12 keys to better project leadership
- Understand why a servant leadership approach gives you the best chance of doing the right work, the right way, for the right people

LEADING A PROJECT

Why do we include a chapter on leading a project when most introductory project management books won't go near it? Quite simply, a person "manages" processes but "leads" people...and people accomplish projects.

Although the skill set for effective project management consists of the project management fundamentals discussed so far in this book (along with general business management, communication, and technical skills mentioned in Chapter 2, "The Project Manager"), they are all interlaced with leadership skills as depicted in Figure 16.1.

In today's world, there is an overwhelming need for individuals who can serve both as project manager and project leader, yet it is a challenge to find individuals who can perform both roles effectively. Why is this? In general, it's the difference between the art and the science of project management—the difference between the soft skills and the hard skills and knowing how much of which one to apply. And on many unfortunate projects, the lack of leadership or the use of an ineffective leadership approach actually creates problems that did not otherwise exist.

FIGURE 16.1

Integration of leadership skills.

In this chapter, we review the aspects of a project that need leadership and how leading a project is different from managing a project. In addition, we explore the key components of project leadership, the power of the servant leadership approach, and the common traits of effective project leaders. With this awareness and understanding, you will be much more prepared to serve as both project manager and project leader, even on your first assignment.

More Than Managing

The process of leading a project is more than managing the project. The process of leading a project entails the approach utilized to guide the people involved (team, stakeholders, organization) toward the accomplishment of the project's objectives. This process involves your mindset and leverages key skills such as dedication, interpersonal skills, adaptability, and customer orientation. If we look back at Chapter 2, many of the roles a project manager performs involve leadership, including the following:

- **Planner**—Ensures the project is defined properly and completely for success, all stakeholders are engaged, work effort approach is determined, required resources are available when needed, and processes are in place to properly execute and control the project.

- **Point person**—Serves as the central point of contact for all oral and written project communications to key stakeholders.

- **Facilitator**—Ensures that stakeholders and team members from different perspectives understand each other and work together to accomplish the project goals.

- **Aligner**—Gains agreement from the stakeholders on project definition, success criteria, and approach; manages stakeholder expectations throughout the project while managing the competing demands of time, cost, and quality; gains agreement on resource decisions and issue resolution action steps.

- **Problem solver**—Utilizes root-cause analysis process experience, prior project experiences, and technical knowledge to resolve unforeseen technical issues and take any necessary corrective actions.

- **Umbrella**—Works to shield the project team from the politics and "noise" surrounding the project, so they can stay focused and productive.

- **Coach**—Determines and communicates the role each team member plays and the importance of that role to the project success, finds ways to motivate each team member, looks for ways to improve the skills of each team member, and provides constructive and timely feedback on individual performances.

- **Salesperson**—Focuses on "selling" the benefits of the project to the organization, serving as a "change agent," and inspiring team members to meet project goals and overcome project challenges.

In addition, many qualities of successful project managers described in Chapter 2 have strong leadership elements, including the following:

- **Takes ownership**—Takes responsibility and accountability for the project, leads by example, and brings energy and drive to the project; without this attitude, all the skills and techniques in the world will only get you so far.

- **Savvy**—Understands people and the dynamics of the organization, navigates tricky politics; has the ability to quickly read emotionally charged situations; thinks fast on feet; builds relationships; leverages personal power for benefit of the project.

- **Intensity with a smile**—Balances an assertive, resilient, tenacious, results-oriented focus with a style that makes people want to help; consistently follows up on everything and their resolutions without annoying everyone.

- **Eye of the storm**—Demonstrates ability to be the calm eye of the project hurricane; high tolerance for ambiguity; takes the heat from key stakeholders (CxOs, business managers, and project team); exhibits a calm, confident aura when others are showing signs of issue or project stress.

- **Strong customer-service orientation**—Demonstrates ability to see each stakeholder's perspective; able to provide voice of all key stakeholders (especially the sponsor) to the project team; has strong facilitation and collaboration skills; has excellent active listening skills.

- **People-focused**—Takes a team-oriented approach; understands that methodology, process, and tools are important, but without quality people it's very difficult to complete a project successfully; acts ethically; protects the team; and takes a teaching approach.

- **Always keeps "eye on the ball"**—Stays focused on the project goals and objectives. There are many ways to accomplish a given objective, which is especially important to remember when things don't go as planned.

- **Controlled passion**—Balances passion for completing the project objectives with a healthy detached perspective, which enables the project manager to make better decisions, continue to see all points of view, better anticipate risks, and better respond to project issues.

- **Context understanding**—Understands the context of the project—the priority that the project has among the organization's portfolio of projects and how it aligns with the overall goals of the organization.

- **Looking for trouble**—Constantly looking and listening for potential risks, issues, or obstacles; confronts doubt head-on; deals with disgruntled users right away; understands that most of these situations are opportunities and can be resolved up front before they become full-scale crisis points.

Where Is Leadership Needed on a Project?

There are three key points to know about leading a project:

1. There are many aspects of project leadership.

2. The project manager is not the sole provider of project leadership.

3. Specific leadership providers vary depending on the project environment.

To clarify this idea, let's take a look at project areas where leadership is needed and who could provide it in Table 16.1. Please note that for agile projects, the reference to "Team leader(s)" in Table 16.1 would include the Scrum Master and Product Owner roles.

TABLE 16.1   Project Leadership Areas

Project Area	Leadership Provided By
Direction and plan	Project sponsor
	Senior management
	Project manager
	Technical leader(s)
	Product management
Organizational influence	Project sponsor
	Senior management
	Project manager
	Technical leader(s)
	Product management
Commitment	Project sponsor
	Senior management
	Project manager
	Project team
	Product management
Stakeholder expectations	Project manager
	Project sponsor
	Senior management
	Product management
Facilitation	Project manager
	Team leader(s)
Communications point	Project manager
	Team leader(s)

Project Area	Leadership Provided By
Project team	Project manager
	Team leader(s)
	Technical leader(s)
Conflict resolution	Project manager
	Team leader(s)
Managing business change	Project sponsor
	Senior management
	Project manager
Technical issues	Project manager
	Technical leader(s)
Business issues	Project sponsor
	Senior management
	Product management
	Project manager
	Team leader(s)
Managing risks	Project sponsor
	Senior management
	Product management
	Project manager
	Team leader(s)
	Technical leader(s)

We explore managing stakeholder expectations, managing project communications, and building an effective project team in greater detail in Chapters 17, 18, and 19, respectively.

 TIP The ability to effectively communicate (in all forms) is a fundamental skill for project leadership.

12 Keys to Better Project Leadership

In the modern world of projects, project leaders cannot rely on position power or traditional, autocratic leadership approaches to get the job done. To guide a group of unfamiliar project stakeholders and project team members to accomplish something that has not been done before, you must rely on a different set of skills and leadership principles. As we review the 12 keys to more effective project leadership, please remember this is not an all-or-nothing deal—it is a continuum. The more of these that you demonstrate, the better leader you will likely be.

1. **Focus on the people**—There are those who maintain that project management is about managing a process (or a work plan) and not about managing people. Are they serious? Who does the work? People. An effective project leader takes a holistic view that puts people first. This approach results in a focus on establishing and building relationships and a focus on gaining an authentic understanding and buy-in from each stakeholder.

2. **Visualize the goal...and the way there**—This is the traditional leadership ability of providing direction to the team. Not only does a project leader need to clearly see the end and be able to create this picture for everyone else, but they must also understand how the team is going to get there. The ability to see this big picture is vital to keeping the project focused on its primary objectives.

3. **See with "their" eyes**—This is a skill that is not natural for many, but an invaluable one if you can do it. Look at your project from the perspective of the other stakeholders. What do they see? What are they thinking? What do they need? This ability to take another's perspective is foundational to building better relationships, developing requirements, managing communications, managing expectations, and building a productive project team.

4. **Earn their trust**—Effective leaders are trusted by senior management to do the right thing and get the job done. They are trusted by other stakeholders because they manage with integrity and consistently seek win-win scenarios to any project challenge.

   TIP   Be the first to take responsibility and the last to take credit.

5. **Earn their respect**—How do you earn the respect of project stakeholders when you do not have position power? There are four key behaviors that affect the level of respect granted you by project stakeholders:

   - **Show respect**—First of all, show respect to each person you are dealing with. Listen to them—I mean, really listen to them, respect their time, and respect their knowledge, experience, and perspectives.

   - **Be real**—Deal with reality, not what it should be or could be. Your willingness to acknowledge and confront the realities of the project will be key to your overall effectiveness.

   - **Be fair**—People might not always like final decisions, but they will respect the decision and you if they feel you handled the situation in a fair manner. An approach to team management, decision-making, and conflict resolution that emphasizes fairness is key to earning the respect of others.

   - **Be consistent**—Lead by example, stick with your decisions, maintain your principles, do what you say you are going to do, and be emotionally steady.

6. **Facilitate progress**—As a project leader, you are focused on accomplishing the project objectives, and you realize that one of the most important jobs you have is to make it as easy as possible for your team to complete its work. How do you do this? Think of yourself as a conduit for progress, an enabler, a productivity enhancer. Some key actions include the following:

   - Anticipate issues, work to prevent them, and confront and resolve the ones that do occur—quickly

   - Create an open and honest team environment where members are encouraged and comfortable to exchange their thoughts and ideas

   - Facilitate the decision-making process

   - Get needed information quickly

   - Ensure the team has the structure, process, and tools to be as productive as possible

   - Work to reduce the doubt and uncertainty factor for others

7. **Take ownership**—Let there be no doubt in anyone's mind who is responsible for this project. An ownership mindset manifests itself in a persistent, results-focused, no-excuses attitude that is undeniable and contagious to the other team members.

8. **Be resilient**—Like the proverbial willow tree that shows its true strength when confronted with a ferocious wind, a project leader is able to quickly adapt his approach and style to best meet the needs of the project. Through a creative and flexible mindset, a project leader understands that there are many ways to achieve the targeted goals and works to make it happen.

9. **Be a teacher**—A great model for the modern project manager is that of a teacher. In many situations, you are literally educating all stakeholders regarding their roles and responsibilities in a project approach. But in all project situations, taking a teaching mentality—a mindset that sincerely wants others to learn, grow, and improve—rather than a judgmental view will be paramount to your leadership effectiveness.

10. **Strive for excellence**—An important trait of effective project leaders is their ability to create confidence that the project will be well managed and that it will accomplish its goals. How do you do this? Be very good at what you do, know what you are doing, and exude competence and professionalism (note—I did not say arrogance). The three simple keys here are be prepared, be organized, and never stop learning and improving.

11. **Compensate for weaknesses**—A leader is humble enough, has enough self-awareness, and is team-focused enough to recognize personal weaknesses. From this recognition, the leader then builds a team and delegates responsibilities to properly compensate. Again, it is difficult to be proficient at everything, and it is much easier to leverage the strengths of yourself and of your team to get the job done.

12. **Showcase self-control**—As a rule, most effective project leaders are models of self-control. They are consistent and positive in their behaviors and are generally immune from egocentric approaches and significant shifts or swings in their emotional stability (especially negative ones). In addition, they are able to remain calm under pressure and serve as a model for others during stressful times.

Depending on your experiences, organizational culture, and education, these project leadership keys might seem perfectly natural to you or they might seem like the ramblings of academia management theory. In either case, I can attest that each is important to your ongoing project leadership effectiveness.

 NOTE The servant leadership approach to project management gives you the best chance of doing the right work, the right way, for the right people.

 TIP When dealing with people, nothing beats a face-to-face meeting and a humble spirit.

Power of Servant Leadership Approach

Although we discussed numerous project leadership keys in the previous section, it really boils down to a simple, practical mindset that drives the thoughts, words, and actions of an effective project leader. It is a mindset of "service first" and not "me first." Personally, I had served as a project manager for many years before I ever learned that there was a name for the natural approach that I took to managing projects. The approach is called servant leadership, and it was popularized by Robert Greenleaf in 1970 in his book *The Servant as Leader.* Since then, the philosophy of servant leadership has been steadily growing in popularity and now serves as the foundation for most modern leadership training programs.

One of the main reasons I took this type of approach naturally is because it just made sense. In a project environment, where you are stakeholder-focused, where you must rely on yourself, where you must effectively relate to others to get work done, and where you must completely understand the needs and requirements of your customers to deliver the proper solution, it just seems to be a very practical path to take.

To me, it is a synergistic approach for any organization (or project) that values strong customer-service and team-focused approaches in their leaders.

To better illustrate what is meant by a servant leadership approach, and why I think this approach gives you the best chance of doing the right work, the right way, for the right people on your project, let's look at the prominent characteristics of this philosophy:

- Asserts a strong service orientation; lead by expanding service to others

- Emphasizes listening, patience, respect, and responsiveness

- Takes the perspective of others; maintains the best interest of others

- Accepts responsibility; takes initiative

- Encourages collaboration and trust; empowers individuals

- Seeks growth and improvement in all team members, organization, and community

- Solicits input and feedback from all stakeholders, especially in the decision-making process

- Insists on the use of skills to influence and persuade, not manipulate

- Spotlights a strong integrity principle—the ethical use of power

Again, like all project management and leadership skills, a servant leadership mindset is not an all-or-nothing approach. It is a spectrum between a total egocentric, leader-first mindset on one end and a complete servant-first thought pattern on the other end. The goal is to do your best, continue to learn, and work to improve over time, just as you do with the other skill set areas.

THE ABSOLUTE MINIMUM

At this point, you should have a solid understanding of the following:

- You lead people but manage processes.
- All project management skill sets are interlaced with leadership skills.
- Project leadership is not the sole domain of the project manager.
- The 12 keys to better project leadership include the following:
  - Focus on the people
  - Provide a clear picture of the project goals and how to get there
  - Look at the project from the perspective of the other stakeholders
  - Earn their trust
  - Earn their respect
  - Facilitate progress
  - Take ownership and responsibility
  - Be resilient, adaptable, and flexible
  - Be a teacher
  - Strive for excellence
  - Compensate for any weaknesses
  - Demonstrate self-control
- A servant leadership approach to project management is a practical, common-sense mindset that gives you the best opportunity for project success.
- For more information on servant leadership, check out the Greenleaf Center for Servant Leadership at www.greenleaf.org.

Figure 16.2 summarizes the main points reviewed in this chapter.

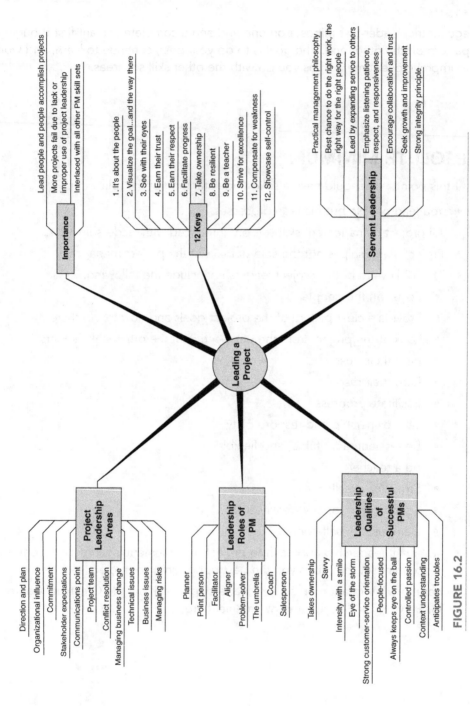

FIGURE 16.2

Overview of leading a project.

MANAGING PROJECT COMMUNICATIONS

Communication is the fuel that drives project success, and the mishandling of it is a top-five reason why projects struggle. You've likely heard this mantra before, but what does this really mean, why is it true, and more importantly, how do we handle our project communications effectively?

In this chapter, we answer these questions, review what we mean by project communications, think about why effective communication cannot be taken for granted, and study the key principles and best practices leveraged by effective communicators. With this knowledge, you will greatly increase your own personal effectiveness and position your project for the best outcome possible.

NOTE Per PMI (Project Management Institute), project managers should spend 90% of their time communicating.

What Are Project Communications?

The communications of a project include all means and manners by which the project interacts with all its stakeholders. This not only includes the standard, formal communication items such as

- Status reports
- Progress review meetings
- Kickoff meetings
- Executive reports
- Presentations
- Financial reports
- Government (or external agency) reports
- Issue logs
- Risk logs
- Change request logs
- Role-responsibility matrix
- Project organization chart
- Any project meeting (in any form/option)
- Any project deliverable
- Project collaboration tools

It can also include organizational change management communications, such as

- Project name/identity
- Project website (portal)
- Enterprise social networking platforms
- Organizational change management plan

- Frequently Asked Questions (FAQs) references

- Awareness campaigns

- Newsletters

- Public relations notices

- Roadshows

- One-on-one meetings with key stakeholders

Although the nature of your individual project (number and type of stakeholders, location of stakeholders, and overall project risk level) dictates how many of these elements are part of your project, the next set of project communications is included on every project, and is likely the most important part of project communications: the day-to-day, interpersonal communications that occur between the project team and the project stakeholders. This includes interactions in the following forms, plus others:

- Face-to-face

- Telephone

- Email

- Instant messaging (individual or group)

- Voice mail

- Texting

- Conferencing (audio, web, or video)

- Meetings

- Team collaboration tools

Later in this chapter, we review simple but powerful tips to improve your interpersonal communication skills, and we review important reminders to help you choose the best medium/tool for your desired message.

 NOTE Solid project managers know there are two skills that will carry them in almost any project situation: organization and communication.

The Importance of Project Communications

Project communications are not only important for the obvious reason—keeping individual stakeholders properly and consistently informed on the status, progress, and impact of the project—they are a determinant factor to the overall success of the project. Why is this? Here are a few key reasons:

- **Managing expectations**—We discuss managing expectations in greater detail in the next chapter, but for now, we'll just say that the quality and effectiveness of your communications will have a tremendous impact on stakeholder perceptions regarding the project and your role as a leader.

- **Managing the project team**—Your ability to communicate is the prominent factor affecting how well you manage and lead the core project team.

- **Reducing conflicts**—There are enough challenges executing your average project with the customary time, fiscal, and resource constraints without adding unnecessary conflicts that result from misperceptions, lack of information, or nonexistent issues, all of which result from ineffective communications.

- **Saving grace**—Solid project managers know there are two skills that will carry them in almost any project situation: organization and communication. Being excellent in these areas, especially project communications, will compensate for shortcomings in almost every other area.

Why Communicating Can Be Tough

Before we review key principles and best practices, let's make sure we understand why we cannot take communications for granted. On one hand, we know instinctively that there are many factors that impact the communications process—primarily because we live it every waking minute. On the other hand, many of us don't seem to incorporate this reality into how we communicate.

The goal of any communication is to have the receiver end up with an understanding (resulting perception) that equals the meaning intended by the sender (intended message). It sounds so simple, doesn't it? Yet, as Figure 17.1 depicts, there are many challenges facing the accomplishment of this simple goal.

Challenges Facing Effective Communications

FIGURE 17.1

Challenges facing effective communications.

For any message to accomplish its goal, it must clear two key hurdles. First, it must register with the receiver—it must hit their radar screen. Depending on the current state of the receiver (physical state, emotional state), other things happening in the environment (noise), and ability of the receiver to focus and listen to the message, this may or may not occur. Second, if it does land on the receiver's radar screen, the message must then pass through a series of filters in the receiver's mind, including past experiences, assumptions, expectations, cultural influences, values, and beliefs. And then, even when the message clears these two primary hurdles without significant distortion, the receiver's general ability to decode the message will vary depending on their natural learning style (such as auditory, visual, or kinesthetic). Heck, when you think about it, it's a wonder we ever clearly communicate anything.

So why bring all this up? Three reasons:

1. As a sender, recognize that successfully getting your message across is not trivial and cannot be assumed.

2. As a receiver, recognize the factors that can affect your ability to accurately understand (or hear) what the sender is trying to communicate.

3. Most importantly, it gives your ego an out. Too many people let their egos get in the way of improving their communications. Don't take it personally if you are not understood the first time. As mentioned, there are many challenges. The more you can take your ego out of the equation and focus on understanding, the better your communication abilities will become.

Seven Powerful Principles

Let's take a look at the seven key principles employed by most effective project communicators:

 CAUTION In organizations with standard project reports, don't assume these meet the information needs of your individual stakeholders. Be willing to adjust to better meet their needs.

1. **Plan your communications**—Like every other aspect of managing projects, you want and need to plan your project communications. The goal of communications planning is to ensure that all the stakeholders involved in the project have the information they need, when they need it, to fulfill their responsibilities. The key factors that affect communications planning and the communication requirements for a project include the following:

    -   Sponsoring organizational structure

    -   Results of stakeholder analysis

    -   Reporting relationships

    -   Functional areas involved in the project

    -   Number of people involved in the project

    -   Physical location of the project stakeholder

    -   Information needs of each stakeholder

    -   Experience level of project team members

    -   Availability of technology

    -   Immediacy and frequency of information needs

    -   Desired form of project communications

- Expected length of the project

- Organizational risk level of project

- Expected change impact on end users

- Organizational culture

- Level of external communications needed

- Procurement contracts

- Any constraints advised by legal counsel

After the specific communication requirements are determined for your project, make sure to do these two things:

- Document this information in a project communications management plan.

- Ensure that all formal project communications (and the work to produce them) is included in the WBS and project schedule.

2. **Remember the basics**—The three most powerful communication techniques are also the simplest. Why are these techniques powerful? They work and most people don't do them, so the contrast is very noticeable.

- **Make it a high priority**—Don't shortcut project communications; show respect for stakeholders.

- **Use your manners**—Be polite; show appreciation and gratitude.

- **Follow through**—If you say you are going to do something, do it.

3. **Five Cs of communication**—Keep the five Cs in mind when composing or delivering any project communication:

- **Clear**—State the subject; stay on subject; hold the receiver's hand through the message; use appropriate terms.

- **Concise**—Get to the point; limit scope of the message.

- **Courteous**—Be polite; watch your tone.

- **Consistent**—Use appropriate tone, medium for intended message; all message elements should support intended meaning.

- **Compelling**—Give them a reason to pay attention.

4. **Take responsibility for understanding**—This hits at the mindset you need for effective communications. Key points include the following:

   - Invest the effort, patience, and determination to make sure you are clearly understood.

   - Employ effective listening skills to ensure you have clearly understood what the other person has intended.

   - Be flexible.

   - Tailor your communications content to best fit the information needs of each target audience (project team, customers, senior management, or personnel management).

   - Pay attention. Notice the feedback. If what you are doing is not working, be willing to adjust.

   - Don't assume understanding—always clarify, ask questions, verify. Focus on taking the other person's perspective in all communications.

5. **Build relationships**—Effective communicators know that the bridge between people is built on trust, rapport, and personal connection. Be eager and willing to invest the time to build one-on-one relationships with your key stakeholders, especially early in the project. In addition, a relationship focus helps create an open and honest environment, which is better suited for dealing with natural project challenges.

 TIP Responsibility for project communications is an excellent project management apprentice opportunity.

6. **Be proactive**—Your enemies in project communications are surprise, doubt, and uncertainty, so being proactive is another key mindset and approach principle. Per the communications plan, keep your targeted audiences informed on a consistent basis. Anticipate any additional information needs. Never leave stakeholders wondering or needing to call you first.

7. **People and politics go together**—Another name for this is "don't be naïve." Effective communicators demonstrate an understanding and savviness for the political nature of the project environment. They understand the political implications of any potential communication and make sure to look at it from other perspectives before delivering the intended message.

 TIP Send emails to stakeholders that contain direct URL links to the targeted project communication.

Best Practices of Effective Project Communicators

To better understand these communication principles and improve your communication abilities, let's review the common best practices used by effective project communicators. We'll look at general communications management, status reports, conducting meetings, interpersonal skills, and the best use of the common communication media.

General Communications Management

First, review the best practices of general project communications management:

- **Assign a point person**—To ensure quality and consistency in project communications, make sure to make specific project team members accountable for official project communications. On most projects, you (the project manager) will serve as the communications point. However, on larger projects, you might need to delegate responsibility for certain communication items or for communication to targeted stakeholders. This might include working closely with the company's human resources, marketing, or corporate communications departments.

- **Leverage natural strengths**—Although you will always need to leverage many communication forms and media, take advantage of any natural communications strengths you might possess and use the other methods to support those strengths.

 NOTE Researchers believe 50%–90% of a message is conveyed via nonverbal means (cues, signals, and symbols). Thus, the more nonverbal language present, the richer the communication.

- **Perform stakeholder analysis**—As part of your communications planning, perform a stakeholder analysis. This analysis should provide insights into the needs and motivations of each stakeholder. In addition, use this assessment to validate what type of project communications are needed to properly support each stakeholder audience and manage their expectations.

 TIP Set up distribution lists (voice mail, email, group messaging, and collaboration portals) to streamline communicating with project team members and project stakeholders.

- **Use push and pull**—Effective project communicators use both push (send it to them) and pull (make it available to them) communication methods. With the advent of central project repositories, the pull method has experienced growing popularity. Although the use of this method is excellent for anytime, on-demand information needs by stakeholders, do not rely on it for important or urgent project communications. Make sure to send (push) any important, urgent project communications directly to the targeted stakeholders. In addition, if you are using team collaboration technologies (such as Microsoft Teams or SharePoint), you can leverage both push and pull methods simultaneously by having stakeholders subscribe to alerts that notify them automatically (push) if there is an update to a given artifact. The alert contains a link that the stakeholder can use to access the targeted artifact (pull).

 CAUTION Closely monitor how any pull communications are working. If stakeholders are not staying informed or engaged in a timely manner, guide them to push communication methods and/ or sign up for alerts.

- **Make it easy**—If you want to score big points with your stakeholders, make it easy on them to understand what you are sending them (provide summaries) or asking them to do (provide context and purpose). Don't make them search for things (include referenced items with your communication or links to those items). Your stakeholders are busy with many tasks and priorities, and they don't enjoy feeling confused and unsure. Any efforts you make that enable them to quickly understand what you're delivering or what you're asking them to do will always be appreciated, and these efforts will increase your value to the overall project.

 TIP Send project documents as PDF files or send links to those documents to reduce potential conflicts with software tools, minimize the size of email attachments, and protect communication content.

- **Keep the information flowing**—A simple but powerful service provided by many effective project communicators is to make sure the right people have the right information to perform their roles. In many organizations, information tends not to flow easily from one group to another. An effective project manager looks for these bottleneck points and simply acts as a conduit for better information flow.

- **Take communication decisions seriously**—Consider your relationship, the message content, and available media options when making any communication decision. In general, certain communication options are better for different types of situations, and effective communicators choose wisely.

- **Confirm technology and user training**—Always ensure that the technologies to be used for your particular communication are working properly and that the affected stakeholders understand how to leverage them correctly.

Communications Options

Now more than ever, many communication mediums are available to your project. To best manage project communications, you need to understand the strengths and limits of each option, so that you use the medium that is most appropriate for the type of relationship you have with the targeted audience and for the content of the message. The right choices can improve project productivity, facilitate open communications, and build stronger stakeholder relationships. The wrong choices create misperceptions, confusion, and weaker stakeholder relationships.

To assist your communications decision making, Table 17.1 reviews the best uses and important notes for the common communication options.

 TIP   When possible, leverage online team collaboration tools and enterprise social networking tools to manage project communications.

 TIP   Whenever possible, ensure that any project communication method and tool supports the ability to securely access information anytime from anywhere using the common technology platforms (such as smartphones, tablets, laptops, and so on) leveraged by the project stakeholders.

 CAUTION   Be wary of the use of unsecured communication tools by project team members while conducting project work/business, especially where there are any possible confidentiality concerns/risks.

 TIP   Establishing and building stakeholder relationships is a higher priority than enforcing a strict meeting protocol.

 NOTE   Effective interpersonal skills are a trademark of servant leaders.

TABLE 17.1 Summary of Project Communication Options

Communication Option	Best Use(s)	Important Notes
Face-to-Face	Best method to start business relationships and earn trust. Best for sensitive, interpersonal, or difficult messages. Best for communicating emotional and nonverbal messages.	Richest, most efficient method. Only way to do business in many cultures. "Showing up" demonstrates commitment.
Videoconferencing	Best substitute for face-to-face meetings.	Increasing availability thru web conferencing tools. Make sure technology works in advance. Reduces meeting participants' ability to multitask during meeting.
Direct Audio (Telephone)	When interactive conversation is needed. When visual communication is not needed. When urgency is important. When privacy is important.	If placed on speaker phone, assume there are others in the room.
Voice Mail	Short messages. When common message needs to be sent to multiple people. When targeted stakeholder is auditory-oriented or is inundated with email.	If lengthy message, summarize message content up front. Avoid for controversial or sensitive communications. Make sure stakeholder checks voice mail regularly.
Electronic Mail	When common message needs to be sent to multiple people. When targeted stakeholder is visually oriented or prefers email communications. When communication record is needed.	See the section "Tips for Email (and Other Text-Only) Communications."

Communication Option	Best Use(s)	Important Notes
Instant Messaging	For daily interactions of project team. For virtual project teams. Group/team IM tools can facilitate team collaboration.	Helps to build community and project team intimacy. Not appropriate for formal work relationships. Keeps the office quieter. Most group/team IM tools can record discussions. Monitor privacy and confidentiality concerns.
Texting	When brief, one-on-one information needs to be shared between people where informal, friendly relationship is established. When immediate response is not needed. When communication does not warrant a phone call or people cannot take or receive a phone call.	Although technology is improving, you should not assume message is always received or received in correct order (if more than 160 characters).
Audio Conferencing	When group collaboration is needed and face-to-face meeting is not possible. When a desktop or document does not need to be shared in real time.	More social presence than email or IM. Allows participants to multitask and do other things, which makes level-of-engagement and meeting quality an ongoing project risk. Most web conferencing tools provide audio too. Most systems allow conference to be recorded.
Web Conferencing with Audio	When group collaboration is needed and face-to-face meeting is not possible. When data or presentation needs to be shared. Virtual training sessions.	Same challenges as audio conferencing. Invest more prep time on technology readiness and training. Able to record questions. Record and make available for later access.

Communication Option	Best Use(s)	Important Notes
Web Conferencing with Video	When visible group collaboration is needed and face-to-face meeting is not possible.	Participants need enough privacy and environment control to allow for video cameras.
	When facial expressions and/or nonverbal communications need to be visible.	Ensures higher level of engagement and participation; reduces multitasking.
	When data or presentation needs to be shared.	Invest more prep time on technology readiness and training.
		Record and make available for later access.
Project/Team Collaboration Tools	When ongoing group collaborations on work products or topic discussions need to be documented.	Builds community and project team intimacy.
Social Networking Tools	When project information needs to be shared outside of core working team.	Must determine use level of social networking tools by targeted audiences (comfort, frequency, and so on).
	When a sense of community needs to be established or improved, especially for external stakeholders.	Enterprise social networking tools (such as Yammer) can be used when access to project information must be secured and limited to authorized users.
	When quick, real-time feedback is needed from external stakeholders to facilitate project decisions.	

Tips for Email (and Other Text-Only) Communications

In the world of project collaboration and social networking tools, email might seem downright archaic, but there are reasons why it is still around, especially in the business world. Everyone uses it, especially senior management; it's more private; it provides a searchable and retrievable record of your communications; it enables you to send a communication without interrupting the recipient and enables this person to respond at a time that is convenient; and most people can get to their email from anywhere (given the increased use of smartphones and other mobile devices). That being said, review the following key tips that will improve the quality of your email (and perhaps other text-only) communications:

- Use email when a message needs to be communicated consistently to more than one stakeholder.

- Limit use of email for work product reviews, other collaboration activities, and topic discussions, especially when you're using team collaboration tools.

- If sending a message containing protected data whether in the body of the message or as an attachment, make sure email is sent with the proper encryption method for your organization.

- Avoid use of text-only communication for controversial or sensitive communications.

- Do not send text-only communication when you are feeling negative emotions.

- Clarify how frequently the intended recipient checks and responds to email.

- Gauge and clarify the organizational culture for email communications.

- Clarify how supporting materials should be handled (sent as attachments, direct links to materials on project repository, and so on).

- Avoid lengthy emails whenever possible.

- If a lengthy message is required, summarize content upfront, and highlight any actions that you are requesting.

- Use the subject line effectively—ensure it is consistent with topic/focus of message, and use it to highlight action needed.

- Use numbered lists to assist replies and references to original message topics...avoid using bullets.

- Limit the use of the carbon copy (Cc:) function to those who truly need to have awareness of the message or those who have requested to be copied.

- Use the blind carbon copy (Bcc:) function when you need to protect the privacy of distribution group membership.

- If written communications are not your strength, consider delegating important project communications to someone on the team who is skilled in this area.

- Although email, text messaging, and instant messaging are more direct and more private than project collaboration and social networking sites, do not forget that any text-only communication can be printed, read over someone's shoulder, and forwarded.

Status Reporting

The following are the best status reporting practices of effective project communicators:

- **Be consistent**—Provide progress status reports on a consistent, regular basis as defined in the project communications plan.

- **Target reports**—Provide the appropriate level of detail for the targeted audience.

- **Use bullets and numbered lists**—Use bullet points and numbered lists to summarize key facts; keep it short; enable the reader to quickly gauge the state of the project.

- **Employ visuals**—Because most people are visual learners and most senior management types need to get a thorough understanding of project status and/or the project issue quickly, look for opportunities to provide information in a visual format.

- **Use color-coding**—If not defined for the organization, establish three general threshold levels for key project metrics and critical success factors. For each level, associate the appropriate stoplight color: green, yellow, or red. Then use these colors to communicate the health of each key project metric on the status report. This enables senior management to get a quick reading on the project's health.

- **Leverage exception-based approach**—Use the main (first part) of the status report to highlight any exceptions or variances to the project plan. Then provide details in the appendix section. This format should enable you to provide one status report that meets the needs of most, if not all, of your key stakeholders.

Meetings

The best meeting practices of effective project communicators include the following:

- **Know your game plan**—Determine the overall goal and objectives for the meeting; invite the right people; structure the meeting appropriately; determine what preparation is needed by the meeting participants to make the meeting useful.

- **Post an agenda**—Whenever possible, post an agenda in advance of the meeting. In either case, make sure to review the agenda at the start of the meeting and check whether any modifications are needed.

- **Facilitate**—Be the meeting director. Review and set meeting context; review meeting ground rules upfront; keep everyone engaged; keep the meeting flowing; solicit feedback; summarize key points; seek consensus.

- **Stay on track**—Keep the meeting on topic; set time limits (timebox) for agenda items; avoid trying to solve problems in meetings—schedule a follow-up meeting instead.

- **Leverage conferencing tools**—When some people are participating virtually, leverage combinations of audio, video, and web conferencing tools to improve meeting quality.

- **Take notes**—Delegate someone to take notes of meeting decisions and action items.

- **Attain closure**—Before adjourning the meeting, review all action items (including responsible owners and targeted completion times), summarize meeting results, schedule any necessary follow-up meetings, and thank attendees for their active participation and time.

- **Post minutes**—Distribute (post) meeting minutes to meeting participants and affected parties within 24 hours of the meeting whenever possible. If action is required from nonattendees, seek their commitment before distributing minutes, or note items on which they have not been consulted.

Interpersonal Skills

The next set of best practices is likely the most important because it impacts the quality of all your project communications—the formal and the more frequent day-to-day interpersonal communications that occur between the project team and the project stakeholders. The following list notes the key interpersonal skills demonstrated by effective communicators:

- Listen with a purpose.

- Be humble.

- Think before responding.

- Take their perspective.

- Don't be judgmental.

- Be interested in others.

- Seek to understand what they do, why they do it, and what pains they are experiencing.

- Validate perceptions before responding.
- Show appreciation for their time and contributions.
- Ask questions to confirm and improve your understanding.
- Summarize what the speaker said.
- Make people feel heard.
- Focus on building relationships.
- Stay in control of your emotions.
- Don't assume that a negative response by others is personal—most of the time it's not.
- Avoid interrupting, if at all possible.
- Validate that you are being understood.
- Avoid terms and tones that imply judgment, guilt, or wrongdoing on other parties.

THE ABSOLUTE MINIMUM

At this point, you should have a solid understanding of the following:

- Effective communications are important to managing perceptions, managing expectations, managing the project team, reducing conflicts, and overcoming any project management gap in other areas.
- The five Cs of effective communications are clear, concise, courteous, consistent, and compelling.
- The most important communication skill is listening.
- The three most powerful communication techniques are also the simplest: Give it your full attention, use your manners, and follow through.
- Always match the communication tool/method with the message content, purpose, and audience.
- Consistently strive to improve the effectiveness of email communications.
- The most important mindset trait for effective communications is taking responsibility for understanding.
- Leverage web conferencing tools to improve the quality of virtual team meetings.
- Improve your knowledge and prowess of meeting collaboration tools, especially the one used by your organization to enhance your meeting management processes.

The map in Figure 17.2 summarizes the main points reviewed in this chapter.

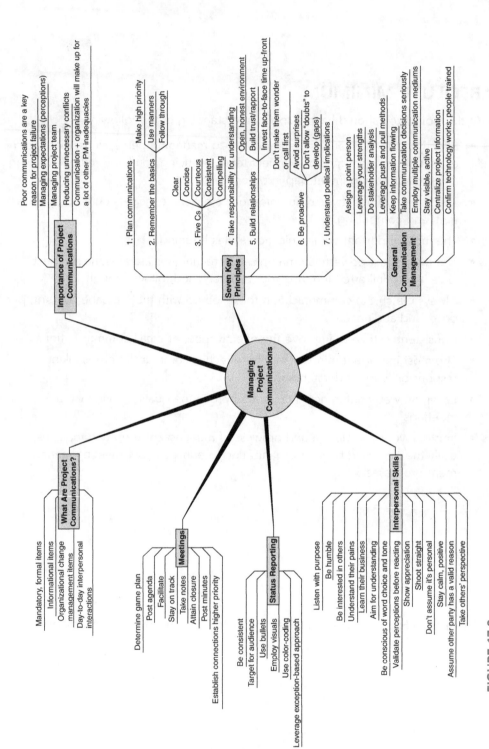

FIGURE 17.2

Overview of managing project communications.

IN THIS CHAPTER

- Discover the essential components for successfully managing stakeholder expectations

- Understand why managing expectations is not the same as managing scope

- Find out the four critical aspects of stakeholder expectations

- Understand why completing a project on time, on budget, and within scope does not guarantee success

- Learn why many expectation issues originate during requirements definition

- Review proven guidelines to better requirements definition and management

18

MANAGING EXPECTATIONS

Do you believe that managing stakeholders' expectations is nothing more than properly managing project scope? Do you believe that managing stakeholders' expectations is nothing more than effective project communications? Do you believe that every project is successful that completes on time and on budget? If you answered yes to any of these questions, then this chapter is for you.

Value of Reviewing Stakeholder Expectations Management

Although managing stakeholder expectations speaks to the essence of project management and is a key objective of all project definition, planning, and control activities, it is often ignored in introductory project management books. Why? Well, I think there are many reasons, but there are two main ones:

1. Many consider it to be an advanced project management topic.

2. Many people do not know how to manage expectations and thus just lump it with other project management activities.

Although I agree that it is very difficult to isolate strict expectations management activities or talk about managing expectations without discussing other aspects of project management, there is tremendous value in taking a concentrated look at this:

- **Expectations are a critical success factor**—Although scope, budget, and schedule are core elements of managing expectations, there is more—and if you ignore it, the odds for real project success are greatly diminished. We get into this more later in this chapter.

- **You can make a difference**—Because expectations deal with perceptions and often get into the "art" of project management, they can be less tangible, which makes it more challenging to offer guidance. This won't stop us. We review several powerful, tangible techniques you can employ to better guide stakeholder expectations.

- **Sign of project management maturity**—Nothing says "experience" and "I'm not a rookie" more than a project manager who understands the importance of guiding stakeholder expectations and who constantly focuses on this aspect of their project.

Although we have referenced many tools and techniques in earlier chapters that help manage expectations, this chapter provides the opportunity to highlight those important items one more time and the opportunity to take a focused look at this vital area of project management. We explore the critical aspects of expectations, the key components of successfully managing stakeholder expectations, the common mistakes to avoid, and the essential principles and techniques that will guide us in any project environment.

Critical Aspects of Expectations

If you are going to attempt to influence something, you first need to know what makes up that "something." For expectations, there is one key concept and four critical components that need to be understood for effective management.

Balancing Reality and Perception

The key concept is that expectations are shaped by both reality and perception. In an ideal project, both the reality and perception of project objectives, performance, targeted results, and expected impact are aligned upfront among all stakeholders during project definition and planning, and then remain this way throughout the project. However, this ideal situation is elusive. Even when expectations are aligned during planning, there are many influences and factors that can alter expectations during the course of the project. This relationship is depicted in Figure 18.1.

FIGURE 18.1

The expectations balance.

As a project manager, your challenge is to guide the actual "real" performance of the project while simultaneously aligning and balancing the perception of each stakeholder. This work is a dynamic, ongoing venture that is only complete when the project is closed.

Not Just Scope Management

There is more to managing expectations than just managing scope. Now, don't get me wrong; managing scope is a very important part of managing expectations, but it's not everything. There are four critical components of expectations. Each expectation element is important to the success of the project and is subject to the natural push and pull between project reality and stakeholder perceptions. This relationship is portrayed in Figure 18.2.

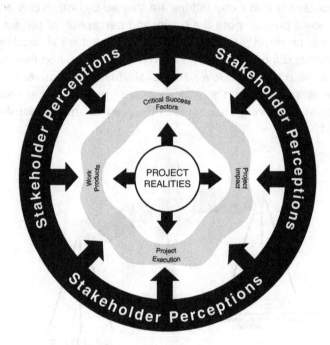

FIGURE 18.2

Aspects of expectations management.

Let's review each expectation component in greater detail, explain the specific elements included in each group, and discuss some of the tools and techniques that you can use to help manage each part.

- **Critical Success Factors**—This aspect includes the traditional measuring rods of scope, schedule, and budget. In addition, it includes any additional acceptance criteria that you established with your key stakeholders during project definition and planning. The heart of project management (and nearly this entire book) is focused on managing expectations around these elements, but the key tools are a solid project definition document, a realistic schedule, a baseline budget, early detection of performance variances, and disciplined change control.

- **Project Impact**—This component highlights the change impact of the project output (results, solution, and work products). It accounts for any work, process, or organizational change experienced by any stakeholder as a result of the project outcome. This aspect is commonly neglected by less-experienced organizations and project managers. As Dr. Stephen Covey (a world-famous personal development coach and author of *The 7 Habits* book series) always says, the key here is to think (and plan) with the end in mind. With this clarity, you can better communicate a common vision of the project outcome and help stakeholders prepare for the changes that will affect them.

 NOTE The expectation component classifications are academic in nature and are there to serve discussion and review. Many expectation elements could be placed in more than one of these categories.

A common mistake made in expectations management is to sell or commit to requirements that cannot be met given the project constraints. This is often done in efforts to get business, make the customer happy, or instill confidence in the team's abilities. The "under-promise, over-deliver" principle is one that reminds us that it is much better with regard to expectations management to promise less and deliver more.

- **Work Products**—This category covers things such as "that's not what I asked for," "that's not what I meant," and "oh no, you gave me exactly what I asked for." This could be considered a part of project scope, but depending on the level of detail in your scope statement, it might not be adequately addressed. This category deals with the detailed expectations surrounding the individual work products that each stakeholder has. At a minimum, it focuses on requirements management, quality management, and overall project approach. We discuss key requirements management techniques that greatly improve your effectiveness here.

- **Project Execution**—This final component deals with the day-to-day execution of the project. Although not as critical as the other aspects, a lack of attention to these elements will certainly create situations that can easily lead to underperforming projects, and then to major expectations management activities. This category deals with the efficiency and effectiveness of the project team, and with the confidence the stakeholders have in them to successfully deliver the targeted solution and in you to lead them there. Common elements in this group include interactions between team and client stakeholders, and clarity of roles, responsibilities, work processes, and work assignments.

We review many of these elements in greater detail in Chapter 19, "Keys to Better Project Team Performance." In addition, many of the communication and leadership techniques we reviewed in Chapters 16, "Leading a Project," and 17, "Managing Project Communications," come into play here. Important principles to remember here: Make sure team members are prepared for their interactions with stakeholders; do not assume stakeholders have a clear understanding of project processes and their work assignments; always look at the project from their perspective; and proactively review (with a gentle touch) key tasks and targeted completion dates.

Although we have broken down expectations into various components, which are summarized in Table 18.1, it's important to remember that effective expectations management is not complicated. The success formula for each aspect of expectations management is relatively straightforward:

- **Get real**—Set realistic expectations; get initial agreement (buy-in) from affected stakeholders; review assumptions and constraints; talk about it; address it; get clarity and understanding.

- **Keep it balanced**—Manage changes; align project reality with stakeholder perceptions; proactively communicate; educate; constantly validate and affirm perceptions; regularly assess performance; reset expectations as needed.

- **Follow through**—Deliver; honor the agreements; get the work done; "under-promise, over-deliver."

 NOTE Most of the principles depend greatly on the effectiveness of your communication and interpersonal skills. Your ability to manage the perceptions of each individual associated with the project is the key to managing expectations.

 NOTE The main factor affecting the nature of kickoff meetings is, "Where are you in the planning process?" If detailed planning is complete, the kickoff meeting is more of an informational session. If not, the kickoff meeting can be used as a detail planning workshop.

 TIP Utilize mini-kickoff meetings at the beginning of each project phase, not just the start of the entire project, to reset expectations.

Note that agile approaches have this concept built in through regular planning and review sessions for each sprint or increment.

TABLE 18.1   Summary of Critical Expectation Components

Expectation Area	Elements	Key Tools and Techniques	Notes
Critical Success Factors	Scope statement Project budget Target dates Performance versus cost versus time Acceptance criteria Agreement on what defines success	Project definition document Project plan Change control Performance reporting Realistic schedule Kickoff meetings Milestone reviews	Be proactive No surprises Ensure right people are informed of changes Forecast missed deadlines
Project Impact	ROI Key Performance Indicators (KPIs) Individual work task changes Business process flow changes Organizational change impact	Acceptance criteria Stakeholder analysis Prototypes, simulations Future workflow models Pilots Phased implementations	Often neglected May need separate deployment project Organizational change management plan needed
Work Products	Requirements Deliverables Interim deliverables	Requirements management Quality management Iterative development Prototypes, scenarios, and simulations Pilot implementations Product reviews and sign-offs	Get something tangible early Heavy customer involvement Use internal team QA reviews
Project Execution	Decision-making process Roles and responsibilities Work assignments Project processes Common goals	Responsibility matrix Realistic schedule Resource plan Team charter	Take other perspective Don't assume understanding or clarity Be aware of busy team members

Expectation Area	Elements	Key Tools and Techniques	Notes
	Personal credibility	Kickoff meetings	Use gentle touch to proactively remind team of key tasks, responsibilities, and dates
	Avoids issues	Walkthrough schedule, processes	
	Team interactions with stakeholders	Coaching team members	
	Leadership confidence	Internal reviews	Always set context to improve understanding
			Educate along the way

TIP Understanding the process flow helps you identify stakeholders, scope boundaries, change impact issues, and better requirements.

EDUCATE YOUR STAKEHOLDERS

Appropriate stakeholders should be educated on the following points at a minimum:

- Requirements serve as the primary target for the project and as the foundation for detailed project planning.

- Walk stakeholders through the various techniques and methods to be employed in the requirements definition process.

- If using an agile approach, educate stakeholders on the process for capturing and managing requirements in this environment and how it is different from a traditional waterfall methodology approach.

- Changes to requirements affect cost and schedule, and they cost more the later in the project they are made.

- Requirements can serve as provisions in the contract.

CAUTION Expectations that cannot be quantified should be identified as project risks. Make sure your project assumptions are consistent with your final requirements.

 TIP Translate performance and quality expectations into tangible, documented requirements.

Seven Master Principles of Expectations Management

Now that you have a good feel for the breadth of managing expectations, you can understand the value of many key project planning and project control fundamentals we reviewed in prior chapters. Before we do a quick encapsulation of those items and then delve into two other powerful tools for managing expectations—requirements management and kickoff meetings—let's look at the seven master principles that drive all expectations management activity:

1. **Get buy-in**—Whether it's the critical success criteria, resource and time commitments, or individual work assignments, invest the time and energy to gain their trust and to make sure you have genuine buy-in from the affected parties. This is why effective planning is a must.

2. **Take care of business**—This is the "blocking-and-tackling" fundamentals of project management. Set your baselines, manage to them, and properly handle and communicate any variances.

3. **Communicate the big picture**—With the end goal in mind, clearly sell the vision on where the project is going, what the targeted solution will be like, and why each work assignment is important. People want to know "why" and understand the importance of their role.

4. **Listen and be alert**—If stakeholders are not on the same page or have unstated expectations, there are always cues and signals. Look and listen for them and make it a priority to deal with them quickly. When we discuss managing requirements, probing for unstated expectations will be a key focus.

5. **Take their perspective**—We discussed leadership in Chapter 16, but its importance is worth re-emphasizing. This ability is a mainstay for effective expectations management, and it empowers you to anticipate the needs and concerns of your project stakeholders. It also drives a flexible mindset

that allows you to adapt approaches, plans, and specifications to best meet the situation at hand.

6. **Never assume**—This key principle needs constant attention. Many don't realize the assumptions they are working under until it is too late. To help you avoid assumptions, keep the following in mind:

   - Err on the side of overcommunication.

   - Always set context for all your communications.

   - Constantly confirm understanding.

   - Clearly communicate what is expected from each team member.

   - Continuously reset expectations.

   - Verify whether you have the correct solution to meet the project's objectives (rather than just validating documented requirements).

7. **Understand priorities**—There are always many stakeholders, often with their own distinct views of the world and sets of priorities. Although you always aim to find compromises that appeal to the entire group, it is important to understand the decision-making process and whose voices have greater influence and priority. In particular, always be very clear on who controls the budget for your project.

Essential Elements of Managing Expectations

Let's take a look at the essential tools and techniques that are available to the project manager to effectively manage stakeholder expectations.

Project Planning and Control Elements—A Quick Review

At many times during the chapters on defining, planning, and controlling a project, we referenced managing expectations as a key reason or benefit of specific project management tools and techniques. Table 18.2 and Table 18.3 summarize the most important project management tools, techniques, and actions to manage stakeholder expectations.

TABLE 18.2   Summary of Essential Planning Elements to Manage Project Expectations

Element	Impact on Expectations
Project Definition Document	Defines why we are doing this.
	Defines what organizational-level goal(s) is supported.
	Defines how this project fits/aligns with the other projects.
	Defines expected benefits from this project.
	Defines what will be done.
	Defines who is impacted.
	Defines how success will be measured.
Scope Statement	Sets boundaries for what will be done and what will not be done.
WBS	Enables stakeholders to see the work that must be done.
Project Budget	Sets cost and ROI expectations.
Estimates	Foundation for budget and schedule.
Assumptions and Constraints	Key for better expectations around estimates, scope, budget, and schedule.
Project Schedule	Sets time expectations.
Project Plan	Sets expectations for how project will be managed.
Project Organization Chart	Identifies and communicates who is involved and how team is structured.
Stakeholder Analysis	Defines who is affected and what their needs are.
Communications Plan	Defines how the communications needs of project stakeholders will be addressed.
Responsibility Matrix	Sets expectations regarding role and work tasks.
Project Approach	Stakeholders need to know what is going to happen and why approach needs to be tailored to best manage stakeholder expectations.

TABLE 18.3 Summary of Essential Control and Execution Elements to Manage Project Expectations

Element	Impact on Expectations
Kickoff meetings	Notification project is underway; facilitates expectation setting for the group.
Project approach	Maximizes requirements definition and product/system development approaches that provide early and frequent feedback loops and that focus on demonstrating tangible aspects of the targeted solution.
Status reports	Regular, consistent performance monitoring and reporting keeps everyone informed.
Change control	Allows scope, time, and budget expectations to be reset and controlled along the way.
Quality management	Focused on satisfying real customer needs and ensuring the solution does the right thing.
Risk management	Anticipates, forecasts, and attempts to avoid impacts to the critical success factors.
Issue management	Communicates issues to the right people.
Requirements management	Drives expectations on the product of the project (more on this later in this chapter).
Completion criteria	Clarifies expectations for any work package.
Formal sign-offs	Documents acceptance of work products at points in time. Used with milestone and work product reviews.
Reviews	Validates expectations of work products along the way.
Milestones and checkpoints	Validates expectations of project performance along the way.
Requirements traceability matrix	Keeps visibility of targeted requirements throughout the project process.
Product backlog	For agile projects, keeps visibility on targeted requirements. Entries are prioritized and continuously refined during the project.
Team charter	Communicates team rules and procedures (more on this in Chapter 19).

Leveraging Kickoff Meetings

Kickoff meetings are simple but powerful tools to help manage expectations. We could have discussed these in the chapter on project communications (Chapter 17), as is typically done, but kickoff meetings are such an instrumental tool in managing expectations, I felt it was better to do it here.

In general, a kickoff meeting is simple. Get all the targeted stakeholders together to officially review the project and get it underway. So why focus on this technique? Kickoff meetings are invaluable for accomplishing certain things related to expectations management, and many people either do not do them properly or underutilize them.

Primary Goals

The three primary goals for any kickoff meeting should include the following:

- Give official notification that the project (or project phase) is underway.

- Achieve a common expectation baseline for all stakeholders.

- Start the relationship-building process between project team, customers, and other stakeholders.

Key Recommendations

With these goals in mind, here are some key recommendations for better kickoff meetings:

- The meeting size, length, and logistics will vary depending on organizational culture, project size, number of stakeholders, project methodology, and project importance. Plan your kickoff meetings accordingly.

- As a rule, don't try to do too much or cover everything. Use follow-up, mini-kickoff meetings with focused groups or specific individuals to cover the details.

- For general kickoffs, get everyone there if possible, especially the executive sponsors.

- Set context for everyone. Focus on the "why." Review project purpose, objectives, and value to the business.

- Clarify the priorities, target goals, and critical success factors.

- Paint the picture. Enable everyone to visualize how the final solution will look, how it will affect them, and how all the pieces fit together.

- Get to know each other. Start the relationship-building and teamwork processes. Introduce everyone.

- Review roles and responsibilities and project team organization. Emphasize each person's role, expected time commitment, and value.

- Establish your leadership and the energy for the project. Set the tone; generate enthusiasm and motivation.

- Review important project plan items:
  - Scope and major deliverables
  - General approach (methodology)
  - Critical milestones
  - WBS
  - Schedule
  - Estimated effort and budget
  - Key assumptions, risks, and constraints
  - Key project communications processes
  - Process/procedures for monitoring project performance
- Whenever possible, hand out team keepsakes (or promotions) at the beginning of the project. It helps to build team unity and project awareness.
- Ask for feedback. Clarify any confusion now.
- Ensure people know what to do first/next (short-term). They should be clear on their next steps.

Requirements Management—The Difference Maker

A large percentage of expectation misunderstandings have their origins in the requirements gathering and requirements management processes. The frustrating thing about these situations is that most of them can or could be avoided. Although the subject of requirements definition is a field of study itself, we will leverage the Pareto principle here. We focus our attention on addressing the common requirements-related problems and the key principles and guidelines that make the most difference in your future requirements definition and management efforts.

Common Problems to Avoid

To better understand the value of the recommended principles and guidelines, let's take a quick review of the common problems with gathering and defining requirements:

- **Not well written**—Requirements are ambiguous, inconsistent, too high-level, or not clear.

CAUTION If requirements are not detailed upfront, be prepared to spend more time in testing or more time in evolutionary cycles.

- **Incomplete**—The list of requirements is not complete to properly define the solution.

- **Unstated expectations**—The list of requirements does not accurately reflect all the expectations held by the stakeholders for the targeted solution.

- **Inflexible process**—Although specifications do need to be agreed on and finalized at certain points, defining requirements is an evolutionary process and things do change. The system for managing requirements must anticipate this reality. This is one of the strong aspects of using an agile approach.

- **Inadequate definition process**—Using statements to describe a targeted solution creates many opportunities for misunderstandings and misperceptions—the age-old problem with language. In most cases, you need to employ other techniques and methods to verify that you are defining the right solution. Techniques that help stakeholders visualize the final work product or solution are especially helpful.

TIP Leverage techniques and methods that help stakeholders visualize the targeted solution during the requirements gathering and definition process.

- **Lack of education**—Often, the stakeholders who are defining the solution requirements don't fully understand the entire requirements process and the significance or impact of their decisions.

- **Ineffective review process**—Some examples include using a process that is not a good match for the reviewers' natural working method or schedule; using a process that does not ensure reviewers are engaged; or using a process that does not make it easy to see what changed from the previous version.

- **Using the wrong tool for the job**—In addition to the challenges with leveraging the right techniques and methods to elicit requirements, the wrong tool is used to capture, store, and manage the documented requirements. In many situations, a requirements management tool that uses a centralized database foundation is needed to properly handle the needs of the project, solution, or organization versus the document-based approach. See Chapter 25, "The Fun Never Stops," for more information on when a requirements management tool is needed.

Principles to Remember for Better Requirements Management

To help you develop better requirements and improve your ability to manage both requirements and expectations throughout the project, review the following principles:

- Requirements definition is an evolutionary process. Plan your project approach and requirements management tools accordingly.

- The requirements definition process should consist of a combination of gathering techniques. The specific techniques you choose should be based on risks and characteristics of the project.

- The requirements review and approval process should facilitate clear understanding and engaged participation, and ensure feedback is properly handled.

- Requirements should describe *what*, not *how*.

- Requirements should avoid any unnecessary constraints.

- Requirements should be complete, explicit, realistic, and understandable by all parties.

- Requirements should be linked to the intended solution.

- Requirements should be prioritized.

- Listen; do not pre-judge or draw conclusions too quickly.

- Strive to convert expectations into requirements.

- Educate appropriate stakeholders on the requirements process.

- If requirements are for an enhancement, change, or addition to an existing solution, update the original requirements artifacts that define the total working solution versus relying solely on new, specific, separate artifacts for the requested change.

- Use a tool to manage requirements that meets the needs of the project, solution, and organization.

CAUTION If requirements are for an enhancement, change, or addition to an existing solution, update the original requirements artifacts that define the total working solution versus relying solely on new, specific, separate artifacts for the requested change.

Guidelines for Better Requirements

To avoid the common problems identified earlier and greatly increase your requirements definition prowess, note these guidelines:

- Focus on user experience. Understand how the user interacts with the targeted solution.

- Understand the user's workflow.

- Understand the user's work environment.

- Always ask "why?"

- Include other non-language exhibits or models as part of the requirements definition.

- To drive out unstated expectations, understand the following from each user representative:

  - What are the biggest problems now, and why?

  - What functions or features will be the most useful, and why?

  - What aspect of the new solution are you most anticipating, and why?

  - What are your quality and performance expectations for the final solution, and why?

- To help make better design decisions, define requirements in both present and future needs whenever possible.

- Identify each requirement with a unique ID.

- Document any accompanying assumptions.

- Use a quality checklist to improve the effectiveness of your requirements.

- Monitor and control changes to requirements.

- Whenever possible, involve the people who will be testing the targeted solution in the requirements definition process.

- Use a requirements traceability matrix (RTM) to link each requirement to one or more aspects of the final solution. This is a powerful tool to ensure that every requirement is accounted for and to better control "gold-plating."

 TIP Leverage development approaches that enable stakeholders to see the product as soon as possible. Early feedback helps ensure alignment on requirements and engagement from customers.

THE ABSOLUTE MINIMUM

At this point, you should have a solid understanding of the following:

- The goal of managing expectations is to have a common set of expectations shared by all stakeholders in terms of what is being delivered, what it will accomplish, when, and at what cost.
- Managing expectations is more than managing project scope.
- The master principles of expectations management are the following:

  1. Get buy-in

  2. Take care of business

  3. Communicate the big picture

  4. Listen and be alert

  5. Take the stakeholders' perspective

  6. Never assume

- Two key tools for managing expectations are kickoff meetings and requirements management.
- Requirements management mistakes to avoid:
  - Poorly written requirements
  - Incomplete set of requirements
  - Unstated expectations
  - Inflexible process
  - Inadequate definition process
  - Lack of stakeholder education
  - Ineffective review process
  - Using the wrong tool for the job
  - Focus on the user experience for better requirements

- Other key expectations management tips include the following:
  - Avoid surprises
  - Keep people informed of status (project health)
  - Avoid last-minute communications
  - Clearly communicate what is expected by team members

Figure 18.3 summarizes the main points reviewed in this chapter.

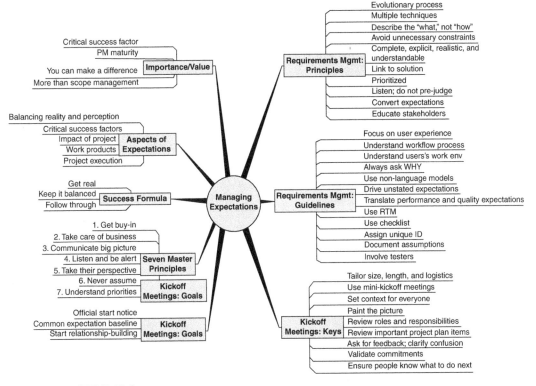

FIGURE 18.3

Overview of managing expectations.

## 19

IN THIS CHAPTER

- Review the primary traits of high-performing teams
- Understand the key principles that lead to better project team performance
- Review proven techniques to improve project team performance
- Learn effective responses to special situations, including poor performers, high-maintenance team members, and team conflicts

KEYS TO BETTER PROJECT TEAM PERFORMANCE

When it comes right down to it, you've got to deliver. And the key to doing this is having a high-performing project team. You can have the greatest plan in the world, but if your core project team can't get the work done as expected, it really doesn't matter. Conversely, a high-performing project team can go a long way in compensating for inadequate planning and other less-than-ideal project environments. Although effective leadership and communication skills are key ingredients of a successful project team environment (and we reviewed these important facets in Chapters 16, "Leading a Project," and 17, "Managing Project Communications," respectively), there is tremendous value in understanding the specific principles and techniques that we can apply to maximize the performance of our project team.

In this chapter, we review the common characteristics of high-performing project teams, explore the management principles and techniques that foster better team performance, and offer key advice on how to best handle challenging project team situations frequently encountered by project managers.

High-Performing Teams

Before we delve into the management principles and techniques that can lead to better project team performance, let's be clear on the goal. In other words, what do high-performing teams look like? What do they have in common? Do they all look and act the same? While no two teams ever perform in precisely the same manner, and every team will have their particular strengths, I have found a core set of traits that are shared by high-performing teams:

- **Clarity**—This trait is likely the most important. High-performing teams know where they are going, what they are doing, and why they are doing it. They understand the project goals and priorities, they have clear roles and responsibilities, and they understand their assigned work tasks and how their piece fits in with the rest.

- **Commitment**—Members of high-performing teams are committed to the success of the project. They demonstrate a persistence and determination to get the job done. The source of the commitment is not always the same. It might be personal, to the team, to the customer, or to the organization.

- **Professional**—High-performing teams are professional about their work. Members take individual responsibility for the quality of assigned work, personal communications, and interactions with all stakeholders.

- **Synergy**—High-performing teams develop a synergistic force about them that allows them to accomplish more as a combined team than they could do collectively as individuals. This synergy is developed over time, but generally results when the team has the right mix of skills and experiences, has a healthy team orientation, and has clearly defined roles and responsibilities.

- **Trust**—High-performing teams display a great deal of trust in each other and in their project leader. Trust is earned over time, and demonstrating effective leadership and creating a collaborative team environment with an open exchange of ideas are keys to building this trust level.

Ten Key Management Principles

Now that we have a better sense for what a high-performing team looks like, let's review ten key management principles that are paramount to our efforts to guide our team's performance:

1. **Adapt management style**—Although as a rule, a collaborative, servant-leadership management approach to leading project teams will be the most effective in most situations, you might need to adjust your style depending on the project phase, the needs of your particular team, and the project environment.

2. **Get the right people**—Whenever possible, personally select the members of your core team. You should have the best understanding of the skills, abilities, and behaviors that are needed for project success. In particular, get people who have a track record of success. As any successful project manager will attest, having the right people is 80% of the battle. Of course, in the real world, you don't always have this luxury, and we'll talk about that in the "Special Situations" section later in this chapter.

3. **Plan as a team**—A major component of modern project management is the idea that planning is a team activity. This was a heavy emphasis in our planning chapters. Why is this key? If the team develops the project plan, it becomes "their" plan and "their" schedule. With this comes a much higher level of commitment, buy-in, and accountability, and much less time spent battling the issues you get when this is not present.

4. **Keep the team focused**—One of the most important things a project manager can do is to make sure each team member is simultaneously crystal clear on the big picture of the project (mission, objectives, and priorities) on one hand and focused on their immediate task on the other. To focus, not only must each team member have clear work assignments and roles, but the project manager needs to be an umbrella for them. As an umbrella, the project manager protects the team from the politics, noise, and other factors that distract them and slow their progress.

5. **Set clear expectations**—To encourage maximum team productivity, nothing is more important than making sure team members understand what is expected from them in advance. This applies to both work assignments and team protocols. A key aspect of this expectation-setting activity is to review the completion criteria for any work assignment up front. This step alone goes a long way in preventing rework and increasing productivity.

6. **Facilitate productivity**—Continuing our productivity theme, the focus of the project manager should be on doing everything to enable each team member to be as productive as possible. What does this mean? It means the following:

   - Ensure that work assignments are clear and understood.

   - Provide the tools, resources, and procedures to facilitate team collaboration.

   - Provide all resources that are needed to accomplish the work in a timely fashion.

   - Facilitate resolution to any issue impeding work assignment completion.

   - Anticipate issues that might affect work productivity and take action to mitigate or prevent them (risk management at the work task level).

7. **Improve marketability**—A key goal I have for every person on my team is to improve their marketability through their experiences on the project. In the end, the only real job security one has is to always be "marketable"—and to continuously improve one's marketability. Look for ways to improve skills, build résumés, and help each person make progress on their career goals. This mindset is key to both how you assign and sell work tasks. Personally, I like to find out who desires to become project managers or gain project management skills, and then assign roles and responsibilities throughout the project to facilitate this marketable growth.

8. **Leverage individual strengths**—An extension of the previous principle, this one has three primary components:

   - Look for the strengths that each person brings to the table, but understand their weaknesses. This approach keeps you positive and is especially important when you have not personally selected your team or when you have been given a team member with a reputation.

   - Understand what drives people, their motivators, and what they care about. Not only will this help you position people to do better, it will also enable you to reward and recognize them more effectively.

   - Align project roles and responsibilities with each team member's "sweet spot" as much as possible. The sweet spot is the combination of natural strengths and personal motivators.

9. **Recognize and reward**—This principle has three primary aspects:

TIP   Always be looking for opportunities to recognize and reward the behaviors and accomplishments that will lead to project success.

- **PR agent**—Pretend you are the public relations agent for each one of your team members. In addition to providing timely feedback and appreciation to each person, make sure the right people (especially the people who influence their career advancements and compensation) know about the excellent work your team members are doing throughout the project. Don't wait to do all this at the end of the project or at annual review time; it is much more effective and meaningful if it is communicated as it happens.

- **Celebrate**—Take the time and make plans to celebrate interim milestones along the way. This forces you to acknowledge the efforts to date and helps to build team momentum.

- **Rewards**—There are two key items here: First, look for ways during initial project planning and throughout the project that will allow the team members to share in the rewards (profits) if the project accomplishes certain goals. Second, if the project team or specific team members are asked to perform heroic efforts, set up an incentive that will both reward and acknowledge the special efforts.

10. **Facilitate team synergy**—Especially early on in the project, use methods to help build the cohesiveness of the team. Most teams naturally go through the traditional "forming, norming, storming, and performing" stages, but there are things you can do to be a positive influence on this process. Depending on how much the given project team has worked together before and where they are physically located, the specifics will differ, but as a guide, you want to focus on the following:

    - **Build relationships**—Set up team-building outings, team lunches, team meetings, and so on that will enable relationships to begin and grow.

    - **Foster team collaboration**—Set up the tools that make it easy for the team to work together regardless of work locations; look for opportunities to have multiple team members work together on a single assignment to encourage knowledge sharing and reduce risk around isolated pockets of expertise, in addition to improving overall team performance.

    - **Set up team procedures**—Determine what rules, guidelines, and protocols are needed to help establish team productivity (such as modes of communication, core hours, standard meeting times, work standards, work processes, and administrative procedures).

- **See progress**—Structure the project approach so that the team can get some early, visible progress. Not only does this create enthusiasm for the stakeholders, but it does the same for the core team, too. In addition, track the team's progress and accomplishments in a very visible fashion. This helps build enthusiasm, but also encourages pride and accountability in project efforts.

Proven Techniques for Better Team Performance

With the ten key management principles as our foundation, let's take a look at a few proven techniques that generally lead to better project team performance:

- **Conduct team kickoffs**—Conduct separate kickoff meetings with your core team at the beginning of each phase. This is an excellent way to reset expectations on project context, project goals and priorities, team member roles and responsibilities, team member assignments, project schedule, and team procedures.

   TIP Utilize mini-kickoff meetings at the beginning of each project phase, not just the start of the entire project, to reset expectations.

- **Collocate**—Congregating team members in one place is not always possible, and it is becoming more uncommon as project work becomes increasingly distributed. However, results speak for themselves. When project team members are physically located in the same area, it is much easier to build relationships, share ideas and experiences, collaborate on assignments, develop answers to problems, and increase team synergy.

- **Use meeting time wisely**—To communicate both respect and value for individuals' time, and to help team productivity, have a definite purpose or need for any team meeting and confirm that this purpose is understood by all team members. At a minimum, conduct a general team status meeting each week to share knowledge and lessons learned, and to provide gentle peer pressure accountability. The need for formal meetings varies depending on the project approach utilized, how the team is naturally collaborating, the composition of the team, team productivity, and the list of outstanding issues.

- **Develop a team charter**—To align individual expectations with desired team behaviors, develop a team charter that defines the guidelines, procedures, and principles by which the team will operate. The important thing here is not whether you take the time to document this, but it is the act of working with the team to develop these guidelines and procedures. This way, much like the overall project plan and schedule, the charter becomes theirs.

- **Set standards**—Especially on projects where multiple individuals might be doing the same type of work or when work is outsourced, develop and communicate the standards the work must meet to be accepted. This helps clarify expectations, reduces rework activity, improves quality, and leverages expert knowledge.

- **Leverage expertise**—This is an invaluable method to improve team performance and improve the skills of multiple individuals, especially in cases where the project involves newer technologies, the primary resource pools do not have adequate skill levels, or the organization needs to avoid allocating their most senior, sought-after talent on a single project.

- **Resolve conflicts right away**—High-performing teams do not let intrateam conflicts or project issues linger, because they can adversely affect team productivity if they do. As the project manager, you need to facilitate resolutions quickly. This does not mean that you do not listen and make rash judgments. It means that you deal with it—don't avoid it. In all cases, it is very important that you stay objective, treat all sides with respect, place your focus on potential solutions, and seek out win-win scenarios.

- **Prepare for client interactions**—To better manage client expectations and avoid unproductive issues, prepare the team for direct client interactions. Make sure they understand the project from the client's perspective, the expectation the client has of the team's abilities, specific actions to take if they need assistance when they are with the client, and any talking points to either avoid or emphasize.

- **Set up a project repository**—To help facilitate team productivity, share knowledge, and protect project assets, set up a common repository that is accessible by all core team members to store project work products and project management deliverables. We discussed this in greater detail in Chapter 12, "Managing Project Deliverables."

- **Set up a team collaboration environment**—To encourage and make it easy for the team to work together on project work items—especially when the team is distributed or virtual in nature—set up the appropriate collaboration tools and environments. This normally means setting up one or more online tools to enable team members to do one or more of the following: discuss topics (group chat), facilitate team meetings (web conferencing), view and edit a common work product, and track changes to a work product. See Chapter 25, "The Fun Never Stops," for more information on project collaboration tools.

- **Develop team rituals**—To help build team unity, develop specific rituals that engage the entire team. Examples include going out to lunch together on a certain day each week, sharing breakfast together on a certain day each week, celebrating individual birthdays or anniversaries, and so forth.

- **Effective task assignments**—I've talked about this one in various ways many times already, but the point I want to emphasize here is that you can't just assume a task assignment is understood and will be done because it appears on the schedule and there is a person's name beside it. The keys here are the following:

  - Instill a sense of ownership on assigned tasks. Look for modules or domains that specific people can have lead responsibility over.

  - Verify that the person assigned the work is clear on task completion criteria. This will avoid the need to micromanage (per M-W) your team. (Because I'm naturally lazy, this is an important one for me.)

     NOTE   The Pareto principle is also known as the "80-20" rule. It's a common rule of thumb and an effective management tool that states, "20 percent of something is always responsible for 80 percent of the results."

  - Ensure that one person is primarily responsible for a task and that you have buy-in on that responsibility.

  - Ensure that the level of schedule detail is appropriate to effectively assign and monitor work.

- **Plan for orientation**—For any new team member joining your project, there is an introductory orientation period. Your goal is to streamline this period and have each team member at maximum productivity as soon as possible. The four specific actions I employ are the following:

  - **Protect your schedule**—Do not assume the new team member will be 100% productive on day one. The length of the ramp-up period will be specific to the project, work assignments, and previous work experiences.

  - **Prepare an orientation packet**—Put yourself in the new team member's shoes and think about what you need to know to get a solid understanding of the project environment.

  - **Set up the work environment in advance**—In any project environment where team members need specific equipment, tools, or access privileges to do their work, do whatever you can to get this set up before the team member starts. If you can't, account for this in your schedule.

  - **Invest the time up front**—Plan on spending time with any new team member up front. By investing focused attention with any new team member, you can better communicate your energy for the project and the expectations for the project, their role, and their contributions. As an avid follower of the Pareto principle, this is a clear case where spending a little extra time up front prevents the need to spend a lot more time down the road on team productivity issues.

- **Plug in**—To help facilitate team performance, you must stay connected with the team. Keys here are to stay visible, use the same communication channels the team is using, take time to meet with each team member one-on-one, and make sure the team knows you are there to help them be productive.

- **Share leadership responsibilities**—To help team members develop leadership skills and to help build commitment to the project, look for opportunities to share leadership responsibilities. This is natural on larger and cross-functional projects.

Special Situations

There are going to be project situations in which you won't have a stellar, high-performing team. There might be times when you have just the opposite situation to deal with. In either case, you still need to get the work done. It's in these situations where your goal is to get better team performance. Although we could spend an entire chapter on all the problem situations you might encounter, I at least want to spend a section examining some special situations related to project team performance that you are likely to encounter and offer a few helpful recommendations in each case.

- **Poor performers**—Poor performers generally fall into two categories: unacceptable work results or unacceptable behaviors. In many cases, the poor performance is a result of unclear expectations. If faced with this situation, keep these action items in mind:

   TIP Keep in mind that the rest of the team is watching how you deal with these situations. Your challenge is to strike the balance between handling the person fairly and not letting the poor performance become a drag on the team.

  - **Verify expectations**—On first occurrences, don't overreact—verify the expectations that the team member had and take responsibility for any lack of clarity.

  - **Provide feedback**—After you have proper information, provide specific feedback to the team member as soon as possible in a private setting. Focus on the behavior or result, not the person.

   TIP Performance feedback should be timely, discreet, and specific.

- **Enable success**—Do everything that you can do to enable each team member's success. Provide resources. Knock down obstacles. Provide every opportunity for their performance to improve.

- **Initiate backup plans**—At the same time, you cannot assume their performance will get better. At the first signs of performance issues, start thinking about what you can do to mitigate the impact to the project if you do need to replace the team member or if the performance does not improve.

- **Cut your losses**—Assuming you've done everything mentioned so far, there comes a time when you must cut your losses. The main reason why a poor performer needs to be removed is the effect it can have on the performance and morale of the rest of the team.

- **High-maintenance staff**—This group of team members includes those individuals who have a reputation of either being difficult to work with or possessing unusual personalities. In most cases, these are the people you need for your key critical path tasks—of course. From experience, here are my two key recommendations for these situations:

  - **Check for yourself**—Don't assume the reputation (the perception) is totally true. Verify for yourself. I have found that in many cases, these individuals are unfairly labeled. These labels often say more about the people who are uncomfortable working with individuals who are different from them than anything else.

  - **Treat them the same**—Use the same approach with them as you would any other team member. Work to understand their motivators, clarify expectations, avoid surprises, and help them be successful.

- **Schedule developed without team**—I know I emphasize the importance and the value in developing the detail project plan and schedule with the team. I also realize this does not always occur in the real world (shocking, I know). If you find yourself in a situation where either you or your team is asked to take responsibility for a schedule that you or they did not help develop, you must take the time to review the schedule. You need to get buy-in from the team members before continuing. Two important items for consideration here:

  - **Understand the schedule assumptions**—In many of these situations, team members totally dismiss the merits of a schedule because they are not aware of the assumptions that serve as the foundation for the schedule. Key assumptions include those about resource ability and quality level of work product (completion criteria).

  - **Identify risks**—If there are gaps between the schedule assumptions and project reality, or if you cannot get commitment from the team, you have some new project risks, if not outright issues. Follow your designated risk and issue management procedures to handle it.

THE ABSOLUTE MINIMUM

At this point, you should have a solid understanding of the following:

- The core traits for high-performing teams are clarity, commitment, professionalism, synergy, and trust.
- In most situations, a participative approach to project management, decision making, conflict resolution, and brainstorming leads to better project team performance.
- The key project management skills that are needed to lead better project team performance include leadership, communication, facilitation, interpersonal, and team-building skills.
- The ten key management principles that lead to better project team performance are

  1. Adapt management style to best meet the needs of the project.
  2. Select your project team yourself whenever possible.
  3. Develop the project plan and schedule with the team.
  4. Keep the team focused on both their immediate tasks and on the project's big picture.
  5. Set clear expectations.
  6. Enable each team member to be as productive as possible.
  7. Strive to improve the marketability of each person on your team.
  8. Leverage the individual strengths to best accomplish the project goals.
  9. Constantly look to recognize and reward the accomplishments and good work of your team members.
  10. Use team-building methods and procedures to help develop team synergy.

Figure 19.1 summarizes the main points reviewed in this chapter.

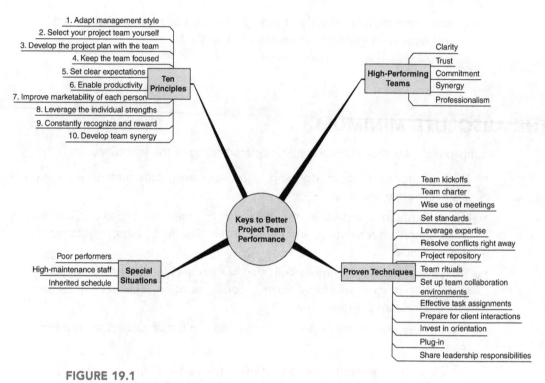

FIGURE 19.1

Overview of keys to better project team.

20

MANAGING DIFFERENCES

With the current trends in business and technology, the odds that you will manage a project consisting of stakeholders from the same culture, located in the same environment, and representing a common business function decrease as each day passes. In the past, these more complex project situations were assigned to proven, experienced project managers. Today, you are likely to deal with cross-functional, cross-cultural, or virtual environments (or combinations of these three) in your initial project management opportunity. This is why I feel it is important to review key aspects of managing differences in project environments.

In this chapter, I want to accomplish two primary goals. One, I want to share with you the unique aspects of each of these project situations, the common problems to watch out for, and, most importantly, the key principles and lessons that I have learned managing these types of projects. Two, I want to emphasize how these special situations do not require any additional project management techniques—just disciplined application of the principles and techniques we covered in earlier chapters. With this knowledge and awareness, you will be more confident and better prepared to manage these aspects of your project environment.

Five Key Principles

No matter the situation, there is a common set of principles that you can apply to better manage any project where there are significant differences in the composition of the team. The differences can include location, business function, or cultural aspects. Let's take a look at the five fundamental principles that will guide your efforts in any of these situations:

CAUTION   These project environments can, and usually do, create risks around work productivity and communication effectiveness because there is often a greater chance for misunderstandings.

1. **It's the same, but more**—The first principle to understand is that it does not take additional or new management techniques to be effective at leading these types of projects. These project situations just place more emphasis and importance on the project management fundamentals reviewed in earlier chapters. In particular, these aspects of project management become essential:

   • Well-defined and properly planned project

   • Effective project sponsorship

   • Buy-in and commitment on success criteria

   • Well-managed expectations

   • Clear roles and responsibilities

   • Effective communications

   • Effective risk management

   In addition, the discipline to properly document plans, meeting minutes, decisions, and issues is generally more important due to the need to ensure proper and clear communications.

2. **The right leadership approach**—The best project leaders in these situations are ones who possess the right mix of communication, facilitative, interpersonal, and expectation management skills to accomplish the following:

NOTE A servant leadership approach is often most effective for these types of projects. See the discussion of servant leadership in Chapter 16, "Leading a Project."

- Instill confidence in the stakeholders that they can lead the team to the accomplishment of the project objectives.

- Take the perspective of each stakeholder group to ensure each group believes they are included, understood, valued, and heard in the project process.

- Create alignment around the project goals and concentrate the team's focus on what unifies them (the common ground).

- Help each stakeholder group understand how their piece (work process, interests, and needs) fits into the overall puzzle.

- Take a flexible approach by maintaining focus on the major project priorities and an understanding that everything else is just a means for getting there.

3. **Communication is king**—As we reviewed in Chapter 17, "Managing Project Communications," effective project communications are a bedrock aspect of project management. Specifically, in these types of project situations, here are the key points to keep in mind:

   - Use communication mechanisms that are accessible to everyone.

   - Use project collaboration environments and techniques that are accessible to everyone.

   - Develop a project vocabulary. Be willing to use their terms and terms they understand. Be mindful of any confusion over terminology being used.

   - Plan on frequent touchpoints to compensate for the lack of face time, especially in virtual project team settings.

   - Document project communications, especially anything discussed verbally, to ensure mutual understanding and agreement.

   - Ensure that each team member is clear on the following at all times:

     - Project context

     - Project goals

     - Team members' roles and responsibilities

     - Team members' assignments

- Project schedule
- Project collaboration environments and tools
- Chain of command and reporting relationships

CROSS-FUNCTIONAL PROJECT ISSUES

A prime cause of issues on cross-functional projects is neglect of a specific functional area or group. Make sure each affected stakeholder group is properly represented, consulted, respected, and kept informed.

Another prime cause for issues on cross-functional projects is poor performance by a functional leader. Common performance issues include the following:

- Not fulfilling role responsibilities
- Lack of functional knowledge or experience
- Misalignment of priorities; unable to meet time commitments for role
- Not consulting other members of their functional group
- Not keeping other members of their functional group informed
- Unable to complete reviews in a timely fashion

4. **Verify understanding**—In these project situations, more time is necessary to verify that you are being understood and that you (your team) accurately understand the other stakeholders. A few specific things to be mindful of include the following:

   - Be wary of any assumptions.
   - Ask the extra question to make sure.
   - Establish and clarify team norms and procedures.

- Explain project processes and the value they serve.

- The larger the project, the more effort to get through requirements definition and review cycles.

- Requirements gathering needs to use multiple methods to ensure completeness and understanding.

- Take the time to walk through their current processes.

5. **More project management effort**—This is somewhat implied by the first principle in this list, but it is important to understand that the project management component of these type of environments is more significant (as a rule). There can be a misperception that the effort to leverage these latest technologies and business trends to gain efficiency and accomplish projects faster also means less project management effort. Incorrect. The effort to lead, facilitate, ensure understanding, and build teamwork in these situations is at least equal to, and in most cases much greater than, the effort to do the same with a co-located team.

Reminder: To help build the sense of ownership, work with the designated functional leaders to perform the detail planning for the project.

Proven Techniques for Leading Cross-Functional Projects

With the prior principles understood, let's review a few proven tips and techniques specific to leading cross-functional projects that I have either confirmed or realized over the years:

- **Ensure proper project sponsorship and governance**—Any time a project's scope addresses more than a single business function, it is critical that the project sponsor have jurisdiction over all the business functions affected. If the sponsor does not have this jurisdiction, then a process (often by a senior-level committee—steering committee, change control board) needs to be established up front to deal with any territorial issue or change request that affects the cross-functional environment.

- **Designate functional leaders**—As part of your project organization and your role-responsibility matrix, include functional leader positions as the primary representatives from each distinct group. These roles are instrumental in facilitating the project process and reducing your workload.

- **Acknowledge the importance and value of each group**—Although you might serve as the ringmaster and steadfastly communicate the vision and process approach for the project, you should be quick to acknowledge the importance, value, and role that each group contributes to the success of the project. You don't have all the answers, so you need to facilitate the execution of the project and instill a sense of ownership into each of your functional leaders.

- **Get commitments from respective resource managers**—As part of the collaborative approach that is needed for these types of projects, make sure to work closely with the various resource managers who are responsible for assigning the appropriate personnel to the project. In many cases, the resource managers are the bosses of the individuals who will serve as your designated functional leads. Invest the time with them. Review the project definition with them. Include them on the review and acceptance of the project plan, especially the resource plan and project schedule.

 TIP Make sure to include the resource managers and, if they're not the same person, the bosses of the functional leaders in your project communications.

- **Ensure project alignment**—If you were not involved in the project definition process, make sure your cross-functional project is aligned with the other projects underway or planned in the enterprise. There is nothing worse for team spirit and commitment than starting a project that has an obvious conflict with other initiatives.

- **Focus on workflow process**—To add more value to the project, to better serve your role as facilitator, and to help you make better decisions, invest the effort early to understand the complete workflow process that is affected by the project. In many cases, your functional leaders will have silo outlooks and will not fully understand how they get the inputs they do or how their outputs affect the rest of the operation.

- **Kickoff meetings are essential**—Kickoff meetings are always excellent tools for setting expectations and communicating the same message to the key stakeholders. On cross-functional projects, where multiple departments or business units are involved, this type of event is critical to getting the project started correctly and improving the chances for success.

- **Resolve issues aggressively**—On cross-functional projects, you are likely to see issues occur that do not have a clear owner. As discussed in detail in Chapter 13, "Managing Project Issues," it is imperative that you take an aggressive attitude toward finding resolutions to any issue to protect the project's critical success factors.

- **Look out for dysfunctional relations**—Now, you would think that because the various functional areas are all members of the same, common organization that it would be one big happy family. Well, people are people, families are families, and dysfunction is always close by. Just understand that in many organizations, there can be historical disputes between functional groups or individuals within the group that affect your project's performance.

- **Invest time on communications planning**—As mentioned many times in many different ways, communication is key to project success. For cross-functional projects, you need to invest additional time in planning your project communications due to the heightened importance they will have in this setting and to the increased number of stakeholders that need to be included.

- **Invest time on requirements definition**—As discussed in Chapter 18, "Managing Expectations," the requirements definition process is often the source for missed expectations. This is especially true with cross-functional projects due to the increased breadth of scope, the number of stakeholders, and the team dynamics that can come into play. In addition, as mentioned in the fourth principle in managing these types of projects, more effort is needed to verify understanding. The key is to plan adequate time and effort for a thorough requirements definition phase, so you can avoid the common problems that contribute to insufficient requirements definition, including the following:

   NOTE Cross-functional projects are excellent candidates for conducting project and requirements definitions as a project by itself (as discussed in Chapter 4, "Defining a Project") due to the number of stakeholders that need to be consulted and the potential change impact.

  - **Reluctant signatures**—Stakeholders who approve requirements without a real understanding or buy-in. Be especially cognizant of stakeholders who are quiet, susceptible to peer pressure, or offer no nonverbal signs that the light bulb has gone on.

     CAUTION Watch out for stakeholders who are signing off on (accepting) requirements without complete understanding. Although this might get you through a milestone, it will come back and bite you before you're done.

  - **Misunderstandings, assumptions, and unstated expectations**—Use multiple requirements gathering methods, leverage visual models, ask extra questions, and focus on change impact.

TIP To better achieve a common understanding of requirements on cross-functional projects, leverage visual models and prototypes of those requirements as early and often as possible.

Proven Techniques for Leading Cross-Cultural Projects

With the prior principles understood, let's review a few proven tips and techniques specific to leading cross-cultural projects that I have either confirmed or realized over the years. Keep in mind that a project does not need to be global in nature to be a cross-cultural project. Many times, projects with stakeholders from different parts of the United States can qualify as cross-cultural projects, too, especially if the project touches a combination of the distinct regions (such as Northeast, Midwest, South, Texas, and West Coast).

- **Be respectful**—Take time to consider the effect that the different cultures, time zones, holiday schedules, and workday schedules will have on the project. Common impact areas are terminology, risk management, communications planning (including best times for status meetings), and the project schedule.

- **Potential cultural impacts**—Understand potential cultural effects on project communications and team interactions. Specifically, be aware that due to cultural differences, others might not be as assertive or willing to speak up to the degree you would expect. In addition, review any conventions that you plan to use for status reporting. Make sure the conventions do not convey some unintended meaning and that everyone is comfortable using them.

- **Listen for understanding**—Even with a common language (in most cases, English), the use and the sound of the language can vary dramatically. The key here is to kick your active listening skills into high gear and focus on understanding. Don't let yourself get distracted or tune out because of accents or the irregular use of certain words. Stay engaged, be patient, ask questions, clarify terms, and don't stop until you are comfortable that you're on the same wavelength with your cross-cultural partners.

- **Plan on more formality**—To reduce the impact of cultural differences and ensure mutual understanding, cross-cultural projects are more mechanical, formal, and by the book. You just need to plan on this and realize that project management shortcuts are not as likely in these environments.

- **Capture and publish detailed meeting notes**—One aspect of planning on more formality that is worth calling out is the importance of capturing and publishing detailed meeting minutes when the language spoken is not native to all participants. This can go a long way in ensuring that everyone really understands the main points of the meeting and that there were no misunderstandings.

Proven Techniques for Leading Virtual Projects

Any project that consists of team members not in the same physical location is a virtual project to some degree. The more geographically dispersed the team members and the more interaction that is done with non–face-to-face communications, the more virtual the project is.

With the continued advances in communications and information technology, and the common everyday use of mobile phones, remote network access, email, web mail, pagers, and instant messaging, the ability of people to productively collaborate on common work is increased dramatically. And, of course, the reduced office costs and the increased ability to leverage outsourcing options are very attractive to most organizations.

However, these potential productivity gains and cost reductions do not happen automatically—especially in the demanding environment of most projects. A tremendous amount of energy is needed to plan, coordinate, and manage a virtual project team. Let's review a few key tips and techniques specific to leading virtual project teams that I have either confirmed or realized over the years:

- **Get some face-to-face time, especially early**—If there is any way possible to get face time with your virtual team members, do it. It has been my experience that face-to-face interaction is instrumental in building trust, developing relationships, and jump-starting project momentum. I recommend the following scenarios for your consideration:
  - Get everyone together for the project kickoff meeting.
  - Try to collocate the team for the first stage (or as long as you can), and then let team members return to their remote locations.
  - If neither of these are possible, try a mini-kickoff session that focuses on the work planning and identifying risks, and strongly encourage everyone to use videoconferencing, especially for initial meetings.

- Depending on the project phase and the nature of the work, look at split work environments (such as two days on-site, three days remote, or one week on-site every month).

- If it's available, look to leverage videoconferencing as much as possible, especially for initial team meetings. If not, consider creative use of digital pictures.

- **Establish team norms**—Facilitate the rules and procedures that will guide team interactions and productivity with the team. Key items include the following:

  - Core hours during which everyone needs to be available (online)

  - Access to team members during non-core hours

  - Preferred team communication and collaboration mechanisms

  - Preferred meeting times, especially important when members are in different time zones

  - Reporting status

  - Project repository

  - Contingency plans for network or phone outages

  - Team directory

- **Responsiveness is the difference-maker**—The key to successful virtual project teams is responsiveness. If people are easily accessible and respond quickly, most organizations couldn't care less where people are working. These environments do require team members to be professional and mature.

- **Set up protocols for virtual meetings**—Virtual meetings are the lifeblood of a virtual project team. Here are some key reminders to make these meetings more productive:

  - Use technologies that are available to everyone.

  - Use technologies that are reliable for everyone.

  - Use technologies that meet the security requirements of the project and sponsoring organizations.

  - Ensure that everyone understands how to use the technologies.

  - Make sure to send agenda and reference materials in advance of the meeting (or just post to the project repository and send a link to it).

  - Review protocols for asking questions.

- Keep discussions focused on items that pertain to all participants. For other items, take them offline. Stop the discussion and assign an action item to schedule a separate meeting with those involved.

- Instant messaging conferences might be appropriate for core team meetings.

- **Establish clear time zone references**—This might not be as much of an issue for you, but in this age of multiple time zones and daylight savings time, take the time to review and clarify time-zone designations and conventions. This goes a long way in avoiding meeting time conflicts. I have two recommendations here:

  - Use the newer time zone references such as Eastern Time (ET) to refer to whatever time it is on the east coast rather than Eastern Standard Time (EST) or Eastern Daylight Time (EDT).

  - Reference city or state to clarify the intended time, such as Chicago time, London time, or Arizona time.

- **Verify productivity early**—To ensure that the virtual work environment generates the expected level of productivity needed for project success, pay close attention to initial work efforts. The fundamentals of work assignments apply the same here, but they're even more important:

  - Invest time to clarify work expectations and completion criteria.

  - Provide all necessary resources.

  - Keep work packages small—less than the standard reporting period.

- **Use preferred communication methods of customer and sponsor**—Either as part of your initial communications planning or as an observation you make during the project, make sure to communicate with your sponsor and your key customers in the manner they prefer and in the manner that best fits their learning style. If this is in person, meet them in person. If it is via phone at 7:30 a.m., call them at 7:30 a.m. If it is email at the end of the day, email them. The two important things to note here are the following:

  - The communication mechanisms you use for the core project team might likely be different than what you use for sponsor and customer communications.

  - Use the methods they prefer, not what you prefer. This approach leads to fewer miscommunication and expectation management issues.

THE ABSOLUTE MINIMUM

At this point, you should have a solid understanding of the following:

- The key principles to note in leading cross-functional, cross-cultural, or virtual project environments include the following:

  1. The same project management fundamentals apply.

  2. A leadership approach that emphasizes effective communication, collaboration, interpersonal, and expectation management skills tends to work the best.

  3. Communication, communication, communication.

  4. Invest more time to ensure understanding.

  5. More project management effort is needed.

- Proven tips and techniques for leading cross-functional projects include the following:

  1. Ensure that the project has the proper sponsorship and governance procedures.

  2. Designate functional leaders to represent each distinct group.

  3. Consistently acknowledge the importance, value, and role that each group contributes to the success of the project.

  4. Get buy-in and commitment from resource managers.

  5. Ensure that the project is aligned properly with other organizational initiatives.

  6. Invest the effort early to understand the complete workflow process that is affected by the project.

  7. Kickoff meetings are essential.

  8. Resolve issues aggressively.

  9. Look out for dysfunctional interactions.

  10. Invest time in communications planning.

  11. Invest time in requirements definition.

- Proven tips and techniques for leading cross-cultural projects include the following:

  1. Be respectful of cultures, customs, time zones, and holiday schedules.

  2. Recognize the potential culture effects on project communications and team interactions.

  3. Turn your active listening skills into hyperdrive.

  4. Plan on more formality.

- Proven tips and techniques for leading virtual projects include the following:

  1. Get some face-to-face time, especially early in the project.

  2. Establish team rules and procedures.

  3. Focus everyone on the importance of responsiveness.

  4. Set up protocols for virtual meetings.

  5. Establish clear time zone designations.

  6. Verify productivity levels early.

  7. Use the communication methods preferred by the customer and the sponsor.

The map in Figure 20.1 summarizes the main points reviewed in this chapter.

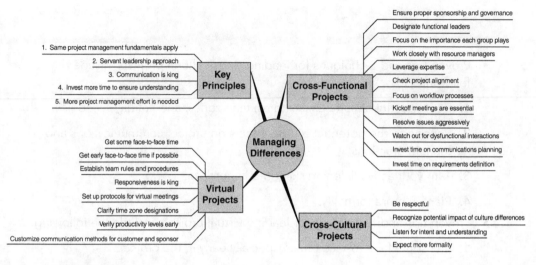

FIGURE 20.1

Overview of managing differences.

IN THIS CHAPTER

- Understand why managing vendors is important to even first-time project managers

- Understand the key principles that lead to better vendor management

- Learn to avoid the common mistakes made on out-sourced projects (they are not all due to the vendor)

- Review tips and techniques for both the client (buyer) and vendor (seller) organization and project manager

- Understand the key skills that have the greatest impact on managing vendor situations

- Learn contract fundamentals and how different contract types impact your approach

21

MANAGING VENDORS

As more and more organizations look to focus on their core competencies and reduce their fixed operating costs, while simultaneously attempting to execute more projects, it is very likely that your project, even your first one, will involve collaboration with other organizations.

Although the specific process for establishing working relationships with other organizations depends largely on the industry in which you work, many project managers lack considerable exposure to procurement and vendor management. Often, this is due to organizational structures and the common use of procurement specialists who have specific education and training to understand the legal and contractual nature of this activity.

For these reasons, I felt it was important to include this chapter, so you can be better prepared for whatever you face on your initial project assignment.

This chapter is not meant to be a comprehensive overview of procurement or vendor management, and I encourage you to study these areas further. Instead, this chapter focuses on the outsourcing of project work (as opposed to outsourcing entire departments or other operational work) and on the key fundamentals and frontline tips that make the greatest difference in your ability to manage these project relationships and avoid the mistakes made by both first-time and experienced project managers.

Specifically, we review what activities are actually included in vendor management, the core principles that should drive your work, and helpful advice for both the buyer and seller project manager. In addition, we touch on the important basics of contracts, including the impact certain types of contracts have on the project manager, and we highlight the skills that make the greatest impact on your ability to effectively manage outsourced projects.

First, Let's Clarify a Few Terms

For the sake of clarity and brevity, let's review a few terms and touch on the focus of this chapter. By *vendor*, I mean the seller organization—the organization that is contracted to provide product or services. I generally refer to the client organization—the organization purchasing the services—as the buyer. The use of buyer and seller terms here is consistent with the current PMI standards on procurement management.

In addition, we focus on arrangements that involve the outsourcing of entire projects, project phases, or specific project deliverables to external entities. Thus, this excludes "staff augmentation" arrangements where a vendor is contracted to provide a resource to fill a role on your project team.

With these clarifications, we're now ready to take a look at the principles that provide the foundation for effective management of the buyer-seller project relationship.

Ten Proven Principles of Vendor Management

The following ten fundamental principles will guide your efforts in managing vendor relationships:

1. **Solid project management goes a long way**—Outsourced projects place more importance on the project management fundamentals reviewed throughout this book. Although you might be able to get by with less on internal projects, outsourced projects bring a visibility and accountability (both financially and legally) that make solid project management and leadership a requirement

to make the relationship work. In particular, the following aspects of project management become essential:

- Well-defined and properly planned project
- Effective project sponsorship
- Buy-in and commitment on success criteria
- Well-managed expectations
- Clear roles and responsibilities
- Effective communications
- Formal change control management
- Effective issue management

 TIP The principles and techniques in managing virtual and cross-cultural teams in Chapter 20, "Managing Differences," are valuable in outsourced project arrangements.

 NOTE Just because procurement and vendor management require formal communications and processes, it does not mean that only formal communication methods are used. In fact, the formal communications should just follow (and document) what has already been discussed and agreed to.

2. **Vendor management is multifaceted**—Effective vendor management has four distinct elements that need attention:

- Evaluation and selection
- Contract development
- Relationship management
- Delivery management

3. **"See" the contract, "be" the contract**—Borrowing an expression from the sports world, you need to be fully aware of what the contract states. Ideally, you are involved in the development of the contract or, at the very least, the project definition document that is referenced by the contract. In either case, you need to have full knowledge of what the contract states for three reasons:

- To ensure that you clearly understand what the vendor is responsible for
- To ensure that you are managing the project and vendor consistently with the contract
- To understand what incentives are motivating your seller

4. **Formality rules**—Due to the legal implications of the work relationship, all changes must be in writing and formally controlled, no matter who originates the change. In addition, all project communications dealing with procurement management should always be formal and written.

 NOTE In many organizations, a natural conflict exists between the contract administrator and the project manager. There are three reasons for this:

- The contract administrator is the only one authorized to change the contract.
- The contract includes or references the project definition document or project plan.
- The project manager owns and manages the project definition document and project plan.

5. **Contract complexity should be consistent with project risk**—Both the procurement process and the level of contract detail should be consistent with project risk. The same due diligence process needed for a multimillion dollar project should not be used for a $50,000 project.

6. **If it is important, put it in**—Any aspect of an outsourced project that is important to either party should be in the contract. This includes, but is not limited to, deliverable specifications, the methodology used to create the deliverable, specific resources, roles, and responsibilities, planned communications, deliverable acceptance criteria, and project success criteria. Do not rely on assumptions.

7. **Management commitment is key**—Partnerships between organizations are the result of demonstrated management commitment. More important than what the contract says or doesn't say, the commitment level and flexibility demonstrated by senior management (from each party) to make the relationship work will be the determining factor.

8. **Focus on "win-win"**—This principle is a cultural shock to many organizations, but both parties should focus on building win-win relationships throughout the project. When issues and tensions occur (and they will), actions should be focused on mutually beneficial resolutions and on easing tensions—not escalation and provocation.

9. **Clarify terms and processes**—Take the time to review, explain, and clarify all terms and processes involved in the project. More conflicts result from misunderstandings than anything else.

10. **Clarify internal roles and responsibilities**—Make sure to clarify the roles and responsibilities for the procurement (purchasing) department versus the project team, especially between the contract administrator and the project manager. Conversely, the seller project manager needs to clarify his role and responsibilities in this arrangement with his sales, accounting, and legal departments.

12 Tips for Buyers

The following tips and techniques have been picked up from the front line of project management and might be helpful to both buyer organizations and project managers in their efforts to get the most from their outsourced project arrangements:

1. **Align sellers' goals with yours**—This could be a principle of managing vendors. To get the most from your vendors, make sure their goals are aligned with your goals (which should be in sync with the project goals). The terms of the contract should be set up so that all parties win together. The use of incentives, risk-reward scenarios, and requiring accepted deliverables for payment approval are popular techniques here.

 NOTE The motivation behind incentives is to align the seller's objectives with the buyer's.

2. **Ensure WBS is appropriate**—Make sure the work to be outsourced is clearly defined, complete, and appropriate for the given environment. Consider the following questions:

   - If the vendor is off-shore, can the work be done with limited interaction with your organization?

   - Do you expect the vendor to help with training?

   - What documentation do you need or expect?

   - How will you transition the final deliverable(s) to your organization?

3. **Tie acceptance of deliverables to payments**—A key condition to associate with any payment is formal acceptance of the targeted deliverable(s). This works better when clear acceptance criteria are established in advance.

4. **Use phases to reduce risk**—An excellent way to manage the natural risk involved in outsourcing project work is to limit the commitment length by project phases. By limiting the scope of the contract to one or two project phases (specifics will depend on project risk and methodology used), you minimize

your dependency on a vendor that might be underperforming, and you force a systematic review of vendor performance before committing to additional work.

5. **Understand resource and process dependencies**—Get a clear understanding of the resources that the vendor needs from your organization to effectively perform their work and when those resources are needed, and then proactively manage those dependencies. Use the same approach on project processes—especially deliverable reviews and testing stages.

6. **Use project management fundamentals to reduce risk and improve quality**—Besides the tips already mentioned, focus on these other solid project management fundamentals to reduce risk, improve quality, and meet expectations:

   • Request and review interim deliverables

   • Request tangible results early in the process

   • Focus on clear specifications

   • Establish clear acceptance criteria for each deliverable

   • Leverage a requirements traceability matrix

   • Establish frequent status reporting cycles

7. **Integrate vendor teams whenever possible**—Whenever the nature of project work allows it, always look for opportunities to integrate the vendor's project team with yours. Besides creating better teams and working relationships, this technique is effective for knowledge transfer and more proactive risk and issue management.

8. **Use a third party to QA vendor's activities**—If the risk of the project warrants, consider using a third-party resource as a quality auditor on your primary vendor, including another vendor. This can be an additional project expense, and you are adding potential complexity to your management efforts, but if there is not an in-house quality department or there is lack of experience with this type of project, it is an investment that can pay considerable dividends. This arrangement helps protect the interest of the client and helps keeps everyone accountable to the contractual arrangement.

9. **Evaluate vendor estimates**—Determine how you will validate the integrity and reasonableness of the vendor's cost and time estimates. Common methods include the use of multiple vendor bids, requesting a WBS to support the estimate, and review by subject matter experts.

10. **Look for "go-to" partners**—Encourage your organization to seek true vendor partners rather than just view them as disposable, interchangeable suppliers. Vendors that have demonstrated the ability to get the job done, the management commitment to meet your expectations, the flexibility to resolve conflicts and honor the spirit of contractual agreements, and the ability to establish synergy and trust with your enterprise give your enterprise a strong operational advantage.

11. **Try out a new vendor**—To reduce the risk of going with a new vendor, consider giving any new vendor a tryout. Use a new vendor for a smaller project or a piece of a larger project before making a commitment on a higher profile engagement. There's nothing like seeing a vendor in action to determine whether they are a good fit for your enterprise.

12. **Beware of certifications**—As the advantages of organizational process maturity are understood by more and more industries and enterprises, more organizations are placing a higher priority on process maturity certifications such as CMMI and ISO. Consider the following three questions in regard to these certifications:

    - When did they earn the certification and who performed the audit?

    - Does the certification apply to the entire organization or only to a specific project or department?

    - What evidence exists that proves the organization is still operating at the certified level?

Seven Tips for Sellers

The following tips and techniques have been picked up from the front lines of project management and might be helpful to both seller organizations and project managers in their efforts to get the most from their contracted project work and business relationships:

1. **Get formal acceptance**—Make sure to get some form of formal verification or sign-off from the client to document acceptance of the targeted deliverable(s).

2. **Clarify standards and acceptance criteria**—Make sure to understand what standards you are expected to adhere to before you begin your work (put in the contract) and document what criteria will be used by the client to officially accept each deliverable.

3. **Define review process**—Make sure to clarify with the client what process will be used to review and accept each deliverable. In particular, specify who will be

involved in the review process, how much time will be allowed for the review, and how many iterations (for refinements) should be expected and included as part of the scope.

4. **Control invoicing process**—There is nothing worse than visiting with the client project manager or project sponsor after they have received an inaccurate project invoice that you did not know had been sent or had never seen. To prevent these situations and manage the credibility of your organization, ask to have review-and-approve powers on any project invoices before they are issued.

5. **Keep a close eye on resource dependencies**—From the start, understand what elements of the WBS need collaboration with resources from the client (or other) organization and make sure the client clearly understands these dependencies and realizes the impact (time, cost, quality) of not having the resources when needed.

6. **Manage communications**—Take control and ownership of all communications between your team and the client organization and communications with your senior management.

7. **Be transparent**—The more open, transparent, and visible you are regarding your team's activities and progress, the more trust and confidence you build with your client. If you happen to find yourself in a crisis, your "truth and nothing but the truth" approach and the relationship you have established might be the only things that get you through these times.

12 Key Project Management Skills for Better Vendor Management

To better help you prepare for responsibilities of vendor and procurement management, let's review the type of skills and knowledge a project manager should possess to be effective in these areas. The key project management skills needed for procurement and vendor management include the following:

1. Managing expectations

2. Effective verbal and written communications

3. Managing virtual and cross-cultural teams

4. Defining a project

5. Proficient negotiating

6. Vendor selection and evaluation

7. Strong interpersonal skills

8. The ability to identify risks and develop appropriate responses (managing risks)

9. Contract knowledge

10. The ability to manage to a contract

11. Understanding when and how to use legal assistance

12. Managing changes

Stuff You Need to Know About Contracts

I mentioned earlier that contract knowledge is a key project management skill for procurement and vendor management. So, what exactly do I mean by contract knowledge? Although there is no substitution for actual experience, in-depth study, and formal training, here is a quick synopsis of the key contract facts that you need to understand to improve your effectiveness in this area of project management.

Conditions for a Legal Contract

The four conditions that make a contract a legally binding agreement are the following:

- It must be voluntarily entered into.

- It must contain mutual consideration.

- It must be created for legal purposes.

- It must be signed by authorized parties.

Key Contract Elements

Not every contract is the same, and not every contract will contain all these sections (they might not apply), but the common contract components include the following:

- Scope statement, including deliverables, requirements, out-of-scope items, and assumptions

- Timetable and milestone dates

- Acceptance criteria

- Responsibilities of each party

- Financial arrangements, including payment schedule, invoicing arrangements, and incentives
- Identification of the person authorized to make changes
- Change control procedures
- Issue resolution and escalation procedures
- Performance measurement and reporting
- Communications plan, such as status reporting, senior management meetings
- Procedures or penalties for ending the contract prematurely
- Liability for failure to perform
- Ownership and property rights of project deliverables
- Security agreements
- Nondisclosure agreements

Primary Contract Types

The three common contract types are as follows:

- Time and materials (T&M)
- Fixed price (FP)
- Cost reimbursable (CR)

The three variations of cost-reimbursable contracts are as follows:

- Cost Plus Fixed Fee (CPFF)
- Cost Plus Percent of Cost (CPPC)
- Cost Plus Incentive Fee (CPIF)

A common variation of T&M contracts is to cap the top end (T&M with a Cap).

The Impact of Each Contract Type

In the previous section, we mentioned the three key contract types. In this section, we review the points you need to understand about each type. The key categories include the following:

- The contract's advantages and disadvantages
- What situation is best for the contract's use

- Who owns the risk

- The required project management tasks

Table 21.1 summarizes these key facts about each contract type.

TABLE 21.1   Summary of Contract Types

	T&M	FP	CR
Advantages	Quick to create. Brief duration. Good choice when hiring people to augment your staff.	Less work for buyer to manage. Seller has strong incentive to control costs. Buyer knows total project price. Companies are familiar with this type. Can include incentives.	Simpler scope of work. SOW is easier than one for an FP. Lower cost than FP because the seller does not need to add as much for the risk. Can include incentives.
Disadvantages	Profit in every hour billed. Seller has no incentive to control costs. Good only for small projects. Requires most day-to-day oversight by the buyer.	Seller might under-quote and make up profits with change orders. Seller might reduce work scope if it is losing money. More work for the buyer to write the SOW. Can be more costly than CR if the SOW is incomplete. Seller will increase the price to cover risk.	Must audit seller's invoices. More work for buyer to manage. Seller has only moderate incentive to control costs. Total project price is unknown.
Best to use when...	You need work to begin right away. You need to augment staff.	You know exactly what needs to be done. You don't have time to audit invoices.	You want to buy expertise in determining what needs to be done.

	T&M	FP	CR
Who has the risk?	The buyer.	The seller (cost), or both the buyer and seller if not well defined.	The buyer.
Scope of work detail	Brief. Limited functional, performance, or design requirements.	Extremely complete. Seller needs to know all the work. "Do it."	Describes only performance or requirements. "How to do it."
Project management tasks	Providing daily direction to seller. Striving for concrete deliverables. Close monitoring of project schedule. Looking for a situation to switch the contract type.	Establishing clear acceptance criteria of deliverables. Managing change requests. Monitoring project task dependencies. Managing risks. Monitoring project assumptions.	Auditing seller's costs. Monitoring seller work progress. Ensuring added resources add value to the project. Watching for shifting resources. Watching for unplanned seller charges. Rebudgeting.

THE ABSOLUTE MINIMUM

At this point, you should have a solid understanding of the following:

- Solid project management is essential to reducing risk and improving quality on outsourced projects.
- Vendor management is composed of four distinct elements:
  - Evaluation and selection
  - Contract development
  - Relationship management
  - Delivery management

- Effective vendor management requires more formality with regard to communications and change control.
- Do not assume anything. If it is important to you or your organization, put it in the contract.
- Focus on "win-win" to build better vendor relationships.
- Make sure the vendor has the same goals that you do. Use incentives to align their goals with yours.
- Make sure the WBS is appropriate for effective outsourcing.

The map in Figure 21.1 summarizes the main points reviewed in this chapter.

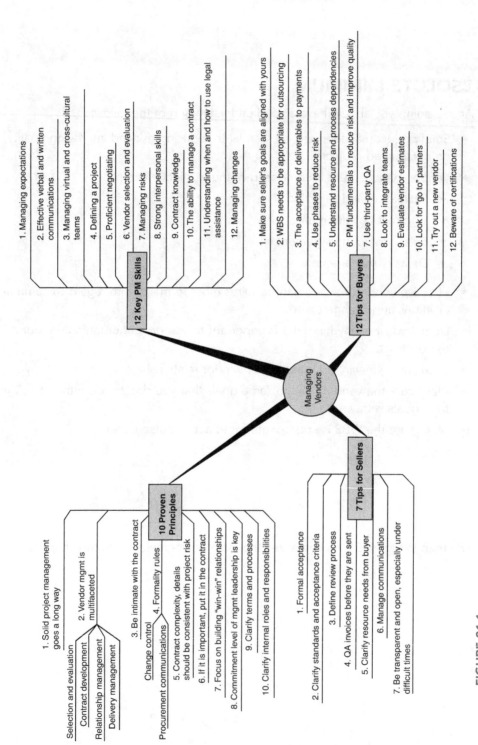

FIGURE 21.1

Overview of managing vendors.

IN THIS CHAPTER

- Find out how to properly bring closure to your project
- Use the Project End Checklist to make sure your projects end in style
- Understand the common challenges to overcome when ending your project
- Review the different reasons a contract and project can end

22

ENDING A PROJECT

As in most personal interactions, how we begin and end the process can make all the difference. The same can be said for projects. Continuing to use the personal interaction analogy, we know how initial impressions and the relationship we establish can make our "goodbye" extremely awkward or very exciting for the promise of what is yet to come. In addition, there is nothing more frustrating in personal relationships than a lack of closure. Our goal, as a project manager, is to bring proper closure to our project for all parties involved and to make sure the last impression everyone has of our work is professional and positive.

In this chapter, we review the key principles that drive successful project closures, the different ways a project can end, the challenges many organizations have in ending a project properly, and of course, the invaluable checklist for ending a project in style.

Three Key Principles

Before we review the checklist items that will drive our project-ending efforts, let's touch on the key principles that drive a successful project close:

- **It is earned along the way**—The main purpose of project management is to achieve the success criteria set forth at the beginning of the project and to meet stakeholder expectations throughout the project. If this is done, a successful project close is almost guaranteed. If not, this is generally why unofficial games like "activate the spin machine," "pick the fall guy," and "bring in the lawyers" were invented.

> **TIP** Develop a Project End Checklist to improve both your and your organization's performance.
>
> Leverage a standard form to document client acceptance and approval of project deliverables. This streamlines the process and helps condition the stakeholders to perform this important activity.
>
> Requirements for formal contract closeout procedures should be defined in the contract's term and conditions.

- **Think end from the start**—A key part of the project plan must focus on how the end of the project will look when we are done, who will own and operate the deliverables, and how to transition those deliverables to them. Many projects have difficulty ending because this process is not clear or understood.

- **Bring closure**—To avoid the emptiness and frustration that is frequently experienced when there is not proper closure, make sure to properly acknowledge the contributions of all project participants, close out the legal and accounting elements, and officially signal that the project is complete.

Project End Checklist: 13 Important Steps

With these principles in mind, the 13 steps included in the project end checklist will ensure that you perform a complete project close and leave the stakeholders with a positive lasting impression of your project management abilities.

> **NOTE** Other common names for Project End Checklist include Project Closure Checklist and Project Closeout Checklist.

1. **Gain client acceptance**—Personally, I would make sure you have this completed before you attempt to close the project. This is most often handled as

exit criteria for user acceptance, post-implementation walkthrough, or a final tollgate meeting (or a combination of these). The key here is to make sure the client has formally verified and accepted the project deliverables. You need to have this documented.

2. **Transition deliverables to owner**—Complete the necessary steps to properly hand off the project deliverables to their intended owner.

3. **Close out contract obligations**—Work with your procurement advisors to make sure that all obligations of the contractual relationship have been met and that all exit criteria have been satisfied.

4. **Capture lessons learned**—Both the positive and negative aspects of the project should be recorded. Ideally, this allows future projects to duplicate the constructive aspects of your project and avoid similar downfalls or mistakes. Of course, this is easier said than done. See the section "Common Project Closing Challenges" later in this chapter for more on this.

 NOTE Lessons learned are part of the project life cycle and include both positive and negative aspects of the project. This allows future projects to duplicate the constructive aspects of your project and avoid similar downfalls or mistakes.

5. **Update the organization's central information repository**—Archive all project management records and as many project deliverables as possible to the organization's central information repository (or knowledge management system). Assuming the repository is easily accessible, searchable, and the contents are protected by a configuration management process, this is a powerful way to reduce learning curves and gain efficiency on future projects.

6. **Issue final financials**—Depending on the nature of the project, work with accounting and procurement to make sure that all financial transactions have taken place, such as invoice generation and final payments. In addition, you should develop the final project financial reports, such as budget summary and variance analysis.

7. **Close accounts and charge codes**—While working with the accounting department, make sure that the process for closing all associated accounts and charge codes is completed.

8. **Update resource schedules**—This is a step that should occur throughout the project. Make sure that the resource scheduling arm of your organization knows well in advance when your project team members will be completed with their assignments on your project and will be available for other opportunities.

9. **Conduct performance evaluations**—Although you should offer performance feedback to team members throughout the project, make sure to complete the formal performance evaluation forms and process when their work assignment is completed. This formal documentation is often key to the individual's career and compensation growth.

 TIP   Most of the project end checklist tasks can be performed at the end of each project phase, too.

10. **Update résumé**—Make sure to update your personal résumé to accurately reflect your project experience, including your roles, responsibilities, accomplishments, and impact. Encourage your other team members to do the same.

11. **Market project accomplishments**—The organizational résumé is a trademark of professional services organizations, but one that can be employed by all organizations and departments. Capture the project highlights and accomplishments in a format that enables the organization to effectively communicate its successes and the value it has offered.

 NOTE   A common approach for creating an organizational résumé is to develop a *white paper* that summarizes the business challenge, goals, approach, key deliverables, and value achieved by the project and organization.

12. **Ask for referrals/references**—Of course, the best testament to client satisfaction is whether the sponsoring individuals (organization) will officially endorse your work. At both a personal and organizational level, this should be the goal from the start. Make sure to ask for it, if the goal has been achieved.

13. **Celebrate!**—Nothing helps bring closure to a project better than an official celebration that recognizes the team's contributions and the accomplishment of the project goals. Make sure to plan the celebration event from the start.

Common Project Closing Challenges

The proper ending of a project is the most neglected project management process. To understand why and to better prepare yourself for this important activity, let's review the common challenges that project managers and organizations have at this stage:

- **Rush to the next project**—Due to the pace of business in today's times, there is often zero downtime between project assignments, and in many cases, the next project is getting started before you have completely ended your previous one. This mode of operation often results in an incomplete project close, especially if the project is completely in house.

- **No accountability**—If there is no one (or department) making sure the project close activities occur or if completion of these activities is not part of your evaluation, it is very easy to let this go. After all, you've delivered the goods, the client is happy…you're done…right?

- **Not seen as "value-added" activities**—As a project manager, if you do not see your organization putting a priority on project close activities, you are going to be much less likely to follow through here. By *priority*, I mean does the organization include this process as part of your evaluation? Does it leverage lessons learned from past projects? Does it value the support, development, and use of a knowledge management system?

- **Lack of transition plan**—Quite simply, there was not enough attention paid at a detailed level to how the project would end and how the deliverables would be handed off to the eventual owners. In some environments, separate *deployment* projects are established to deal with the logistical and detail issues that come into play here.

- **Sanitization of lessons learned**—The most valuable lessons to be learned are often "what not to do." But who wants their faults or bad decisions to be recorded for posterity's sake? It takes strong executive management support and a politician's touch to record useful lessons learned for an organization.

Methods for Ending a Contract or a Project

To simplify the coverage of this process, I have assumed that our project completed as planned, and that any contracts involved also ended at the same time the project completed. In reality, many of these project-ending steps could and should be done at the end of each project phase and not just at the end of the project. These are part of the closing project management process described in the PMI *PMBOK Guide*.

Also, there are other scenarios that can occur to either your project or contractual relationships, and we will quickly review these next. In each of these cases, you should review the project end checklist to see how many of these you can perform.

 NOTE Contract duration does not always equal project duration.

Terminating a Contract

In many cases, the duration of your contract is shorter than the duration of the project, especially if you have only outsourced a specific phase or a portion of the project work. In these cases, your work to bring closure to the contract and vendor relationship is separate from the steps to end the project.

In other cases, the contract might end early because of mutual agreement between the parties or because of a breach of the contract terms. To clarify, a contract can end in one of three ways:

- Successful performance
- Mutual agreement
- Breach

Successful performance is what we think of as getting the work done. All the work specified in the contract was performed by the seller and formally accepted by the buyer. The term *contract termination* refers to the other two ways a contract can end: mutual agreement or breach.

If there is *mutual agreement*, the contract is terminated because both the buyer and the seller involved in the project agree that the project work should not continue. However, if a project contract is terminated due to *breach*, a party involved in the project work has failed to uphold its side of the contract.

Terminating a Project

In the preceding section, we reviewed how a contract can be completed or terminated, and I mentioned that a contract closeout does not always signify the end of a project. However, the end of a project almost always forces a related contract to end. For your reference, Table 22.1 lists the various ways a project can be terminated—all of these would trigger some or all aspects of your project end checklist.

TABLE 22.1 Methods of Project Termination

Method	Description
Completion	Successful performance; getting the work done.
Cancelled	Portfolio management decision due to poor performance, better resource utilization, or realignment with organizational goals.
Displacement	Project becomes obsolete due to another project.
Collapse	Project ends due to external factors, such as natural disasters, corporate mergers, and so on.

Method	Description
Absorption	The project becomes a permanent part of the sponsoring organization (a new department or division).
Deterioration	A "slow death." Neglect. The sponsoring organization gradually reduces its support and budget for the project.

THE ABSOLUTE MINIMUM

At this point, you should have a solid understanding of the following:

- Many of the steps involved with ending a project might need to be performed at the end of each project phase.
- Client acceptance of project deliverables should be formal and documented.
- Ensure that the transition plan of project deliverables is performed.
- Capture lessons learned from the project (both positive and negative) to help the organization in the future.
- Take care of your project team members—give them official performance feedback, offer to serve as a reference (if appropriate), and help them transition to their next assignment.
- Archive all project management items and all project deliverables (if permitted) to your organization's knowledge management system for future use and reference.
- Ensure that contractual obligations have been met and that all contracts are finalized properly.
- Tie up the financials, including final transactions, reports, and closing of associated charge and accounting codes.
- Capture and market the accomplishments of the project.
- Make sure to celebrate and recognize the achievements of the project.

The map in Figure 22.1 summarizes the main points reviewed in this chapter.

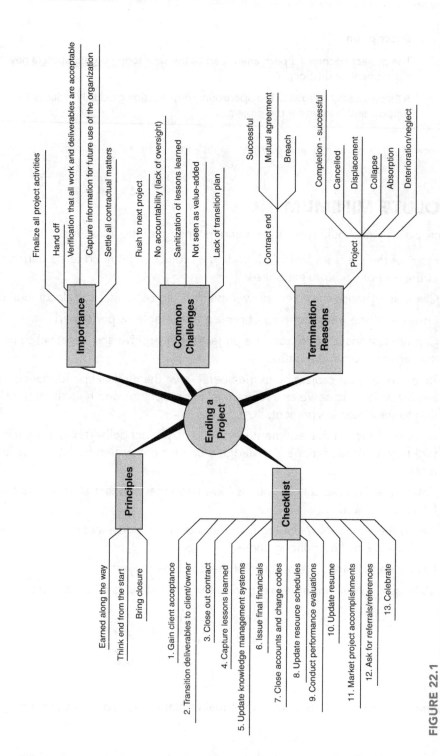

FIGURE 22.1

Overview of ending a project.

23

MAKING BETTER USE OF MICROSOFT PROJECT

It's not perfect. It has limitations. It can be frustrating. But, with a little experienced insight, you can quickly learn how to make Microsoft Project your friend and, more importantly, how to use Microsoft Project to be a better project manager.

This chapter is not a comprehensive instruction manual on Microsoft Project. This chapter focuses on accelerating your learning curve. It assumes you have some working knowledge of Microsoft Project already and that you are using Microsoft Project to manage an isolated, single project that does not include Microsoft Project Server.

Specifically, this chapter reviews the key design elements that drive how Microsoft Project behaves, the key features in Microsoft Project that you need to know about, the best practice for starting any new project, ten must-know features of Microsoft Project, tips for avoiding common frustrations, powerful techniques for effectively reporting from Microsoft Project, and the key differences in the versions of Microsoft Project that are still supported.

At the time I am updating this book for the fifth edition, the available versions of Project for purchase from Microsoft are Microsoft Project 2019, Project Online, and Project for the Web.

Microsoft Project 2010 went out of support in 2020. Microsoft Project 2013 and Project 2016 are still supported, with Project 2013 expected to be out of support in 2023. We will review the key updates in each of these releases and the key differences in the three current versions, so that you are up to speed.

It's important to understand that although I have acquired a great deal of experience with Microsoft Project, have received consistent positive feedback for how I've used the tool from my circle of peers (of course, this may more be a reflection of my peers), and can share lessons, tips, and insights that will greatly reduce your learning curve, I am still learning too. The continuous learning is due to three primary factors: Microsoft Project is a feature-packed application, new versions bring additional and revised features, and you learn what you need to know to accomplish the task at hand.

Understand This...and It All Becomes Easier

As is the case when learning any new concept, skill, or tool, if you are taught the supporting principles first, everything else that follows is much easier to learn. Why? Because you have a framework, a context, to organize the details and explain the specific behaviors. It's no different here. Let's review the key design fundamentals behind Microsoft Project that will help you better understand how the tool works and help you avoid many frustrations that others commonly experience.

- **It's a database**—This is an important one. Microsoft Project is not like most other Office products. There is a relational database engine behind it. Why is this good to know?

  - First, it helps explain all the View, Display, and Table options from which you have to choose. These are all just different slices (views) of the same set of core database tables.

- Second, you can include any of these standard fields in any view you want. Do not limit yourself to what you first see. You are not limited to the default column displays that you are first presented, and you can easily insert new columns at any time.

> **NOTE** Take the time to review the available tables in Microsoft Project. It reinforces the idea that Microsoft Project is indeed a database, accelerates your awareness of all the data points that are available, and opens your mind to new ways to leverage the tool.
>
> The tables can be accessed from the View, Table menu. In addition, a complete description of the available tables is available from the Project Help system (Help, Microsoft Project Help).

- **Dates are serious business**—Two of the most powerful and useful aspects of Project are its capability to develop an accurate calendar-based schedule based on the tasks, effort estimates, and assigned resources, and its capability to provide "what-if" impact analysis based on any proposed change to those elements. However, these can both be neutralized by doing one simple thing: manually entering values for either the start date or finish date for a task. When a start or finish date is manually entered, a constraint is established for this task, either a Start No Earlier Than or Finish No Later Than constraint. Either prevents Project from scheduling the task, and the task does not respond to changes to predecessor tasks or resource assignments as you would expect due to this fixed constraint. We cover the best practice for entering tasks on new projects later in this chapter. To be clear, I'm not saying that you will *never* enter a fixed date for a task, because there are times it will be appropriate. However, it should be the exception.

> **CAUTION** Avoid entering a start or finish date when adding new tasks.

> **TIP** Set a deadline date on a task rather than entering a finish date to prevent Project from establishing a hard-coded constraint on the task.

> **NOTE** Microsoft embraces the capability to enter your own start and finish dates with the introduction of manual (or user-controlled) scheduling versus automatic scheduling performed by the tool. Specifically, the new Top Down Summary Task feature makes it much easier to do high-level plans and rolling wave planning now.

- **Task Duration = Work Effort × Resource Units**—If you understand the fundamentals behind schedule development, as were reviewed in Chapter 6,

"Developing the Work Breakdown Structure," Chapter 7, "Estimating the Work," and Chapter 8, "Developing the Project Schedule," this formula is easy to understand; however, if you do not understand the fundamentals, it can frustrate you. What does this formula mean? It means that the amount of time it takes to complete a given task is a product of the total work effort involved and the number of resources applied to the task, not to mention the availability of those resources. So, why does it cause confusion at times?

- Many people assume Duration is the same as Work Effort, and Duration is a default column displayed by Microsoft Project on many popular views.

- When you update or change any of the three components of the formula, Project updates the other values accordingly. This routinely occurs when resources are assigned to tasks.

- **Multiple calendars**—Although most people are aware that there is a calendar for the project—after all, it is the ability to easily capture the time dimension for our WBS and task lists that makes Project an attractive work tool option—many people do not leverage the project calendar properly nor realize that each resource can have its own calendar too. This provides a great deal of flexibility and accuracy when scheduling resources and evaluating impact to your overall project timeline. In addition, a specific task can even have its own calendar (which overrides the calendars of any resources assigned to that task). Calendars are available from the Tools, Change Working Time menu item, and they are summarized in Table 23.1.

TABLE 23.1 Summary of Microsoft Project Calendar Types

Calendar Type	Description	Notes
Project	Calendar applied as default for all project tasks	Standard is the default.
		Apply organizational calendar and any nonstandard productivity levels here.
Resource	Calendar for specific resource	Project creates one for each resource.
		Apply resource-specific schedule constraints (vacations) and availability levels here.
		Overrides project calendar.
Task	Calendar applied to specific task	Ignores project calendar.
		You control whether this ignores resource calendars.

TIP   Remember to Apply the new or updated calendar to the view you are working with...not just Change Working Time. Project does not always do this automatically.

- **Planned versus Actual versus Baseline**—Microsoft could have avoided a lot of confusion by simply adding one word to two fields in the Project database. If the Start Date field was named "Planned" Start Date and the Finish Date field was named "Planned" Finish Date, most users would have a quicker understanding of what the fields actually represent and how these fields relate to their Actual and Baseline versions.

- **Default settings**—Like any software application, Project has default settings. The key is to understand what they are, what they impact, and how you can change them to make Project work the way you want it to. The default settings are found primarily on the Tools, Options dialog. We'll review the key default settings to consider as part of the "Best Practices for Setting Up a New Project" section later in this chapter.

Need-to-Know Features

With those fundamentals in mind, let's review specific features of Project that will help you make better use of the tool. Four complaints often heard about Project include "It's hard to develop schedules that reflect reality," "It's difficult to show all the information to others," "It's tough to read or understand a Project schedule," and "It's good for planning, but not very helpful as a tool to manage the project." These features address those complaints. They will help you develop a more accurate schedule, communicate more effectively, and make it easier to use as a management tool. Most importantly, these features are *not* obvious to new users.

NOTE   There are a couple of ways to accurately account for part-time resources in your schedule. You can adjust their resource calendars to show how many hours a day they are available. This is best when the availability level is constant for the duration of the project. You also can indicate the availability level at the task level when the resource is assigned (that is, Horine [50%]). This is best when the availability level is not constant or is unique for this specific task.

It is also the best approach if you need to clearly and explicitly communicate the part-time level of the given resource for the task.

- **Calendars**—By default, Project uses a calendar that recognizes no holidays and assumes all resources work five days a week, eight hours a day. This can result in a schedule that is not as realistic as it should be. All Project calendars are found (and can be adjusted) from the Tools, Change Working Time menu option, including the individual resource calendars. Normally, you want to adjust the default project calendar to account for organization-wide resource availability factors, such as standard holidays and standard productivity levels. For availability factors that apply only to a specific resource, you want to adjust the respective resource calendars. The common reasons to do this would be to accurately account for days the resource is not available to the project effort (planned vacation days, planned paid time off, planned conferences, and so on) and to account for non-full-time availability levels.

- **Custom fields**—A powerful and useful feature of Project is the availability of custom fields. Custom fields can be added to any view, and they can be used to store or display any data item. They can be used to help you better manage the project or to help you better communicate project status to others. In a custom field, you can store any type of data, you can define a value list, and you can even incorporate visual indicators (graphic symbols).

  Personally, I use custom fields for visual indicators (I cover this next), to capture resource notes (especially if I want to show assigned resources at the summary task level), to save a previous set of baseline (or target) dates, or to show which deliverable is associated with the task. You can leverage custom fields by first defining your custom field (via the Tools, Customize, Fields menu option or by selecting Customize Fields from the right-click menu) and then inserting the field into your desired table or view.

   NOTE Since Project 2010, Microsoft introduced many more Excel-type features to Project, including the capability to add new fields (table columns) dynamically. There's no need to select the data type first now.

- **Visual indicators**—As hinted earlier, the custom field enables you to incorporate visual (graphical) indicators into your project file. Project provides a set of visual symbols that you can use to provide better reporting and better communication. You can define the field to change the graphical indicator (symbol) displayed based on the value associated with the field. The value could be a value you manually enter (and control) or the value could be automatically determined by a formula you define. See Figure 23.1, Figure 23.2, and Figure 23.3 for examples of using a formula with a custom field (Baseline Check) to automatically display a visual status for each task when comparing against the Baseline Finish date. Table 23.2 provides a summary of the logic and parameters used. Graphical indicators are defined by selecting Customize Fields, Values to Display, Graphical Indicators.

FIGURE 23.1

Formula assigned to custom field (Baseline Check).

FIGURE 23.2

Assigning formula values for Baseline Check to graphical symbols, part 1.

FIGURE 23.3

Assigning formula values for Baseline Check to graphical symbols, part 2.

The most popular indicators are the three-dimensional color symbols, the three-dimensional arrows, the colored flags, the emoticons, and the light bulb icon. See Figure 23.4 for a partial list of the available symbols.

TABLE 23.2 Summary of Parameters Used for Baseline Check Example

Test	Value	Action	Notes
If no baseline finish date for task	10	Do not display anything	Baseline Finish has NA value.
If task is not completed and variance cannot be determined	5	Display question mark symbol	
If task is completed	4	Display check mark symbol	
Finish variance more than 4 days	3	Display RED three-dimensional square	Formula uses 480 minutes to represent an 8-hour day. 4 days = 1920 minutes.
Finish variance between 2–4 days	2	Display YELLOW three-dimensional square	2 days = 960 minutes.
Finish variance less than 2 days	1	Display GREEN three-dimensional square	Formula returns this value if none of the other conditions are satisfied.

FIGURE 23.4

Partial list of available graphical indicators.

- **Gantt bar format**—Another default setting that contributes to the perception that Project is difficult to use for status reporting is the Gantt bar default format. Many users of Project do not realize that the format of the Gantt bar can be changed. You can change the size, the color, and the end point symbols used. You can have different task types automatically use different Gantt bar format settings (Bar Styles), and you can determine what field values (if any) that you want to display alongside the bar. The Gantt bar format can be modified by right-clicking directly on the displayed Gantt Bar or by selecting Format, Bar or Format, Bar Styles.

- **Task format**—Closely related to the Gantt bar formatting feature, you can also control the textual display format of each task. Many new users of Project get frustrated with the default task displays, especially if they attempt to use their Project file for communication or reporting purposes. You can have different task types automatically use different display format settings, and you can change the background cell color, text color, size, and font of any task.

  It's worth noting that after you have a format you like, you can quickly apply the same format to other selected tasks by using the Format Painter function. Task Display format can be modified by right-clicking directly on the highlighted task and selecting Font or Text Styles or by selecting Format, Font or Format, Text Styles.

  TIP Use the standard Microsoft Office Format Painter function to quickly apply a desired display format to other tasks.

- **Timescale**—Another feature that greatly improves reporting and communicating from Project is the capability to adjust the timescale that is displayed. Many new users of Project do not realize this can be modified. By altering the timescale displayed, you can better control how much of your project timeline (Gantt bar) can be seen on one page (or screen). In other words, you can make the Gantt bar fit. The timescale can be modified by right-clicking directly on the displayed timescale in the Gantt bar view or by selecting Format, Timescale.

- **Copy Picture**—Here's another powerful reporting feature that even many experienced Project users do not know how to leverage properly. Rather than trying to insert an entire project (.mpp file) object into a Word document or PowerPoint presentation and then spending time attempting to get it to display in a semi-legible manner, you can use the Copy Picture function to take a snapshot directly from your Project file and then paste the resulting image into your target Word file or PowerPoint presentation slide. In addition, you do not have to copy all the currently displayed tasks. If you want to copy only certain tasks, you can select those targeted tasks before you choose the Copy Picture function. You can access the Copy Picture function from the standard toolbar or from Edit, Copy Picture.

 TIP   Make sure to hide any columns you do not want (or need) to display before you activate the Copy Picture function.

 NOTE   Since Project 2010 improved the capability to share information from Project by introducing the new Timeline View feature, maintaining task organization and formatting when doing a copy/paste, providing the capability to enter notes in any cell (including dates), providing for use of drawing tools in Gantt Bar view, and providing richer color palette and text formatting options.

- **WBS**—Another common complaint with Project files, especially for files that have a large number of tasks, files that have a lot of detail, or files that have multiple levels of task detail, is that it can be very challenging to see the organization (the context) of the work tasks. It can be difficult to see how one task relates to another task.

  A simple, but powerful, way to enhance the organization and readability of your schedule is to display the Work Breakdown Structure (WBS) field. This provides a numeric identification for each task that quickly communicates how it relates to the other tasks. There are two methods for displaying the WBS value. If you want the WBS value to appear in its own column, you need to add the column by selecting Insert Column and choosing the WBS field from the list. If you want the WBS value to appear as a prefix to the task name, you need to enable Show Outline Number from the Tools, Options, View tab— Outline Options section.

- **Detecting Resource Overallocation**—Another common issue with schedules created with Project is that users do not check for overallocated resources, often because they do not know how to do this. This is actually an easy aspect to check. If you select View, Resource Allocation or View, Resource Usage, Project displays any overallocated resource in red text. In addition, it shows you in which time period(s) the resource is overallocated. Knowing this, you can decide what action to take to resolve each overallocation situation. Of course, you might simply need to perform *resource leveling*, and we discuss this in more detail later in this chapter.

NOTE In Project Professional 2010, the Team Planner feature provides a visual mechanism to easily assign resources to tasks, quickly identify unassigned or unscheduled tasks, and manage resource leveling.

- **Displaying Tasks**—Many new users do not realize that you can easily control what level of task detail is displayed, which tasks are displayed, and even how the tasks are organized when they are displayed. With this control, you create much more flexibility in how you communicate and report using your Project file. These task display control features are readily available from the standard Project toolbar (and from the Project menu), but they are frequently underutilized. See Figure 23.5 for the toolbar references.

  - **Show Outline**—Enables you to display the tasks by WBS hierarchical level. It enables you to control how much detail is displayed. In many cases, I use this feature to reset my display to base level. Then I selectively expand certain tasks to show the associated detail.

FIGURE 23.5

Task selection functions on toolbars.

 TIP When re-baselining a schedule, capture the event (issue, delay, decision) that is responsible for change and link this to impacted tasks rather than directly modifying the date fields.

- **Filters**—Enables you to display only the tasks that meet certain criteria. This is commonly used to show only tasks assigned to specific resource(s) or to show only tasks within a certain time period. Project provides a comprehensive set of predefined filters, but it also allows you to define custom filters, including filters based on your own custom fields. In addition, you have the same auto-filtering capability you are accustomed to using in Excel.

- **Group By**—Enables you to categorize and report project information in a variety of ways. Grouping also enables you to view rolled-up summary information for tasks, resources, or assignments on each field in the group. Like filters, Project provides a solid predefined list of groups, but also enables you to define your own groups, including ones based on your own custom fields.

- **Baselining**—A closing step in the schedule development process and an essential tool for proactively controlling project performance is to establish a baseline (see Chapter 8, "Developing the Project Schedule," and Chapter 10, "Controlling a Project," for more details on this). The baseline captures the data entered to date (estimates, tasks, resources, assignments, and even actual work) as permanent reference points that can be used as a point of comparison. You save a schedule baseline by selecting Tools, Tracking, Save Baseline (or Set Baseline). Project stores up to ten different baselines for you (in case you need to re-baseline). Project provides several ways to compare actual performance against the baseline, including the Tracking Gantt view (View, Tracking Gantt). In addition, if I do need to re-baseline the project schedule, I like to do three things to link the schedule with the project change control system:

  1. Update the baseline version number (and display the baseline version somewhere in the footer or header).

  2. Capture the event that is responsible for the re-baseline as a new task or milestone (if you have not already done so) and link this to the tasks that are affected.

  3. Capture the associated change request number that documents the schedule change in the Project file—either on the task mentioned in #2 or as a project note.

Best Practices for Setting Up a New Project

Now that we've reviewed the key fundamentals and need-to-know features of Project, let's run down the best practices for setting up a new file. Many of the frustrations experienced by new Project users originate from the start in part because they do not build their schedule file with these practices in mind. By following this approach, you can build a schedule file that allows for what-if analysis, a file that becomes a useful management tool throughout the project. In addition, these practices are consistent with the schedule development process covered in Chapters 6 through 8. Here are my recommendations for starting a new project:

 NOTE Microsoft made it much easier to do what-if analysis using Project by introducing the ability to make tasks active or inactive.

- **Set Project Start Date**—Control the date Project uses as the beginning date for your schedule by setting the project start date. This is done in the Project Information dialog shown in Figure 23.6.

> **TIP** To help ensure that any future project file you create has the desired default setting, click the Set as Default button on the General tab before closing the Tools, Options dialog.

FIGURE 23.6

Dialog used to set the project start date.

- **Set Project Summary Task (Row Zero)**—Go to Tools, Options, View, and in the Outline options area, select the Show Project Summary Task checkbox. With this set, Project adds a row zero to the top of your schedule that summarizes all your project information. This is a tremendous timesaver for identifying the planned finish date and the total work effort.

- **Review default settings**—There are a handful of default settings under Tools, Options that can be troublesome if you're not aware of what is going on (see Figure 23.7).

FIGURE 23.7

Use the Tools, Options dialog to review settings.

- **Autolink tasks**—On the Schedule tab, clear the Autolink on Inserted or Moved Tasks checkbox if you do not want Project to automatically create predecessor links (dependencies) between tasks as you enter them. I turn this off (uncheck, clear) because I want to purposefully set the logical dependencies between my tasks.

- **Tasks honoring constraint dates**—On the Schedule tab, clear the Tasks Will Always Honor Their Constraint Dates checkbox. This causes a warning indicator to constantly appear in the Indicators column whenever the given task is violating a constraint date. Otherwise, you only receive an initial warning. You want to be sure you are aware of these constraint violations:

 TIP After you set up a project file (*.mpp) with the custom columns, formats, and settings you like, you can use this file as a template for future projects.

- **Multiple critical paths**—Most users want to deal with only one critical path at a time. You want Project to clearly identify the single critical path driving your planned completion date. To be sure this happens, go to File, Options, choose Advanced, scroll to the bottom, and clear the Calculate multiple critical paths checkbox.

- **Adding new resources**—This is personal preference. By default, Project automatically adds resources for you as you assign them to tasks. This sounds great, and it can be a timesaver; however, it does not perform any validation on your resource entries. You can end up with a lot of typos as resources and a lot of multiple references to the same resource. Both are problematic. On the other hand, if you turn off this feature, you need to enter your resources in advance (on the Resource Sheet) before you can assign them to tasks. If you want to turn off this setting, go to the General tab and clear the Automatically Add New Resources and Tasks checkbox.

- **Default scheduling mode**—New tasks are scheduled manually by default. To change this, go to File, Options, Schedule; then scroll to Scheduling options for this project section set the value for New Tasks Created to Auto Scheduled.

- **Set project calendar**—Go to Tools, Change Working Time to modify the standard calendar that should be used for the project.

- **Set header and footer**—To better prepare your Project file for reporting and distribution, set up the header and the footer sections. I like to add the project name to the header section, and I like to add the following to the footer section: filename, baseline version number, and page X of Y. You can access the header and footer under File, Page Setup.

- **Enter and organize tasks**—If we followed our schedule development process, we'll enter the tasks using our deliverable-based WBS. Besides the reminder *not* to enter a start or finish date for the task, I strongly encourage use of the Notes field to capture any assumptions that will be important to reference. In addition, it is easy to see these notes because Project includes a notes icon in the Indicators column, and it automatically displays the note when you put your cursor over the icon.

- **Set milestones**—If there are any milestone or fixed target dates that must be honored, enter those dates for the respective tasks as deadlines on the actual tasks or as "milestone only" tasks. Both the deadline attribute and the milestone attribute for a task are set on the Advanced tab in the Task Information dialog; see Figure 23.8 for clarification.

FIGURE 23.8

Set the milestone flag and deadline date in the Task Information, Advanced dialog for a task.

 NOTE A milestone task has zero duration and will not impact calculations for work hours, duration, or cost.

- **Set external dependencies**—I would also enter placeholder tasks for any external dependencies that your project has, and I would establish a link (predecessor relationship) to those tasks. This way, you can clearly communicate these dependencies so that they are not just assumptions that get lost in other planning documents. And if the completion dates for those dependencies change, you can clearly identify the effect to your project.

- **Capture logical dependencies**—After your tasks are entered and organized, you want to purposefully capture the logical dependencies between your tasks. Do not consider any resource dependencies. Again, if you have followed the schedule development process discussed in Chapters 6 through 8, you will have this information from your team work sessions.

 CAUTION Avoid establishing dependencies between tasks based on resource assignments whenever possible.

- **Set up custom fields**—Insert and set up any custom columns you want or need for this project.

 TIP For better control of resource leveling, set the priority level of your tasks (Priority field).

- **Enter estimated durations or work efforts**—For each task, enter the estimated duration or work efforts by resource. Until a resource is assigned, no work effort is calculated for the task.

- **Assign resources to each task**—Now you are ready to assign resources to the tasks and continue the schedule development process.

Keys to Making Resource Leveling Work

One of the key need-to-know features of Project mentioned earlier is the capability to detect resource overallocation. A step that you can take to be sure your resources are not overallocated is to perform resource leveling on your schedule. If used correctly, resource leveling is a powerful tool to help you identify and remove resource allocations, especially with large, detailed schedules. Often, these overallocations identify the tasks that might benefit from additional resources. However, in my experience, many project management professionals underutilize this feature. One of the main reasons for this is the lack-of-control feeling that many people experience when attempting to use it. I can't promise to alleviate all your frustrations, but here are some keys to making resource leveling work for you rather than against you:

- **Use manual resource leveling**—The resource leveling function is sensitive and might give you some unanticipated schedule changes if Project does this automatically. If you want to control when resource leveling occurs, select the Manual radio button in the Leveling Calculations area on the Tools, Level Resources dialog.

- **Capture task dependencies**—Make sure to follow the schedule development best practices and capture the logical dependencies between your tasks. This goes a long way in getting logical results from the resource leveling process.

- **Be cautious assigning resources to summary tasks**—This issue applies to several behaviors of Project, and resource leveling is one of them. For summary tasks, make sure a resource is *not* assigned to both the summary task and to one or more of the detailed tasks. It's okay to assign a resource to a summary task if all the detail tasks are assigned to that resource. Often this situation occurs when a task is further detailed (subtasks added) after the initial resource assignment is made.

- **Use the Priority column**—In my experience, this is the least understood key to making resource leveling work for you. Often, when all tasks have the same default priority value, Project does some funny things when leveling resources. A common result is that Project bounces a resource between two separate summary tasks for no logical reason, or it assigns a resource to a less important task first. But, if we have not told Project which tasks are more important (by adjusting the task priority level), then how will it know? Again, this is an issue for tasks that do not have logical dependencies established but that have the same priority level. To do this, insert/display the Priority column and adjust the priority values for each task accordingly. Then when you execute resource leveling (Tools, Resource Leveling), be sure that the Leveling Order is set to Priority, Standard (see Figure 23.9).

FIGURE 23.9

Set the leveling order in the Tools, Resource Leveling dialog.

- **Set the Level Only with Available Slack option**—When you prepare to execute resource leveling (Tools, Resource Leveling), make sure the Level Only with Available Slack checkbox is selected. This prevents Project from moving the finish date and forces the overallocations to be identified. When you feel most of your overallocations that are due to a lack of resources have been resolved and you want Project to give you a more realistic finish date, then clear this checkbox.

One way to check the results of the resource leveling process is to use the Filters view to show only the tasks for a selected resource (Project, Filtered For, Using Resource). With this view, you can quickly check whether the resource has been logically assigned to tasks and that this availability has been maximized. For individuals who are new to resource leveling, this can be an educational exercise and it can help build confidence in the resource leveling engine.

In addition, you can use the Team Planner feature to manage the resource leveling process.

 CAUTION Remember, resource leveling does not guarantee you the best plan; it only guarantees to remove resource overallocations.

Powerful Reporting Secrets

What do we frequently hear when it comes to generating Project reports or when other stakeholders attempt to read a Project schedule: "I can't show all the data I need," "I can't get the Gantt Bar to fit on one page," "I don't like the appearance of the schedule," "The reports are boring," "There's too much detail—I can't tell where I am," "It's too hard to read," "It takes a lot of effort," "I can't share my project file with anyone because they don't have Project." Yeah, that's a fair sampling. Does it have to be this way? No, it does not—and by now, you likely have a good feeling for how you can address many of these complaints.

The three primary keys to better reporting with Project are awareness of capabilities, clarity of audience needs, and creativity. A significant portion of this chapter has focused on raising awareness of Project capabilities and options, and we'll revisit the ones that deal with reporting. Next, the more you understand about what your audience wants, the better. It will help you focus on where to invest your effort. What do they need to see? What level of detail are they concerned with? How will they read your report? If you combine the answers to these questions with your knowledge of what Project can do, you can develop a targeted approach to best share your Project schedule information. Let's review the keys to improving your reporting efforts:

NOTE While this section on Powerful Reporting Secrets was written with pre-2010 versions of Microsoft Project in mind and Microsoft has greatly improved reporting capabilities since then, these fundamentals will help you improve your ability to effectively share project status information with stakeholders.

- **Take care of the basics**—How many times have you seen a Project printout and you have no idea what project it is from, when it was printed, when it was last updated, what page number you are looking at, or what baseline it is from? A simple, yet often overlooked, step you can take to improve the readability of your Project file is to use a header and footer. At a minimum, I like to show the project name in the header section, and the filename, baseline version, and page number X of Y in the footer section.

 TIP Include an organizational logo picture in the Header section of your Project file to further personalize for your targeted audience.

- **Control the fields you are displaying**—Often, users have a difficult time getting everything to fit because they are showing fields/columns they do not need. Remember to hide any columns that are not essential for your given audience. In addition, you can adjust the width of any of your columns.

- **Tailor with custom fields**—As we've discussed earlier with custom fields, you can show practically any type of information alongside each task row. You are not limited to the standard columns that Project shows in a given view. On past projects, I've used custom fields to show information such as Status Comments, Resource Notes, and Deliverable Notes. In addition, I've used a custom field like Resource Notes to show resource assignments at the summary task level without impacting the actual work effort calculations in Project.

- **Control the tasks you are displaying**—Use the outlining, filtering, and grouping features (discussed earlier) to control which tasks are actually displayed. In most cases, showing summary tasks at a given level is sufficient for reporting purposes. This step can go a long way in providing reports that are understandable and useful for your audience. In my experience, I find that the level of detail I need to show is not consistent for the entire schedule. For example, phases that have already been completed can easily be shown at a high summary level, whereas activity for the current phase can be displayed at a lower level of detail.

- **Modify formats**—As mentioned before, you have the power to change the format of the displayed text. I often develop a style for tasks at a certain hierarchical level. They have the same font, size (normally larger), and color. This way it is even easier to see and understand the organization of the project.

- **Determine whether you need to show the Gantt Bar**—This might sound like heresy, but check to see whether your audience wants to see the Gantt Bar. If they do, you need to decide what data to show with the task Gantt Bar, what format to use for the Gantt Bar at each level, and which data to show in the table columns. If they do not, you end up with a table and space to show much more information. I have found the Gantt Bar to offer the most value in high-level summary presentations of my schedule. To convey detailed schedule information, I rarely use the Gantt Bar.

- **Modify timescale**—This is important if you are displaying the Gantt Bar, and we talked about this feature earlier, too. In many cases, to show the entire Gantt Bar on one page, you need to adjust the default timescale that Project is using.

- **Add attention-getting visuals**—Use custom fields with graphical indicators to add stoplight status to each task or to visually highlight other aspects about the task, such as risk level, task has associated issue, task is in progress, or importance level of task. See Figure 23.10 for an example of a schedule that uses two custom graphical indicator columns.

 TIP If you use any other calendar for the main project calendar besides the Standard calendar, be sure you also update the Gantt chart timescale format to use this calendar by going to Format, Timescale, Non-working Time tab and select your nonstandard calendar as the one to use.

	0	Focus	WBS	Task Name	Baseline Status	% Complete	Start	Finish	Dur
0			0	- **Phase1 - QC Interfaces**	▫	38%	Tue 6/3/08	Wed 4/15/09	45.4
1			1	Project Management - Monitoring and Control	▫	53%	Tue 6/3/08	Mon 4/6/09	44 wks
2		⚑	2	- **Vendor Interface Development & Testing**	◆	78%	Wed 7/2/08	Wed 1/7/09	27.2
3	✓		2.1	+ Review and Approve DRS and Test Plans	✓	100%	Wed 7/2/08	Fri 8/22/08	7.6 w
67		➡	2.2	+ Review Test Results	?	37%	Tue 9/16/08	Fri 10/10/08	3.8 w
70		➡	2.3	- Sample Files Delivered	◆	41%	Thu 8/14/08	Wed 1/7/09	21 wk
71			2.3.1	+ Data Feeds (Inbound)	◆	42%	Thu 8/14/08	Wed 1/7/09	21 wk
108			2.3.2	+ Report Feeds	▫	33%	Mon 9/15/08	Wed 12/31/08	15.6
114		➡	3	- **Develop Client Interfaces & Reports**	▫	28%	Mon 8/18/08	Fri 1/16/09	22 wk
115	▣		3.1	QC Reviews - BRDs	▫	90%	Mon 8/18/08	Fri 11/21/08	70 day
116	▣	⚑	3.2	QC Reviews - UT Plans	▫	0%	Mon 9/15/08	Fri 12/19/08	70 day
117	▣		3.3	QC Reviews - UT Results	▫	0%	Mon 9/15/08	Fri 1/16/09	90 day
118			3.4	+ BRDs Approved	▫	99%	Fri 8/29/08	Mon 11/17/08	11.2 w
140			3.5	+ Unit Test Results Approved	▫	0%	Thu 1/15/09	Thu 1/15/09	0 wks
162	▣		3.6	Move Interfaces to UAT Environment	▫	0%	Thu 1/15/09	Fri 1/16/09	2 day
163			4	+ Data File Validation	▫	77%	Mon 6/16/08	Tue 4/7/09	42.4
238	▣		5	<Dependency> BPO Acceptance Test Execution	▫	0%	Tue 11/25/08	Mon 2/2/09	10 w
239			6	- Downstream Acceptance Testing	▫	19%	Mon 7/7/08	Wed 4/15/09	40.6
240			6.1	+ Planning	▫	20%	Mon 7/7/08	Wed 1/28/09	29.6
378			6.2	+ Test Execution	▫	0%	Thu 1/29/09	Wed 4/15/09	11 wk

FIGURE 23.10

Example of attention-getting visuals.

- **Leverage Copy Picture**—Leverage the Copy Picture function to include your Project information in other document format types such as PowerPoint and Word. Just be sure to tailor the columns and tasks you want to display first. This feature is found on the Task tab, Clipboard group, Copy button, Copy Picture.

- **Use the power of Page Setup**—The Page Setup options are certainly not unique to Project, but it seems like many users forget about the flexibility they offer. In my experience, the most useful Page Setup features are scaling adjustments (just like in Excel), margin adjustments, and, on the View tab, Fit Timescale to End of Page and Print First *X* Columns on All Pages. See Figure 23.11 for a reference to the Page Setup, View dialog.

FIGURE 23.11

Page setup options are set in the Page Setup, View dialog.

- **Determine how users will read it**—This goes hand-in-hand with controlling the tasks you display. You need to know how your audience will read your report (or schedule view). Do they have Project or Project Viewer? Do they want to see it as a part of another report or presentation? Do they want it online or just as a hard copy? The answers to these questions tell you whether you need to create snapshots and, if so, what format you need to target.

 TIP If your stakeholders do not have Project, distribute your report (schedule views) as PDF files.

- **Leverage canned reports**—Project provides a significant list of canned reports that most people never look at. The following are three reasons why:

  - The standard views end up meeting 80% to 90% of the information needs.

  - Users have not invested time to become aware of what reports exist.

  - Users do not like the standard information or appearance of the reports. This area is an untapped resource for most people.

    Nearly all the canned reports that are available under View, Reports can be customized. At a minimum, you can adjust appearance details such as color, font style, and font size, and this is often by row or data category. However, for many reports, you can control the data displayed with task selection and the use of groups and filters.

     NOTE Starting with Project 2013, Microsoft significantly improved the reporting capability. A user can create rich dashboard-style professional reports directly from Project. In addition, there are more preconfigured reports, including work reports, project overview reports, burn-down charts, and task boards, that leverage the new built-in graphic, charting, and formatting capabilities.

- **Leverage visual reports**—Project offers a solid set of summary and pivot table reports that use Visio and Excel templates, and these can be used as is or tailored as needed.

     TIP Consider setting up a custom text field as resource notes to control the display of resource information without affecting resource work assignments.

- **Distribute multiple views**—If you have a schedule with multiple levels of work detail, it can be challenging to provide views at the detail level while also ensuring the reader maintains perspective with the overall schedule. This challenge increases with additional levels of work detail and with stakeholders who do not have Project. In these cases, I do not hesitate to provide multiple views (or snapshots) of the schedule: a high-level summary view that provides overall schedule context, and additional detail views for each current or hot area of the schedule.

- **Use callout features**—This is one feature I wish Microsoft would incorporate directly into Project. If you find yourself having to use PowerPoint or Word to deliver your schedule updates, consider the use of callouts to highlight key risks, dependencies, assumptions, and target dates (see Figure 23.12). I normally use Copy Picture to get the base Gantt chart view from Project, then access the callout object from the Drawing toolbar (AutoShapes, Callouts).

TIP   If you are defining a new work process that will be repeated, nail down the process first before you propagate the detail. It will save you a lot of rework or editing.

FIGURE 23.12

Example of using the callout feature.

- **Consider using two versions**—In many situations, it might be simpler and less time-consuming to work with two versions of your Project schedule. You can use one version to manage the project and another version to report the status. This approach can free you to capture all the details you want and need in your day-to-day working schedule without affecting the clarity and conciseness of your reporting process.

- **Timeline View**—Since Project 2010, instead of having to build your own custom timeline reporting structures in Visio, PowerPoint, or some other graphical drawing tool, you can just do it all within your Project file. With the Timeline View, you can easily show as much or as little detail as you need, control which tasks are included, and completely customize the look and feel of the timeline. And most importantly, you can easily copy the final Timeline to other applications to quickly share with others.

NOTE Since Microsoft Project 2016, you can now have multiple Timeline views. This makes it even easier to quickly generate effective and easy-to-understand reports directly from Project.

More Insights to a Better Project Schedule

Here's a list of additional tips and insights from my experience that can help you build a better schedule with Project:

- **Managing timeline expectations**—Often, people avoid using Project to communicate during the project definition or project planning stage because Project incorporates the calendar aspect, and when stakeholders see real calendar dates even in preliminary, high-level schedules, their expectations can be influenced. A simple way to manage these expectations is to change the timescale labels that Project displays. As previously mentioned, the timescale can be modified by right-clicking directly on the displayed timescale in the Gantt Bar view or by selecting the Format, Timescale menu option. After the Timescale dialog is displayed, you will want to change the label format used. Simply select an option that does not use an actual calendar date, such as "Week 1, Week 2...Week N."

- **Assigning resources to summary tasks**—If you are using Project to estimate, schedule, or manage resource work hours, be wary of assigning resources to summary tasks. In Project, the resource assignment to a summary task is separate from the resource assignments to the detail tasks belonging to the summary task. In many cases, the resource is assigned to the summary task either for display purposes or before the detail tasks were added. I am not saying that you cannot assign resources to a summary task; there are times it is very appropriate. I am saying be sure you understand how this works and review any resource assignment that has the same resource assigned at both the summary and detail level.

NOTE You can assign a "budget-only" to a summary task.

- **Displaying assigned resources**—If you have a task that happens to have a few resources assigned, or you have resources with long names or you are assigning resources at less than 100% availability, it can be very challenging to fully display the assigned resources along with the task, especially if you are using the Gantt Bar view. Here are a few suggestions to better manage this display situation:

- Use a custom text field, such as Resource Notes, to display what you want for the resource names.

- Use the Resource Initials field/column instead of the default Resources field/column.

- Assign the list of resources to a group, and then assign the group resource to the task.

- Further decompose the task, so you can assign resources to their own tasks.

- If the task cannot be broken down, consider duplicating the task, and then assign a different resource to each instance of the task.

- **Capturing impact of issues and delays**—Rather than simply updating the start date for a given task when a new baseline needs to be set, capture the reason for the schedule impact (event, issue, delay, or change request) as a new task in your schedule. This way, the source of the impact has visibility and you do not forget why the schedule change was made (see Figure 23.13).

	O	Focus	WorkStatus	WBS	Task Name	% Complete	Work
606		😊	◆	6.3	‑ User Acceptance Testing (UAT)	98%	294 hrs
607	✓			6.3.1	Setup Test Environment	100%	16 hrs
608	✓	😊		6.3.2	<<Delay - Security Migration Issues, 8.8 Infrastructure>>	100%	0 hrs
609	✓			6.3.3	Execute UAT Test Plan	100%	88 hrs
610	✓			6.3.4	Address Issues	100%	84 hrs
611	✓	⚑		6.3.5	<Additional Test Cycle Needed>	100%	100 hrs
612		➡	○	6.3.6	+ UAT Summary Report	0%	6 hrs

FIGURE 23.13

Example of showing impact.

- **Updating tasks with progress already captured**—Remember, after progress is recorded against a task, it does not automatically calculate planned dates. I often see people get frustrated because they assign resources to a task and the planned finish dates do not change. In most cases, the task already has a percentage complete amount recorded against it.

- **Saving baseline dates**—Until you get comfortable with how Project manages baselines, you can always save your own copy of your baseline dates and duration by using custom fields.

- **Managing buffers**—Rather than burying buffers or contingencies throughout the schedule in individual tasks, use specific tasks for buffers (contingencies) to simplify management throughout the project. It makes showing impact much easier when issues or proposed changes come up.

- **Using similar subtask names across summary tasks**—A common issue people face when dealing with task names that have similar if not the same name across summary tasks is that it is difficult to tell which specific task it really is. The three best ways to reduce these occurrences are to use the WBS field when possible, include a reference to the summary task in the task name, and create a custom field that combines the summary task and task names.

 NOTE   In Microsoft Project 2019, you can display a Task Summary Name column in Task View to help clarify task references.

- **Managing overhead tasks**—To better manage overhead hours and activities to a project, I recommend using recurring tasks rather than a "hammock" task. The recurring task offers more detail, flexibility, and control, and the hammock task construct in Project is subject to issues due to the Paste Link (OLE technology) approach that is used to tie the task date to the Project dates.

 NOTE   A *hammock* task is a task used to capture overhead items such as PM time, meetings, and miscellaneous costs that change as the project date changes.

- **Assigning resources to fixed duration tasks**—When assigning resources to fixed duration (versus effort-driven) tasks, make sure the resource has availability during that period. If the resource is not available, Project does not make the assignment (does not assign any work hours) but does not notify you about this.

- **If whacked, do over**—If all else fails and you cannot get the values of a resource assignment to make sense to you (dates, hours, or resource allocation), simply enter a new task and rebuild the resource assignment. After the assignment is rebuilt, you can delete the one that was giving you fits. This technique seems to work 99.9% of the time.

Ten Key Helpful Features

In summary, since Project 2010, it has been much easier to use Project as the primary working environment for managing your project. You can use the tool to do your initial, high-level planning; to keep all project information and decisions in one place; to do what-if analysis; to manage your active project; and to meet all of your reporting needs. Although not a complete list, here are 10 key features that have helped me in my use of Project:

NOTE Since Project 2010, Microsoft has continued to improve the collaboration, reporting, and task list management aspects of the tool while simultaneously advancing the higher-end financial, resource, and portfolio management capabilities available in the product.

1. **Timeline View**—This might be the feature that excites me the most because it addresses one of, if not the biggest, pain points with using Project: summarizing and communicating the details of your detailed schedule to a mass audience. With the Timeline View feature, you can do that without having to leave the tool. The Timeline View enables you to capture the key tasks and milestones from your detailed schedule and present them in a clean, appealing graphic that can be easily understood by all stakeholders.

 CAUTION New tasks are manually scheduled by default. To change this for the entire project file, go to File, Options, select Schedule, scroll to the Scheduling Options for This Project section, and set the value for New Tasks Created to Auto Scheduled. For individual tasks, you can set to Auto Schedule by selecting the target task(s) and choosing the Auto Schedule option from the right-click menu or the Project Ribbon.

2. **User-Controlled Scheduling**—With this capability, you can manually schedule individual tasks (versus having the task automatically scheduled using the Project scheduling engine). Not only does Microsoft make it easy to visually distinguish a manually scheduled task, but it has implemented an "anything goes" approach with these task types. There are no default values for start date, duration, or finish date, and you can enter any text value in these fields. Plus, none of the normal Project scheduling engine qualities are enforced—constraints and calendars are ignored, dependencies do not change the scheduled dates, and resource assignments do not change duration. The task is totally controlled by what you (the user) enter. Thus, if you just need to use Project as a task list manager or just need to capture high-level summary dates (which is common for initial high-level planning or rolling wave planning), you will greatly appreciate this new feature. See Figure 23.14 for examples of both the Timeline View and aspects of user-controlled scheduling.

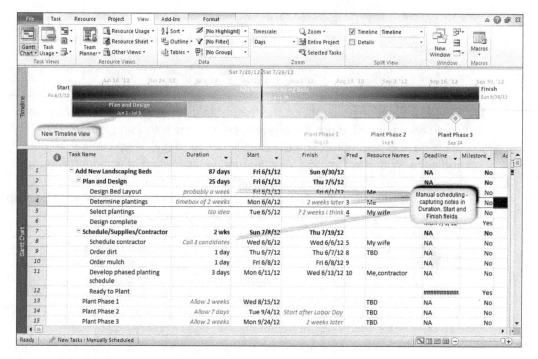

FIGURE 23.14

Simple project to show Timeline View and manual scheduling features.

 NOTE A manually scheduled task can contain any text value in the Duration and Date fields.

3. **Top-Down Summary Tasks**—Not only does Project create the summary task and the first subtask for you in one step (which is a nice little time-saver), but you can manually set the value for the summary task. Then as you flesh out the details, you can add the subtasks to it. In addition, Project lets you know via the red squiggly line feature on the Summary Task Finish Date if the total duration for the subtasks are extending past the end date you set for the summary task.

4. **Task Inspector**—Using a Backstage View construct in Task Inspector, Project provides a full array of information that could be affecting the scheduling of a task and a list of possible actions you can take to resolve it.

5. **Team Planner**—With Team Planner, it is much easier to see what each team member is assigned to do at each point in the project, to find and resolve task assignment conflicts, and to find and resolve resource overallocations.

6. **Enhanced Copy/Paste**—Now it is much easier to collaborate with others using different applications because when you copy and paste, your task organization and formatting are maintained.

7. **Automatic Text Wrapping of Task Names**—What was always a major pain with Project in versions prior to Project 2010 is no longer a concern. The tool automatically wraps each task name now. When this feature is combined with the other enhanced capabilities to control the look and feel of each cell, the capability to use Project to display information to a wide range of audiences is greatly improved.

8. **Drawing Tools**—In another example of the improved capability to present project or schedule information directly from Project, you can now leverage the Drawing Tools palette directly on the Gantt Bar view.

9. **PDF/XPS output**—Saving/printing your schedule to PDF and XPS formats is integrated into the product. Everyone can now share their schedule views by distributing PDF or XPS versions of their schedules.

10. **Move Project**—If you want to reuse past schedules as a template or there has been a major rescheduling of your current project, this is a powerful new feature. Move Project reschedules constraints and deadlines relative to the former project start date; just changing the project start date does not do this.

 CAUTION When switching a task from manually scheduled to automatically scheduled, Project makes decisions for you, especially if the values you have for duration or dates are not standard. In general, any duration field with a text value will get the default task duration value ("1 day?"), and any date field with a text value will get the project start date value.

What You Need to Know About the Different Versions of Microsoft Project

In past editions of this book, I've covered versions of Microsoft Project going back to Project 2003. And when Project 2010 (the game changer) was released, I put a lot of focus there. For this edition, I am going to assume you are working with something newer than Project 2010, and I will focus on the offerings still officially supported by Microsoft. In this section, I bring you up to speed quickly on these versions by sharing the key updates and/or differences in each of them, including two project management "light" tools available from Microsoft.

In summary, these latest offerings have not seen a major change like we saw with the introduction of Project 2010. However, Microsoft has continued to build upon the foundation it established with that Project 2010 version.

Project 2013

In Project 2013, Microsoft made a major upgrade in the reporting capabilities from Project. No longer do you need to pull data from Project and incorporate it into other presentation tools just to meet minimum reporting standards. Starting with Project 2013, you can generate reports from Project that are professional with an emphasis on charts and graphics. Microsoft made it easier to generate better-looking reports and also provided new sets of predefined reports for work tracking and project overviews. Plus, Microsoft made it much easier to design custom reports. Also in Project 2013, it is much easier to share files and communicate with resources due to the much tighter integration with other Microsoft technologies, especially Lync (now Skype for Business) and Office 365. On top of the significant reporting and collaboration advancements, the coolest feature from a pure project manager "geek" standpoint might be the capability to trace a task path with one click. With one click, you can now see all predecessor tasks and all successor tasks for the given task, making it much easier to see relationships.

Project 2013 is scheduled to be out of support in 2023.

 NOTE The standard Microsoft product lifecycle support is five years for mainstream support and five additional years of extended support. Please check Microsoft's Product Lifecycle site for the latest information. The current URL for this is https://docs.microsoft.com/en-us/lifecycle/.

Project 2016

With Project 2016, Microsoft continued to power up the enterprise and portfolio management capabilities of the product. The biggest upgrade is the resource management functionality. In summary, you now have a full-fledged enterprise resource management tool built in to Project with the capability to communicate directly with resource managers, develop and maintain resource plans, and request resources directly from within Project.

From a reporting standpoint, the coolest change in Project 2016 is the capability to generate multiple Timeline views for your project. This makes it much easier to clearly show an overview of project status and further reduces any need to go outside Project for status reporting. The other promising feature provided in Project

2016 is the "Tell Me" feature, which incorporates some artificial intelligence (AI) behavior to quickly help the user do things in Project.

On the back end, significant strides were made in Project 2016, including the implementation of a power business intelligence reporting capability, the integration of the OData service, and the consolidation of one database for both Project and SharePoint (for sites using an on-premises Project Server installation).

Project 2016 is scheduled to be out of support in 2025.

Project 2019

With Project 2019, Microsoft continues to improve the efficiency and accessibility of the application and provides advanced security and cloud interaction capabilities. In addition, there are incremental improvements in team collaboration, agile and Kanban management support, portfolio management, and analytical reporting capabilities. Some of the coolest new features include the ability to visually track task relationships with task path highlighting, an enhanced Copy Project information feature, more built-in report options, the ability to link tasks using a dropdown menu (no longer have to remember the task number), enhanced Timeline features (task progress displayed, timeline bars can be labeled), and the availability of a new Task Summary Name field now in Task View.

 NOTE Project 2019 is backward compatible with Project 2013 and Project 2016.

In addition, Project 2019 makes it much easier for Windows Narrator and other assistive technology to read more elements of a Project file. Plus, there are improvements to contrast and keyboard support.

And as with past desktop Project offerings, there is an option between the Standard edition and the Professional edition. You need the Professional edition if you want to manage resources, sync with Project Server or Project Online, or allow users to submit timesheets.

Project Online

Project Online is Microsoft's full-featured, cloud-based project management and portfolio management tool offering and is built on the SharePoint platforms. This application allows organizations to manage projects, programs, and portfolios across the organization, as well as track the utilization and availability of resources in the organization. There are three versions of Project Online available via the subscription plan offerings from Microsoft: Essentials, Professional, and Premium.

The Professional and Premium editions offer the same features as the latest Project desktop version, currently 2019, and include the ability to download a desktop version. The Premium version offers more advanced demand management, resource management, analytical reporting, and portfolio reporting capabilities. The Essentials version is an add-on purchase that allows users to do time reporting and basic task status updates.

 NOTE As you can see, Microsoft has no intention of losing ground as the most-used project management tool in the market anytime soon. Per Microsoft plans, you can expect the Project offering to continue to evolve with continued improvements in agile development support, portfolio management reporting, financial cost planning, business intelligence capabilities, Kanban work management, and mobile device and application support.

Project for the Web

As popular as Project has always been, it was facing competition from tools that were focused on easy work collaboration and task management. In addition, the consistent move to more agile development approaches has created a growing need for tools that provide simple visual task management, support frequent changes, make it easy to share documents, and serve as a repository for team communication, especially at the task level. Project for the Web is Microsoft's response to that need. It is a cloud-based, streamlined product intended for small and simple projects. It provides a quick and easy way to create simple work schedules and to collaborate with team members. The functionality is just a small percentage of the features available in Project 2019, but it does offer Grid views, Kanban boards, Gantt timelines, capture of task dependencies, and integration with Microsoft Teams.

Microsoft Planner

Microsoft Planner was Microsoft's original offering to meet the need for easy work collaboration and task management in 2016. Microsoft Planner is a free tool that is utilized within the Office 365 subscription licensing package and is integrated with the rest of Office 365 and Microsoft Teams. In fact, you can find it under Teams as *Tasks by Planner and To Do*. Microsoft Planner features a Kanban board methodology for simple task management geared toward ad hoc projects and teams that allow team members to work together on the board and update tasks.

For a quick comparison summary of the different Microsoft Project versions available, please refer to Table 23.3.

TABLE 23.3 Summary of Microsoft Project Version Differences

Project Version	Key Features	Notes
Project 2013	Improved professional reporting capabilities Tighter integration with other Microsoft technologies	Trace task path feature added
Project 2016	Improved resource management Multiple Timeline views "Tell Me" AI feature	Focused on enterprise and portfolio management capabilities
Project 2019	Enhanced task path highlighting and Copy Project information Link tasks via drop-down task selection Timeline bars show task progress and can have labels Task summary Name field in Task View	Enhanced security and cloud interaction Accessibility improvements
Project Online	SaaS delivery mechanism for Project Built on SharePoint platform Cloud-based Project Portfolio Management (PPM) tool Robust reporting capabilities using Power BI	Professional edition same features as Project 2019 Can include desktop client as well
Project for the Web	Small team, simple project management Subset of features available in Project 2019 Offers grid view, dependencies, scheduling, and a timeline (Gantt) view	Web based Step up from Planner Integrates with Teams
Microsoft Planner	Online group collaboration tool Used for ad hoc, small projects Simple task management using Kanban board	Independent of Project Included with Office 365 subscription In Teams, called *Tasks by Planner and To Do*

THE ABSOLUTE MINIMUM

At this point, you should have a solid understanding of the following:

- Project is a database application.
- Task Duration = Work Effort × Resource Units.
- Project utilizes multiple calendar types—project, resource, and task.
- The three main date types that Project uses are Planned, Actual, and Baseline.
- Custom fields can be added to any view and can be used for visual indicators, too.
- The best practices for starting a new project schedule file.
- The keys for making resource leveling work.
- The techniques for effective reporting from Project.
- The 10 key capabilities to be aware of in Project.
- Clear understanding of the differences between the versions of Microsoft Project.

Figure 23.15 summarizes the main points reviewed in this chapter.

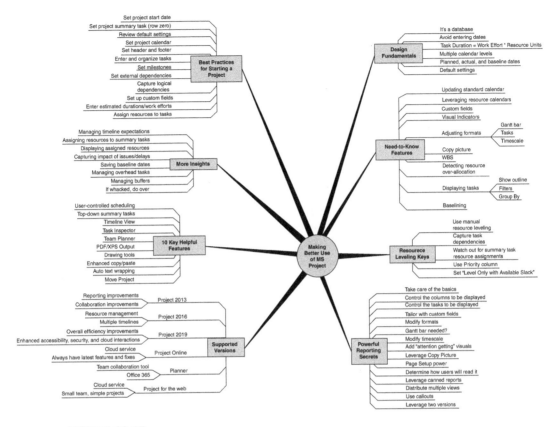

FIGURE 23.15

Overview of making better use of Microsoft Project.

## 24

IN THIS CHAPTER

- Understand how to manage a project in a project management "lite" culture

- Find out what to do when a detailed schedule cannot be developed

- Review insights for managing a project with a hard milestone date

- Learn how to deal with difficult resources

- Review steps to better prepare for and manage turnover

- Discover powerful tips for managing a selection process

- Learn how to improve any testing process

WHEN REALITY HAPPENS

Whereas the last chapter focused on accelerating your knowledge and use of Microsoft Project, this chapter focuses on accelerating your project management effectiveness by taking a closer look at common scenarios and challenges you are likely to encounter—even on a first assignment.

The first four parts of this book addressed the fundamental project management concepts and processes. With this knowledge, you have a solid foundation for handling any project situation. However, there is nothing like real-life project scenarios to make us question all of this. In this chapter, we review a few of those common challenging situations. Each review emphasizes the fundamentals that apply and provides additional recommendations to better prepare you for when these realities happen in your work life.

What If I'm in a Project Management "Lite" Culture?

Let's face it. There are environments, situations, and organizations that are not supportive of ideal project management practices. The reasons for these project management "lite" cultures can vary. The organization or industry might be new to project management. The organization might have been burned by ineffective Project Management Office (PMO) experiments or frustrated by past project managers who emphasized administrative details at the expense of critical success factors. In some organizations, the project manager is responsible for several projects simultaneously. In other situations, the project manager is serving multiple roles on the team. Whatever the reason, you might find yourself in an environment where you cannot implement the full arsenal of project management best practices. Yet, you are still accountable for successfully managing the project. What can you do?

First, take confidence in knowing that many successful projects have been managed using project management lite approaches. You can do it too. In many cases, it is in these environments where a project manager must use all their skills and leverage their creativity. In most project management lite environments, the "lite" pertains more to the level of documentation, planning detail, and tracking administration (project control detail) that is generated. Let's review the keys to thriving in a project management lite culture:

 TIP   No matter the environment, you must document and communicate the core project definition items of context, scope, approach, success factors, timeline, and key team roles. See Chapter 4, "Defining a Project," for additional details.

- **Focus on the core**—No matter the project situation, you (and your team) must have clarity on the following:
  - **Project context**—Why are we doing this project?
  - **Project scope**—What are we doing on this project?
  - **Success factors**—How will we be measured?
  - **Approach**—How will we get the work done?
  - **Roles and responsibilities**—What are these for each team member?
  - **Timeline**—When does work need to be completed?
  - **Management approach**—At the minimum, what meetings, tools, or reports will be used to check and facilitate team progress?

- **Focus on communication, relationships, and managing expectations**—
These are always important, but in these environments, you must be very
effective in all three areas to successfully lead and manage a project.

> **TIP** No matter the environment, always emphasize effective
> communication, positive relationships, and clear expectations with
> all project stakeholders.

- **Lead the project**—In these environments, you cannot be successful by simply
managing the project. You must lead it. See Chapter 16, "Leading a Project,"
for a review of these principles and skills, especially servant leadership.

- **Emphasize personal contact and relationships**—Especially in these environments, you need to get to know your team, the key expert resources you will
need, and anyone else who will need to provide work to your project. Take the
time to learn what drives them, how they work, and what other priorities they
are managing. Look for ways to help make them successful, and always show
your appreciation for their willingness to help you.

- **Emphasize value-added deliverables only**—You should only require a deliverable (work product) that is value-added to the overall process, especially if you
are asking others to generate effort that is not directly related to their targeted
work products (such as project administration or management items). Look for
opportunities to right-size or combine your list of required deliverables.

- **Tailor your scheduling approach**—In environments like this, you might not be
able to develop a detail work schedule, and we discuss how to manage this
in more detail in the next section. At the minimum, what is important is that
everyone is clear on what they are working on (responsible for), the quality
level that is expected or the process that needs to be followed, and when the
work product is due.

> **TIP** Leverage iterative, agile approaches in project manage-
> ment lite environments.

- **Right-size your monitoring and tracking procedures**—This is closely related
to the emphasis on value-added deliverables. For both yourself and your
team, be sure that all project monitoring and tracking procedures are streamlined, necessary, and not duplicated.

- **Generate work products as early as possible**—In environments where it is
either difficult or impractical to perform detail planning or detail requirements
definition, an approach that generates tangible results early can be invaluable.

This approach is one of the tenets of iterative, agile methodologies that I talk more about in Chapter 25, "The Fun Never Stops." The approach is invaluable because until stakeholders are able to experience the targeted concepts or products, they are not able to consider all their requirements.

- **Plan on multiple iterations**—For the same reasons as mentioned earlier, you should plan on multiple iterations of your process. To assume that any work product will be correct with only one iteration is not practical. This applies to definition, design, development, testing, and deployment approaches.

What If I Can't Develop a Detailed Schedule?

In spite of all the logical and practical benefits we reviewed in Chapters 5–8 for leveraging a detailed schedule development process, you might actually find yourself in an organization or a project situation where you cannot build a project schedule to the level of detail or completeness that you would ideally like. In other cases, you cannot develop a detailed multiphase schedule because there is too much unknown, too much uncertainty in the early stages of the project. What can you do in these cases? The best approaches are to leverage one or more aspects of quality schedule development. Here are techniques to consider:

- **Detail what you can**—Include as much WBS detail as you can. This is one of the advantages of building a schedule using a WBS. At a minimum, you should always know the first few levels of your WBS. Do what you can.

 NOTE With the current versions of Microsoft Project, it is much easier to build schedules that are incomplete, evolve over time, or are primarily focused on milestones.

- **Manage to milestones**—Set target dates for key deliverables, events, and decision points, then monitor progress against these dates. The key with this approach is to target the right milestones and include enough interim checkpoint milestones so you can identify any major issues and variances early enough to take corrective action.

- **Manage to deliverables**—This is a similar approach to "managing to milestones" except the emphasis is on the targeted work products. The work details are delegated to the respective deliverable owner, but they are accountable to the target completion. The key with this approach is to ask for enough interim deliverables so that you can identify any major issues and variances early enough to take corrective action.

NOTE   A quality schedule leverages combinations of these techniques.

- **Manage to project phases**—In this approach, you organize the project into phases with a defined checkpoint (gates, review session, go/no-go decision point) at the end. The appropriate stakeholders review the health of the project and determine whether the project should proceed to the next phase. The keys here are to clarify what the project health evaluation criteria will be and which stakeholders will participate in the evaluation process.

- **Manage to short duration detail plans**—This is a common technique with iterative, agile projects, troubled projects that are in recovery mode, projects with a lot of uncertainty and schedule risk, and projects that are managed by phases. In this approach, your focus is on the next milestone. What are we getting done in the next 2 to 4 weeks, or the next 30, 60, or 90 days? By ensuring that the work details (process, assignments, roles, and expectations) are clear to your team, they stay focused and productive. This helps the team experience accomplishment more often, and it is essential to building overall project momentum.

What If I Must Manage to a Hard Milestone Date?

If you have not already, you will soon find yourself managing a project that absolutely, positively must be completed by a certain date, a project in which being late or saying, "It can't be done," is not an option. What do you do in these cases? What do you need to focus on? Here are my recommendations for managing a project that has a hard milestone date:

 TIP   For any project that has a true hard milestone date, the project's milestone completion date should be set well in advance of this date whenever possible. Give yourself a contingency buffer whenever possible.

- **Clarify the real driver for the milestone date**—As with any project goal, you must be clear about what is behind the milestone date, what is driving it. In the case of milestone dates that are imposed on a project, there are several common sources:

  - External event

  - Business/organizational goal

- Business/organizational budgeting cycle

- "Stretch" goal from project sponsor to make sure the project is completed by the actual/real target date

- **Give yourself a contingency buffer**—For any project that has a true hard milestone date, the project's target completion date should be set well in advance of this date whenever possible to provide a contingency buffer and increase the probability that you will be ready for the actual, hard milestone event.

- **Competing project demands**—Remember the classic project management triangle discussed in Chapter 1, "Project Management Overview": If time is fixed, then our management focus turns to the other factors. The common responses are increasing resources and decreasing scope or quality.

- **Clarify what "done" looks like**—Especially for these situations, you need to make sure your vision of the solution is the same as your project sponsor's. This is the core of your expectations and scope management efforts and includes a detailed review of project success factors, assumptions, priority requirements, and implementation or deployment strategies.

- **Get crystal clear on must-have functionality**—As mentioned previously, you need to have clear priority on your solution requirements, including quality standards. This clarity helps drive and focus your team's work efforts and provides a basis for a staged (or incremental) delivery approach.

- **Manage scope diligently**—When you must hit a specific date, you must be diligent about scope management. Invest the time up front to get buy-in on requirement priority levels and common understanding of the final solution. From there, use your change request process to manage any requests (or decisions) to modify scope, approach, priorities, assumptions, and so on. See Chapter 11, "Managing Project Changes," for a review of this process.

 TIP Scope management is critical if the milestone date cannot be moved.

- **Focus the team's work effort**—Focus on the productivity level of your team and any key resources. Review Chapter 19, "Keys to Better Project Team Performance," for a reminder of powerful techniques you can leverage. Here is a quick summary to keep in mind:

  - Get dedicated resources whenever possible.

  - Co-locate your team whenever possible.

- Conduct frequent touchpoints with your team.

- Remove any overhead or non-value-added tasks from their plates.

- Avoid downtimes and delays. Be sure your team members have the information, deliverables, and resources they need to stay productive each day.

- Resolve issues quickly.

- **Prioritize testing efforts**—Often in a fixed-time project, the work effort that is squeezed—asked to do their work in less time—is testing. It is always important to prioritize testing efforts based on two primary factors: requirement priorities and risk levels. If you have limited time, you want to get the biggest bang for your buck in your testing efforts. Focus on your high-risk items and set these expectations with your stakeholders.

- **Mini-milestones**—When the final milestone cannot be moved, make sure to set frequent, interim milestones in your schedule, so you can accurately gauge progress and take appropriate corrective actions while there is still time. Plus, the accomplishments of these mini-milestones help build momentum and team confidence.

 TIP If the final milestone date cannot be moved, make sure to set frequent, interim milestones so progress can be accurately gauged and appropriate corrective actions can be taken while there is still time.

- **Strongly consider phased implementations**—Leveraging a phased implementation (incremental delivery, multiple releases) approach for deploying the project solution is not only invaluable for change management and risk management reasons, it can also be a powerful mechanism for balancing the needs of the project sponsors with the capacity of the project to get work done within a given time frame. This technique can be considered as a response (corrective action) to a project issue, even if it was not part of the original plan.

 NOTE Many of these recommendations for managing a hard milestone date are inherent using an agile approach...specifically, the use of mini-milestones, clarifying "must-have" functionality, focusing the team's work efforts, and use of phased implementations.

What If I Have Difficult Resources?

On occasion, you might have resources that do not seem to be concerned about the success of your project. Their lack of concern can come in various forms, from subtle or passive on one end to more direct, aggressive actions on the other end. These situations can be tough, and the best response can be less than obvious. Here are a few observations and recommendations for your consideration if you happen to find yourself in this situation:

- **It's not about you**—Remember that 99.9% of the time, the source of their less-than-cooperative attitude has nothing to do with you personally, so stay calm, stay detached, be the eye of the storm, and don't react emotionally.

- **Difficult or different**—Many people confuse difficult with different, especially those who are new to an organization. There is a wide range of personality types out there. Some people just naturally have more challenging styles. I always check with other people—people who have more experience with the given resource—before determining whether the observed behavior is normal.

- **Diamonds in the rough**—In many cases, resources are difficult when they are frustrated, especially if they feel they are not being heard or if they are not clear on the project context and purpose. Take the time to meet with them and listen purposefully. They can often provide early insights to risks you need to manage. In addition, people generally appreciate the opportunity to vent and offer counsel.

- **Don't avoid**—Remember, good project managers do not avoid risks and issues. You need to proactively manage any potential resource issue. You need to clarify whether you have a really difficult resource issue as soon as possible.

- **Focus on results**—In most cases, after my initial investigation, I flag any difficult resource situation as a risk. It only becomes an issue if the resource is not delivering quality work on time, or if they are impacting the work of other team members. This helps to take the emotion out of things and helps make sure you are not overreacting to a "different personality" situation.

- **Look for win-win**—Although most people want to do their best and be part of successful endeavors, it might take more incentive for others. This occurs more frequently with shared resources that are not 100% dedicated to your specific project. Continue to build relationships with these people and look for opportunities to help them, recognize them, and make them care about your request or need.

- **Avoid silos**—If you have a resource who has a difficult work history or who is a known turnover risk, you want them to work on tasks where the knowledge and skills it takes to generate their deliverables does not reside solely with them.

- **Assign noncritical tasks**—If you have a quality of work concern from a resource that you have to keep, reduce your risk by assigning them noncritical, less visible tasks.

- **Outsource the role**—If you have known organizational resource difficulties, you should give strong consideration to a risk avoidance strategy—outsourcing the roles.

- **Meet with supervisor**—If you have not had any success in changing the resource's behavior on your own, or learn that the real problem is a matter of priorities, reach out to the appropriate supervisor and discuss your situation. Often, immediate supervisors are much better equipped to change behavior.

What Can I Do About Turnover?

Nothing can put a project schedule more at risk than the sudden loss of key resources. As a project manager, you hope you are aware of these potential events well in advance, but this is not always the case. Let's take a look at a few observations and recommendations that might help you prepare for and manage a turnover situation:

- **The longer the project, the more likely turnover will occur**—If you manage a project that is scheduled to last more than six months, you should assume that you have resource turnover risks, especially with your core team members. Circumstances change: People receive other opportunities, their personal or family situations change, their career interests shift, and they can lose interest. To the extent possible, leverage compensation packages, project incentives, and quality of work assignments to minimize this risk.

- **Prepare for turnover**—A benefit of documenting the definition of the project, your management plans, and your detailed work schedule is that it makes it much easier for a new resource to come up to speed in the context of their work. I think about how I would quickly orient any new person to the project. If you don't have these materials, develop them.

- **Avoid silos**—To the extent that you can build in mentoring arrangements to your project teams, the better. Not only does it build work satisfaction, it also reduces impact if a resource leaves. In addition, encourage work processes that encourage openness and sharing of all work products.

- **Increase visibility**—If you are concerned about a key resource leaving, consider increasing the visibility and importance this person has on the project. This is generally done by a combination of the roles and work tasks assigned. Common examples include providing more exposure to senior management, providing more exposure to customers, assigning leadership roles, assigning mentoring roles, and assigning quality assurance tasks.

- **Assign noncritical tasks**—If you are concerned about a resource leaving, you can take the opposite approach to reduce your risk. You can assign them non-critical, less visible tasks. If the resource is part of an organization, this should be a decision made in collaboration with other impacted managers.

- **Outsource to transfer the risk**—If you have known organizational resource turnover risks, you should give strong consideration to a risk avoidance strategy—outsourcing the roles.

- **Transition period or not?**—What do you do if you actually lose a resource? First, determine whether you want a transition period. In some cases, it may be better to make a sudden, no-notice change. In most cases, especially if replacement resources cannot be found quickly, a transition period is helpful—the longer the better.

- **Promote from within, backfill less-senior positions**—Next, you need to determine how to replace the departing resource. Various strategies are available, but the one I encourage you to consider whenever possible is to fill the position by promoting from within, and then backfill the promotee's former position.

Tips for Managing a Selection Process

 NOTE Selection processes are all about managing risk.

Chapter 21, "Managing Vendors," mentioned that the evaluation and selection process is a core aspect of effective vendor management. Because outsourcing continues to grow as a business management selection process, the odds are very good that you will direct a selection process, in one form or another, early in your project management career. Given the importance that this process has to your project success criteria, your funding efforts, and your ability to establish valuable vendor partnerships—not to mention the visibility you have to senior management and the marketplace—it is critical that you handle these endeavors well. To help you with this, consider these tips and observations from my experience as you plan your next evaluation or selection process:

- **Understand why you are doing this**—Due to the number of stakeholders and accompanying agendas to be managed, the logistical details involved, and the effort it takes, it can be easy to forget why we do evaluation and selection processes in the first place. The main reason that organizations perform selection processes is to reduce risk. There can be other, closely related reasons including gaining consensus, developing the business case, and satisfying due diligence requirements.

- **What are the real goals?**—One of the common complaints of these processes is that the organization ends up selecting the option that was not recommended by the evaluation team. This generally happens because the real purpose of the selection process or the actual decision criteria was not clear to the evaluation team. In addition, what is your organization really after? The answer can guide the focus and the specific approach you take. Do you just need competitive bids? Are you performing market research? Do you need to satisfy procurement requirements? Do you need to satisfy due diligence requirements?

- **Clarify the driving strategies**—Designing your selection process is easier if you have agreement and clarity on answers to the following questions:

  - Which is more important: partner relationships or lowest price?

  - Do we want a custom solution?

  - Are we willing to adapt the best practices of available market solutions?

  - Which is more important: the best solution or the best working relationship fit?

 TIP Whenever possible, maintain ownership of all selection documents (RFI, RFQ, RFP, and so on). Assign procurement review and approval responsibilities only.

- **Scale process to risk level**—Selection processes can range greatly in activities, stages, time, cost, and effort. The important principle is to scale the process to the level of risk involved. For high-risk decisions, the process can include steps such as the following:

  - Current State Assessment

  - Future State Analysis

  - Develop Long List of Candidates

  - Develop Evaluation Criteria (Knockout)

  - Develop Scoring Process

- Request for Information (RFI)
- Request for Quote (RFQ)
- Request for Proposal (RFP)
- Bidders Conferences
- Information Gathering Sessions by Candidate Vendors
- Demonstrations (onsite, online)
- Reference Checks
- Client Site Visits
- Vendor Site Visits
- Financial Health Assessments
- Quality Audits
- Executive Relationship Building
- Gap Analysis
- Business Case (Benefit-Cost Analysis)
- Final Rankings/Recommendations
- Contract Negotiations

- **Partner with procurement**—Be sure to involve your procurement representative from the start. Clarify any, and all, procurement requirements and procedures that you need to follow. Clarify who owns vendor communications. Clarify your role versus the role of the procurement lead.

- **Establish a clear process**—With your evaluation team, develop a clear game plan for the overall selection that emphasizes objectivity and neutrality. Review the approach with your key stakeholders. This goes a long way in building confidence in your direction.

- **Consider other factors**—In addition to aligning with the risk level involved, make sure to consider these other factors before finalizing your selection methodology:

  - How much time do you have?

  - How many vendors/options do you need to evaluate?

  - What is the normal level of investment that vendors are willing to make in an evaluation process?

- How many evaluators are involved?

- Where are your evaluators located?

- How available are your evaluators?

- **Tailor process to evaluators**—As you develop your selection process with your evaluation team, determine what methods would work better for your team. This is closely related to understanding the learning styles and personalities of your team members (and organization). For some, reviewing and scoring a 100-page RFP response is a great fit; for others, not so much. For some, participating in an interactive, online demonstration works great, because they can see something in action, they can ask direct questions, and it's a flexible use of their time. For others, they might lose context perspective or might not fully engage due to multitasking lures.

 TIP   To improve the quality of your evaluation scoring process, conduct preview (or readiness) sessions with all stakeholders who will provide feedback to review logistics, scoring process, and related assumptions.

- **Establish evaluation criteria**—Determine what criteria will be evaluated. Develop a small set of must-have requirements—often referred to as "knock-out" criteria—that can be used to quickly narrow your candidate list. In addition, for your longer list of evaluation criteria, establish a priority level for each criterion. You need this for your scoring process.

- **Establish evaluation scoring**—As part of your goal to have an objective process, it is imperative that your scoring process be determined in advance, agreed to by key stakeholders, documented, communicated clearly to all evaluators, and executed as designed. Here is a list of key considerations for your evaluation scoring process:

  - Score against evaluation criteria and requirements "fit."

  - Use a scoring scale with clear differentiators between each score value.

  - Use an even number of scoring options whenever possible to avoid a middle-of-the-road, on-the-fence option.

  - Determine how nonresponses will be handled; make sure they do not skew the final scores.

  - Ensure there is a clear method to distinguish between a poor score and a nonapplicable criteria.

  - Ensure the stakeholder community is fairly represented.

- Determine whether scores from specific stakeholder groups will carry greater weight.

- Encourage each stakeholder group (department, business unit) to reach a consensus score to ensure that the number of final scores considered remains proportional.

- Conduct preview (or readiness) sessions with all evaluation participants.

- Ensure that all participants are clear on evaluation logistics, the scoring process, and related assumptions.

- Archive the original evaluation scores from each participant.

- **Use an open-book approach**—From my experience, I favor an open-book approach with the candidate vendors. You can mitigate your risk with sharing confidential information with nondisclosure agreements (NDA) or confidentiality agreements. The benefits far outweigh the risks. The more open, the more complete, the clearer you are with your candidates about your requirements, your context, and your expectations, the better the candidate responses will be and the more efficient your selection process will be.

- **Clarify timing of each process step**—As an essential aspect of managing expectations for both you and your candidate vendors, make sure to communicate the timetable for your overall selection process to the candidate vendors. This helps the candidates plan appropriately, which should help increase the quality of your selection process. In addition, you should clearly communicate the specific timing expectations for any scheduled events or expected responses. If you need to have a documented response by Friday, provide the exact time the response is to be received, such as 12 noon Eastern Time.

 CAUTION The nature of negotiations and contract development efforts make them automatic schedule risks.

- **Control vendor communications**—As part of your effort to manage expectations and keep the process objective, clarify who owns what aspects of vendor communications with your own team. In addition, clearly set expectations with your candidate vendors, such as who they are authorized to contact within your organization.

- **Be consistent and fair**—Be diligent that your process is consistent and fair. Be sure each candidate follows the same steps, is given the same opportunities, has access to the same information, and is evaluated using the same criteria.

- **Value your vendor contacts**—Handle all interactions with your candidate vendor contacts with professionalism, candor, and respect. Show appreciation for their interest and investment. Even if you do not select the vendor for this opportunity, you might need their services down the road. Plus, it never hurts your career to showcase your skills and professionalism with others in your industry and marketplace.

- **Leverage expertise**—There are times, often as a step to further reduce risk, that organizations hire firms (or individuals) to help them with the selection projects. The help can range from background consulting or advisory roles to out-in-front leading the project roles.

- **Get to the short list quickly**—The key to streamlining a selection process is to get to your short list as fast as you can. The short list represents the candidates who have a real opportunity to be selected. Depending on the level of due diligence that is required on a final recommendation, you might need to go from a short list to a list of finalists to control the effort and cost required to get to a final recommendation.

- **Document gaps**—As part of your evaluation process, make sure to document the gaps between the candidate vendor's solution and your required future state. You need to develop the plan and figure the additional costs to address these gaps. This is a factor when evaluating your options.

- **Focus on partnerships for strategic projects**—When dealing with strategic initiatives, encourage your senior management to focus on partnership relationships versus the lowest cost option.

- **Include negotiation and contract development times**—When developing schedules for selection processes, make sure to allocate sufficient, realistic time blocks for negotiations and contract developments. It is common to underestimate this time, especially in corporate environments. When building your schedule, ask the procurement and legal groups for their input on this, and then keep them in your information loop throughout the process.

Tips for Managing a Testing Process

Here's a list of tips and insights from my experience that can help you manage a testing process and avoid many of the common pitfalls:

NOTE   Review Chapter 15, "Managing Project Quality," for more tips on how to better manage an effective testing process.

- **Leverage expertise**—As with any skill or experience that is in low supply on your team, consider procuring testing professionals to assist your effort.

- **Trace to requirements**—Think "testing" from the start of the project. Use a requirements traceability matrix to ensure that the final work product satisfies the targeted requirements and that all those requirements were properly validated.

- **Develop a test plan**—Take the time to plan your testing effort and to document your plan. This is critical when your testing process involves resources that are not dedicated to the project effort. In addition, the test plan should address the test data that is needed and how it will be managed, and it should address how the actual test execution will occur.

- **Determine types of testing**—Determine what types of testing you will perform. This is generally a factor of risk, schedule, and budget.

- **Think customer experience**—Do not limit your focus to functional testing. Place your focus on the overall customer experience. Key aspects of most customer experience are usability, data, and performance. If the performance risk is sufficient, I strongly recommend the use of load-testing tools.

- **Identify high-risk items**—Clarify the high-risk areas in your solution or in the customer's acceptance of your solution. These should be your priorities. Start testing these as early as possible.

 TIP For systems managing any personal identifiable information (PII), ensure the testing process focuses on the parts of the system that store, display, or transmit these data elements.

- **Plan on multiple iterations**—When estimating the time for test execution, make sure to include time for multiple iterations. Because it is difficult to know how many iterations will be necessary, estimates for test execution are often time-blocked and based on historical experiences.

- **"To script or not to script"**—This is often a controversial subject in testing endeavors. Do you need to document (script) how the tester performs each test case? Well, it all depends. If it is a requirement of your organizational methodology, then you'll need to do it. Otherwise, it depends on the value it would provide. If your testers do not have knowledge or experience with the targeted work product, then you might need to script. If your testing efforts will be repeated or are a candidate for automated testing, then you might want to do it. Another benefit of test scripts is that it can make it easier to communicate test defects.

- **Don't forget the data**—Data drives organizations. If your project involves data migration, data conversion, or data loading, realize that you need to develop procedures for validating that the data is correct and acceptable, too.

- **Simulate production**—Closely related to the "think customer experience" recommendation, your test plan should include a testing stage that occurs in an environment that mirrors (or gets as close as possible to) your production environment, the environment in which your customer will actually interact with your solution. If you cannot do this, you have a major project risk.

- **Leverage checklists**—Checklists are simple, yet powerful. They clearly capture and communicate the quality standards that must be met by the targeted work package, and they improve project team productivity. They are flexible—separate checklists can be developed for each work product or project management process. They provide a mechanism to capture the lessons learned from past projects. They can also provide a mechanism to document the verification performed on the work package.

- **Identify completion criteria**—This starts during project definition with defining the acceptance criteria for the project, and it continues for each deliverable and work assignment. Answer this question in advance for each deliverable: "How will we know when it is done?" Understanding the completion criteria up front increases productivity and prevents much of the rework that can occur when quality requirements are not understood from the start.

- **Leverage DevOps methodology**—If dealing with software projects, the use of DevOps methodology can be a huge asset in improving the quality of your testing process. By setting up the processes to integrate testing automation early and testing each software build, you can catch defects early, improve the quality of the product, and reduce the number of issues that have to be triaged and resolved later.

 CAUTION Many testing issues result from a lack of forethought on the management of test data and the detailed logistics of test execution.

- **Schedule readiness checkpoints**—To improve the quality of test execution, to better manage expectations of all testing process participants, and to ensure all prerequisite test execution events are completed, schedule testing readiness checkpoints before the start of any new test execution phase.

- **Capture metrics**—To increase the professionalism of the testing process, keep track of the following in your testing process:

- Traceability to requirements

- Number of test runs

- Number of total test cases

- Number of total defects

- Number of defects by severity level

- Number of defects resolved

- Number of defects closed

- **Determine defect tracking process**—Determine how test defects will be captured, documented, and logged. From there, decide how each defect will be assessed and assigned and who is involved in each step. After the defect is resolved, determine who needs to verify (retest) that the corrective action meets expectations.

- **Pretest customer acceptance**—Here's an excellent expectation-management technique. Always test whatever your customer is going to test first; there should be no surprises. This also applies to verifying any resolved defects.

- **Use a defect tracking/management system**—Whenever possible, use an online defect management system to capture the defect tracking process you develop. The system helps implement the process, provides visibility, and enforces accountability.

THE ABSOLUTE MINIMUM

At this point, you should have a solid understanding of the following:

- In project management lite environments, remember the following:
- Nail the core project definition and planning fundamentals.
- Focus on communication, relationships, and managing expectations.
- Emphasize value-added deliverables only.
- Right-size your monitoring and tracking procedures.

- If you are unable to develop a detailed schedule, leverage one or more of the following techniques:
    - Manage to milestones, deliverables, and/or project phases.
    - Focus on detail plans for the next 30/60/90-day milestone.
- When your project must hit a hard milestone date, keep these tips in mind:
    - Give yourself a contingency buffer.
    - Manage scope tenaciously.
    - Focus on team productivity.
    - Clarify what the end result looks like and get buy-in from stakeholders.
    - Set mini-milestones.
    - Strongly consider phased implementations.
- If you encounter difficult resources, consider the following pointers:
    - Stay calm and clarify whether your perception is correct.
    - Remember that difficult resources are often passionate, but frustrated, people who can be great assets to your management efforts.
- The longer the project, the more likely that resource turnover will occur.
- Keys to managing a selection process include the following:
    - Clarify the purpose and goals of the selection process.
    - Scale your process to the risk level involved.
    - Partner with your procurement representative.
    - Establish a clear, objective, and fair process.
- Keys to managing a testing process include
    - Trace back to requirements.
    - Focus on high-risk items and the customer experience.
    - Develop a test plan.
    - Capture testing metrics.
    - Leverage a defect management system whenever possible.

Figure 24.1 summarizes the main points reviewed in this chapter.

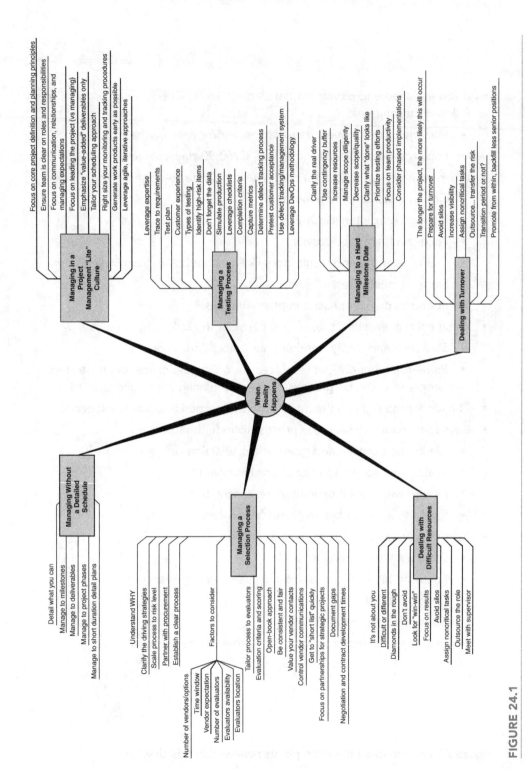

FIGURE 24.1

When reality happens overview.

25

THE FUN NEVER STOPS

One of the wonderful things about the project management field is there is always more to learn. With this in mind, I want to offer information and insights on additional project management concepts, tools, trends, and topics that you are likely to encounter in the workplace to further accelerate your learn-ing curve—or at the very least allow you to discuss these topics with confidence among your peers.

Agile Approaches

The term *agile* is used often these days, but there are still misunderstandings about what an agile project approach is and how it is different from more tradi-tional project approaches. I believe this occurs for three primary reasons:

- The agile approach is still relatively new as a business practice in many circles.

- There are several terms that are used interchangeably with "agile," including iterative, flexible, adaptive, and extreme.

- It is rarely implemented as a pure methodology.

 NOTE As a sign that agile approaches are becoming more common and accepted, PMI now offers five certifications in agile project management, including the PMI-ACP (PMI Agile Certified Practitioner), and the seventh edition of the *PMBOK Guide* now fully incorporates agile practices and principles.

In most cases, agile techniques are incorporated into more traditional approaches. In fact, many organizational project methodologies are evolving to adopt the agile practices that work well in their environments.

To help your understanding of agile project management techniques and increase your confidence in discussing agile methodologies, let's do three things. First, let's review the common characteristics of agile project management approaches. Then, for those who may be in a truer agile environment, we touch base on the key terms used in an agile methodology, and highlight a few practices that will help you become more effective quicker.

To start, let's run down the common characteristics of agile project management approaches:

- **Iterative development**—Agile approaches take an iterative approach to the development of the targeted solution. It is an excellent technique when the complete set of requirements cannot be gathered, visualized, or agreed to. In some circles, these iterations are called waves, sprints, phases, or even mile-stones. Other iterative development techniques can include prototypes, pilot projects, and focus groups. The principle behind the approach is to focus on priority requirements, deliver tangible solutions for evaluation as early as possible, and finish with the desired result.

- **Phased deployment**—In most cases, agile approaches also emphasize an iterative or phased approach to deployment, techniques that we have discussed before as excellent risk management approaches. Any use of test markets, beta releases, pilot projects, phased implementations, or staged rollouts are examples of phased deployments.

- **Detailed, short-term schedules**—Agile approaches focus on detailed schedules for the near-term milestone (iteration, sprint, phase, or wave). The schedule for the rest of the project is kept high-level, general, and frequently time-boxed based on historical performances. This is done because the future path of the project is determined (and can be adjusted) based on the actual results and findings of the current iteration. In most cases, an iteration is between 30 and 60 days.

- **Customer value–driven**—Agile approaches are focused on customer satisfaction. The emphasis is on delivering value, and delivering tangible solutions as early as possible. The goal is to get feedback and clarify requirements as soon as possible. With an iterative approach, the customer stays involved, makes decisions with better data (reviewing tangible results), and remains in control throughout the project.

- **Timeboxing**—Timeboxing is a trademark characteristic of iterative software development methodologies, but it has use in many project environments and has grown in popularity as a project scheduling technique. In a pure sense, the work requirements (scope) for a given timebox are set (fixed), and little, if any, change is allowed to occur. The time element is strictly enforced, regardless of work completion status. At the end of the timebox, a customer review is conducted to evaluate the results and plan the scope of the next iteration. Requirement priority, refinement of requirements, and progress-to-date all determine the scope of the next iteration. Timeboxing is an effective technique in situations with high uncertainty or situations that need frequent review and evaluation.

- **Change expected**—This is a core differentiator of agile approaches. Agile approaches expect change and are ideal when the unknowns and unpredictability factors are high.

- **Plan-do-review**—Agile approaches emphasize the plan-do-review model. Subsequent planning increments are driven by results achieved at the finale of the recently completed iteration, sprint, milestone, or timebox.

- **Solution focused**—Agile approaches focus on the customer experience and on what the customer is after: the targeted solution. There is a strong results orientation with an emphasis on early value and clarifying requirements based on experience and evaluating tangible results.

- **People-focused project management**—Agile project management emphasizes the "people" aspect of projects over the bureaucratic, administrative procedures. The focus is on relationships, leading (versus managing), and value. Project management deliverables are limited to the minimal set that offers the most value. Servant leadership principles are a strong fit for agile approaches.

- **Collaborative**—Collaborative development approaches are another common trait of agile methodologies. There is a partnering arrangement between the customer and the design-development team, and the normal boundaries are minimized, if not removed. Customers are placed on the core team and, in many cases, co-located with the project team. In addition, the iterative development approach emphasizes frequent feedback loops and continuous focus on the customer's requirements.

- **Risk management focused**—You can argue that the main purpose of an agile project approach is to manage risk, the key risk being that the final solution will not meet the satisfaction of the customer. The agile techniques of progressive requirement development, short iterations, partnering close to your customers, prototyping, attacking high-risk solution aspects early, and people-focused management all contribute to managing this essential risk.

Next, if you happen to be working in a truer agile development environment, let's review a few key definitions that will help accelerate your learning curve and effectiveness:

- **Sprint**—A timeblock (timebox) for development. This time period is normally 2–4 weeks.

- **Epic**—Major items (group) of scope. Think of this as a functional area of the system or key process workflow.

- **Stories**—Aspects and/or components of an epic. Use cases or function points would be similar concepts.

- **Tasks**—Specific work items needed to accomplish (develop) a story.

- **Backlog**—The inventory of prioritized work items for the project. This will include the original features (stories, tasks) to be developed, plus defects found during testing and enhancements identified during the process.

- **Daily standup**—The daily checkpoint meeting during a sprint. It is time-boxed at 15 minutes and held at the same time each day. It is meant to encourage communication, sharing, and accountability. Each participant provides a concise update addressing these three questions:

  - What did you do yesterday?

  - What will you do today?

  - Are there any obstacles in your way?

- **Retrospective**—The review meeting held at the end of a sprint for the purpose of continuous improvement. This checkpoint allows for early identification of anything not meeting expectations or agreement on the corrective actions to take to improve performance in the next sprint.

- **Scrum**—One of the most popular ways to implement an agile methodology for software development. It is an iterative software model that follows a set of roles, responsibilities, and meetings that never change. Sprint development cycles are used to deliver software on a regular basis.

- **XP**—The acronym for another type of agile software methodology called *extreme programming*. It is similar to Scrum, because they are both agile-based approaches, and frequently project teams will adapt elements and practices of both methodologies. The key differentiators of XP include use of 1-week iterations (versus 2–4 week sprints), a strict adherence to developing scope in priority order, and emphasis on software engineering practices like test-driven development, automated testing, and pair programming.

Now that we've hit a few key terms, let's next talk about a few practices that will help you manage an agile-based project:

- **Leverage skilled SMEs**—To support the tight time frames and need for quick decisions, it is imperative that the business assign skilled subject matter experts (SMEs) to the project team. Without them, there will be gaps and negative impact to the development process.

- **Use the right tool**—Whenever possible, leverage a software development process and management tool that is designed for agile development. This will make it easier to implement the agile processes and ensure a higher level of communication among the team.

- **Clarify big-picture scope**—While agile approaches are great tools for situations when scope details are ambiguous or the customer is not sure what they want, it is still important to clarify and define the big picture as soon as possible. Ideally, when the initial definition phase of the project is complete, you will have a comprehensive list of stories that define desired functionality, the integration points, both internal and external stakeholders, and any key dependencies. The better the definition of the scope boundaries and key function points is up front, the better the estimates can be, the better alignment of epics and stories within a sprint, and the better the sprint plans will be overall. Without this, there is a higher probability of project delays, sprints completing with planned work not done, and rework of previous developed scope.

- **Determine the sprint duration**—When deciding what sprint duration your project will have, you need to balance how frequent progress needs to be displayed to the stakeholder, the experience of the project team, the capacity of the development team, the estimated work efforts of the key stories, the tolerance for outstanding defects, and the overhead impact of supporting processes (testing, code reviews, and so on).

- **Allocate a sprint(s) for requirement refinement**—Because the nature of agile development encourages early and frequent reviews and refinement of business requirements, it is essential to allocate at least one sprint in your plan for this refinement to be developed (especially if it must have features for the initial version of the product).

- **Allocate a sprint(s) for planned work rolled back into backlog**—It is a good idea to allocate at least one sprint in your plan to address the work that was not completed as originally planned in earlier developments. In most cases, because work planned in early sprints usually includes high-priority items, that work normally gets reallocated to the next sprint. This results in a cascading impact to the scope of future sprints unless development capacity is increased to help compensate.

- **Allocate a sprint(s) for test defect resolution**—In a similar vein, there will be test defects identified during the sprint that might not be resolved within the sprint. These outstanding defects will be added to the backlog and must be prioritized along with every other item in the backlog for future sprints. In most cases, you will need a sprint focused on test defect resolution before the product is deployed to production.

DevOps and DevSecOps

For those working in the IT space, especially with application/software development, you are most likely to come across the growing trend of DevOps and DevSecOps…and that is almost a guarantee if you operating within an agile environment. So, let's cover what these terms mean, why more organizations are adopting these practices, and the key focus areas for the project manager.

While agile development was born out of a desire to build applications faster and tear down the walls between development and the business, DevOps practices were created to do the same between development and operations. Hence the term "DevOps" is a merger of the terms Development and Operations, and the practice of DevOps is a natural extension of agile development.

In a DevOps culture, DevOps is a set of practices that combines software development and IT operations. It aims to shorten the systems development life cycle and provide continuous delivery with high software quality. It provides tighter alignment and collaboration between once siloed roles and strives to avoid the handoffs and the deployment and sustainment issues that are common in the traditional approach. In short, it moves the Operations function to the left in the lifecycle process flow and embeds the Operations personnel within the project team.

In a mature DevOps culture, you will see applications developed, tested, and deployed faster with minimal issues and defects and with a better ability to monitor the health of the application in production. So, you might be asking, "Well, if this is true, why aren't all organizations using DevOps already?" Well, that's because you are dealing with major organizational change management and in most cases a whole new set of tools and way of working.

To make all this happen, one key aspect of DevOps is to automate as much of the IT workflow as possible. This requires a new set of tools, new way of architecting applications, new knowledge, new roles, and new approaches to the work. The focus areas of DevOps include, but are not limited to, source code management, code builds, continuous integration, continuous deployment, testing, configuration, and performance monitoring. And when we discuss *DevSecOps*, the focus areas also include security tools for continuous threat and vulnerability management. The number of available tools for each automated function is lengthy, but common tools you are likely to encounter include, but are not limited to, GitHub, Jira, Docker, Kubernetes, Jenkins, Maven, Ansible, Nagios, Splunk, JUnit, Load-Runner, and GitLab.

As you can imagine, since DevOps is a relatively new methodology (a set of practices), there are new tools to acquire, learn, and adopt, and every industry and organization has its own unique set of change management challenges—the level of DevOps maturity and implementation varies greatly within organizations at this point in time. Not unlike the shift to agile approaches, it is common to see a lot of hybrid approaches as organizations make this transition.

Before we review what this all means to the project manager, let's review DevSec-Ops in more detail first. As you probably guess by now, the term *DevSecOps* is a merger of Development, Security, and Operations, and the methodology resulted from some of the shortcomings of DevOps. In a strict DevOps culture, you could still end up with security testing not being part of the main workflow and security risks not being identified until later in the life cycle when the time and cost to resolve can be exponentially more. Thus, DevSecOps fulfills the desire to integrate security concerns and security testing (automated security testing ideally) into every phase of the development life cycle. Again, like DevOps, it moves the Security function to the left in the life-cycle process flow, embeds the security personnel within the project team, and includes a new set of tools, technologies, and approaches.

But other than the security component, DevOps and DevSecOps have a great deal in common and share these features:

- A culture of collaboration and communication among once siloed groups/functions

- Shared responsibility across the team for application performance and security, especially the developers

- Focus on faster delivery

- Transparency of work

- Maximize automation—reduce, if not eliminate, any manual development, operations, testing, and performance monitoring tasks

- Maximize customer value

- Monitor and measure performance and health of systems and software

- Capture feedback and continuously improve "the system"

Okay, at this point, you might be saying, "This all sounds very technical; why do I, as a project manager, need to know about this?" Well, much like with agile approaches, to be more effective, you need to understand the work process your team is using and the tools involved. Specifically, here are the key focus areas for the project manager working in a DevOps or DevSecOps environment:

- Servant leadership to foster the collaboration/trust needed and handle the change management aspects involved in your organization

- Need to understand the processes involved to properly plan, define roles needed, understand the dependencies, and ensure processes are working

- Use the same tools the team is using for work tracking and communication

- Ensure feedback and defects are captured and incorporated in replanning efforts

- Ensure automated testing is kept current

- Ensure continuous integration/continuous deployment (CI/CD) workflow is functioning as expected

- Remember that automation is a component of DevOps and DevSecOps, but not the only component

HIPAA, Privacy, and Security

At one time, privacy and security were of concern primarily to national defense systems and financial institutions. Now all systems must have privacy and security concerns embedded within not just the system requirements, but also within all aspects of the team and organization, including physical location of the team, team procedures, testing procedures, tools used, and communication methods allowed.

The Internet and most applications developed in the past few decades were not developed with security in mind, nor with awareness of how their systems could be exploited and how customers' data could be stolen. Well, those days are over. Now, due to federal requirements, serious financial liability concerns, and demands from the marketplace, organizations and systems must be more focused on systems security and data privacy. Although we could spend an entire book (or two) on this subject matter, what I want to do in this section is provide some guidance to the project manager who might be new to all of this. These notes will enable you to conduct an intelligent conversation about these matters and, more importantly, help you ask the right questions when you are planning and executing your project.

To start, here are the definitions for three common acronyms:

- **HIPAA**—The Health Insurance Portability and Accountability Act, passed by Congress in 1996. The act accomplished several things, but for our focus here, it requires the protection and confidential handling of protected health information. In particular, it ensures only the minimum information necessary is used or shared.

- **PHI**—Protected health information, as defined in HIPAA. As a general rule, PHI covers any information for past, present, and future medical conditions, including patient identifying information and payment provisions. It applies to all forms of this data: paper, oral, and electronic.

- **PII**—Personally identifiable information, any information that can be used to uniquely identify, contact, or locate an individual, or can be used with other sources to uniquely identify a person. While part of HIPAA, PII has become a focus for all systems doing business on the Internet.

Here are some things to consider when dealing with HIPAA, privacy, and security:

- **Get educated**—As a new project manager, understand which privacy and security standards are important to the organization and which standards must be met so that your project is accountable. In addition, clarify what training your team must complete to ensure adherence to these standards.

- **Set up projects with security in mind**—You need to ensure the following:

  - Access to any system and project resource is individually authenticated.

  - Access to the physical location(s) of the project is secure.

  - Any remote access by team members is secure.

  - Any tool used supports the necessary security protocols.

  - All project team communications abide by security protocols.

  - All team members know what to do if any device is lost or stolen.

- **Design your system with security in mind**—The days of "open" default access are over. Systems must be defined with encrypted channels as the preferred choice. The proper audit trails and checks should be built in to the system.

- **Protect production data at all times**—Protect the need to access any production data during systems development and testing. If it must be done, ensure access is limited and any key PII data elements are masked. Focus on limiting any printout of this data.

- **Plan for security audits**—Assume your project will be accountable to security audits. These audits will likely target physical locations, networks, applications, procedures, systems access, and especially any area where the organization has been exposed before. Plan not only for the audits, but for time and resources needed to analyze the audit results and provide action plans to remediate any gaps.

- **Plan testing with security in mind**—Not only do test plans need to ensure the targeted business and functional requirements are met, but they also need to take a hacker mentality and include test cases and/or testing tools that will proactively identify any data privacy or security holes.

Project Management Offices

The nature, scope, and overall effectiveness of a given Project Management Office (PMO) vary from organization to organization. As a result, perceptions of the value that a PMO offers vary widely, and there is a lack of consensus on what a PMO is supposed to do. As a project manager, you must be clear on the responsibilities that your PMO has, how it can assist you on your project, and how you need to work with it during your project. In many situations, your PMO reports are separate and distinct from your status reporting and implemented as an individual line item on your communications plan.

 NOTE   In some organizations, the PMO is referred to as the Program Management Office.

To start, the organizational scope of a PMO can vary tremendously. Some of the first PMOs were developed to manage enterprise projects, such as enterprise resource planning (ERP) implementations. Since then, the scope of PMOs has expanded. In some organizations, the PMO is at the corporate, enterprise level. In others, it is positioned at the business unit or department level. The level is often determined by organizational culture, stage of PMO evolution within the organization, and organizational priority.

In either case, the nature and authority of the PMO fall somewhere on a spectrum. On one end of the spectrum is the support mode. In support mode, a PMO provides project managers with training, guidance, templates, and best practices. On the other end of the spectrum is the central planning, project oversight mode. In this mode, the PMO provides all the project managers, controls the portfolio management process, manages resource allocation, and closely monitors the performance of each project. In addition, the scope of a PMO is not always limited to projects. In some organizations, PMOs are used to monitor and oversee service-level agreements (SLAs) with vendors. Specifically, the responsibilities of a given PMO are a combination of the following:

- **Project support**—Provide project management guidance to project managers in business units.

- **Methodology**—Develop and implement a consistent and standardized project management process.

- **Training**—Conduct or outsource project management training.

- **Consulting and mentoring**—Coach employees on best practices.

- **Tools**—Select and administer project management–related tools for use by the organization.

- **Program management**—Provide management and oversight of multiple, related projects.

- **Portfolio management**—Establish a process for requesting, prioritizing, and approving projects. In addition, establish a process for canceling projects that are not meeting portfolio performance standards.

- **Resource management**—Establish and execute processes to ensure resources are allocated effectively based on the portfolio priorities.

- **Monitor SLAs**—Monitor performance of and adherence to service-level agreements.

 NOTE In most organizations, the PMO is charged with directing the project portfolio management process.

Historically, most PMOs were started by CIOs to provide the needed structure to standardize project management practices, facilitate IT project portfolio management, and develop methodologies for repeatable processes. Today, the best PMOs leverage the organization culture to successfully deliver the project portfolio in a way that satisfies both senior management and the targeted customers. By enabling better resource management, reducing project failures, and supporting projects that offer the biggest return on investment, PMOs can provide the foundation for effectively managing any business.

The specific organization and staffing model for a PMO depends on a myriad of organizational factors, including key organizational pain points, targeted goals, natural organizational strengths, strengths of existing resources, and corporate culture.

Traits of Successful PMOs

Now, for all the value that a PMO can provide, there are many organizations that have not experienced success with PMOs. Rather than focus on where many PMO implementations have failed, let's take a more positive tact. Let's review common traits of successful PMO implementations, and you can infer the reasons why some have been less than successful.

- **Aligned with corporate culture**—PMO implementations are change management exercises. Developing an effective PMO involves strategy, reviewing industry standards and best practices, process tailoring, patience, and persistence. This process can be a challenge and requires some finesse, especially if the culture has not valued disciplined approaches in the past.

- **Communicate purpose and vision clearly**—Effective PMOs develop and implement a consistent and standardized project management process.

- **Garner senior management support**—A key part of the PMO implementation strategy is to understand the best ways to involve senior management. Common methods are through sponsorship or direct reporting relationships. It is essential that senior management understands the value of the PMO and serves as a champion for the PMO purpose.

- **Learn from pilot projects**—Many successful PMO implementations start with well-defined pilot projects for a given business area or type of project. The projects rely heavily on the feedback from the project managers and senior management involved to tailor the PMO approach.

- **Evolve over time**—Many PMOs have started with a support focus and then moved down the service spectrum over time. In other instances, a PMO implementation focuses on immediate pain areas (such as improving planning efforts) and then expands into other areas once consistency is achieved.

- **Standardize the fundamentals**—Every project is different, but the core project management fundamentals can be standardized. Effective PMOs ensure that the processes, techniques, and tools around project, planning, estimating, and reporting are consistent, predictable, and value-added. This includes providing a repository of project templates and checklists.

- **Focus on value-added deliverables**—Effective PMOs want to streamline paperwork and reduce the document approval cycles in a given project. As a result, they seek to combine deliverables when possible and attempt to leverage online, collaborative project management information systems.

- **Provide project administration support**—Rather than require additional project administration efforts from the project managers, PMOs that assign project administrators to work with the project managers enable the project manager to focus on leading the project team, resolving issues, and clearing the path of obstacles.

- **Focus on getting projects done**—Effective PMOs encourage and support their project managers to be project leaders, to be people on the ground, with the troops, and focused on project execution.

 TIP   The best PMOs are business-driven and focused on continuous improvement.

- **Bring objectivity to the project initiation process**—The last thing the PMO needs is to have people believe that projects are subjectively approved. When this happens, people circumvent normal channels for getting projects approved, resulting in increased lobbying and political end-runs, both of which do not work in favor of the organization's well-being and long-term success. By adopting a pragmatic approach that is based on quantifiable criteria for evaluating, approving, and prioritizing the project, the PMO can stand above the fray and avoid getting caught in political crossfire, while still acknowledging and balancing the political realities of the process.

- **Justify projects on pessimistic scenarios**—This is an organizational executive management decision. However, when it comes to estimates for budget, work effort, and completion dates, the PMO should encourage the development of multiple scenarios for any project request, especially pessimistic or worst-case ones. This is especially important because most project estimates are way too optimistic. Because project portfolios should be managed like investments, this allows for safer, more conservative financial projections. The key here is to understand the difference between justifying (or funding) a project investment and the expectations for the actual execution of the project. A pessimistic basis for justification can be totally independent from the assumptions and estimates used to guide the delivery of the project.

- **Allocate resources intelligently**—Effective PMOs monitor resource schedules and limit, if not prevent, resources from being overallocated and from having to focus on more than one major initiative at a time. Although this ties in to our discussion of critical chain project management later in this chapter, it really is common sense. Results have shown that multitasking is not productive and leads to longer work days and weeks, which can lead to frustrated workers.

- **Align strategy with delivery**—Effective PMOs partner closely with the executive team to make sure the project portfolio investments are aligned with the corporate goals and strategies.

Portfolio Project Management

Portfolio project management (PPM) describes various approaches to managing projects as part of an overall project investment portfolio. PPM focuses on project initiation (determining which projects should be funded), aligning projects with corporate strategy, aligning resources with those project priorities, and monitoring performance of the project portfolio throughout the year. The practice evolved out of the growing reality that more and more business is accomplished through projects, the concern that too many projects did not succeed, and the lack of visibility that many executives had on ongoing project performance.

Here's a list of additional insights and observations to help you better understand portfolio project management topics:

- **Portfolio project management is NOT program management**—This is a natural point of confusion due mainly to the terms used and to the role of many PMO organizations. Portfolio project management is focused on the investment aspect of the project funding decisions. Program and project management is focused on the delivery (execution) of those projects in the portfolio.

- **Never be totally objective**—Implementing portfolio management is political by nature. Most PPM advocates emphasize the dimension of objectivity and the focus on quantifiable metrics introduced into the project request evaluation and approval processes for an organization. To their credit, PPM processes do reduce the degree of political influence. However, people make these final decisions and the profit centers still carry tremendous influence in determining what projects are funded.

- **Element of corporate governance**—In many organizations, project portfolio management is closely tied to the corporate governance process. The senior management (or executive) group that determines the project portfolio is the same group checking project performance status on a periodic basis.

- **PPM software**—A full PPM solution manages demand (work requests) and resource allocation, prioritizes requests, and monitors investment performance.

- **May or may not include resource management**—Some organizations include resource management as part of PPM while others do not. This is something to clarify when starting in a new organization. If it is not included, there should be tight integration with the corporate resource planning and allocation processes.

- **Separate reporting process**—In most organizations, the status reporting you do for your PPM tool and the corporate governance process is different than what you do for the project leadership team. This occurs because of the limitations of the PPM tool and because of the amount of detail that the executive committee wants to see. From the advancements I see in PPM solutions and the current state of many web-based project management software offerings, I think this will change in the future.

- **Finding the balance**—You must find balance for your given organization. Although most senior management types do not want (nor have time for) the details of your project, they also do not want to be surprised. They do not want to see a project "green" (it's going great) one reporting period and then "red" (help me, I'm in big trouble) the next. This is one of the main advantages of exception-based or stoplight-based status reporting approaches. From my experience, I tend to go "yellow" on any dimension with a high-impact risk or current issue.

Governance Processes

Okay, corporate governance is not exactly a hot (or new) concept, but it is a term that gets thrown around a lot and is often not explained to people who are new to the scene. Because it is closely associated to PPM and PMOs, I thought it would be helpful to put this concept in proper context, too.

Here are a few insights and observations from my experience that can help you better understand corporate governance topics:

- **Portfolio project management is part of corporate governance**—This is discussed in the previous section.

- **Other elements of corporate governance**—Corporate governance can include more than just project portfolio management. In most cases, the additional governance scope is needed to ensure compliance with strategies, standards, policies, and regulations. Specifically, other corporate governance processes can include the following:

  - IT governance (compliance with architectural standards)

  - Procurement

  - HR

  - Resource management

  - Legal

  - Regulatory

  - Quality assurance

Critical Chain Project Management

Critical chain project management (CCPM) is a management practice beginning to gain momentum. As a relatively new project manager, you might find yourself working in an organization using CCPM, or you might be hearing more about it and just wondering what is so different about it. My objective is to give a brief synopsis of CCPM, clarify the key unique features, and provide a basis for further discussion and discovery.

CCPM is a method of planning and managing projects based on Eliyahu M. Goldratt's Theory of Constraints. It is a method that emphasizes resource management and speed. It is a method that aims to remove the slack that is built in to most schedules. It is a method that requires a different approach to schedule development, project execution, and monitoring project performance. Let's take a closer look at some specific features to help you better understand the principles and uniqueness of CCPM:

- **Critical chain**—CCPM identifies and focuses on the critical chain, as opposed to the critical path. Resources are then assigned to each task, and the plan is resource leveled using the 50% estimates. The longest sequence of resource-leveled tasks that leads from the beginning to the end of the project is then identified as the critical chain. If there are no resource constraints (and resources are leveled), then the critical chain and the critical path are the same.

- **System**—In CCPM this term refers to all tasks in the schedule.

- **Two estimates for each task**—When estimating the work effort or duration for a task, two estimates are developed. One estimate is called the 50% probability estimate; the other one is the 90% probability estimate. The 50% probability means exactly that; the task has a 50% chance of completing within the effort and time estimate. The assumption is that most schedules are based on 90% probability estimates.

- **Schedule on the 50% probability estimate**—A CCPM schedule is built based on the 50% probability estimates. The justification for using the 50% estimates is that half the tasks will finish early and half will finish late, so that the variance over the course of the project should be zero.

- **Pool the differences into a buffer**—The difference between the two estimates are pooled into a buffer, called the *project buffer*. This buffer is added to the end of the project schedule to protect the targeted completion date.

- **Feeder buffers**—In addition to the project buffer, CCPM also uses a series of feeder buffers to further protect the critical chain. Any noncritical chain task that feeds into the critical chain sequence has a buffer, a *feeder buffer*, inserted between the noncritical chain task and the critical chain.

- **Resource focus**—CCPM is focused on resource constraints and resource productivity. You will read and hear a lot about "throughput." It is a requirement that schedules are resource leveled in order to reduce, if not avoid, multitasking.

- **Resource transition**—The CCPM references discuss a third buffer type—a *resource buffer*. This is a bit confusing, because it is not a buffer in the same sense of the project buffer and the feeder buffers. The resource buffer focuses on project execution and on the process of transitioning a task sequence from one resource to another. The process involves direct communication between the resources (performers) assigned to the two tasks. The predecessor task resources notify the successor task resources on regular, predetermined intervals about their expected completion date. Furthermore, a final confirmation should be given a day or two before task completion so all successor task performers are ready to start work exactly when needed. Goldratt calls this notification process the *resource buffer*. It is a simple, yet effective method to ensure that a task starts exactly when it should. Early finishes are not wasted.

 NOTE   *Student syndrome* is the term used to describe the common tendency to procrastinate until the last moment.

Parkinson's Law states that work expands to fill the allocated time.

- **Relay runners**—As hinted at in the previous section, the mode that resources operate in a CCPM project is that of a relay runner. The resource knows when the baton is coming (predecessor task completed), as soon as the baton arrives the resource stays focused and gets the task completed as fast as it can, and then hands off the baton to the next runner (resource assigned to successor task).

- **Efficiency of pooled buffers**—This is a strong component of CCPM. By pooling the usual slack found in task estimates into buffers and setting up task management procedures that encourage and reward speed, a project can take advantage of the time gains that would normally be hidden or eaten up from multitasking, student syndrome, Parkinson's Law, inbox delays, lack of prioritization, or task handoff inefficiencies. If any particular task is delayed or completes later than the 50% estimate, the project manager "borrows" time from the project buffer and adds it to the offending activity. On the other hand, if an activity finishes early, the gain is added to the project buffer.

- **Monitor the buffers for project health**—Overall project health is measured by monitoring the feeder and project buffers. If the rate of buffer consumption is low, the project is on target. If the rate of consumption is such that there is likely to be little or no buffer at the end of the project, then corrective actions or recovery plans must be developed to recover the loss. When the buffer consumption rate exceeds some threshold value (a rate that puts the buffer at risk of being consumed before the project is complete), then those response plans need to be implemented. CCPM advocates feel that buffer management is better than earned value management (EVM) for measuring project performance because the EVM technique can be misleading. EVM does not distinguish progress on the project constraint (the critical chain) from progress on nonconstraints.

 TIP Always look to pilot any new tool or process so the lessons learned can be applied before any type of wider implementation. This helps manage the change factor and increase the level of acceptance.

Web-Based Project Management and Collaboration Tools

If your project requires (or could benefit from) sharing project information with clients, vendors, subcontractors, a mobile or geographically dispersed team, or anyone located outside your corporate networks, you should consider web-based project management and team collaboration software solutions. The purpose of this section is to make sure you are aware of those options and to offer some recommendations on what to consider when evaluating them.

To start, some of the attractive features of these tool options and the reasons you want to consider them include the following:

- No software installation required except your web browser (that is, cloud-based).

- Web-based solutions can be much less expensive. Depending on the features you require and your ability to leverage open-source options, a web-based solution can even be free.

- Ability to update tasks and project plans from anywhere.

- Ability to establish a centralized, private, secure environment connecting people, process, and product regardless of team member location.

- Provide for better visibility and openness.

- Streamline communication and work effort.

- Can assign tasks to individual team members and track progress.

- Can be deployed within a day, depending on need and licensing arrangement.

- Most vendors offer Software as a Service (SaaS) models.

- Many vendors offer hosted or installed "on premises" options for environments that have tight security requirements.

- Faster and enhanced working processes.

- Short learning curves.

- Most offer group discussion/chat capabilities.

- Most offer version control of project documents.

- Most offer web conferencing tools.

- Can serve as project repository—easy to locate documents and artifacts; keeps documents current and synchronized.

- Reduce the need for email collaboration and the challenges that can come from that, especially when multiple team members are reviewing the same artifact or responding to the same topic.

Many options are available now, and the list continues to grow. If you can consider web-based solutions, here are key elements to consider in your selection and evaluation process:

- Project management feature set required

- Enterprise visibility

- Cost

- Return on investment

- Ease of use; training required

- Platform independence

- Scalability

- Integration ease

- Ability to focus on work and not status reporting effort

- Level and granularity of security needed

- Ability to use for client access

- Disaster recovery services offered (backups or prevention of data loss)

TIP   When evaluating any cloud-based collaboration tool, ensure that it offers the level of security to meet the requirements of your participating organizations.

Requirements Management Tools

The purpose of this section is make sure you are aware of requirements management tools and to provide criteria to help you determine whether your project or organization needs to consider using one.

First, a requirements management tool is a centralized, collaborative, and database-centric approach to managing requirements, versus the document-based approach that has traditionally been used to capture, communicate, and review the specifications for a project or product.

In many environments, simply moving the document-based approach to a project team collaboration tool can alleviate many issues. However, there are many cases when even that might not be enough. To determine whether your project or organization could benefit from a requirements management tool, consider these factors:

- The complexity level of the targeted product or solution

- The size of the stakeholder team participating in the requirements definition process

- The need for multiple people to modify the same set of requirements simultaneously

- The change frequency level of the requirements

- The efficiency and effectiveness of the requirements review process

- The need and ease of tracing source requirements to design specifications or test cases

- The need to integrate requirements with a test management tool

- The need and ease to link to related and supporting requirements

- The need to store a common set of attributes about each requirement

- The need to manage requirements that are planned for different releases or products

- The need to reuse or access the original product/solution/system requirements for future enhancement projects

- The need to store requirements that were deprioritized or rejected

- The need to reuse requirements for future projects

CAUTION The introduction of any new tool requires proper planning and an investment from the sponsoring organization.

Mind Mapping Tools

 CAUTION Although visual thinking is exciting and most people prefer it, it will seem awkward to others, especially those who are more comfortable with linear organizational structures.

 TIP One simple, but powerful, productivity enhancer for project managers is to use mind maps for meeting notes.

 NOTE Tony Buzan, a British psychology author and educational consultant, is regarded as the modern father of mind mapping techniques.

Mind mapping software allows you to build, modify, and share mind maps electronically. A *mind map* is a diagram that contains information pieces (words, ideas, pictures, tasks, and so on) arranged radially around a central theme (key word or idea).

A mind map enables you to do visual thinking. It enables you to capture and communicate related information in a manner that is aligned with how the brain organizes data and information. Mind maps have been used successfully in brainstorming environments to generate, visualize, and structure ideas. They have also been used as powerful aids in learning new concepts, note taking, problem solving, decision-making, and writing. I have provided basic, simple mind maps at the end of each chapter using the MindManager tool from Mindjet (www.mindmanager.com).

So, why do I include this in a project management book? Why is the use and acceptance of mind mapping tools growing rapidly? Why are more and more organizations adding mind mapping tools to their productivity tool arsenal? To help answer these questions, let me offer these insights based on my own experience:

- **Ability for one-page communications**—The ability to communicate large amounts of information and the most complex concepts on a single page in an easy-to-understand manner is powerful.

- **Visual appeal**—There is a "wow" factor. It's different, but at the same time more natural for many audiences. It catches your attention and draws you in.

- **Collaborative nature**—It was built for collaborative work sessions. For a project manager, it is a powerful medium for planning a project.

- **Integration power**—Mind maps provide a portal-like home base for all documents, deliverables, or artifacts associated with the subject of the mind map. In addition, the best mind mapping software provides for easy integration with your other productivity suite software (such as Microsoft Office and Project).

- **Streamline paperwork**—Due to the organizational power and visual appeal of mind maps, you can effectively share and communicate information simply by sharing the mind maps. There is a reduced need for additional documents to be created.

- **Working smarter**—As the pace of work increases and the nature of work becomes more collaborative, organizations and knowledge professionals continuously look for ways to work smarter and be more productive. Mind mapping tools can facilitate these goals.

Value of Certifications

This is always a hot topic, and not just in the project management circles. What is the value of certifications? What does having one mean? What does it really measure? These questions are fair, especially in a profession like project management that requires skills and talents that are difficult to measure in standardized testing approaches. The most popular project management certification is the Project Management Professional (PMP) from PMI. It is the gold standard for a project management professional certification. In addition to the PMP, PMI offers a number of other certifications and micro-credentials. Since the last edition of this book, PMI has added four new certifications focused on agile/hybrid project approaches. See Table 25.1 and Table 25.2 for a summary of PMI's offerings as of 2021.

TABLE 25.1 Summary of 2021 PMI Certifications

Certification	Name	Notes
PMP	Project Management Professional	Gold standard; world's leading project management certification. Proves project leadership experience and expertise in any way of working (predictive, agile, and hybrid approaches).
PgMP	Program Management Professional	Senior level; advanced certification. Designed for those who manage multiple, complex projects to achieve strategic and organizational results.
PfMP	Portfolio Management Professional	Senior level; advanced certification. Designed for those who manage a portfolio of projects and programs aligned with organizational strategy and focused on doing the right work.
CAPM	Certified Associate in Project Management	A stepping-stone certification to a PMP. Demonstrates your understanding of the fundamental knowledge, terminology, and processes of effective project management.
PMI Project Management Ready	PMI Project Management Ready	Newest certification. Introduces high school and post-secondary students to the concepts and skillsets of project management.
PMI-ACP	PMI Agile Certified Practitioner	Demonstrates a proven ability to apply agile principles and practices on projects.
PMI-PBA	PMI Professional in Business Analysis	Demonstrates knowledge and expertise in business analysis.
PMI-RMP	PMI Risk Management Professional	Demonstrates knowledge and expertise in the specialized area of assessing and identifying project risks along with plans to mitigate threats and capitalize on opportunities.

Certification	Name	Notes
PMI-SP	PMI Scheduling Professional	Demonstrates knowledge and advanced experience in the specialized area of developing and maintaining project schedules.
DASM	Disciplined Agile Scrum Master	Newer certification; expires in one year; can be renewed.
		Requires a course on the PMI Disciplined Agile (DA) tool kit.
		Teaches how to apply the DA tool kit (Scrum, Kanban, SAFe) to determine the most effective way of working (WoW) for your team/organization.
DASSM	Disciplined Agile Senior Scrum Master	Newer certification; expires in one year; can be renewed.
		Teaches experienced agile practitioners how to use the Disciplined Agile tool kit to optimize how teams work, work with allies within their organization, and solve a variety of advanced problems.
DAVSC	Disciplined Agile Value Stream Consultant	Newer certification; expires in one year; can be renewed.
		Requires DASSM and 3 years of agile experience.
		Teaches how to combine practices from Flow, Lean, the Theory of Constraints, and Organizational Development into Disciplined Agile to give you the tools to optimize enterprise-wide value streams.
DAC	Disciplined Agile Coach	Newer certification; expires in one year; can be renewed.
		Requires DASSM and 3 years of agile coaching experience.
		Teaches how to coach teams across the enterprise organizations to achieve true agility by applying Disciplined Agile and choose their best way of working.

TABLE 25.2 Summary of 2021 PMI Micro-Credentials

Micro-Credential	Name	Notes/Focus Area
AHPP	Agile Hybrid Project Pro	Validates you are aligned to the new PMI/PMP standards for Agile and Hybrid approaches.
Agile Metrics	Agile Metrics	Teaches how to select agile metrics that matter and that help meet your team and organizational objectives.
CD-P	Citizen Developer Practitioner	IT application focused. Provides the tools and methodologies to efficiently create effective and scalable applications using low-code and no-code platforms.
OTF	Organizational Transformation Foundation	First course in the OT Series. Provides the fundamental knowledge of transformation initiatives.
OTO	Organizational Transformation Orchestration	Second course in the OT Series. Provides the framework for transformation execution.
OTI	Organizational Transformation Implementation	Third course in the OT Series. Provides the leadership and strategic knowledge of transformation initiatives.
BEPCP	Built Environment Project Communication Pro	Construction industry. Focuses on the power of effective communication and how to improve on this skill specifically in a construction environment.

In addition, for those of you focused on agile/hybrid projects, there are other industry standard certifications that are highly regarded. Primarily, the certifications offered by the Scrum Alliance (www.scrumalliance.org) and the Scaled Agile Framework (SAFe) certifications from Scaled Agile, Inc. (https://scaledagile.com).

Okay, I might not be the most objective person in the world, because I am a PMP, but I think I can offer helpful insight on the value of project management certification:

- **Get serious**—By earning a certification, you demonstrate a mindset that says to others that you take your work and your profession seriously.

- **Common understanding**—A certification does not guarantee performance or results, but it does ensure that you share a vocabulary and a common understanding of fundamental project management processes.

- **Differentiator**—In a competitive marketplace, any method to further differentiate yourself from your peers never hurts, and earning a credential is good way to do that.

- **Marketability**—More and more employers are using the PMP credential as a base requirement for their project management positions.

- **Compensation**—Studies have shown that the average compensation level of certified professionals is higher than their uncertified counterparts.

 NOTE A *micro-credential* from PMI is an industry specialization and does not have the same qualification or renewal requirements as a traditional certification. Generally, obtaining a micro-credential involves taking a course and passing a nonproctored exam.

Micro-credentials can also help meet the continuing education (PDU) requirements to renew your PMP.

Current micro-credential offerings include AHPP, CD-P, OTF, OTO, OTI, BEPCP, and Agile Metrics.

Project Management Training

When it comes to project management training, a wide variety of options is available. In the same way it can be difficult to test for project management skills, it can be equally challenging trying to train someone to be a project manager. From my experience, here are a few insights and observations I've accumulated over the years on project management training:

- **Mentoring**—The absolute best way to learn project management is to observe it being done well. When possible, newer project managers should serve on a project team with a more senior project leader. This could be as a project manager with a senior program manager, or it could be as a project coordinator, a project administrator, a business analyst/lead (if skill set applies), or as a technical lead (again, if the skill set applies) with a senior project manager who enjoys the opportunity to mentor others.

- **Focus on specific skills**—Another worthy training strategy is to focus on one skill set at a time. In most cases, professionals have specific areas they need to improve, and often when these skills are improved, it will have a cascading effect on other areas of performance.

- **Simulations**—Given the nature of projects, it is difficult to anticipate the specific situations and scenarios that a project manager will face or to bring the reality of projects to the classroom environment. Due to the improvements in technology over the years, a tremendous advancement in training is the use of computer and gaming simulations. I am convinced this is the future for all training efforts.

- **Computer based**—I find computer-based, web-based, virtual training offerings (webinars, online seminars, and so on) to be an efficient and convenient method for staying informed on current trends and tools and refreshing key fundamentals.

- **PMI special interest group conferences**—I have received a lot of benefit from attending the educational conferences provided by the PMI special interest groups. I believe the main reason for this is the presentations are provided by practitioners from the field and the content is very current and relevant.

- **Skills to target**—As you gain experience in project management and attain a certain mastery of the project management fundamentals, it can be more difficult to find project management training that offers a lot of value to you. Well, one of the great things about project management is that it covers almost all aspects of business, management, and your industry, so there is never a shortage of things to learn about or improve upon. For most people, there is value in acquiring additional training in the following areas:

  - Business management

  - Procurement

  - Leadership

  - Quality techniques

  - People management

- **Tool-specific**—Especially tools used for project management, communication, and collaboration.

THE ABSOLUTE MINIMUM

At this point, you should have a solid understanding of the following:

- Agile project management approaches are characterized by change expectancy, iterative development, phased deployments, collaboration, people focus, customer focus, timeboxing, detailed near-term schedules, frequent feedback loops, and constant risk management.

- DevOps and DevSecOps practices are an extension of agile approaches, include a new set of tools, technologies, and approaches, rely on a culture of collaboration, and are characterized by integrating the infrastructure operations and/or security quality into the entire systems development life cycle.

- Security and data privacy concerns impact your entire project and organization.

- The scope and responsibility of a PMO varies by organization and maturity level.

- Common traits of successful PMO implementations include alignment with corporate culture, clear purpose, senior management support, evolution over time, focus on getting projects done, and a focus on aligning strategy with project delivery.

- Project portfolio management focuses on project initiation, aligning projects with corporate strategy, aligning resources with those project priorities, and monitoring performance of the project portfolio.

- Unique features of critical chain project management include the focus on throughput, task execution speed, resource constraints, scheduling on 50% probability task estimates, and the use of buffers to protect the completion date and to monitor project performance.

- Web-based project management and team collaboration software solutions are excellent options for virtual, geographically dispersed teams.

- Requirements management tools need to be considered when document-based approaches no longer serve the long-term interest of the sponsoring organization.

- Mind mapping tools foster collaboration, simplify communication, and provide potential for increased work productivity.

- Certifications demonstrate that you take your work and profession seriously.
- PMI certifications:

  www.pmi.org/certifications
- PMI certification micro-credentials:

  www.pmi.org/certifications/micro-credentials
- Effective project management training approaches include mentoring and simulations.

The map in Figure 25.1 summarizes the main points reviewed in this chapter.

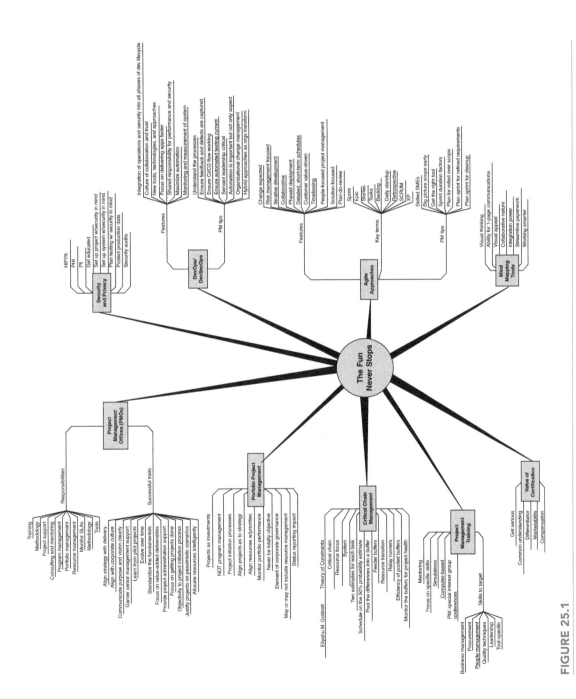

FIGURE 25.1

The Fun Never Stops chapter summary.

IN THIS CHAPTER

- Discover the recent significant changes to the PMP exam

- Learn how to best prepare for the PMP exam in the shortest time possible

- Understand what to expect on the PMP exam

- Learn how to avoid the common trouble areas that cause people problems on the exam

- Review powerful test-taking strategies

POWERFUL PMP EXAM TIPS

As has been the theme of this book, I want to share with you the insights and knowledge that will accelerate your learning curve and make you effective as fast possible. Since I have mentioned the value of the PMP certification a couple of times, and I have co-authored a PMP exam preparation book in the past, I felt it was only right to extend this focus to preparing for the PMP exam.

In this chapter, we will get right to it. I am not going to waste time covering the process for applying for the exam, general study approaches, or how to actually sign up for the exam. I am confident you have this covered (and I did include the primary PMI links you need for this at the end just in case).

We focus on the concepts, knowledge, and strategies you need to ensure exam success. We review what is important to PMI and why you need to understand this to ensure exam success. We review what areas can cause people problems on the test and how to avoid them. We review what you can expect on the test, and we discuss the key areas you must focus on in your preparations.

To get started, let's review what's changed in the 2021 version of the PMP exam.

 NOTE To be eligible to take the PMP exam, a candidate must have one of the following:

- Four-year degree
- 36 months (4500 hours) leading and directing projects
- 35 hours of project management education

  Or have

- Secondary degree (high school diploma, associate's degree, or the global equivalent)
- 60 months (7500 hours) leading and directing projects
- 35 hours of project management education

What Is Different About the 2021 PMP Exam?

The new version of the Project Management Professional exam was released by PMI in 2021, and there are significant changes to the scope and the structure of the test. Please refer to Table 26.1 for a summary comparison of the new exam versus the prior exam format.

 NOTE Per PMI, *enablers* are illustrative examples of the work associated with the task. The enablers referenced are not meant to be an exhaustive list but rather offer a few examples to help demonstrate what the task encompasses.

TABLE 26.1 Comparing 2021 PMP Exam Version with Prior Version

Category	Prior to 2021 Version	2021 Version
Domains with Percentage of Questions	Initiating (13%)	People (42%)
	Planning (24%)	Process (50%)
	Executing (31%)	Business Environment (8%)
	Monitoring and Controlling (25%)	
	Closing (7%)	
Tasks	42	35
Enablers	No	Yes
Total Number of Questions	200	180
Number of Questions Scored	175	175

Category	Prior to 2021 Version	2021 Version
Types of Questions	Multiple choice with single response	Multiple choice with single response
		Multiple choice with multiple responses
		Matching
		Hotspot
		Fill-in-the-blank
Project Management Approaches	Predictive	Predictive (50%)
		Agile or Hybrid (50%)

While the new exam was released prior to the *PMBOK Guide* – Seventh Edition, and PMI states the PMP exam is not based on the PMBOK, it is easy to see the same influences that drove the latest PMBOK changes are apparent in the new exam too, especially the focus on the 8 performance domains, the 12 project management principles, and inclusion of agile and hybrid project approaches. The new exam is more focused on measuring a practitioner's ability to take a holistic, value-focused, people-first, work-smarter approach to their craft. Of course, these attributes have been the focus of this book from the first edition. A common complaint about the PMP exam in the past was that it largely measured an academic understanding of the project management fundamentals and did not gauge a person's ability to apply this knowledge in real-world situations. The latest PMBOK and this new version of the exam are definite steps to change this.

For starters, the exam content is now organized into three basic domains for any project—People, Process, and Business Environment—and the scope now includes both traditional/prescriptive project approaches and agile/hybrid project approaches. Now, does this mean the former focus on the five process groups and the ten knowledge areas is no longer needed? Of course not…that is fundamental project management intelligence, and this information simply exists as a subset of the three new domains: People, Process, and Business Environment. In addition, the ten knowledge areas all map to the different process groups, which all closely relate to tasks that fall under the three new domains.

Speaking of…an essential tool for your exam preparations will be the PMP Examination Content Outline document (see link at the end of the chapter). This exam outline provides the checklist for what you need to know for the test. For each domain, you will see each task that is included, and for each task the set of enablers (activities, examples) that apply. I mention this here for two reasons. One, these tasks and enablers tell you what is important to PMI. And two, there are tasks and points of emphasis now on the test that were either not covered or not emphasized before. Specifically, refer to Table 26.2 for a summary of these tasks to assist your study preparations. Of the 35 tasks in the new 2021 PMP Examination Content Outline, 12 of them are on this list. Upon review, you will notice PMI is placing an increased importance on people skills, team-building, cooperation, agile and hybrid project management, compliance management, project value, and organizational change.

TABLE 26.2 New or Increased Emphasis Tasks for 2021 PMP Exam

Domain	Task	Enablers
People	Lead a team	Set a clear vision and mission
		Support diversity and inclusion (e.g., behavior types, thought processes)
		Value servant leadership (e.g., relate the tenets of servant leadership to the team)
		Determine an appropriate leadership style (e.g., directive, collaborative)
		Inspire, motivate, and influence team members/stakeholders (e.g., team contract, social contract, reward system)
		Analyze team members' and stakeholders' influence
		Distinguish various options to lead various team members and stakeholders
People	Ensure team members/ stakeholders are adequately trained	Determine required competencies and elements of training
		Determine training options based on training needs
		Allocate resources for training Measure training outcomes
People	Build a team	Appraise stakeholder skills
		Deduce project resource requirements
		Continuously assess and refresh team skills to meet project needs
		Maintain team and knowledge transfer
People	Promote team performance through the application of emotional intelligence	Assess behavior through the use of personality indicators
		Analyze personality indicators and adjust to the emotional needs of key project stakeholders
Process	Ensure knowledge transfer for project continuity	Discuss project responsibilities within team
		Outline expectations for working environment
		Confirm approach for knowledge transfers

Domain	Task	Enablers
Process	Execute project with the urgency required to deliver business value	Assess opportunities to deliver value incrementally
		Examine the business value throughout the project
		Support the team to subdivide project tasks as necessary to find the minimum viable product
Process	Plan and manage schedule	Estimate project tasks (milestones, dependencies, story points)
		Utilize benchmarks and historical data
		Prepare schedule based on methodology
		Measure ongoing progress based on methodology
		Modify schedule, as needed, based on methodology
		Coordinate with other projects and other operations
Process	Determine appropriate project methodology/methods and practices	Assess project needs, complexity, and magnitude
		Recommend project execution strategy (e.g., contracting, finance)
		Recommend a project methodology/approach (i.e., predictive, agile, hybrid)
		Use iterative, incremental practices throughout the project life cycle (e.g., lessons learned, stakeholder engagement, risk)
Business Environment	Plan and manage project compliance	Confirm project compliance requirements (e.g., security, health and safety, regulatory compliance)
		Classify compliance categories
		Determine potential threats to compliance
		Use methods to support compliance
		Analyze the consequences of noncompliance
		Determine necessary approach and action to address compliance needs (e.g., risk, legal)
		Measure the extent to which the project is in compliance

Domain	Task	Enablers
Business Environment	Evaluate and deliver project benefits and value	Investigate that benefits are identified
		Document agreement on ownership for ongoing benefit realization
		Verify measurement system is in place to track benefits
		Evaluate delivery options to demonstrate value
		Apprise stakeholders of value gain progress
Business Environment	Evaluate and address external business environment changes for impact on scope	Survey changes to external business environment (e.g., regulations, technology, geopolitical, market)
		Assess and prioritize impact on project scope/backlog based on changes in external business environment
		Recommend options for scope/backlog changes (e.g., schedule, cost changes)
		Continually review external business environment for impacts on project scope/backlog
Business Environment	Support organizational change	Assess organizational culture
		Evaluate impact of organizational change to project and determine required actions
		Evaluate impact of the project to the organization and determine required actions

 TIP Use the PMP Examination Content Outline document provided by PMI to focus your exam preparation efforts. The tasks and enablers emphasize what is important to PMI.

In addition to the scope changes, the new exam includes different types of questions now. Previously, the exam consisted solely of multiple-choice questions with one best response. In the new 2021 version of the PMP exam, the question types consist of the following:

- Multiple choice with single response

- Multiple choice with multiple responses

- Matching

- Hotspot

- Fill-in-the-blank

What Is the PMP Exam Like?

The Project Management Professional exam is a computer-based exam composed of 180 questions; 175 questions are actually scored, but you will not know which 5 are not, so you need to take the same approach for all 180 questions. As noted in the previous section, the question types are more varied now. It is not all multiple choice with single response questions anymore. Approximately 4 hours is allowed for the exam (230 minutes and a 10-minute break).

As mentioned earlier, the exam is evenly split between traditional/predictive and agile/hybrid methodologies and the questions are distributed across the three domain areas (50% from Process domain, 42% from People domain, and 8% from Business Environment domain). In addition, the domain questions are randomly dispersed throughout the exam.

The intent of the questions is to test a thorough understanding of project management. To this end, many questions are creatively designed to check both key understanding (knowledge) and the ability to practically apply these concepts at the same time. A part of this creative exam design is to utilize many different types of questions. To better prepare you for the PMP exam experience, let's review the key question types and formats you are likely to encounter:

- **Situational questions**—These questions require you to rely on your knowledge, real-world experience, and judgment to answer them correctly.

- **Conceptual understanding**—For these questions, you must apply concepts to a new situation by using more than simple memorization. Often, PMI intentionally uses different terminology for the same concepts. This is done to test your understanding of the topic rather than your ability to simply recall a term.

- **Memorization questions**—The PMP exam will have some questions that are short and direct and can be answered in less than 20 seconds. For example, you might encounter some fill-in-the blanks and factual-type questions.

- **Double-reverse logic questions**—A popular technique of wily test designers, these types of questions ask about a topic using reverse or double-reverse logic. Generally, you need to select the exception from the four possible options.

- **Story problem questions**—There are long, drawn-out, story problem questions that can take several (2–5) minutes to process. The key to these question types is deciphering what information presented is essential and needed to answer the question.

- **"Use the pencil" questions**—There are questions that will require you to perform simple calculations and/or draw simple diagrams to select the correct answer. Frequently, questions regarding earned value, financial accounting, project network diagrams, and project schedules require the use of the pencil to get the right answer.

- **Non-PMBOK questions**—Estimates vary, but most people feel around 60% of the exam questions come directly from the PMBOK. The other questions originate from other reference materials, subjects related to project management, and real-world situations. In addition, past exam takers have noted "out-of-the-blue" type questions that test specific knowledge points. Project management is a broad field of study, so you can never be too prepared.

- **"I need to change careers" questions**—Somewhat related to the note above regarding out-of-the-blue questions, there are a few questions placed in every PMP exam to rattle the exam taker. These questions will be difficult, if not impossible, to answer with confidence. Just expect these, and see our exam-taking tips on how best to deal with them. This may be PMI's way of testing how you respond under pressure and when things do not go as expected.

Next, let's review the common gaps that test takers experience between their own real-world experiences and PMI expectations. These gaps will vary depending on the industry in which you work. For the IT industry, these gaps are very common.

 TIP A common feedback point from many exam takers is that several questions seemed to have *more than one correct answer*. Often, most, if not all, of the answers are reasonable responses to the question at hand. However, there is always one best response, as determined by PMI.

Common "Context" Differences

Because it is important to answer the exam questions from PMI's perspective, and not necessarily from your real-life experiences, let's first review several key high-level differences between the PMI vision and common experiences of project managers:

- **Not exactly like we do it**—Because nearly every organization implements project management differently, we generally find that most implementations are not entirely consistent with PMI's view of the world. You will want to identify those differences for your own situation.

- **"The" project manager**—Given the wide range of "project manager" experiences (for example, technical team leader, project administrator, project analyst, project leader, project coordinator), you might be surprised by the expectation PMI has of the project manager role and the powers that come with it.

- **Unapproved practices**—There are several project management practices and techniques used routinely that are considered inappropriate by PMI (for example, the use of overtime, forcing estimates down). These will appear on the exam as incorrect options.

- **Bigger ballpark**—For most project managers, the PMI PMBOK describes a field of project management that is much broader and more complex than what they have experienced in real life.

- **The whole story**—Many project managers lack experience in the complete life cycle of project management. Generally, there is minimal exposure to the Initiating and Closing phases, focus on measuring project value, and organizational change management. You must understand the complete project management process as described by PMI.

Common "Experience" Differences

This section reviews common gaps between the experiences and practices of many project managers (and their respective organizations) and what PMI expects the project manager to do:

- **Project planning**—PMI's definition is much more encompassing than the project plans routinely developed by many project managers in their own organizations.

- **Developing a project schedule**—It is still rather uncommon to find organizations and project managers who build a project schedule the "right way." As you can imagine, the right way is much more involved than the method routinely employed. If you do not use a four-step process, use network diagramming techniques (there are more than one), understand the three estimating methods, account for all WBS dictionary items, or identify all dependencies and level resources, you probably have some work in this process area.

- **Planning project management**—Yes, we still have not left this planning theme yet. PMI expects that all project management activities be planned and documented. So, if your project plan does not include supplementary plans such as a staffing management plan, a responsibility matrix, a communications management plan, a quality management plan, a scope management plan, and a risk management plan (for starters), you will want to focus on these and understand their value.

- **Tracking project performance**—For traditional projects, "earned value" is PMI's recommended technique for tracking and controlling project costs, schedule, and scope. Earned value analysis is not a generally applied technique in many industries, and many project managers have limited experience in managing project costs.

- **Risk management**—Because a full-scale risk management process, as described by PMI, is rarely implemented in many industries, many people have not been educated in this area either.

- **Quality management**—Quality management, like risk management, is rarely implemented at full scale as described by PMI. However, most organizations do have some levels of quality programs in place. The issue here is that your organization's philosophy, terminology, and processes may not match those espoused by PMI.

- **Procurement management**—This is not as frequent a gap as it used to be, but if you haven't had experience dealing with soliciting, selecting, and managing vendors, you will have gaps to close in this area.

- **Project selection**—Although the practice of applying sound business principles to prioritizing and selecting projects is increasing each year, there are still many project managers who have not been exposed to business case development and official cost-benefit analysis using financial techniques such as NPV, IRR, and payback period.

Common Terminology Differences

A common revelation of many project management professionals, when they are first exposed to the PMBOK, is that they find terms and concepts they know in one fashion do not necessarily mean the same thing to PMI. It is important to become aware of these terminology differences to ensure exam success.

- **Project charter**—To PMI, this is the document that authorizes (initiates) the project and the project managers to do their work, and it's the key output from the initiating process. In many organizations, this document is often given other names (for example, Project Initiation form, Business Case).

- **Project plan**—To PMI, this is the key output of the planning process and contains many subdeliverables (for example, the project schedule, WBS, and all the supplementary project management plans). In many organizations, this document may be known as the Project Charter, Project Contract, Statement of Work, and so on.

- **Project plan versus project schedule**—A Gantt chart (Microsoft Project) project schedule is not a project plan. A project plan contains the project schedule.

- **WBS versus Gantt chart**—To PMI, a work breakdown structure (WBS) is not equivalent to a Gantt chart (Microsoft Project) project schedule. The WBS is a key input into the schedule-development process, and the project schedule accounts for calendar time and resource leveling.

- **Terms to verify**—Here are several other common project management terms you use that might not have the exact same definition as PMI's (these differences are less critical than the ones previously mentioned):

  - Audit

  - Baseline

  - Corrective action

  - Kickoff meeting

  - Procurement management

  - Risk management

- **Uncommon terms to notice**—Several terms used by PMI are not that well known in many industries. You will want to make sure you review these terms too:

  - Gold-plating

  - Integration management

  - Project expeditor

  - PMIS (project management information system)

  - Work Authorization System

What's Important to PMI?

To better appreciate why these common gaps exist and better prepare for the exam, let's review some of the underlying principles guiding PMI's vision of project management:

- The project manager makes it happen and brings it all together. The role of project manager is extremely important and extremely valuable.

- Servant leadership and emotional intelligence are key fundamental project manager attributes.

- A project manager is always seeking "win-win" solutions.

- Planning is very important.

- Coordinating with other projects and operations is very important when both planning and managing a project.

- All management activities should be analyzed and planned in advance. These supplementary management plans are part of the overall project plan.

- Agile project management is much more flexible, but it still includes planning, scheduling, identifying key milestones, managing risks, and resolving issues.

- The project plan should accurately describe project activity, is based in reality, and is used as the baseline to measure progress.

- The WBS is a very important project management tool.

- Communication is the most important activity of the project manager (90% of the PM's time is spent here). Other communication-based principles that are extremely important to PMI include the following:

  - Coordinate with stakeholders on all project aspects.

  - Clearly assign all project roles and responsibilities.

- The risk management process is very important and is a continuous project management activity.

- All estimating should be completed by the people who will actually do the work.

- All projects, regardless of outcome, should complete the closing process. The emphasized outputs from this are as follows:

  - Capturing lessons learned

  - Executing proper administrative closure

- Knowledge transfer is important and should be maintained throughout the project.

- Training of team members and stakeholders is important and training outcomes should be measured.

- Supporting organizational change is important.

- Projects should be focused on delivering value and benefits, and systems should be in place to measure both.

- The project approach taken should be tailored to manage the risk involved, skills of the team members, expectations of the stakeholders, and maturity level of the organization.

- The use of iterative and incremental practices should be encouraged.

Key PMI Assumptions and Themes

To further understand these common gaps—but more importantly, to better prepare for the exam—let's review some of the key assumptions that guide PMI's vision of project management:

1. The project manager is selected when the project is authorized—before any estimating or preliminary requirements gathering.

2. The project manager is ultimately accountable for the project.

3. The project plan is the baseline that the PM uses to control the project.

4. The project plan is an all-encompassing document and must contain cost and schedule baselines to determine project performance during execution.

5. PMI assumes your organization has project management methodologies and quality assurance procedures.

6. The project manager does have human resources and team development responsibilities.

7. PMI assumes the project team is involved in all planning decisions and problem-solving situations.

8. Projects should be aligned and prioritized with the organization's strategic direction.

9. The earlier in the project life cycle, the more risk for the project and the more influence management has on it.

10. Stakeholder management is an ongoing, continuous process throughout the project life cycle.

11. The success or failure of a project is determined during project planning.

12. The WBS is a "must-have" for any project manager and serves as the basis for most project planning.

13. The WBS is the basis for all project planning.

14. The person (people) who will do the work should do the estimating.

15. The most important task and skill of the project manager is effective project communication.

16. The project team should be involved in all project planning activities.

17. Project changes will occur. Changes should be expected, planned for, and well managed when they occur.

18. Earned value is the best project-controlling technique for traditional projects.

19. The project team should solve its own problems and resolve its own issues whenever possible.

20. Quality is planned into a project, not inspected in.

21. Risk management is an ongoing, continuous process performed by the entire project team.

22. Preventing a risk event is always preferred to mitigating a risk event.

23. Closing processes (administrative closure) should occur at the end of each project phase, not just at the end of the project.

24. Lessons learned describe the knowledge the team and stakeholders gain by executing the project and are an invaluable source of project management information.

25. Historical records and lessons learned are very valuable.

26. PMI assumes you have historical records of past projects.

Exam Topics Not Covered by PMBOK

Although the PMP exam is based primarily on the PMBOK, and the PMBOK should be a central reference in your exam preparation efforts, several exam topics originate from general business management knowledge or other PMI publications and are not addressed in the PMBOK.

 NOTE This point also demonstrates one of the major values of practice exams. The questions you will encounter will help you find the topics you might need to study outside the PMBOK.

Although this list is not meant to be exhaustive, here are some key non-PMBOK exam topics you should understand:

- Business case development and benefits realization
- Conflict-resolution techniques
- Interpersonal skills, including active listening
- Organizational theories
- Problem-solving techniques
- Professional responsibility

- Project finance principles

- Theories of motivation

 TIP Use the PMI PMP Examination Content Outline as a preparation checklist. This outline contains the key tasks and enablers you need to understand for each domain, as well as the key skills and concepts you should be knowledgeable about outside the specific PMBOK content.

Exam Preparation Strategies

Here are key strategies to ensure that you get the most benefit from your exam preparation:

- Understand how you learn and what you need to be successful.

  - If you need to hear the material, get audio books or sign up for a class.

  - If you need to see the material, get books, sign up for an online course, or sign up for an onsite exam prep class.

  - If you need to be accountable to someone else, join a study group or sign up for an exam prep class.

  - If you learn best independently, get the learning materials that work best for you, set your schedule, and get started.

  - If you need or do better with a focused immersive learning approach, consider a 3- to 5-day exam preparation crash course.

  - If you learn best by doing, then plan to focus on taking practice exams.

- Get your target materials and/or sign up for your preparation courses.

- Schedule your study time into your calendar.

- Understand the differences between the current version of the PMBOK (that you will be tested on) and the previous version. You can expect around 20% of the questions to be focused on these areas.

- Get inside the heads of the PMI test creators. Understand what's important to PMI and their vision of the project manager role. (This chapter focuses on this.)

- Know the Seventh Edition of the *PMBOK Guide*:

  - Fully understand the 12 Principles of Project Management

  - Fully understand the 8 performance domains.

- Know the 5 process groups and the 10 knowledge areas:

  - Memorize the Process Group and Knowledge Area Process Mapping.

  - Focus on the data flow diagrams for each process.

 TIP Understanding the 5 process groups and 10 knowledge areas will help you grasp the natural flow of projects through the life cycle and deepen your understanding of the fundamental principles, tools, and techniques used to guide a project through that life cycle.

- Focus on the 2021 PMP Examination Content Outline:

  - Know the tasks and enablers for each domain.

  - Spend time on the new and/or emphasized tasks (see Table 26.2 for a reminder).

- Memorize the PMI definition of a project management plan and what supplemental management plans it contains.

- Memorize Earned Value calculations.

- Understand the differences between process groups and project phases.

- Drill, drill, drill. Take as many practice exams as you can, and continue to take them until you are scoring 90% or better on them.

Exam-Taking Tips

Let's review some key test-taking tips to help you during the actual exam procedure.

- Anticipate that many questions will have multiple correct answers. It is your challenge to pick the best answer based on how PMI feels the situation should be handled.

- Remember to answer questions from PMI's perspective, not from your real-life experience. Think "What should I do?" rather than "What did I do?"

- Pace yourself, and be sure to read all four answers completely. Do not just choose the first correct answer that you see.

- Be cautious of the following:

  - Answers that attract the attention of less knowledgeable, less experienced professionals.

- Answers that reflect common project management errors and unapproved practices.

- Answers that are factually correct but are not the correct response to the question.

- Answers that are sweeping generalizations (that is, *always*, *never*, and so on).

- Questions that have extraneous information not relevant to the topic or question.

- As a key strategy, keep in mind the following points when you are actually taking the exam:

  - The exam allows you to mark any question for later review.

  - Plan on making several passes (iterations) through all 180 questions of the exam.

  - On the initial pass through the exam, mark any question that you are not 100% sure of the answer.

     NOTE There is not a universal passing score for the PMP exam. PMI uses a formula that factors the difficulty of the question. Thus, the passing score for your test experience will depend on the set of questions you were given, the difficulty of those questions, the unscored questions, and which ones you got correct.

  - On the second pass, review all the marked questions. You will often find that the answer to a given question becomes clear after dealing with the other questions and/or after a second review of the question and potential answers.

  - If you are now sure you have answered the question correctly, unmark it. If you are still not comfortable, leave it marked.

  - Continue through all the marked questions to complete your pass (iteration).

  - Continue this iterative process until the number of marked questions gets down to approximately 20 or fewer. This would mean you are very confident about 160 of the 180 questions. This should leave you with a comfortable margin.

  - At this point, just give your best guess at the remaining questions.

THE ABSOLUTE MINIMUM

At this point, you should have a solid understanding of the following:

- What has changed in the new 2021 version of the PMP exam.
- The common trouble areas people encounter on the exam.
- The primary principles and assumptions that are important to PMI.
- The types of questions and the types of content to expect on the exam.
- The key areas to focus on while preparing for the exam.
- Powerful tips to assist the test-taking process.

Key PMI resources include the following:

- PMI 2021 PMP Exam Updates: www.pmi.org/certifications/project-management-pmp/earn-the-pmp/pmp-exam-preparation/pmp-exam-updates
- PMI PMP Examination Content Outline: www.pmi.org/-/media/pmi/documents/public/pdf/certifications/project-management-professional-exam-outline.pdf
- PMI Certifications Handbook: www.pmi.org/-/media/pmi/documents/public/pdf/certifications/project-management-professional-handbook.pdf
- PMI Certification Process: www.pmi.org/certifications/certification-resources/process
- PMI Online Proctored Exams: www.pmi.org/certifications/certification-resources/process/online-proctored-testing
- PMI PMP Exam Preparation Guidance: www.pmi.org/certifications/project-management-pmp/earn-the-pmp/pmp-exam-preparation
- PMI *PMBOK Guide*: www.pmi.org/pmbok-guide-standards/foundational/pmbok
- PMI *PMBOK Guide* – Seventh Edition On Demand Webinars: www.pmi.org/-/media/pmi/documents/public/pdf/pmbok-standards/past-pmbok-seventh-edition-event-links-19-july-2021.pdf?v=1a0ebd25-a729-4ee2-a3a3-f915def67a21
- PMI PMIstandards+: https://standardsplus.pmi.org/home

The map in Figure 26.1 summarizes the main points reviewed in this chapter.

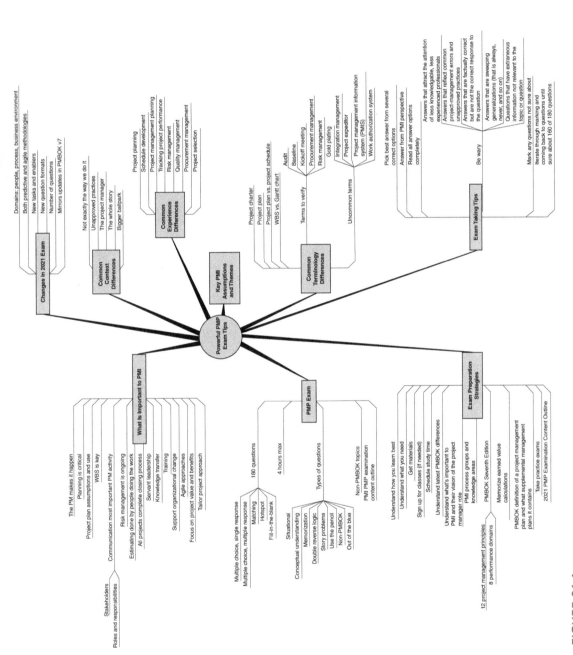

FIGURE 26.1

Powerful PMP Exam Tips chapter summary.

Index